D1591184

THE CAMBRIDGE COMPANION TO
PAUL TILLICH

The complex philosophical theology of Paul Tillich (1886–1965), increasingly studied today, was influenced by thinkers as diverse as Augustine, Luther, Schelling and Heidegger. A Lutheran pastor who served as a military chaplain in the First World War, he was dismissed from his university post at Frankfurt when the Nazis came to power in 1933 and emigrated to the United States, where he continued his distinguished career.

This authoritative *Companion* provides accessible accounts of the major themes of Tillich's diverse theological writings and draws upon the very best of contemporary Tillich scholarship. Each chapter introduces and evaluates its topic and includes suggestions for further reading. The authors assess Tillich's place in the history of twentieth-century Christian thought, as well as his significance for current constructive theology. Of interest to both students and researchers, this *Companion* reaffirms Tillich as a major figure in today's theological landscape.

Russell Re Manning is a University Lecturer in Philosophy of Religion at the Faculty of Divinity, University of Cambridge and Fellow of St Edmund's College, Cambridge. He is author of *Theology at the End of Culture: Paul Tillich's Theology of Culture and Art* (2005).

CAMBRIDGE COMPANIONS TO RELIGION
A series of companions to major topics and key figures in theology and
religious studies. Each volume contains specially commissioned chapters by
international scholars which provide an accessible and stimulating
introduction to the subject for new readers and non-specialists.

THE CAMBRIDGE COMPANION TO KARL RAHNER
edited by Declan Marmion and Mary E. Hines (2005)
ISBN 0 521 83288 8 hardback   ISBN 0 521 54045 3 paperback

THE CAMBRIDGE COMPANION TO FRIEDRICH SCHLEIERMACHER
edited by Jacqueline Mariña (2005)
ISBN 0 521 81448 0 hardback   ISBN 0 521 89137 x paperback

THE CAMBRIDGE COMPANION TO THE GOSPELS
edited by Stephen C. Barton (2006)
ISBN 0 521 80766 2 hardback   ISBN 0 521 00261 3 paperback

THE CAMBRIDGE COMPANION TO JONATHAN EDWARDS
edited by Stephen J. Stein (2007)
ISBN 0 521 85290 0 hardback   ISBN 0 521 61805 3 paperback

THE CAMBRIDGE COMPANION TO EVANGELICAL THEOLOGY
edited by Timothy Larsen and Daniel J. Trier (2007)
ISBN 0 521 84698 6 hardback   ISBN 0 521 60974 7 paperback

THE CAMBRIDGE COMPANION TO LIBERATION THEOLOGY,
SECOND EDITION
edited by Christopher Rowland (2007)
ISBN 9780521868839 hardback   ISBN 9780521688932 paperback

THE CAMBRIDGE COMPANION TO THE JESUITS
edited by Thomas Worcester (2008)
ISBN 9780521857314 hardback   ISBN 9780521673969 paperback

THE CAMBRIDGE COMPANION TO PURITANISM
edited by John Coffey and Paul Lim (2008)
ISBN 9780521860888 hardback   ISBN 9780521678001 paperback

THE CAMBRIDGE COMPANION TO CHRISTIAN ORTHODOX THEOLOGY
edited by Mary Cunningham and Elizabeth Theokritoff (2008)
ISBN 9780521864848 hardback   ISBN 9780521683388 paperback

Forthcoming
THE CAMBRIDGE COMPANION TO JOHN HENRY NEWMAN
edited by Ian Ker and Terrence Merrigan

THE CAMBRIDGE COMPANION TO ANCIENT CHRISTIANITY
edited by Rebecca Lyman

THE CAMBRIDGE COMPANION TO

PAUL TILLICH

Edited by Russell Re Manning

CAMBRIDGE
UNIVERSITY PRESS

BX
4827
.T53
C36
2009

CAMBRIDGE UNIVERSITY PRESS
Cambridge, New York, Melbourne, Madrid, Cape Town, Singapore, São Paulo, Delhi

Cambridge University Press
The Edinburgh Building, Cambridge CB2 8RU, UK

Published in the United States of America by Cambridge University Press, New York

www.cambridge.org
Information on this title: www.cambridge.org/9780521677356

First published 2009

Printed in the United Kingdom at the University Press, Cambridge

A catalogue record for this publication is available from the British Library

Library of Congress Cataloguing in Publication data
Cambridge companion to Paul Tillich / edited by Russell Re Manning.
    p.   cm. – (Cambridge companions to religion)
Includes bibliographical references and index.
ISBN 978-0-521-85989-9 (hardback)
1. Tillich, Paul, 1886–1965.   I. Re Manning, Russell.
BX4827.T53C36   2008
230.092 – dc22   2008037732

ISBN 978-0-521-85989-9 hardback
ISBN 978-0-521-67735-6 paperback

Behold, I am doing a new thing, even now it is springing to light. Do you not perceive it?

(Isaiah 43:18)

Contents

Notes on contributors

Rachel Sophia Baard teaches in the Center for Liberal Education at Villanova University in Pennsylvania, USA, and she is also connected with the Department of Systematic Theology and Ecclesiology at the University of Stellenbosch in South Africa. She specializes in feminist theologies and is currently working on a book on feminist perspectives on the doctrine of sin. She is Co-Chair of the American Academy of Religion Group, *Tillich: Issues in Theology, Religion, and Culture.*

Oswald Bayer is Professor of Systematic Theology and Philosophy of Religion in the Evangelisch-theologische Fakultät at the Eberhard Karls Universität in Tübingen, Germany. His work focuses on Lutheran theology and its philosophical reception in modernity. Recent publications include *Martin Luthers Theologie. Eine Vergegenwärtigung*, third edn (2007; English translation, *Martin Luther's Theology: A Contemporary Interpretation* (2008)), *Living by Faith: Justification and Sanctification* (2003), *Vernunft ist Sprache. Hamanns Metakritik Kants* (2002), *Gott als Autor. Zu einer poietologischen Theologie* (1999) and *Theologie. Handbuch Systematischer Theologie 1* (1994). He contributed the chapter 'Luther as Interpreter of Holy Scripture' to *The Cambridge Companion to Luther* (Cambridge University Press, 2003).

Marc Boss is Professor of Philosophy and Systematic Theology at the Institut Protestant de Théologie in Montpellier, France. He is the editor of the journal *Études Théologiques et Religieuses,* and he co-chairs the Centre Maurice-Leenhardt de Recherche en Missiologie (Montpellier). During the past decade he has contributed, as author, editor and chair of the Association Paul Tillich d'Expression Française, to various publications on Paul Tillich's work.

Christian Danz is Professor of Systematic Theology at the Evangelisch-Theologische Fakultät in the University of Vienna, Austria. His recent books include *Wirken Gottes. Zur Geschichte eines theologischen Grundbegriffs* (2007), *Gott und die menschliche Freiheit. Studien zum Gottesbegriff in der Neuzeit* (2005), *Einführung in die Theologie der Religionen. Lehre und Studienbücher zur Theologie Band 1* (2005) and *Religion als Freiheitsbewußtsein. Eine Studie zur Theologie als Theorie der Konstitutionsbedingungen individueller Subjektivität bei Paul Tillich* (2000). He is an editor of the *Internationales Jahrbuch für die Tillich-Forschung* and since 2006 has been President of the Deutsche Paul-Tillich-Gesellschaft.

John Dourley is Professor Emeritus, Department of Religion, Carleton University, Ottawa, Canada. His doctoral work was on Tillich and Bonaventure at Fordham University, 1971. Continued interest in Tillich led him into Jungian studies and to becoming a Jungian analyst (Zurich, 1980). He has published on Tillich, Jung and psychology, more recently with 'Rerooting in the Mother; the Numinosity of the Night' in *The Idea of the Numinous, Contemporary Jungian and Psychoanalytic Perspectives* (2006) and 'Toward a Salvageable Tillich: the Implications of his late Confession of Provincialism' in *Studies in Religion* (2004). He will shortly publish on the Jung–White dialogue in the *Journal of Analytical Psychology*. He is a Catholic priest and a member of the religious order the Oblates of Mary Immaculate.

John F. Haught is Distinguished Research Professor in the Department of Theology at Georgetown University, USA. His area of specialization is systematic theology, with a particular interest in issues pertaining to science, cosmology, evolution, ecology and religion. He is the author of *Christianity and Science* (2007), *Is Nature Enough?* (2006), *Deeper than Darwin* (2003), *God after Darwin*, second edn (2007), *Science and Religion* (1995) and many other books. In 2002 he was the winner of the Owen Garrigan Award in Science and Religion, and in 2004 the Sophia Award for Theological Excellence. In 2005 he testified as an expert witness for the plaintiffs (*Kitzmiller et al.* v. *Dover School Board*) against the teaching of 'intelligent design' in public-school biology classes.

Martin Leiner is Professor of Systematic Theology and Ethics at the Friedrich-Schiller-Universität in Jena, Germany. He publishes widely in systematic and philosophical theology, including books on the theological reception of Martin Buber's philosophy, the relation between psychology and biblical exegesis, and the theological interpretation of myth. A committee member of the Association Paul Tillich d'Expression Française, he is an editor of the *Internationales Jahrbuch für Tillich-Forschung*.

Frederick J. Parrella is Professor of Theology in the Religious Studies Department of Santa Clara University, USA. In addition to contributing chapters to books, he has edited four volumes, most recently *From Trent to Vatican II: Historical and Theological Investigations* (2006). Paulist Press will publish his book on the theology of the church in 2008. He received the award as the outstanding teacher at Santa Clara University in 1994. He served as President of the North American Paul Tillich Society, and since 1997 he has been its Secretary Treasurer and editor of the Society's quarterly *Bulletin*.

Russell Re Manning is a University Lecturer in Philosophy of Religion at the Faculty of Divinity, University of Cambridge, UK, and Fellow of St Edmund's College, Cambridge. He is the author of *Theology at the End of Culture: Paul Tillich's Theology of Culture and Art* (2005). He is currently writing an intellectual history of natural theology and editing the forthcoming *Oxford Handbook of Natural Theology* with Fraser Watts and John Hedley Brooke. With Rachel Sophia Baard, he is Co-Chair of the American Academy of Religion Group, Tillich: Issues in Theology, Religion, and Culture.

Anne Marie Reijnen is Professor of Systematic Theology at the Faculté Universitaire de Théologie Protestante in Brussels, Belgium, while also teaching at the Institut Catholique de Paris, France. Her publications include a book on the incarnation, *L'Ombre de Dieu sur terre* (1998), and on angels, *L'Ange obstiné* (2000), besides a number of book chapters and scholarly articles on, among other topics, the meaning of ecology for theology and the dialogue between Judaism and Christianity.

Jean Richard is Professor Emeritus at Université Laval, Quebec, Canada. He is, with André Gounelle, co-director of the *Œuvres de Paul Tillich* in French translation. He has published a number of book chapters and scholarly articles on theology and the philosophy of religion, especially on Tillich, in such journals as *Laval théologique et philosophique*, *Science et esprit*, *Études théologiques et religieuses*, *Revue d'histoire et de philosophie religieuses*.

Werner Schüßler is Professor of Philosophy in the Theology Faculty at the University of Trier, Germany. He has written extensively on Paul Tillich, including (with Erdmann Sturm) *Paul Tillich: Leben-Werk-Wirkung* (2007), 'Was uns unbedingt angeht.' *Studien zur Theologie und Philosophie Paul Tillichs*, second edn (2004) and *Paul Tillich* (1997). He is co-editor of the *Tillich-Studien* series (eighteen volumes published to date) and an editor of the *Internationales Jahrbuch für die Tillich-Forschung* (two volumes to date). He has also written on Karl Jaspers and Peter Wust.

William Schweiker is Professor of Theological Ethics at the University of Chicago, USA. He is the author of several books, including *Theological Ethics and Global Dynamics: In the Time of Many Worlds* (2004) and *Responsibility and Christian Ethics* (Cambridge University Press, 1995). He is also the editor of and a contributor to seven volumes, including *The Blackwell Companion to Religious Ethics* (2005), and co-editor and contributor to *Humanity Before God: Contemporary Faces of Jewish, Christian and Islamic Ethics* (2006). He is currently finishing a book with David Klemm entitled *Religion and the Human Future: An Essay on Theological Humanism*.

Mary Ann Stenger is Professor of Humanities at the University of Louisville, USA. She specializes in Christian thought and culture, with interests in philosophy of religion, feminism and pluralism. In addition to numerous book chapters and journal articles, she co-authored with Ronald H. Stone *Dialogues of Paul Tillich* (2002). She currently serves as chairperson of the *Tillich Collected Works Project*.

Ronald H. Stone retired from the John Witherspoon Chair of Christian Ethics of Pittsburgh Theological Seminary, USA, in 2003. He continues to serve as Adjunct Professor of Religious Studies at the University of Pittsburgh. He has written eighteen books on Christian social thought, including *Prophetic Realism* (2005); edited with Robert L. Stivers *Resistance and Theological Ethics* (2004), and with Mary Ann Stenger *Dialogues of Paul Tillich* (2002); and *John Wesley's Life and Ethics* (2001). He is active in the North American Paul Tillich Society, serving as President in 1983 and vice-President in 1996, and is currently on the editorial board of the *Tillich Collected Works Project*.

Erdmann Sturm is Professor at the Institute for Evangelical Theology and Evangelical Theology Faculty at the University of Münster, Germany. He has written numerous articles on various aspects of Tillich's thought and has edited several of Tillich's unpublished lectures for publication, including *Dogmatik-Vorlesung (Dresden 1925–1927)* (2005), *Berliner Vorlesungen (1919–1920)* (2001) and *Vorlesung über Hegel (Frankfurt 1931/32)* (1995). He co-edits the LIT Verlag series *Tillich-Studien* and is an editor of the *Internationales Jahrbuch für Tillich-Forschung*.

Mark Lewis Taylor is Professor of Theology and Culture at Princeton Theological Seminary, USA. Among his several books, his most recent is *Religion, Politics and the Christian Right: Post-9/11 Politics and the Christian Right* (2005). His book *The Executed God: The Way of the Cross in Lockdown America* (2001) won the Best General Interest 'Theologos Award' from the American Theological Booksellers' Association. His *Paul Tillich: Theologian of the Boundaries* (1991) is both a creative interpretation and edited collection of Tillich's work. He is currently editing *Decolonizing Sprirtualities in the Americas* with Nelson Maldonando-Torres and Shelley Wiley for Duke University Press. He is founder and co-director of Educators for Mumia Abu-Jamal.

John J. Thatamanil is Assistant Professor of Theology at Vanderbilt Divinity School, Nashville, USA. He is the author of *The Immanent Divine: God, Creation, and the Human Predicament: An East–West Conversation* (2006). He is currently working on a volume on theologies of religious pluralism and comparative theology tentatively entitled *Religious Diversity after 'Religion': Rethinking Theologies of Religious Pluralism*. Over and above his academic writing, his Op-Ed essays on religion and current events have appeared in the *Atlanta Journal Constitution*, the *Los Angeles Times* and the *Washington Post*. He is a past President of the North American Paul Tillich Society.

Preface

RUSSELL RE MANNING

Who still reads Paul Tillich today? Widely acknowledged as one of the 'giants' of twentieth-century theology and as someone who changed the way modern men (and women) think and talk about God, Tillich is nonetheless the most neglected of the great theologians of recent times. Clearly a compelling, even charismatic, personality, Tillich's personal impact was profound, and he was lauded at his death as something of a theological celebrity. Hailed as a prophet of the 'death of God theology' and bowdlerized by John Robinson's *Honest to God*, Tillich became, for a time at least, the theologian of choice for a new generation attempting to radicalize theology in the revolutionary white heat of the 1960s. Labelled an 'existentialist theologian', Tillich's reputation soared as the theologian of a new reformation in which the dogmatism of creeds is replaced by the 'courage to be' and supernaturalist notions of God are set aside in the pursuit of the 'God above God'. Taken in such a light, Tillich's theology – like so much teenage existentialism – seems hopelessly naïve and frankly embarrassing. It was no surprise that as the spirit of the 1960s waned, Tillich, along with polka-dot mini-skirts, would become unfashionable.

In recent years, however, a number of scholars have rediscovered Tillich, only to find that his impact on late twentieth-century theology has been more profound than expected. Once one returns to Tillich's actual writings – and in particular his pre-emigration German writings – without the presuppositions of reading an existentialist theology, a new and more complicated Tillich emerges, one whose influence has been as pervasive as it has been subtle. While no 'school' took his name, Tillich's ideas and terminology have, as it were, leaked out into the wider theological atmosphere, and it is constantly surprising just how much of Tillich's thought can be found lurking, often unacknowledged, in the background of a diverse range of debates. More than any concrete proposals, it is perhaps the example of Tillich's primary conviction that theology must be done in dialogue – with culture, the arts, the sciences, religious traditions – and his unflinching commitment to the 'both/and' character of such engagement that have proved to be his most enduring legacy to contemporary theology. At a time when theonomous critical thinking is being pressed upon by a militantly atheist science and culture on the one side and the equally strident forms of religious fundamentalism on the other, Tillich's call for a theology of correlation is once again urgently relevant.

This *Cambridge Companion* aims to respond to this situation by presenting the full range of Tillich's thought in accessible, yet nonetheless challenging, essays. The authors are drawn from a wide spectrum of positions, reflecting the renewed interest in Tillich's theology at the beginning of the twenty-first century. While different authors have adopted different approaches, all share the common conviction that Tillich's thinking is profoundly suggestive for us today as we continue the risky enterprise of theological reflection. They aim both to introduce Tillich to those who are not familiar with his writings and to provoke those who are to take a fresh look.

The book is divided into three parts reflecting three foci of Tillich's thought: systematic theology, theology of culture and theology in dialogue.

In the first part, Werner Schüßler traces Tillich's life and the development of his thought, and Oswald Bayer considers Tillich as a systematic theologian, focusing in particular on his methodology and his fundamental assumptions. The following three chapters reflect the Trinitarian structure of Tillich's systematic theology: Martin Leiner considers the various ways in which Tillich approached the question of God, Anne Marie Reijnen engages with Tillich's Christology and Frederick J. Parrella presents Tillich's theology of the concrete spirit. In her chapter, Mary Ann Stenger turns to Tillich's seminal writings about religion and faith, while Erdmann Sturm closes the section with a chapter considering Tillich's sermons.

The second part engages with Tillich's proposals for and writings in the theology of culture. In the first chapter, Jean Richard considers Tillich's analyses of the spiritual situation of his own times, while in the next William Schweiker takes up the future of Tillich's project in the call for a new form of theological humanism. The following four chapters treat different aspects within Tillich's theology of culture: Russell Re Manning discusses Tillich's engagement with art, Christian Danz reconstructs Tillich's philosophy, Mark Lewis Taylor considers Tillich as an ethicist and Ronald H. Stone reviews Tillich's political engagements.

The third part places Tillich's thought into a variety of different dialogues characteristic of contemporary theology. John F. Haught presents Tillich's approach to the dialogue between theology and the natural sciences, while John Dourley considers the particular example of Tillich's engagement with psychology. Marc Boss brings Tillich into the inter-religious dialogue, through a reconstruction of his engagements with Japanese Buddhism as a paradigmatic illustration of his approach. Rachel Sophia Baard tackles the often provocative dialogue between feminist theologians and Tillich, while John Thatamanil's final chapter brings postmodern theology into dialogue with Tillich.

Paul Tillich perceptively characterized his own life and thought in terms of a series of boundaries. For Tillich, theology is to be done, as it were, from the inside looking out: within the theological circle and in the midst of the cultural situation. The theologian has a duty to speak to his contemporaries as contemporaries, not just to the 'cultured despisers of religion' but also to its most enthusiastic defenders. For Tillich, the theological vocation is – and must be – a risk. At the same time, it is precisely in taking this risk that the theologian may bring to light something of the fundamental mystery: the mystery of 'an actuality of meaning, indeed, the ultimate and most profound actuality of meaning that convulses everything and builds everything anew' (*OITC*, 25).

Acknowledgements

This *Companion* is a joint work, and I am immensely grateful to all the contributors, both for the timely delivery of their chapters and the patient manner in which they indulged their editor!

I have had the pleasure of discussing this book and the ideas that lie behind it with members of the three leading scholarly societies dedicated to the academic study of Tillich's thought – the North American Paul Tillich Society (and the AAR Group that it sponsors, Tillich: Issues in Theology, Religion and Culture), Die Deutsche Paul-Tillich-Gesellschaft, and L'Association Paul Tillich d'expression française. I would particularly like to thank Rob James for all his behind-the-scenes advice and friendship.

In Cambridge, I have been much assisted by some able translation work; my thanks are due to Alexandra Wörn, David Leech and Liz Disley. In addition, I have greatly benefited from discussion on Tillich and the prospects for theology of culture more generally with Douglas Hedley, Fraser Watts, Chris Insole, Louise Hickman, Liz Gulliford, Vittorio Montemaggi and, of course, my students.

Finally, I would like to thank Kate Brett at Cambridge University Press, not only for commissioning the book in the first place, but also for her editorial guidance and gentle persuasion.

This book is dedicated to Francesca, companion of my life.

Chronology – a brief outline of Tillich's life and times

1886   20 August, Paul Tillich born in Starzeddel, Germany (now Starosiedle, Poland), where his father, Johannes Tillich, was a Lutheran minister

1900   Family moves to Berlin

1903   Death of Mathilde Tillich, Paul's mother

1904   Begins theological studies at Berlin. Continues his studies in Tübingen and Halle, where he is heavily influenced by Martin Kähler

1909   Takes up first appointment as substitute minister in Lichtenrade; Tillich's earliest sermons date from this time

1910   Awarded PhD in Philosophy at Breslau for his dissertation 'The Construction of the History of Religions in Schelling's Positive Philosophy'

1911   First exhibition of *Der Blaue Reiter*, group of Expressionist artists; Wassily Kandinsky publishes *Concerning the Spiritual in Art*

1912   April: awarded PhD in Theology at Halle for his dissertation 'Mysticism and Guilt-Consciousness in Schelling's Philosophical Development'
        August: ordained Lutheran minister in Berlin; appointed assistant minister in Berlin-Moabit, leading to sustained contact with the urban poor

1914   September: marries Greti Wever
        October: volunteers as army chaplain

1915   Experiences horrors of First World War first-hand, including the battle of Verdun, precipitating a nervous breakdown

1916   Delivers his inaugural lecture at Halle

1917   Rudolf Otto publishes *The Idea of the Holy*

1918   End of First World War, abdication of Kaiser Wilhelm II and establishment of Weimar Republic; Tillich returns to Berlin

1919   Forms '*kairos* circle' of religious socialists
        January: death of Rosa Luxemburg
        April: delivers programmatic lecture 'On the Idea of a Theology
        of Culture'
1921   Divorces Greti Wever
1922   Karl Barth publishes second edition of *The Epistle to the Romans*
1923   Publishes first major work, *The System of the Sciences*, dedicated
        to Ernst Troeltsch
1924   March: marries Hannah Werner
        Appointed Professor for Systematic Theology at Marburg, where
        he befriends Rudolf Otto and encounters Rudolf Bultmann and
        Martin Heidegger
        Delivers formative lecture 'Justification and Doubt' at Gießen, in
        which he applies the doctrine of justification to the intellectual
        life
        Thomas Mann publishes *The Magic Mountain*
1925   Lectures on 'Dogmatics' under the epigraph 'Theologie muss
        Angriff sein' ('Theology must go on the offensive')
        Appointed Professor of Philosophy and Religious Studies at the
        Dresden Institute of Technology
1926   Publishes *The Religious Situation*, in which he applies the prin-
        ciples of theology of culture
1927   Appointed Honorary Professor for Philosophy of Religion and
        Philosophy of Culture at Leipzig
        Martin Heidegger publishes *Being and Time*
1929   Appointed Professor of Philosophy at Frankfurt am Main, where
        he enjoys fruitful collaboration with Max Horkheimer and
        Theodor W. Adorno and lectures on the philosophy of history,
        philosophy of religion, Schelling and Idealism, ethics and the
        history of philosophy; joins Social Democratic Party
1933   January: Adolf Hitler appointed Chancellor
        April: suspended from Chair because of the publication of his
        anti-Nazi *The Socialist Decision* and his positive stance towards
        Jewish students
        May: *The Socialist Decision* is publicly burnt in Frankfurt
        November: arrives in New York at the invitation of Reinhold
        Niebuhr of Union Theological Seminary (whose faculty took a
        5 per cent pay cut to fund Tillich's salary) and Columbia Univer-
        sity
1934   Delivers his first lecture in English – his accent is so bad that few
        understand a word

The Barmen Declaration is issued by the 'Confessing Church'

1936 Chairman of relief organization 'Self-help for German Émigrés'; publishes autobiography, *On the Boundary*

1937 Picasso's *Guernica* first exhibited at the Paris International Exhibition

1939 Outbreak of Second World War

1940 Appointed Professor of Philosophical Theology at Union

1942 Delivers first of 109 radio broadcasts 'to my German friends'

1944 Appointed Chairman of the Council for a Democratic Germany

1945 Atomic bombs dropped on Japanese cities of Hiroshima and Nagasaki

1948 First return trip to Germany, including meeting with Karl Barth in Basle

Publishes *The Protestant Era*, along with first volume of sermons, *The Shaking of the Foundations*; two more collections follow: *The New Being* (1955) and *The Eternal Now* (1962)

1951 Publishes first volume of *Systematic Theology: Reason and Revelation* and *Being and God*

1952 Publishes *The Courage to Be*

1953 Delivers Gifford Lectures at University of Aberdeen

1955 Retires from Union to take up University Professorship at Harvard; lectures widely across the United States on a broad range of theological, philosophical and ethical topics

1957 Second volume of *Systematic Theology: Existence and Christ*

1959 Publishes *Theology of Culture*; appears on front cover of *Time* magazine

1960 Visits Japan

1962 Appointed John Nuveen Professor of Theology at Chicago, where he co-teaches a seminar on the history of religions with Mircea Eliade; awarded the Peace Prize of the German Publishers' Association in Frankfurt

1963 Travels to Israel, where he meets Martin Buber; third volume of *Systematic Theology: Life and Spirit* and *History and the Kingdom of God*; John A. T. Robinson publishes *Honest to God*

1965 11 October: delivers last public lecture, 'The Significance of the History of Religions for the Systematic Theologian'

22 October: dies in hospital from heart attack

1966 Tillich's ashes are re-interred in the Paul Tillich Park, New Harmony, Indiana

Abbreviations

ATR   *Against the Third Reich*, ed. Ronald H. Stone and Matthew Lon Weaver. Louisville, Ky.: Westminster/John Knox Press, 1998.

BOB   *The Boundaries of Our Being: A Collection of his Sermons with his Autobiographical Sketch*. London: Collins, 1973.

BR   *Biblical Religion and the Search for Ultimate Reality*. Chicago, Ill.: University of Chicago Press, 1955.

CB   *The Courage to Be*. Glasgow: W. Collins & Sons/New Haven: Yale University Press, 1952. Repr. Intro. Peter Gomes. New Haven: Yale University Press, 2001.

CEWR   *Christianity and the Encounter of World Religions*, Bampton Lectures, no. 14. New York and London: Columbia University Press, 1963.

CGJ   *Carl Gustav Jung, 1875–1961, A Memorial Meeting, New York, December 1, 1961*. New York: The Analytical Psychology Club of New York, 1962, 28–32.

CHR   *The Construction of the History of Religion in Schelling's Positive Philosophy: Its Presuppositions and Principles*, trans. Victor Nuovo. Lewisburg, Pa.: Bucknell University Press, 1974.

D   *Dogmatik. Marburger Vorlesung von 1925*, ed. W. Schüßler. Düsseldorf: Patmos, 1986.

DF   *Dynamics of Faith*. New York: Harper Brothers, 1957. Repr. Intro. Marion H. Pauck. New York: HarperCollins, 2001.

EN   *The Eternal Now*. New York: Charles Scribner's Sons, 1963.

ENGW   *Ergänzungs- und Nachlassbände zu den Gesammelten Werken von Paul Tillich*, 11 vols. Vols. I–VI Stuttgart: Evangelisches Verlagswerk, 1971–83. Vols. VII–XI Berlin: Walter de Gruyter, 1994–9.

ERQR	*The Encounter of Religions and Quasi-Religions*, ed. Terence Thomas. Lewiston, N.Y.: The Edwin Mellen Press, 1990.
FR	*The Future of Religions*, ed. Jerald C. Brauer. New York: Harper and Row, 1966.
GW	*Gesammelte Werke*, 14 vols., ed. Renate Albrecht. Stuttgart: Evangelisches Verlagswerk, 1959–75.
HCT	*A History of Christian Thought*, ed. Carl Braaten. New York: Harper & Row, 1968.
IH	*The Interpretation of History*, trans. N. A. Rasetzki and Elsa L. Talmey. New York: Charles Scribner's Sons, 1936.
IR	*The Irrelevance and the Relevance of the Christian Message*, ed. Durwood Foster. Cleveland, Ohio: The Pilgrim Press, 1996.
LPJ	*Love, Power and Justice: Ontological Analysis and Ethical Applications*. New York: Oxford University Press, 1954.
MB	*Morality and Beyond*. New York: Harper & Row, 1963. Repr. Forw. William Schweiker. Louisville, Ky.: Westminster John Knox Press, 1995.
MGC	*Mysticism and Guilt-Consciousness in Schelling's Philosophical Development*, trans. Victor Nuovo. Lewisburg, Pa.: Bucknell University Press, 1974.
MTD	*My Travel Diary: 1936: Between Two Worlds*, ed. and intro. Jerald C. Brauer, trans. Maria Pelikan, drawings Alfonso Ossorio. London: SCM Press, 1970.
MW/HW	*Main Works/Hauptwerke*, 6 vols., ed. Carl Heinz Ratschow. Berlin: Walter de Gruyter, 1987–92.
NB	*The New Being*. New York: Charles Scribner's Sons, 1955.
OAA	*On Art and Architecture*, ed. John Dillenberger, in collaboration with Joan Dillenberger, trans. Robert P. Scharlemann. New York: Crossroad, 1987.
OB	*On The Boundary: An Autobiographical Sketch*. New York: Charles Scribner's Sons, 1966/London: Collins, 1967.
OED	*The Concise Oxford English Dictionary*, ed. Judy Pearsall. Tenth edn, revised. New York: Oxford University Press, 2002.
OITC	'On the Idea of a Theology of Culture', trans. Victor Nuovo in *Visionary Science: A Translation of Tillich's 'On the Idea of a Theology of Culture' with an Interpretative Essay*. Detroit, Mich.: Wayne State University Press, 1987.
P	*Perspectives on Nineteenth- and Twentieth-Century Protestant Theology*. New York: Harper & Row, 1967.

PolE   *Political Expectation*, ed. James Luther Adams. New York:
         Harper & Row, 1971.
ProtE   *The Protestant Era*, ed. James Luther Adams. Chicago, Ill.:
         University of Chicago Press, 1957.
PP   *Protestantisches Prinzip und proletarische Situation*. Bonn:
         Friedrich Cohen, 1931.
PTM   'The Problem of Theological Method', *Journal of Religion*
         27:1 (January 1947), 16–26.
RLG   *Die religiöse Lage der Gegenwart*. Berlin: Ullstein, 1926.
RS   *The Religious Situation*, trans. H. Richard Niebuhr.
         Cleveland, Ohio/New York: The World Publishing
         Company, 1932, 1956.
RV   *Religiöse Verwirklichung*. Berlin: Furche-Verlag, 1929.
SD   *The Socialist Decision*, trans. Franklin Sherman. New
         York: Harper & Row, 1977.
SF   *The Shaking of the Foundations*. New York: Charles
         Scribner's Sons, 1948.
SS   *The System of the Sciences According to Objects and
         Methods*, trans. Paul Wiebe. Lewisburg, Pa.: Bucknell
         University Press, 1981.
SSTS   *The Spiritual Situation in Our Technical Society*, ed. and
         intro. J. Mark Thomas. Macon, Ga.: Mercer University
         Press, 1988.
ST I   *Systematic Theology*, vol. I. London: SCM Press, 1951.
ST I (G) *Systematische Theologie*, vol. I. Stuttgart: Evangelisches
         Verlagswerk, 1951.
ST II   *Systematic Theology*, vol. II. London: SCM Press, 1957.
ST II (G) *Systematische Theologie*, vol. II. Stuttgart: Evangelisches
         Verlagswerk, 1956.
ST III   *Systematic Theology*, vol. III. London: SCM Press, 1963.
TC   *Theology of Culture*, ed. Robert Kimball. New York: Oxford
         University Press, 1959.
TP   *Theology of Peace*, ed. Ronald H. Stone. Louisville, Ky.:
         Westminster/John Knox Press, 1990.
TW   'Die Theologie als Wissenschaft', *Vossische Zeitung* 512
         (1921): 2–14.
UC   *Ultimate Concern*, ed. D. Mackenzie Brown. London: SCM
         Press, 1965.
WR   *What Is Religion?* ed. James Luther Adams. New York,
         Evanston and London: Harper & Row, 1969.

A NOTE ABOUT READING TILLICH

Tillich wrote in a wide variety of contexts and for many different audiences. His publications include his famous three-volume *Systematic Theology*; individual monographs and journal articles on a wide range of topics in theology, philosophy and cultural critique; articles in newspapers and religious and political magazines; reviews; university lectures and public presentations; sermons; autobiography; letters; and travel journals. He also wrote and published in two languages, often revising earlier German works for their later publication in English translation. The majority of his output consists of self-contained, short, occasional pieces; and yet there is a remarkable systematic consistency throughout his work.

The accepted scholarly edition of Tillich's work is the fourteen-volume German-language *Gesammelte Werke* (*GW*), edited by Renate Albrecht, and its series of supplements, *Ergänzungs- und Nachlassbände zu den Gesammelten Werken von Paul Tillich* (*ENGW*) (fifteen volumes to date). While well produced, this is not always entirely reliable, with some texts originally written by Tillich in German but first published in English re-translated into German for the *GW*. There is currently no collected works in English (although a project has recently been initiated by the North American Paul Tillich Society). Between 1987 and 1992 de Gruyter published a selection of Tillich's major shorter works in their original languages, arranged thematically in six volumes, as *Main Works/Hauptwerke* (*MW/HW*).

Many of Tillich's works are available in their original editions, while some have been recently re-issued. The majority – with some significant exceptions – of Tillich's major German-language works have been translated into English. One important text as yet unavailable in English (a French translation has been produced) is the series of lectures on dogmatics that was to have been published under the title *Die Gestalt der religiöse Erkenntnis* in 1930. Archival research continues to reveal more unpublished material, especially from Tillich's pre-emigration time, that will be of significant future interest.

There are two editions of Tillich's major work, *Systematic Theology*, published by Chicago University Press from 1951 to 1963 and in London by Nisbet from 1953 to 1964, which was re-issued by SCM Press in 1978 and again by XPRESS REPRINTS in 1997. Annoyingly, the pagination differs between the two editions. References here are to the SCM Press edition.

Part I

Standing within the theological circle

1 Tillich's life and works

WERNER SCHÜßLER

Paul Tillich was born on 20 August 1886 in Starzeddel, Germany (today Starosiedle in Poland), where his father, Johannes Tillich, was a Lutheran minister.[1] In 1890 the family moved to Schönfließ/Neumark (today Trzcinsko Zdrój in Poland), where Johannes Tillich was appointed to the post of chief pastor (*Oberpfarrer*) and district superintendent. From 1900 onwards the family lived in Berlin. The early death of Paul's mother Mathilde (*née* Dürselen) in 1903 must have affected him deeply.

TILLICH'S INTELLECTUAL FORMATION: IDEALISM AND APOLOGETICS

Tillich's fascination with philosophy extends as far back as his final years at the Friedrich-Wilhelms-Gymnasium, and by the time he had completed his *Abitur* and matriculated in the Theology Faculty of the University of Berlin in the winter semester of 1904 he had already acquired a good knowledge of the history of philosophy, in particular Kant and Fichte. In the summer semester of 1905 he continued his studies in Tübingen. For the following four semesters he chose to go to the University of Halle, which at that time had a high reputation in theological circles. The most important theologian at Halle was Martin Kähler, who would exert a long-lasting influence on Tillich.

While studying, Tillich joined the *Wingolf* Christian student fraternity and quickly came to the notice of his fellow members in virtue of his polished debating talents, as a result of which he was elected fraternity representative for the summer semester of 1907. After the end of the semester Tillich continued his studies in Berlin, and in autumn 1908 he passed his first examination in theology with the highest grade of 'Recht gut' ('Very good').

Unusually, Tillich's first appointment was not as a curate, but between March and October 1909 the 23-year-old Tillich replaced minister Ernst Klein as a substitute minister (*Pfarrverweser*) in Lichtenrade, assuming full responsibility for a parish. Several of his sermons survive from this period, which already attest to the early development of the systematic power of Tillich's thinking.[2]

In the meantime Tillich had begun an intensive study of Schelling, which resulted in a philosophical dissertation on Schelling entitled 'Die religionsgeschichtliche Konstruktion in Schellings positiver Philosophie, ihre Voraussetzungen und Prinzipien' submitted to the University of Breslau.[3] After a successful viva voce Tillich received his PhD in Philosophy on 22 August 1910, subsequently taking up his curacy in Nauen on 1 April 1911. On 22 April 1912 Tillich obtained his licenciate at the Theology Faculty in Halle with his thesis 'Mystik und Schuldbewußtsein in Schellings philosophischer Entwicklung'.[4]

At an autumn *Wingolf* conference in Kassel in 1911 Tillich met with some old friends to discuss the question of the repercussions of historical research on Christology. He was later to consider this conference a crucial moment in his theological development:

> I asked how Christian doctrine might be understood if the non-existence of the historical Jesus were to become historically probable, and then attempted to answer my own question. Even now I insist on raising this question radically rather than falling back on the kind of compromises that I encountered then and that Emil Brunner is now offering. The foundation of Christian belief is the biblical picture of Christ, not the historical Jesus. The criterion of human thought and action is the picture of Christ as it is rooted in ecclesiastical belief and human experience, not the shifting and artificial construct of historical research.
>
> (BOB, 320)

After his ordination on 18 August 1912 in the St Matthäus-Kirche in Berlin Tillich worked as an assistant minister at the Erlöserkirche in Berlin-Moabit, where for the first time in his life he came into contact with members of the working classes and became acquainted at close hand with their personal and economic misery. This was his first encounter with the proletariat, and it laid the ground for his subsequent path to religious socialism.

In the summer of 1912 Tillich and his friend Richard Wegener pondered over how the church could be made to appeal once again to the educated classes, who had become distant from its life. The two friends decided to organize talks, to which students, artists and academics were invited. These talks soon came to be known as the 'Vernunft-Abende' and demonstrate the particular apologetic impulse that was to become such an enduring characteristic of Tillich's later thought.

THE FIRST TURNING-POINT: THE IMPACT OF THE FIRST WORLD WAR

After completing his work as an assistant minister Tillich chose to pursue an academic career, beginning post-doctoral work at Halle in 1913 on a theological *Habilitationsschrift*. However, not for the last time, personal and world-historical factors imposed themselves on Tillich's academic development. On 28 September 1914, Tillich married Greti Wever, with whom he had become acquainted in the summer of 1913. Although friends openly warned him against the marriage, Tillich's mind was made up. Greti herself, in whose life religion played no great part, also entertained doubts. Then, at the beginning of October 1914, only a matter of days after his marriage, Tillich voluntarily enrolled as an army chaplain in the First World War. At first, a certain mood of optimism is discernible in his letters; however, this optimism quickly evaporated. In Bieuxy (France), Tillich was involved as chaplain in the first German military operations. On the 30 and 31 October 1915, he experienced horrific hostilities near Sommepy-Tahure, but worse still lay before him, namely the horrors of Verdun in 1916.

After recuperating following the battle of Verdun, Tillich was granted leave to complete his *Habilitation* in Halle. The post-doctoral work that he had meanwhile completed was entitled 'Der Begriff des Übernatürlichen, sein dialektischer Charakter und das Prinzip der Identität dargestellt an der supranaturalistischen Theologie vor Schleiermacher' ('The Concept of the Supernatural, its Dialectical Character and the Principle of Identity in Supranatural Theology before Schleiermacher').[5] Doubts were initially raised in the Faculty at Halle about Tillich's work, which, as Professor Wilhelm Lütgert was to inform him in a letter dated 8 July 1915, was considered too philosophical and not answering to the title; it was in addition felt to be not sufficiently historical, but rather 'purely logical, purely dialectical' ('rein logisch, rein dialektisch'), presupposing as self-evidently true the principles of 'Identity Philosophy' (*Identitätsphilosophie*). Nevertheless, in view of the difficult geo-political situation, the Faculty were reluctant to obstruct Tillich's chances of an academic career; thus, Tillich was not required to make revisions but only to alter his title, making clear that the work was 'rein formal logisch-dialektisch' (*ENGW* V, 101f.).[6]

On 3 July 1916 Tillich delivered a private *Probevorlesung* ('trial lecture') with an accompanying colloquium, and on 20 July 1916 he delivered his inaugural lecture.

In the remaining years of the war (1917–18) Tillich did not return to the hostilities. Nevertheless – or perhaps precisely for that reason – at the end of March 1918 Tillich suffered from an acute nervous disorder, which led to a short stay in hospital. On 30 July 1918 he was stationed back in his home country and on 15 December 1918 was discharged from the army. The sermons composed while he was an army chaplain have recently been published and provide interesting glimpses into Tillich's experience of the war.[7]

During the war Tillich's marriage had suffered. Greti had become involved with Tillich's friend Richard Wegener, and when Greti was finally expecting a second child with Wegener – their first child, born in 1919, lived to be only a few days old – Tillich agreed to a divorce, which was pronounced on 22 November 1921. Returning to Berlin, Tillich became increasingly committed to socialism, considering the recent catastrophe of the war a consequence of a particular ordering of society and of certain ideas bound up with such a social order. Beginning in 1919 Tillich started to meet regularly with Eduard Heimann, Carl Mennicke, Alexander Rüstow, Arnold Wolfers and Adolf Löwe, who formed the so-called 'Kairos Circle' ('Kairos-Kreis'). The *Blätter für Religiösen Sozialismus*, which was published between 1920 and 1927 and to which Tillich contributed various articles, was the public organ of this circle. In the *Blätter* Tillich appealed to the church and its representatives to adopt a positive stance towards socialism and social democracy, and he advocated the possibility of a union between Christianity and socialism. The *Neue Blätter für den Sozialismus*, which was published from 1930 onwards, was also decisively shaped by Tillich.

TILLICH'S THEOLOGICAL VOCATION

In 1919 Tillich began lecturing at the Theology Faculty in Berlin as an untenured lecturer (*Privatdozent*). His first lecture in the summer semester of 1919 was entitled 'Das Christentum und die Gesellschaftsprobleme der Gegenwart' ('Christianity and the Present Problems of Society'), and later lectures (among other things) focused on philosophy of religion (1920 and 1922–3), the religious content and the religio-historical significance of Greek philosophy (1920–1), Western philosophy since the Renaissance (1921), and the intellectual history (*Geistesgeschichte*) of early Christian and medieval philosophy

(1923–4).[8] A work of particular importance from this period is his pro-grammatic lecture entitled 'Über die Idee einer Theologie der Kultur' which he delivered on 16 April 1919 at the Kant-Gesellschaft; this work is a manifesto for Tillich's distinctive revisioning of theology as theology of culture.[9]

In 1920 Tillich met Hannah Werner at a fancy-dress party. Hannah was at this time in a relationship with art teacher Albert Gottschow, whom she was to marry shortly afterwards. One year later, however, she would leave her husband for Tillich; they married on 22 March 1924 in Friedersdorf. Much has been written in recent years about Tillich's mar-riage, although what is true and false in these accounts is impossible for a third party to judge. One thing, however, should not be ignored: despite all the tensions in their marriage Tillich nevertheless always maintained that 'Hannah always stood by me.' Margot Hahl, who has compared the bond between Tillich and Hannah to that between Schelling and Caro-line, has stressed that this marriage should not be judged 'according to conventional standards'.[10]

In the early years of the 1920s Tillich worked hard to make him-self eligible for an academic chair. In 1923 his first major publication, *Das System der Wissenschaften nach Gegenständen und Methoden*, appeared, which Emanuel Hirsch praised as one of the most mature achievements of recent German systematic philosophy.[11] In this work Tillich sought to secure a place for theology within the circle of the sci-ences. It would not be long until Tillich was offered a chair: in 1924, after five years as a *Privatdozent*, Tillich was made an Associate Professor for Systematic Theology at the Philipps-Universität in Marburg.

In his 'Autobiographical Reflections' Tillich wrote the following about his time in Marburg:

> During the three semesters of my teaching there I met the first radical effects of the neo-orthodoxy on theological students: cultural problems were excluded from theological thought; theologians like Schleiermacher, Harnack, Troeltsch, Otto, were contemptuously rejected; social and political ideas were banned from theological discussions. The contrast with the experiences in Berlin was overwhelming, at first depressing and then inciting: a new way had to be found.[12]

Tillich sought this new way in his lectures on 'Dogmatics' deliv-ered between the years 1925 and 1927, which marked a decisive step on the way to his later *Systematic Theology*.[13] In these lectures he formu-lated a principle applicable to his entire theology: 'Theology must go on the offensive' ('Theologie muß Angriff sein'). This 'Dogmatik', which was prepared for publication in 1930 under the title 'Die Gestalt der religiösen Erkenntnis' ('The Structure of Religious Knowledge'), is not, however, Tillich's first attempt at a systematic work. This can be traced back to the year 1913, and the idea of capturing the world through a system of thought had clearly excited Tillich as far back as his student days in Tübingen, as he was to relate in a lecture from the year 1963.[14]

It was also during Tillich's time in Marburg that he encountered Martin Heidegger. As Tillich later remarked: 'It was only years later that I became fully aware of the influence of this encounter on my own thinking. I fought against it and sought only to affirm its new methods of thinking without accepting its results' (*GW* XII, 69). An alternative perspective comes from Hans-Georg Gadamer, at that time a *Privatdozent* in Marburg, who commented retrospectively on Tillich:

> I would like to think that Tillich was not very lucky in Marburg. At that time the Theology Faculty was very much determined by Bultmann, von Soden and indirectly by Heidegger, and the faculty was very critical of Tillich's dialectical skill . . . Those of us who were students of Heidegger found Tillich's work only superficially grounded in real research, and I must say that in certain respects Tillich showed us to be correct. Nonetheless, we were friendly, and he was so charming that it is impossible to speak ill of him. His warmth and tremendous good nature prevented these small academic differences from clouding the atmosphere.
>
> (*ENGW* V, 166)

An important contribution from Tillich's time in Marburg is his lecture 'Rechtfertigung und Zweifel' ('Justification and Doubt') which he delivered in 1924 in Gießen.[15] In this lecture Tillich applied the doctrine of justification to the intellectual life: according to his interpretation, not only is the sinner justified before God, but also the doubter. At this time Tillich's influence began to be felt outside the academy: for example, the 'Berneuchen movement', a reform movement within the Lutheran church, adopted Tillich's concept of symbolic thinking, which corresponded to their firm opposition to all forms of supernaturalistic thinking.

In the summer semester of 1925 Tillich was invited to take up the position of Professor of Religious Studies at the Dresden University of Technology. At this time Dresden was intellectually and culturally an important city. It is unsurprising, therefore, that it was here that Tillich wrote his celebrated work on *Die religiöse Lage der Gegenwart* (1926), which brought his thought to a wider public.[16] In his lectures given during these years Tillich built upon the theological work that he had begun in Marburg. He lectured from his dogmatics, but now under a different title. Not only the title had changed: he now employed new concepts, for example 'lack of being' (*Seinsverfehlung*) instead of 'sin' (*Sünde*), in this way attempting to reach those 'spiritual seekers' who had turned away from the church. However, his language, on the whole, remained too academic. Thirty years later Tillich was to make the following poignant self-criticism: 'The writings . . . that I had written toward the end of the twenties were not written in what I would now identify as the German language, but in what might be called 'philosopher-German' (*Philosophendeutsch*).'[17]

On 24 December 1925 Tillich was awarded an honorary doctorate from the Theology Faculty at Halle. The Dean and former teacher of Tillich, Professor Wilhelm Lütgert, testified in the diploma to the 'conceptual sharpness and dialectical skill' with which Tillich 'developed a programme of the philosophy of religion and a general theory of science, as well interesting and inspiring the younger generation of scholars in their attempt to bring philosophy and the social sciences into contact with living religion' (*GW* XIII, 582).

During the winter semester 1927–8 Tillich received an invitation to take up the position of Honorary University Professor for Philosophy of Religion and Philosophy of Culture at the Theological Faculty of the University of Leipzig. His inaugural lecture, which he delivered in June 1927, was entitled 'Die Idee der Offenbarung' ('The Idea of Revelation'). His lectures in Leipzig – although presented under another title – were the same as those he had given in Dresden.

However, Tillich soon came to feel that Dresden could only be a transitional place for him, and consequently he made every effort from spring 1928 onwards to obtain a chair at the Theology Faculty of the University of Berlin. However, doubts were raised about his theology, which Tillich worked hard to dispel. For example, in a letter to Professor Erich Seeberg dated 1 November 1928 he concedes:

> As far as the 'churchness' (*Kirchlichkeit*) of my theology is
> concerned, I understand your doubts. However, they have their
> essential ground in that I have developed my personal life away
> from the church, while I have developed my professional life
> towards it. This second development is, on account of our present
> situation, very slow and laborious. However, I consider it more
> fruitful than following an obvious employment in the service of

the church. It is for this reason that there are still few published pieces that clearly set out my progress towards that goal. The largest work, my *Dogmatics*, languishes in my notebooks and much work remains to be done before it will be published.[18]

Having exhausted his hopes of moving to Berlin, Tillich finally realized that his only opportunity to leave Dresden lay in switching to a philosophy faculty. On 24 April 1929 Tillich was invited against the will of the Faculty to succeed Hans Cornelius as University Professor for Philosophy and Sociology at the University of Frankfurt am Main; Max Scheler, who had received the invitation before Tillich, died before being able to occupy the chair. Cornelius himself was extremely resistant to Tillich's succeeding him; in a manner not untypical of certain philosophical critiques of Tillich's work, Cornelius proclaimed that *The System of the Sciences* was of a very low level academically, containing banalities of all kinds and employing unclear concepts.

Once installed, however, Tillich was to find Frankfurt very fruitful. He enjoyed good working relationships with his colleagues; particularly stimulating was his close contact with Max Horkheimer and Theodor W. Adorno, later of course leading figures in the Frankfurt School of critical theory. During these years Tillich gave lectures on the philosophy of history, social education and philosophy of religion, on Schelling and the internal crisis of German Idealism, on the development of philosophy from late antiquity to the Renaissance, on the social ethics of Thomas Aquinas and modern Catholic social ethics, on the history of philosophical ethics, on Hegel as well as on the philosophical ideas of German Classicism from Lessing to Novalis. However, his last, great lecture on seventeenth- and eighteenth-century French philosophy was overshadowed by the political events of the winter of 1932–3.

THE SECOND TURNING-POINT: TOWARDS A NEW WORLD

At first Tillich believed he could retain some degree of influence in National Socialist Germany. However, following a warning by Max Horkheimer he eventually came to realize that he would not be able to remain in Germany. On 13 April 1933 Tillich was suspended from his chair on account of his programmatic paper *Die sozialistische Entscheidung* and his positive stance towards Jewish students as Dean of the Philosophy Faculty.[19] In the midst of this fraught situation Tillich received an unexpected offer from Union Theological Seminary in New York inviting him to teach there for a year in the first instance as a Visiting Professor and simultaneously to give lectures in philosophy at nearby Columbia University. Tillich accepted the offer and arrived, together with his wife Hannah and their 7-year-old daughter Erdmuthe, in New York at the beginning of November 1933.

On arrival in New York Tillich was chiefly preoccupied with try-ing to master the English language, a task he would have difficulties with for the remainder of his life. A meteoric rise up the career ladder at Union was out of the question: the lecture timetable at Union for these years shows that from 1933 Tillich was a mere Lecturer on Phi-losophy of Religion and Systematic Theology and from 1936 a Lecturer on Philosophical Theology. Only in 1937 would he become Associate Professor of Philosophical Theology and finally, in 1940, Professor of Philosophical Theology. During these years Tillich lectured on philos-ophy of religion and systematic theology. From 1945 onwards he also gave lectures on 'Church History' and 'History of Christianity' instead of philosophy of religion.

Thanks to his extensive lecturing activities Tillich quickly became known outside Union. As early as 1934 he was invited to the celebrated 'Theological Discussion Group', and only a few years later he was offered membership of the 'Philosophy Club', a privilege extended to only the most exceptional individuals. During these years Tillich was to focus increasingly on depth psychology and its inner relationship to religion. Tillich saw depth psychology as a golden opportunity for theology, just as Kant had seen such an opportunity for philosophy in mathematics, a point he was to stress again and again in his courses of lectures. Tillich was to incorporate depth psychology into his theological thinking and thus explain traditional theological concepts in contemporary language.

If at first only fifteen to twenty students attended Tillich's lectures, this quickly changed: alongside the Union seminarians, graduate stu-dents from Columbia University, members of the general public and German émigrés also attended the overcrowded lectures. In response to the question 'What did they want to hear?' the psychoanalyst Rollo May, an erstwhile student of Tillich's, provided the following answer:

> Tillich sat at the lecture table, trying to pronounce his words in the English he was then just learning. Despite the broken language, I felt I had been waiting all my life for someone to speak out as he did. His words called forth truths in myself that I had known vaguely for years but never dared articulate . . . Tillich spoke with changing expressions of agony and joy reflecting in his face what

was going on in his feeling at the moment. This gripped me with a sense of reality that I had never yet known in the intellectual world.[20]

Ever concerned with political as well as theological matters, Tillich very quickly became known in émigré circles and as a result was elected chairman of the relief organization 'Self-help for German Émigrés', which was founded in the winter of 1936–7 and later renamed 'Self-help for Émigrés from Central Europe'. After the outbreak of war in 1939 Tillich voiced his opposition to National Socialist Germany in various publications. As a result he came to the notice of governmental authorities which encouraged him to participate in the psychological warfare effort against Germany, for the specific purpose of which the Office for War Information had set up a radio station, *Die Stimme Amerikas* ('The Voice of America'). Between 1942 and 1944 Tillich composed 109 speeches addressed 'to his German friends'.[21] When, in June 1944, German émigrés founded the 'Council for a Democratic Germany', Tillich was elected chairman.

In 1948 Tillich was able to return to Germany for the first time since the end of the war. He delivered lectures in various cities, but a permanent return to Germany was out of the question, largely because Barthian neo-orthodoxy had established itself such that theology of the sort Tillich represented was perceived as a threat. Nevertheless, in the following years Tillich would return at regular intervals to give lectures and talks in Germany.

While Tillich elaborated some basic propositions in his lectures on systematic theology at Union, he had still not produced a comprehensive statement of his theology. In 1951 this situation changed with the publication of the first volume of his *Systematic Theology*. The latter work was published in three volumes and consists of five parts: the first volume contains two parts, 'Reason and Revelation' and 'Being and God'; the second volume (1957) consists of just one part, 'Existence and the Christ'; and the third volume (1963) contains the final two parts, 'Life and the Spirit' and 'History and the Kingdom of God'. This is Tillich's major work, which resumes and continues his earlier thinking in a more compressed and in some respects innovative manner. During his time at Union Tillich was occasionally required to preach at church services. The result was three volumes of sermons, *The Shaking of the Foundations* (1948), *The New Being* (1955) and *The Eternal Now* (1962). When asked what he considered the best way into his thinking, Tillich would generally answer: 'First, read my sermons!'

Tillich retired from Union in 1955, but his academic career was far from over. In autumn 1955 he was invited to become University Professor at Harvard, one of the most prestigious academic positions in the United States. During this period Tillich travelled extensively throughout America to lecture, and his fame grew in an unprecedented way: he appeared on the cover of *Time* magazine in 1959 and attended John F. Kennedy's presidential inauguration two years later. After leaving Harvard in 1962 Tillich took up the offer of the John Nuveen Professorship from the Chicago Federated Theological Faculty. Through joint seminars with the historian of religion Mircea Eliade, Tillich's interest in non-Christian religions increased during this period.

On the morning after his last lecture, on 11 October 1965, on 'The Significance of the History of Religions for the Systematic Theologian' Tillich suffered a serious heart attack from which he would not recover.[22] He died on 22 October 1965 at Billings Hospital in Chicago. Tillich's funeral urn was installed in its resting-place in the cemetery at East Hampton, where the family owned a house. On Whit Sunday 1966 Paul Tillich's ashes were entrusted to the earth of the Paul Tillich Park in New Harmony, Indiana.

During his lifetime Tillich had received various honours, for example the *Goetheplakette der Stadt Frankfurt* (1956) and the *Hansische Goethepreis* (1958) and in 1962 he was awarded the *Friedenspreis des Deutschen Buchhandels*. In addition Tillich received various honorary doctorates. As early as 1960 the *Kreis der Freunde Paul Tillichs e.V.* had been formed, which was renamed the *Paul-Tillich-Gesellschaft e.V.* after Tillich's death. In 1980, after additional Tillich societies had been formed in North America (1975) as well as in the francophone world (1978), this was once again renamed the *Deutsche Paul-Tillich-Gesellschaft e.V.* Additionally, a Dutch–Belgian Tillich Society has existed since 1993 and a Brazilian Tillich Society since 1995.

Today the Tillich bibliography boasts over 600 titles, and in addition a whole host of manuscripts lies unedited in the American Paul Tillich Archive in the Andover-Harvard Theological Library, as well as in the German Paul–Tillich Archiv at the University of Marburg; many of them would doubtlessly merit publication. In addition to these should also be mentioned a quantity of shorthand-notated as well as taped talks and lectures. Tillich himself is reported to have said that all of his writings could be burned, with the exception of those on the demonic and the essay 'Rechtfertigung und Zweifel', as well as his best-known work, *The Courage to Be* (1952).[23]

CONCLUSION: ENOUNTERING TILLICH TODAY

Whoever studies Tillich's works carefully will always – consciously or unconsciously – learn something about Tillich himself. For Tillich is no mere intellectualist: his thought did not develop at the writing desk, but rather in personal encounters, out of his own experiences with other human beings and with the world. These experiences find expression in his works, as the following example demonstrates: in his 1957 work *Dynamics of Faith* Tillich writes under the heading 'The Community of Faith and its Expressions':

> The life of faith is life in the community of faith, not only in its communal activities and institutions but also in the inner life of its members. Separation from the activities of the community of faith is not necessarily separation from the community itself. It can be a way (for example, in voluntary seclusion) to intensify the spirit which rules the communal life. Often he who has withdrawn into temporary seclusion returns to the community whose language he still speaks and whose symbols he renews.
>
> (*DF*, 137)

Without a doubt Tillich speaks here from personal experience; it is well known that in the 1920s Tillich detached himself from the life of the church, but he returned to the church later on in his life and enriched it with his thought. Renate Albrecht, editor of Tillich's *Gesammelte Werke* and a former student of his from the Dresden years, said that Tillich never wrote anything in which his personal experiences did not play some role, even in so abstract a work as his *Systematic Theology*.[24] Carl Heinz Ratschow is thus not altogether wrong in claiming that Tillich's works are the immediate expression of his person.[25] It is surely false, however, to interpret Tillich's writings solely in this light.[26] A consideration of Tillich's life may be helpful for understanding his writings; however, that is not to say that the writings do not also speak for themselves. It is not Tillich's own person that is at the heart of his many writings and themes, but rather what he called 'our ultimate concern' ('was uns unbedingt angeht').

Tillich wrote only a very few books. Most of his output is in the form of essays and articles resulting from his talks and lectures. It would be a mistake, however, to think that Tillich frittered away his time in too many different projects. Indeed, Tillich himself had the following to say in answer to this anticipated objection:

Speeches and essays can be like screws, drilling into untouched rocks; they try to take a step ahead, perhaps successfully, perhaps in vain. My attempts to relate all cultural realms to the religious center had to use this method.[27]

When one follows Tillich in understanding theology as necessarily a 'theology of culture', everything becomes a theme for theology – and in Tillich's thought this is realized. Tillich's 'almost boundless impressionability' ('fast grenzenlose Impressionabilität'), as Adorno once put it, must be regarded as a precondition for such a theology. Adorno was correct in characterizing Tillich, in his striking image, as having 'a mobile system of antennae' ('ein wandelndes System von Antennen'), able to tune in perceptively to the spiritual situation around him.[28]

In his 1936 autobiography, *On the Boundary*, Tillich identified the boundary as an apt symbol for his personal and spiritual development:

> At almost every point, I have had to stand between alternative possibilities of existence, to be completely at home in neither and to take no definitive stand against either. Since thinking presupposes receptiveness to new possibilities, this position is fruitful for thought; but it is difficult and dangerous in life, which again and again demands decisions and thus the exclusion of alternatives.
>
> (*BOB*, 297)

Tillich lived his life on many boundaries: between city and country, social classes, reality and imagination, theory and practice, heteronomy and autonomy, philosophy and theology, church and society, religion and culture, Lutheranism and socialism, German Idealism and Marxism, home country and foreign exile. It is perhaps appropriate to give the last word to Tillich himself. Under the heading 'Boundary and Limitation' Tillich concluded his autobiographical reflections in the following way:

> This is the dialectic of existence; each of life's possibilities drives of its own accord to a boundary and beyond the boundary where it meets that which limits it. The man who stands on many boundaries experiences the unrest, insecurity, and inner limitation of existence in many forms. He knows the impossibility of attaining serenity, security, and perfection. This holds true in life as well as in thought, and may explain why the experiences and ideas which I have recounted are rather fragmentary and tentative. My desire to give definitive form to these thoughts has once again been frustrated by my boundary-fate, which has cast me on the soil

of a new continent. Completing such a task to the best of my
ability is a hope that becomes more uncertain as I approach fifty.
But whether or not it is to be fulfilled, there remains a boundary for
human activity which is no longer a boundary between two
possibilities but rather a limit set on everything finite by that
which transcends all human possibilities, the Eternal. In its
presence, even the very centre of our being is only a boundary and
our highest level of accomplishment is fragmentary.

(*BOB*, 349–50)

Notes

This chapter was translated by Alexandra Wörn and David Leech.

1 For Paul Tillich's biography, see Pauck and Pauck (1976), Wehr (1979),
  Bertinetti (1990), Albrecht and Schüßler (1993). The Paucks' biography, in
  addition to containing factual errors, which have been corrected in the
  commentary to *ENGW* V, also suffers from the signal disadvantage that
  the authors are not sufficiently familiar with Tillich's pre-1933 German
  background; it is primarily a biography of Tillich written from an American viewpoint and intended for the American reader. Jerald C. Brauer
  has also noted the inadequacies of this biography in Brauer (1989). Wehr's
  monograph is adequate for a first orientation to Tillich's work but is too
  brief – and offers nothing not already known. Bertinetti's Tillich biography,
  in addition to weaknesses in the biographical account with respect to factual and theological points, also demonstrates a profound misunderstanding
  of Tillich's thought (see Schüßler (1991), 10). In addition to these works
  must be mentioned Rollo May's books (May (1973) and (1988)) and Hannah
  Tillich's memoir (Tillich (1973)). However, these are not Tillich biographies
  in the strict sense: Rollo May's book is primarily a psychoanalytic study,
  which is only interesting when it describes May's own encounters with
  Tillich. Hannah Tillich's book describes various intimate details from her
  own and Tillich's life which may perhaps interest a certain sort of readership
  today but which should probably not be considered a genuine biography. The
  present chapter, which primarily draws on Albrecht and Schüßler (1993), is
  a slightly adapted version of Schüßler (1997), 11–25.
2 *ENGW* VII.
3 *ENGW* IX, 154–272. Translated by Victor Nuovo as *The Construction of the
  History of Religion in Schelling's Positive Philosophy: Its Presuppositions
  and Principles* = *CHR*.
4 *GW* I, 11–108. Translated by Victor Nuovo as *Mysticism and Guilt-
  Consciousness in Schelling's Philosophical Development* = *MGC*.
5 *ENGW* IX, 435–588.
6 *ENGW* V, 101f.
7 *ENGW* VII.
8 *ENGW* XII and XIII.

9 *GW* IX, 13–31. Translated by Victor Nuovo as 'On the Idea of a Theology of Culture' = *OITC*.
10 *ENGW* V, 162.
11 Translated by Paul Wiebe as *The System of the Sciences According to Objects and Methods* = *SS*.
12 'Autobiographical Reflections' in Kegley (1956), 14.
13 *ENGW* XIV = *D*.
14 *ENGW* IX, 273–434. See Albrecht and Schüßler (1993), 14f.
15 *GW* VIII, 85–100.
16 *RLG*. Translated by H. Richard Niebuhr as *The Religious Situation* = *RS*.
17 'Tonbandübertragung vom offenen Abend im Zunfthaus zur Waage' (Zurich, 12.11.1963), cited in Albrecht and Schüßler (1993), 74.
18 Cited in *ENGW* XIV, xxxviif. note 49.
19 Translated by Franklin Sherman as *The Socialist Decision* = *SD*.
20 May (1973), 4.
21 *ENGW* III and *ATR*.
22 *FR*.
23 P. Tillich 'Das Dämonische' (1926) in *GW* VI, 42–71 and 'Der Begriff des Dämonischen und seine Bedeutung für die systematische Theologie' (1926) in *GW* VIII, 285–91. See John (2003), 5.
24 Albrecht (1987), 7–16; 14f.
25 Ratschow (1980), vol. I, 11–104; 24.
26 Ibid., 22.
27 Kegley (1956), 15.
28 Adorno (1967), 25.

Further reading

Albrecht, Renate and Werner Schüßler (1986). *Paul Tillich. Sein Werk.* Düsseldorf: Patmos.
(1993). *Paul Tillich. Sein Leben.* Frankfurt am Main: Peter Lang.
Cali, Grace (1996). *Paul Tillich First-Hand: A Memoir of the Harvard Years.* Chicago, Ill.: Exploration Press.
May, Rollo (1973). *Paulus: Reminiscences of a Friendship.* New York: Harper & Row.
Pauck, Wilhelm and Marion Pauck (1976). *Paul Tillich: His Life and Thought*, vol. I, *Life.* New York: Harper & Row.
Schüßler, Werner (1997). *Paul Tillich.* Munich: C. H. Beck.
and Erdmann Sturm (2007). *Paul Tillich. Leben – Werk – Wirkung.* Darmstadt: Wissenschaftliche Buchgesellschaft.
Tillich, Hannah (1973). *From Time to Time.* New York: Stein & Day.

2 Tillich as a systematic theologian

OSWALD BAYER

MESSAGE AND SITUATION

Characteristically, Paul Tillich begins his *Systematic Theology* (published in three volumes in 1951, 1957 and 1963) with a section entitled 'Message and Situation' (*ST* I, 3–6). This section contains the key to his entire project of a theology developed 'in the tension between two poles'; the tension between 'the eternal truth of its foundation and the temporal situation in which the eternal truth must be received' (3). Tillich never departed from this theological vocation; even in his many works on 'social organization' and the 'critiques of the time' (*Zeitkritik*), notably *The Religious Situation* (1932) and *Theology of Culture* (1959), for which he was initially best known. Tillich always wrote from within 'the theological circle' (10). For Tillich, to do theology is to be situated: the truth of theology is based in a particular time. Tillich's insistence on perceiving the relevant 'situation' as 'the totality of man's creative self-interpretation in a special period' and his willingness to undertake the demanding analytical work that this required (an analysis of 'the scientific and artistic, the economic, political, and ethical forms in which they [a people] express their interpretation of existence') sets him apart from the other prominent kinds of twentieth-century theology (4; 3–4).

For Tillich, the two poles of message and situation stand in the same relationship to each other as the great *kairos* to the many lesser *kairoi* (*ST* I, 3; *ST* III, 369–72). Jesus as the Christ is 'the centre of history', the 'transtemporal' central occurrence of the 'great *kairos*', the only final *kairos*, the Eschaton (*ST* III, 364, 366).[1] As such, he is the 'criterion' of all other *kairoi*, such that we must see the *kairos* that appears in our own life history as embedded in the general cultural, moral and religious context of the age (370). In contrast to Bultmann's more individualistic view, Tillich insists that the perception of the *kairos* in an individual's own decision occurs in the midst of the general historical context and its perception. Of course, the converse is also true: the general situation cannot be grasped in a speculative manner, but only insofar as I participate in it with my own decision. In this sense, Kierkegaard's and Bultmann's accusations of a speculation distanced from actual existence are valid for Hegel's philosophy, but not Tillich's. Of course, not every 'situation' is a *kairos*, and this qualification is crucial to an assessment of Tillich's systematic theology.

Tillich initially experienced the *kairos* in the turmoil of the First World War that 'caused a tear in the deepest foundations for me and my generation so great that it could never be closed up again' (*GW* XII, 34). 'In this present time', wrote Tillich in 1919, theology and ethics must 'step forward in opposition to the capitalist and militarist order of society in which we find ourselves, and whose final consequences became obvious in the World War' (*GW* II, 14). In this time of rupture, in the 'time between times' ('zwischen den Zeiten'), he hoped for a new beginning and announced the *kairos*: the time of great change in which Christianity and socialism should unify to produce a new and meaningful form of life and society. The goal was to 'experience the divine in everything human, the eternal in everything temporal' (33). Tillich described his decision after the First World War as the 'socialist decision', that is 'a decision in favour of socialism' (219). The socialist decision itself is described as a 'prophetic attitude', gleaned from the words of the prophets, whose aim was to hear and to proclaim the first commandment ('I am the Lord your God . . . Thou shalt have no other gods before me' (Exodus 20:2–3)) in a particular historical and geographical situation (362).

APOLOGETICS – ANSWERING THEOLOGY

Apologetic theology has a long tradition; correctly understood, *apologia* forms a constitutive part of Christianity, both substantially and historically (1 Peter 3:15):

> Apologetic theology is "answering theology." It answers the questions implied in the "situation" in the power of the eternal message and with the means provided by the situation whose questions it answers.
>
> (*ST* I, 6)

Tillich distinguishes his position from a 'kergymatic' purism, which claims that theology loses its own foundation if it adapts to the particular situation. By 'apologetic' theology, Tillich does not refer to one aspect or moment of theology, but theology as a whole. It is quite astounding that Tillich fixed on this word and made it into a key term, in spite of its associations with the 'undignified procedure' of the once dominant nineteenth-century apologetics, an approach that was widely recognized to have reduced God to the status of stopgap (6). In no other twentieth-century theological system is apologetics such a defining consideration as it is for Tillich. For him, the apologetic task of theology is not its 'other', second task (as it is for Emil Brunner): it is its only task.[2]

APOLOGETIC DOGMATICS: THREE CHARACTERISTICS

Reflecting on Acts 17:22–32 (the text that might be considered the model *par excellence* for apologetic theology), Tillich identifies 'three tasks of the answering theologian' ('The Theologian (Part III)' in *SF*, 129–32; 130). From these tasks, Tillich derives three features of 'apologetic dogmatics': 1) the ontological *a priori* of creation, 2) the ontical crisis and 3) the ontical healing.

The ontological *a priori* of creation

For Tillich, that no human person can be outside God is an ontological fact. Tillich claims that the first part of Paul's speech means that 'those who ask him the ultimate question are not unconscious of the answer' (130). The Athenians 'adore an unknown God and thus witness to their religious knowledge in spite of their religious ignorance' (130). Even the person who is alienated from the fact of their creation has some idea of their origin and purpose, an idea of that from which they are alienated and separated, and with which they wish to be united. 'God is close to each one of us' (130). Therefore, people must be shown 'that neither they nor we are outside of God, that even the atheists stand in God . . . Genuine atheism is not humanly possible, for God is nearer a man than that man is to himself' (130–1). Just as it would be foolish to want to prove the existence of God, so it would be equally foolish to want to deny it.

The ontical crisis

Although mankind is not strange to God, it is estranged from Him. Although mankind is never without God, it perverts the picture of God. Although mankind is never without the knowledge of God, it is ignorant of God. Mankind is separated from its origin; it lives under a law of wrath and frustration, of tragedy and self-destruction, because it produces one distorted image of God after another, and adores those images.

(131)

With this statement, Tillich clearly accommodates the discontinuity that exists between the created world ('very good' (Genesis 1:31)) and the sinful world with which the creation is perverted. Apologetic dogmatics at this point becomes biting polemic:

> The answering theologian must discover the false gods in the individual soul and in society . . . He must challenge them through the power of the Divine Logos, which makes him a theologian. Theological polemic is not merely a theoretical discussion, but rather a spiritual judgment against the gods which are not God, against those structures of evil, those distortions of God in thought and action. No compromise or adaptation or theological self-surrender is permitted on this level. For the first Commandment is the rock upon which theology stands. There is no synthesis possible between God and the idols. In spite of the dangers inherent in so judging, the theologian must become an instrument of the Divine Judgment against a distorted world.

(131–2)

Tillich here stands in a line of criticism that stretches back to the Old Testament prophets and John the Baptist. He takes up their fight against idolatry and combines it with the radical Reformation interpretation of Paul's understanding of sin. In order to incorporate the radical nature of this prophetic and Reformatory judgement into his apologetics, he broadens it into a principle: the 'Protestant principle' (*GW* VII, 28). Tillich finds the crisis, the judgement of sin everywhere, even among those who consider themselves atheists – for example, the socialists, who Tillich sees as bringing God's judgement on the capitalist world.

Although Tillich expresses this ontical and factual crisis in a universal and radical manner in terms of God's judgement concerning sin as the negation of creation, he also emphasizes the unity of being that still exists between the sinner and God. In every case, the fact remains that 'God is nearer to us than we ourselves' (*SF*, 131). In a closely related manner, Tillich understands sin as the 'estrangement' of man from his true being. The ontical-existential estrangement of humanity from God is not intelligible without our ontological-essential connectedness with him. Of course, this raises the question of whether Tillich's system of differentiation and characterization of essence and existence really corresponds to the 'inexplicable and underivable' fracture that occurs with sin, or whether his is an attempt to understand sin by making it comprehensible, as 'estrangement'.

The ontical healing

The overcoming of estrangement through Jesus Christ is the 'third and final part of the theological answer' and of apologetic dogmatics: 'For we are real theologians when we state that Jesus is the Christ, and that it is in Him that the Logos of theology is manifest' (*SF*, 132). Tillich therefore sees the third part of his systematic theology ('Existence and the Christ') as 'the heart of any Christian theology' (*ST* II (G), 7). In Jesus as the Christ, the New Being (or 'new creation' 2 Corinthians 5:17) becomes present under the conditions of existence. Indeed, it becomes so present that estrangement is overcome and the true essence is revealed under the conditions of the alienated existence:

> To experience the New Being in Jesus as the Christ means to
> experience the power in him which has conquered existential
> estrangement in himself and in everyone who participates in him.
> (*ST* II (G), 144)

At this decisive point in his Christology an ambivalence in Tillich's position becomes clear. On the one hand, Tillich wants to hold on to the contingent nature of Christ's appearance – to its underivability and inexplicability; he does not wish to provide a speculative framework for the Logos being made flesh (John 1:14), nor does he wish to deduce it or to explain it in the manner of Hegel and the young Schelling. By refusing to enter into such speculative explanation, Tillich wishes to preserve the intention of the Kierkegaardian sense of paradox: he does not wish to tamper with the paradox of appearance, in which God is made man and the eternal appears in time. In short, Tillich does not want to turn this secret into a puzzle that can be elucidated by means of a speculative deduction and thereby solved. On the other hand, there is a sense in which Tillich does want to explain the paradox and make it accessible to everyone, while preserving its mysterious character:

> As theologians we must interpret the paradox, and not throw
> paradoxical phrases at the minds of people. We must not preserve
> or produce artificial stumbling-blocks, miracle stories, legends,
> myths, and other sophisticated paradoxical talk . . . We must not

impose the heavy burden of wrong stumbling-blocks upon those
who ask us questions. But neither must we empty the true paradox
of its power.

(*SF*, 132)

In this way, Tillich discusses the three breaches and transitions
which any Christian systematic theology must accommodate: the transition from a created to a fallen world the transition from a fallen to
a saved world and the transition from a world that is saved but still
contested to an uncontested, saved world. The decisive question for
any dogmatics that aims to elucidate the specific character of these
transitions is how the background continuities and discontinuities are
presented. Here the ambivalence that we have seen is crucial, not just
for his sermon on Acts 17 but also in the way that it moulds his entire
theological project.

THE METHODS OF CORRELATION

Point of indifference (*Indifferenzpunkt*)

Tillich considers the method of correlation as the 'backbone of the
entire theological method of thought' (*ST* I (G), 238).[3] Correlation, the
reciprocal relationship of two qualities with one another, determines
the structure of Tillich's systematic theology with its five parts, each
separated into two pairs: 'Reason and Revelation', 'Being and God', 'Existence and the Christ', 'Life and the Spirit' and 'History and the Kingdom
of God'. For Tillich, the word 'correlation' has at least six different
meanings, unified by a particular function: correlation allows the theologian to retreat from a pure identity or unity in which everything is
undifferentiated and to perceive difference in this unity.[4] In this sense,
the method of correlation is functionally equivalent to the use of the
concept of analogy in Karl Barth.[5]

At a central point in his exposition of the method of correlation,
Tillich moves from the epistemological to the ontological, and hence
his question–answer system interweaves with his essence–existence
system.[6]

A symptom of both the essential unity and the existential
separation of finite man from his infinity is his ability to ask about
the infinite to which he belongs: the fact that he must ask about it
indicates that he is separated from it.

(61)

According to Tillich, mankind would not ask questions about God if we were not separated from Him as the infinite essence. We do ask, however, and therefore remain bound to God.

The decisive move in Tillich's thought is therefore the assumption of an original, 'essential unity' of God and humanity and not their differentiation (*ST* II, 55f.). For Tillich, God is not humanity's counterpart. God and humanity, God and World are originally one and the same, an undifferentiated One. Even the differentiation between God and humanity – the paradisic, prelapsarian (and hence essential) difference, which was willed by God and is appropriate to creation as created – even this differentiation is for Tillich a sign of estrangement and sin. The differentiation between God and humanity would not exist if we were one with our origin, i.e. with God. Tillich acknowledges no difference between sinful estrangement and the divinely ordained differentiation between God and humanity.

Instead of this, Tillich claims an *Indifferenzpunkt*: the 'point . . . where question and answer are not separated' (*ST* I, 61). This point 'belongs to man's essential being, to the unity of his finitude with the infinity in which he was created, and from which he is separated' (61). Tillich became familiar with this 'point of indifference', and with its Idealist identity premise, through Schelling. The point of indifference is the point at which Nature and Spirit, God and humanity, recognizing subject and recognized object, ultimately come together and are ultimately one and the same.

Certainly, Tillich does not simply disregard that which theology understands by sin. He is familiar with the paradox that humanity is alienated from its being and is not simply identical, and will not easily become identical, with its origin. However, Tillich places greater importance on the identity of God and humanity than on their difference. The original connectedness of humanity with God – the ground of our being, that which is nearer to us than we ourselves – not only predominates over the sinful and alienated separation, it supersedes the differentiation between God and humanity, God and the world, creator and created, that was willed by God and was appropriate to the creation.

Theological critique

My theological assessment of Tillich's thought takes his understanding of sin as its central point. Clearly, Tillich tries to accommodate sin in accordance with the second article of the Augsburg Confession, but it is his distinctive elucidation of sin as 'estrangement' that is decisive (*ST* II, 47–58). In this way, Tillich effectively explains and positions sin within his philosophical system of essence and existence. As Gunda Schneider-Flume, in a perceptive critique, notes, 'grounding sin in estrangement and the simple opposition of affirmation (estrangement) and negation (no estrangement) in the system of correlation' demonstrates 'the danger that the method of correlation will draw a closed circle'.[7] Tillich's pre-formed philosophical understanding of sin must be contrasted with the theological task to begin with the Bible and avoid all temptation to reduce its unsettling message to a closed philosophical system. 'If sin is simply a sign of existential estrangement and New Being is correspondingly understood as the overcoming of this estrangement', then the gospel is:

> reduced to the recovery of the existence that asks for itself. In the circle of meaningful correlation between question and answer, sin appears as existential estrangement which is negated par excellence in the figure of Jesus as the Christ. From an apologetic point of view, and surely also from a pedagogical point of view . . . sin and mercy are thus reduced to the 'comprehensible' circle of the existence that asks for itself.[8]

In his anthropological delineation of boundaries, Tillich enacts a Kantian-style 'critique' of theological reason. Rather than remaining true to the theological task of listening to the biblical text, Tillich acts as a judge dictating what the Bible is and is not allowed to instruct, even distinguishing the intelligible from the unintelligible and nonsense.

JUSTIFICATION AND ONTOLOGY

The 'Protestant principle'

Influenced by Ernst Troelsch, Tillich was passionately interested in the question of whether 'the Protestant era' was coming to an end, which he interpreted as the pressing theological question of his specific situation. In order to engage with this question, Tillich called upon apologetic theology to seek to analyse and determine features of the situation of the age before becoming answering theology or apologetic dogmatics. In spite of his intentions, however, Tillich's own discussion of historicism and its problems, as with his treatment of the First World War and its attendant political, economic, spiritual, cultural and religious crises, is itself not primarily historical; instead, he proceeds by means of timeless principles. This is most surprising and seems to be paradoxical, until we realize that it is Tillich's treatment of Protestantism that is paradigmatic for his philosophy and theology as a whole. Tillich lifts Protestantism into the atemporal, general sphere by differentiating between the Protestant principle and the concrete historical forms of Protestantism: the concrete forms are perishable, but the principle is enduring and eternal (*GW* VII, 12f., 28). He understands Protestantism as 'a particular historical instantiation of a general and important principle. This principle . . . is effective in all periods of history; it is demonstrated in the main religions of humanity; it was announced powerfully by the Jewish prophets and is manifested in the figure of Jesus as the Christ' (12).

In this approach, Tillich adopts the technique of Hegel's speculative philosophy, which consists in discovering the universal in the particular in order to negate the particular as the particular and 'sublate' it. Hegel discovered Protestantism as the universal and negated the form as the particular in order to grasp it speculatively, and Tillich attempts to form the specifically Christian into a universal, which then disappears in its particularity and becomes plausible through a universal that then makes everything else intelligible, from Buddhism to the theology of Luther. Tillich detaches the Protestant principle entirely from any historical intercession and form, and seeks to demonstrate its validity in a pure sense, free from any concrete representations. All differentiations and definitions are dissolved in this pure principle. The principle guarantees the 'Over-being' (*Uberseiende*), the highest of all, the 'God-above-God', the God beyond all determinations, above the unity of subject and object; it guarantees absolute faith (*GW* IX, 18, 137–9; *GW* V, 125).

Being and non-being

The first commandment of the Decalogue, including the prohibition of images, which Tillich sees as preserved in the Protestant principle, is opposed by Tillich to the positive self-disclosure: 'I am the Lord, your God.' Even this declaration is affected by the commandment 'You shall have no other Gods but me.' Hence, it must be stripped of its symbolic character in order that it can be the last criterion at the ultimate level of abstraction. The criterion of being-itself is undetermined, with no qualities, beyond everything, above and beyond all determinations, above essences.

Being-itself does, however, include some differentiation, in the sense that it is not beyond every attempt to differentiate. It is eventful and alive in itself. However, it is only alive in this sense by virtue of a differentiation which Tillich cannot deny or neglect without destroying and contravening the radical ban on images that he has insisted upon. It is the differentiation between being and non-being that Tillich considers is incorporated into the self of being from eternity. Non-being is brought into being from eternity. This is comparable with Karl Barth's account, in which God eternally approaches the cross, and in this sense, because of his choosing, he incorporates the non-being of death. On this speculative point, Tillich and Barth are intimately connected with one another.

However, despite all that they have in common, the thought is expressed differently. Influenced by Schellling, Tillich says the following:

> Being can . . . only be understood dynamically if Non-Being belongs to it . . . non-being . . . allows God to emerge from His self-closure and show Himself as power and love. Non-Being makes God a living God. Without the negation which he has to overcome in himself and his creation, the divine affirmative would be dead to itself. There would be no revealing of the ground of Being, there would be no life.
>
> (*GW* I, 132)

This crucial and idiosyncratic concept of life as being in oneself, coming out of oneself, and then going back into oneself – God as life, God as living God – can only be conceived if God as being-itself is endowed with non-being through eternity. Tillich explains: 'Non-being makes God a living God' (133).

This thought, for which Tillich once again has Schelling to thank, means that no form of non-being, no form of existential estrangement, can exclude one from essential being. Because God in himself is an 'atheist', every atheist is also in God. The atheist cannot become detached from God. The being-in-God of the atheist is grounded in the innermost doctrine of God. No nihilist is excluded from being-itself; no experience of nothingness can allow one to fall deeper than into the depth of nothingness that is overcome in the self of being. The negations and doubts of the nihilist and the atheist can refer at most only to a theistic God, a personal God, indeed, an anthropomorphic God. They do not refer to being-itself, to the God-above-God that lies beyond the difference between theism and atheism, and beyond any positivity. Indeed, it is a condition of the possibility of doubt that the doubter cannot fall out of the power of being, because it is only thanks to the power of being that he can doubt:

> Genuine atheism is not humanly possible, for God is nearer to a man than that man is to himself.
>
> (*SF*, 131)

This is the only point where Tillich considers that there could be such a thing as atheism in practice, that is, when a person does not passionately doubt God and rebel against Him, but remains indifferent. Then, a person has 'denied his true humanity' ('The Divine Name' in *EN*, 77–84). Like Schleiermacher, Tillich means that a person loses his humanity when he is indifferent to God. By contrast, the passionate atheist is in God, in being-itself; he participates in this being and is justified as a doubter.[9]

The Protestant principle and the problem of the age

Tillich seeks to respond to the situation of modern nihilism and atheism in a theological manner by asking for a 'beyond' both theism and atheism. He combines this attempt with the claim to be a Lutheran theologian and a student of Kähler and Luther, who placed justification by grace at the centre of their theology.

For Tillich, the doctrine of justification is closely related to the Protestant principle. The Protestant principle represents only the negative and critical side of the positive that is to be found in the justification that occurs through grace. The Pauline–Lutheran doctrine of justification is, for Tillich, simply a particularly excellent historical manifestation of a generally valid principle that is demonstrated in all periods of history and in all great religions. In the context of the Pauline–Lutheran justification doctrine, Tillich wants to discover the universal in the particular in order to negate the particular in the theology of Luther. The negation of the particular, the abstraction from Luther's understanding of the doctrine of justification which is based in a particular liturgy and confession, allows Tillich to offer a purified doctrine of justification as a plausible answer to the situation that runs from the early Romantics to the modern nihilists and atheists.

This notion that the 'solution' to the problem of the age – how the Reformation doctrine of justification is valid today – comes to the fore in Tillich's early studies, especially of Schelling. Tillich discussed the results of these considerations in a letter of 5 December 1917: 'Through intensive analysis of the subject of justification, I arrived long ago at the paradox of "belief without God", and the further determination and unfolding of this concept shapes the content of my current religious and philosophical thought' (*ENGW* V, 121).[10] As a student of Martin Kähler, Tillich developed 'a new understanding of the Protestant principle' through his doctrine of justification (*GW* VII, 14f.).

THE SUBJECT OF THEOLOGY

Where Luther spoke of the 'condemnatory judgement of God', Tillich spoke of the 'abyss of meaninglessness'. Where Luther spoke of the liberating word of absolution as a particular, concrete, graspable affirmation, a word that encompasses bread and wine, so Tillich posited such a 'salvation revelation' (*Heilsoffenbarung*), of a 'foundational revelation' (*Grundoffenbarung*) and 'unmediated certainty' as 'freedom from the hopelessness of doubt and meaninglessness' that absorbs all names and categories; a declaration that leads one into the realms of speechlessness and a mystical absence of speech (*GW* VII, 97f.; *GW* V, 135f.; *GW* VIII, 97).

For Tillich, foundational revelation is certain in its unconditional nature, salvation revelation is uncertain in its conditional nature. For Luther, it is the other way round. All men know of God but have no unconditional certainty without the definite and conditional word of Christ.[11] There can be no doubt that Tillich's interpretation is not an extension or a remodelling of an old Reformation truth, but rather a shift of enormous proportions.[12] Nevertheless, Tillich consistently proclaimed his Lutheran orthodoxy: for Tillich, the 'condemnatory judgement of God' is the same as the doubter *qua* doubter being justified in the act of his passionate doubting and therefore, paradoxically, being certain in his doubt. The question as to whether this identity really exists or whether it is only achieved by reaching out into the abstract and general is unavoidable and throws into sharp relief the continuity and discontinuity in Tillich's relationship with biblical and Reformation theology.

Tillich's doctrine of the abyss of meaninglessness and the ground of meaning or of being-itself that carries non-being within it is so unspecific and general that it risks simultaneously saying everything and nothing. Tillich's category of 'ultimate concern' is overly inclusive: anyone can refer to it without contradicting anyone else in their individuality and without having to contradict another denomination or religion – after all, in the context of the ground and abyss of meaning and being, such faiths are arbitrary and one can easily be exchanged for another. The question of what is true and what is false cannot seriously be asked any more, because the alternatives are cancelled out in being-itself that carries non-being within it and collapse along with the question of meaning. The differentiation between belief and unbelief, God and idol, becomes irrelevant, because it evaporates into a single meaning in which this difference is inessential.

By contrast, Luther makes the ontological meaning of the doctrine of justification clear without sacrificing its particularity. Luther answers the question of what would be the 'subject' of theology: 'subiectum Theologiae homo reus et perditus et deus iustificans vel salvator'.[13] Seeking anything outside this subject is null, void and misguided. In short, Tillich's identification of the ontological meaning of justification is certainly to be welcomed; however, his way of portraying it is problematic and loses its concrete shape.

THE AFFIRMATION OF ESSENTIALISM

Tillich attested that without the assumption of the identity of nature and spirit, of thinking and being, of God and humanity, he could not think as a theologian (*GW* XII, 49f.). He is convinced 'that there must be a connecting point (*Anknüpfungspunkt*) in Man for God . . . there must be something in Man which allows him to recognize God, precisely that which Troeltsch has called a religious *a priori* – a "point of identity between God and Man"' (*ENGW* II, 201). In this sense, Tillich affirms the identity premises of idealism:

> I attended the school of German idealism, and I do not think I can forget what I learnt there . . . [I] remained an idealist in epistemological matters, if idealism is considered as the thesis that the identity of thought and being is the principle of truth . . . [It] cannot be denied that there is a correspondence between the human mind and reality that is best expressed in the context of 'meaning', and which led Hegel to speak of the unity of objective and subjective spirit in an absolute spirit.
>
> (*GW* XII, 49–50)

Tillich sees himself as being led towards 'the boundary of idealism', but he does not cross this boundary despite his simultaneous commitment to the truth of existentialism. This commitment, however, is not strong enough to place the identity premises, and with them essentialism, in any serious doubt. For Tillich, the difference between God and humanity, between God and the world, the creator and the created, is never so great that it cannot be swallowed up by a yet greater identity of being. Nonetheless, is he who calls from the depths (Psalm 130:1) identical with him to whom he calls?

If, with Luther, we hold that theology should be concerned not with the identity of creator and created but with the eternally persisting difference that prevails between the creator and the created and that constitutes and enables a relationship and communion between the two, Tillich's affirmation of essentialism – in the sense of the idealistic identity premises – is a fundamental stumbling-block. As a result of its essentialism, Tillich's theology seems to lack reflection on the concrete location of the experience of God, an omission that risks either drifting into the great unknown or turning back to an undifferentiated unity that exceeds all relationships and differences, including that between God and world, creator and created.

Further, Tillich's affirmation of the identity premises has a decisive implication for the character of his method of question and answer. In the context of these premises, the only form of questioning permitted is Socratic or maieutic questioning that brings to light only what is already within the questioner and the questioned. Tillich, like the transcendental theologian Karl Rahner, is interested in a *potentia oboedientialis*, that is, a fundamental and persistent capacity of man to listen. Only those who 'have heard and continue to hear the foundational revelation' hear the Word (*GW* VIII, 94f.).

Tillich's mystical theology of the philosophy of identity is fundamentally irreconcilable with Luther's theology, which concentrates and focuses on Word and faith and thereby on the differentiation, relationship and encounter between God and humanity, the *homo peccator* and the *deus iustificans*. Tillich's doctrine of justification, bound as it is to the category of 'meaning', is not a new interpretation of the biblical and Reformation doctrine of justification – the latter is determined by the Word and not by meaning. Tillich goes too far in his – admittedly understandable and necessary – struggle against personalism. The indispensable moment, or, more specifically, the constitutive personal relationship between God and humanity, and therefore the constitutive and persistent differentiation between God and humanity, that is in no way an expression of estrangement, is something that Tillich wants to account for only in a secondary sense, within the foundation of the Idealist identity premises.

The theologically legitimate and necessary differentiation between God and man was dismissed by Tillich with the term 'supranaturalism': Since supranaturalism assumes a basic dualism between divine and human spiritual life, it is in direct and irreconcilable opposition to the thought of truth and of identity.'[14] This thesis is unsatisfactory. There is a possible third way between a Marcionite dualism on the one hand and an Idealist thesis of identity on the other. The theological task is to avoid hurling the liberating word of Christ like a stone towards another – this much Tillich would agree with – but at the same time, *contra* Tillich, to say this word to the other in such a way that the pre-supposed horizon of the question that is humanity itself will change. The answer to his question is not comprehensible from the outset, but transports him, like Isaiah (Isaiah 6:5), into a state of shock and silence, but also into wonderment and then into great joy.

TILLICH'S AFFIRMATION OF EXISTENTIALISM

Tillich reached a global audience with his book *The Courage to Be* in 1952. This work appeared in a time of increasing cultural skep-ticism. Unlike the situation after the First World War, there was no atmosphere of cultural upheaval and creativity in the years after the Second World War. *The Courage to Be* was released into an intellectual vacuum, which Tillich called a 'sacred void'. This was his interpretation of the *kairos* after the Second World War. Tillich's 'encouragement to be' found resonance in the time of the apogee of existentialism, marked by the influence of Jean-Paul Sartre (*Being and Nothingness* (1943)) and Albert Camus, whose *Myth of Sisyphus* (1942) carried the revealing sub-title 'An absurd reasoning'.

However, Tillich committed himself to the *kairos* of existentialism under the assumption that existentialism simply elucidated a question that is as old as humanity itself, the question that man himself is. In this we see that Tillich, far from embracing existentialism and drawing out its theological consequences, rather limits its theological signifi-cance with his chosen horizon of questioning to such an extent that the Christian understanding of sin and with it Luther's determination of the subject matter of theology – *homo peccator* and *deus iustificans* – has no place. The key feature of Tillich's later theology is that his affirmation of existentialism does not exclude essentialism, but presupposes it.

THE DE-OBJECTIFYING OF THE OBJECT OF THEOLOGY

Paul Tillich follows Martin Luther in appropriating the first com-mandment as the axiom and criterion of all theology. In Luther's famous explanation of the first commandment in his *Great Catechism*, 'to have a God' is defined as 'nothing else than to trust and believe Him from the [whole] heart'.[15] The true God is he whom I can rely on completely; the false one is he who deceives me. For Karl Barth:

> The first commandment is written as a report of an event in time, as an address from one person to another: 'And God spoke all of

these words: I am the Lord thy God! Thou shalt have no other Gods but me!' In such a manner of address: I-Thou! God appears, and the theological axiom is erected.[16]

In marked contrast to Barth's personal discussion, Tillich's account takes up the first commandment idealistically, in a way that leaves room for ontologically mystical immediacy: 'ultimate concern' or, in his German formulation, 'was uns unbedingt angeht' (*ST* I, 11–15). Ultimate concern is, as Tillich says with regard to Kierkegaard:

> the abstract translation of the great commandment: "The Lord, our God, the Lord is one; and you shall love the Lord your God with all your heart, and with all your soul and with all your mind, and with all your strength." [Mark 12:29] The religious concern is ultimate; it excludes all other concerns from ultimate significance; it makes them preliminary. The ultimate concern is unconditional, independent of any conditions of character, desire, or circumstance. The unconditional is total: no part of ourselves or of our world is excluded from it; there is no "place" to flee from it. [Psalm 139] The total concern is infinite: no moment of relaxation and rest is possible in the face of a religious concern which is ultimate, unconditional, total, and infinite.
>
> (11–12)

What makes Tillich interpret the great commandment in such an abstract way? Why does he not concentrate on the literal wording, as Luther and Barth do? The answer lies in Tillich's desire to find a 'formal criterion' that is fitting for 'every' theology and religion, as valid for Buddhism as it is for Judaism or Christianity (11). At the same time, through this abstraction he wishes to secure the conditions of possibility that can make Christianity comprehensible in its concrete form. For Tillich, Christianity is comprehensible when it appears as a specific version of a general religious concept, and he finds in the demand of the first commandment an absoluteness that stealthily removes its controversial character, as well as the particularity that clings to it.

Furthermore – and equally decisively – Tillich's 'abstract translation of the great commandment' into the peculiarly indefinite and undetermined 'ultimate concern' is intended to avoid the religious mistake and theological error of 'personalism'. With his undetermined interpretation, Tillich wants to avoid the discussion about the objectivity of God, understood as humanity's counterpart. Tillich does not acknowledge that it belongs to God's nature as an 'object' that He has the power to oppose me and to stand opposite me (Genesis 32:23–32). However, for Tillich, to conceive of God in his objectivity in this way is equivalent to making Him into an idol. This is precisely what the first commandment forbids: 'You shall have no other Gods but me.' The ban on images is developed into a methodology to such an extent that it is also applied to God's portrayal of himself. Tillich fears that:

> Even God can be made a finite concern, an object among other objects; in whose existence some people believe and some do not. Such a God, of course, cannot be our ultimate concern. [Otherwise] we make Him a person like other persons with whom it is useful to have a relationship. Such a person may support our finite concerns, but He certainly cannot be our ultimate concern.
>
> ('Our Ultimate Concern' in *NB*, 159)

The discussion of Tillich's account of 'essence' and 'existence' shows how he attempts to 'solve' the problem of the personhood of God with a return to what Tillich sees as the only non-symbolic name of God, that of 'being-itself'. Tillich's formula 'ultimate concern' corresponds in its indeterminate and undetermined nature to his discussion of God as 'being-itself'. At the decisive point, being-itself and ultimate concern are identified. Tillich is concerned once again with 'a point of identity between the experiencing subject and the ultimate which appears in religious experience or in the experience of the world as "religious"' (*ST* I, 9).

> The object of theology is what concerns us ultimately. Only those propositions are theological which deal with their object in so far as it can become a matter of ultimate concern for us.
>
> (12)

However, Tillich does not question the relationship between object and act, of *fides quae* and *fides qua creditur*, but conceals it. Nevertheless – what is the relationship between my being completely seized, shocked, delighted and fascinated and that which seizes, shocks, delights and fascinates me? Can the object be brought into the act and identified with it in the way that Tillich implies? 'Ultimate concern' is an object that is in fact no object. Tillich considers talk of the 'object of religion', indeed, any talk of God's objectivity, to be problematic in every respect and tries to avoid it. When he talks of a 'something' which is of my ultimate concern he immediately withdraws even this linguistic formulation by emphasizing 'We cannot speak adequately of the "object of religion" without simultaneously removing its character as an object' (12).

When Tillich continues: 'That which is ultimate gives itself only to the attitude of ultimate concern', it becomes clear what is at issue: there should not be anything between what concerns me and me as concerned or ultimately affected – nothing that would allow a distancing or an escape (12). I cannot escape from God, as Jonah tried to, because God is everywhere: 'if I make my bed in hell, behold, thou art there' (Psalm 139:8). This means there cannot be any distance placed between that which concerns me and me as concerned. That which concerns me is not only always with me, it is in me – it is nearer to me than I can be to myself.

In this way, Tillich isolates the theological truth of immanence and ignores the other moment: that God comes to me in His Word from outside. In so doing, he de-objectifies the object of theology. This finally, then, is the price that Tillich must pay in his attempt to elucidate the Pauline and Reformation doctrine of justification in the context of the modern world.

Notes

This chapter was translated by Elizabeth Disley and Russell Re Manning. For the full German version, which is considerably abridged by this translation, see Bayer (2008). For a comprehensive account, see Bayer (1994), 185–280.

1 See also, *ST* III, 370, 153.
2 Brunner (1929).
3 See also his claim that 'the following system is an attempt to use the "method of correlation" as a way of uniting message and situation'. *ST* I, 8.
4 Clayton (1978).
5 K. Barth (1957a), especially Ch. 5.
6 See *ST* I, 59f. 'The divine–human relation is a correlation.'
7 Schneider-Flume (1979), 510.
8 Ibid.
9 Schleiermacher (1960), 177 [§33].
10 Letter to Maria Klein on 5 December 1917. See also *ProtE*, 'Introduction'; *GW* VII, 11–28.
11 Luther (1883), 19,208; see also 206,31–207,13.
12 For a full discussion of Tillich's distinction between *Grundoffenbarung* and *Heilsoffenbarung*, see Schüßler (1987) and Re Manning (2006).
13 Luther (1883), 40/II, 327,11–328,3.
14 Thesis 118 of the Kassel Spring Conference of 1911 in *ENGW* VI, 45.
15 Luther (1883), 562,2f.
16 K. Barth (1986), 63–78.

Further reading

Bayer, Oswald (2008). 'Grundzüge der Theologie Paul Tillichs, kritisch dargestellt.' *Neue Zeitschrift für Systematische Theologie und Religionsphilosophie* 50.

Bulman, Raymond F. and Frederick J. Parrella eds. (2001). *Religion in the New Millennium: Theology in the Spirit of Paul Tillich.* Macon, Ga.: Mercer University Press.

Clayton, John P. (1980). *The Concept of Correlation: Paul Tillich and the Possibility of a Mediating Theology.* Berlin: Walter de Gruyter.

Foerster, Herbert (1965). *Die Kritik Paul Tillichs an der Theologie Karl Barths.* Diss., Göttingen.

Gilkey, Langdon (1990). *Gilkey on Tillich.* New York: Crossroad.

Kegley, Charles W. and Robert W. Bretall eds. (1956). *The Theology of Paul Tillich.* New York: Macmillan.

Scharlemann, Robert P. (2006). *Religion and Reflection: Essays on Paul Tillich's Theology*, ed. Erdmann Sturm. Münster: LIT Verlag, 2006.

Wenz, Gunter (1979). *Subjekt und Sein. Die Entwicklung der Theologie Paul Tillichs.* Munich: Chr. Kaiser Verlag.

3 Tillich on God

MARTIN LEINER

INTRODUCTION: INTERPRETING TILLICH'S
MULTIDIMENSIONALITY

The intellectual appeal and the hermeneutical challenge of interpreting Paul Tillich's doctrine of God lies in his typical habit of invent-
ing creative formulations and phrases. Tillich seeks to combine diverse
traditions – speculative philosophy and Lutheran theology, proclamation of the gospel and dialogue with other religions or religious 'seekers', fundamental insights of liberal and dialectical theology, modern
existentialism and classical Greek ontology, German Idealism and religious socialism – and equally diverse motives. Tillich often attempts to
combine pastoral and systematic, apologetic and cultural, elementary
pedagogical and complex phenomenological, and academic and ecclesial concerns in order to arrive at a new language. Moreover, one always
has to keep in mind his sensitivity for a specific audience, whether
German or North American, academic or non-academic, religious or
agnostic. Finally, we need to take into account developments and shifts
in his thinking, although these should not be over-exaggerated.

This complex unity or multidimensionality, if you will, helps to
explain three characteristic aspects of the reception of Tillich's work,
which are also important for his doctrine of God: a far-reaching interpretative potential; one-sided interpretations and appropriations; and
one-sided critiques.

Tillich's understanding of God belongs to those parts of his work
that have had the greatest impact in different cultural realms. His concepts of God as 'ultimate concern', 'ground of being', 'being-itself' or
'God beyond God' are discussed in diverse fields, such as theology, philosophy, history of religion, aesthetic theory, political science, psychology and inter-religious dialogue. In the years before and after his death,
Tillich's formulations entered the general discourse of educated circles

and fostered a mutual understanding among different realms that had otherwise become increasingly alienated from each other.

At the same time, the far-reaching potential and the multiple dimensions of Tillich's work entail the possibility of a one-sided focus on one particular dimension at the expense of the others. Hence, we have various images of Tillich: as the liberal theologian of modernity, the Christian existentialist, the Idealist philosopher of religion, the Christian theologian who is open to East Asian religions or the socialist theologian of liberation for the First World. All these images capture one more or less important dimension of Tillich's thought, but they tend to neglect other possible readings of his work.

The reverse of an affirmative one-sidedness is the overly critical interpretations, which have become common since the late 1980s. Anyone who tries to bring together as many aspects from the history of ideas as Tillich did can hardly please everybody. For liberal theologians, Tillich is too theocentric; for Lutherans, he is too much of an Idealist; philosophers find his concepts to be insufficiently clear; existentialists think he is too optimistic; dialectical and postmodern theologians find him too ontological; for theologians of liberation, he is too conservative; and interpreters who look for systematic coherence find him contradictory. One could easily continue the list. Some of these very critical interpreters recognize valid points or weaknesses in Tillich's work, but often they do not do full justice to the complexity of his statements. On the whole, the one-sided critiques, like the one-sided appropriations, tend to prevent readers from perceiving the appeal of Tillich's work and from developing their own interest in it.

Fortunately, recent work on Tillich has found a way beyond this impasse in a strengthened hermeneutical and dialogical effort to interpret his work. In keeping with this new emphasis, this chapter will undertake three tasks, following Nicholas Wolterstorff's distinction between 'authorial-discourse interpretation' and 'performance interpretation'.[1]

(1) Authorial-discourse interpretation 1: the reconstruction of the creative contexts in which Tillich's doctrine of God originated. In accordance with Schleiermacher's theory of understanding as the reproduction of the generation of a statement, we will show how the boundary between different discourses became the location of creative insight for Tillich. In doing so, we have to weigh different influences on his work. Here, the focus of much recent research on Tillich's early German writings and on the influence of Schelling has been particularly productive. The following remarks continue in this vein, but I will put a stronger

emphasis on the constellation of specific problems that Tillich tackled and that, in the first place, created the dynamic tension for finding a new language.

(2) Authorial-discourse interpretation II: in discussing Tillich's work, I will sketch the multidimensionality of his formulations and the use of his concepts in different discursive contexts, as well as the later shifts in his thinking. Gunther Wenz was right on target when he described the basic tendency of Tillich's doctrine of God with the formula 'from subject to being', i.e. from the subjectivity of transcendental idealism to a metaphysics of being.[2] The formula is nicely illustrated by Tillich's early idea of God as our 'ultimate concern' and his later description of God as 'being-itself'. At the same time we have to recognize, following Wenz, that Tillich's early writings are already characterized by ontological concepts and that his later writings did not simply abandon the theme of subjectivity.

(3) Performance interpretation: in a third step, we will test the strength of Tillich's statements in contexts that he himself rarely addressed or not at all and develop a critical conversation with his work. Not surprisingly, some parts of his creative achievements will prove to be more successful than others.

THE KNOWABILITY OF GOD: HOW IS KNOWLEDGE OF GOD GENERATED?

Authorial-discourse interpretation I: The context and genesis of Tillich's doctrine of knowledge of God

At the time of Tillich's theological beginnings, one approach was especially prevalent among German-speaking theologians. It came from Albrecht Ritschl and his school and understood knowledge of God as being made possible exclusively through Jesus Christ. Max Reischle's statement 'Without Jesus I would be an atheist' was often quoted, even though it remained unclear whether the reason for knowledge of God was the historical Jesus or the risen Christ proclaimed by the gospel. In the 1930s, Karl Barth vehemently defended a version of this Christocentric approach in his debate with Emil Brunner as the basis of every proper theology: knowledge of God is made possible exclusively in and through Jesus Christ. Natural theology is the basis for philosophical speculation and the political misuse of the gospel. Revelation itself creates the possibility of knowledge of God, without the need for any pre-existing point of contact on the side of human beings. Tillich's position on this point was very clear: throughout his whole life he consistently refused to accept such a view.[3] The statement 'that without Christ we would be atheists is contradictory in itself, because the understanding of Jesus as God's revelation is possible only on the basis of a prior disposition to evaluate a reality as revelation. If without Jesus we were atheists, Jesus could not free us from atheism, for the vehicle to receive him would be missing' (*GW* VIII, 93).

Tillich sets forth his position in two steps, influenced by the traditional Augustinian idea of an implanted knowledge of God ('cognitio dei insita') and variations of this idea in medieval mysticism, German Idealism, Schleiermacher and Kierkegaard, and in his teacher Martin Kähler. His dissertation in theology, 'Mysticism and Consciousness of Guilt in Schelling's Philosophical Development' (1912), elaborates on the antinomy between the 'feeling of unity with God, who is the principle of the identity of absolute and individual spirit' and the 'experience of the contradiction between the holy Lord and the sinful creature' (*MW/HW* I, 28–9):

> On the one hand, the will to truth finds satisfaction only when unity between the knower and the object to be known is established, when the Absolute is the subject as well as the object of knowledge. On the other hand, the moral law, when it is truly comprehended, reveals the character of the will as being opposed to God, the enmity of the subject against God.
>
> (29)

The second thesis formulates the principle that 'the basis of the doctrine of God . . . must be the idea of truth, not the idea of morality' (25). This implies nothing less than the proposition that the identity principle is the basis of every form of religious or theological knowledge of God.

After some attempts at qualifying his conception of an implanted knowledge of God, especially in his 1917–18 correspondence with Emanuel Hirsch, Tillich arrived at a further clarification that became essential for his later writings.[4] The concept of meaning (*Sinn*) comes into prominence over against the concept of truth. Recent research thus speaks of a *sinntheoretische* turn in Tillich's philosophy of religion.[5] The Unconditional is now defined primarily in terms of meaning.[6] In his essay 'The Overcoming of the Concept of Religion in Philosophy of Religion' (1922), Tillich writes: 'certitude of God is certitude of the Unconditional ('Gewissheit des Unbedingten'), which is contained in the certitude of the self and grounds it' (*MW/HW* IV, 82). The experience of the 'I' is also the experience of being-held by something which is not part of the world. In locating the original knowledge of God in the immediate self-consciousness, Tillich is able to emphasize the non-objectivity of God as well as to apply the basic principle that was formulated for the first time by Irenaeus: 'Impossibile est, sine deo discere deum.'[7] God is known only through God (90). God is co-posited in the self-certitude of the 'I' and is therefore the origin of all knowledge of God. This has four consequences:

(1) With Kant, Tillich rejects the proofs for the existence of God. It is impossible to arrive at a thought of God if one starts from a consciousness without God. Cosmological arguments always tend to think of God as one object among others while ontological arguments do not recognize the fundamental difference between idea and reality.[8]

(2) God is not an idea but an experiential reality and accessible to every human being.

(3) Tillich interprets both religious and non-religious consciousness from the perspective of his idea that the Unconditional is a given:

> Now the self-certitude of the 'I' includes . . . an unconditioned perception of reality beyond subject and object and the participation of the subjective 'I' in this Unconditional-Real, in which it is grounded. The 'I' is the medium of the unconditioned perception of reality, and as such it participates in the certitude of that which it mediates; it participates only as a medium, since it is not the holder but the held. – The 'I' has now the opportunity to experience its self-certitude in such a way that the unconditioned perception of reality, which is a part of [this certitude], stands in the foreground as the *a priori* religious form of self-comprehension; at the same time, [the 'I'] has the opportunity to experience its self-certitude in such a way that the relation to the existence of the 'I' stands in the foreground as the *a priori* non-religious form of self-comprehension. In the first case, the 'I' goes through the form of its consciousness, as it were, and reaches the basis of reality in which it is grounded, in the second case, this basis remains effective – since without it there would be no self-certitude – but it is not touched; the 'I' remains unconnected, in the realm of [its own] consciousness.
>
> (81–2)

Hence, for Tillich, a non-religious consciousness can exist in intention but not in substance. Human beings are always already held by God.

(4) Tillich offers an explanation of how a religious world-view is generated. When one intends to look for the Unconditional, which is experienced in the 'I', in the reality of the world, one finds, through the Unconditional in the conditioned, 'that which holds everything, being its root of existence, its seriousness, its unknown depth, its holiness' (83).

These are the basic contours of Tillich's doctrine of knowledge of God. Its creative achievement lies in the successful combination of Schelling's concept of the Unconditional with Schleiermacher's idea of God as the whence of my immediate self-consciousness. The Irenaean principle that God is known only through God is upheld. Tillich thus combines modern epistemological presuppositions with basic theocentric assumptions: when there is a breakthrough (*Durchbruch*) of the Unconditional in a human being, he or she receives a share in God's self-knowledge.

Authorial-discourse interpretation II: The development of Tillich's doctrine of knowledge of God

Tillich's later works discuss this doctrine in various contexts and enrich it with a number of other elements.

The essay on 'Justification and Doubt' (1924) applies the doctrine pastorally as well as in regard to a theory of Protestantism, to a theology of religion and to contemporary theological debates. Tillich even describes the presence of God in the immediate self-consciousness as a 'foundational revelation' (*Grundoffenbarung*). Protestantism has 'to learn again how to speak of Christ in such a way that the powerful voice of the foundational revelation in all religions and cultures becomes audible' (*MW/HW* IV, 96). Only reflection upon this revelation makes it possible to overcome the doubts regarding the presuppositions of the Lutheran doctrine of justification. 'The response' to the doubt 'can be given only on the broad basis of the foundational revelation that shatters every position from which the skeptic can express his doubt' (96). The overcoming of doubt occurs through the presence and the truth claim of the Unconditional in human self-consciousness, which confronts the skeptic and puts him under its judgement, which is at the same time the gracious breakthrough of the gift of the Unconditional.

The essay on 'The Idea of Revelation' (1927) combines the concept of the breakthrough of the wholly Other and the trust in it with what is co-posited in the 'I':[9]

When the Unconditional-Hidden is revealed, it must be revealed precisely in this quality, as the unconditioned Hidden. It must appear . . . as what can never and nowhere be found in the context of the conditioned . . . The Unconditional-Hidden . . . is at the same time the Unconditional-Alien, which cannot be accessed from our own reality. It is the Wholly-Itself (*Ganz-Eigene*), which is always already present when a path begins. If it were only the one or the other, it could not become manifest. The possibility of revelation depends on the unity of both characteristics.

(102)

In this context, Tillich uses elements of early dialectical theology and transforms them in trying to overcome the critical paradox by means of the positive paradox:

The Unconditional cannot be reached from the conditioned. The two are wholly alien to each other. The Unconditional is the beginning of every path, *das Ganz-Eigene*. It breaks into its own as something alien: it reveals itself. If what is revealed is *das Ganz-Eigene*, then it is my ultimate concern.

(103)

Tillich's lectures on 'Dogmatics' in Marburg (1925) set forth the idea 'that the being-held (*Getragensein*) of being by the Unconditional in the state of ambiguity manifests itself as judgment' (*D* § 38, 197). The experience of separation, loss of meaning and self-destruction, and even the experience of nothingness, are connected to the breakthrough of revelation.[10]

The first volume of *Systematic Theology* (1951) emphasizes other elements besides the breakthrough of the basic ground ('tragender Grund') of the self in the knowledge of God. The theory of subjectivity recedes into the background, while ontology becomes more important. Tillich focuses on external factors, on the media of revelation and eventually on Jesus Christ as God's final revelation. He approaches the idea of knowledge of God through a phenomenology of revelation, characterized by the concepts of mystery, ecstasy and miracle, which Tillich interprets ontologically. The shock of the possibility of nothingness and meaninglessness is experienced. 'Revelation is the manifestation of the mystery of being for the cognitive function of human reason' (*ST* I, 129). This manifestation occurs through the media of revelation. When Tillich speaks about the inner word, he perhaps moves furthest away from the idea of the breakthrough of the basic ground in the self. Moreover, the idea of foundational revelation is missing from his *Systematic Theology*. Instead, he now says: 'Man in a state of existential separation cannot attain the message of the New Being by recollection. It must come to him, it must be said to him, it is a matter of revelation' (125). Revelation and knowledge of God possess an external history of preparation in the Old Testament, final revelation in Jesus Christ and subjective appropriation. Tillich interprets revelation in Trinitarian terms and emphasizes its soteriological impact: through an ecstatic participation in the Holy Spirit, revelation overcomes the ambiguities of existence and makes possible the fragmentary experience of the New Being (155–9).

One could understand the more traditional Lutheran explanations of the knowledge of God in the *Systematic Theology* as a break in Tillich's development, yet he also sets forth his idea on 'depth' (*Tiefe*). His famous New York sermon 'The Depth of Existence' identifies God with the depth and the ground of individual being: 'The name of this infinite and inexhaustible depth and ground of all being is *God*. That depth is what the word *God* means' (*SF*, 63).

This sermon displays a translation of the idea of foundational revelation into a new language, for example, when it identifies atheism with superficiality and separation from one's own depth.

The 'courage to be' replaces the idea of being-held by the Unconditional and becomes the prevalent expression of the experience of God. In the work of the same title from 1952, Tillich says: 'The courage to be in all its forms has, by itself, revelatory character. It shows that the self-affirmation of being is an affirmation that overcomes negation . . . The courage to be in its radical form is a key to an idea of God which transcends both mysticism and the person-to-person encounter' (*MW/HW* V, 224). Hence, the courage to be becomes the condition of the possibility of a deeper knowledge of God.

Performance interpretation

Tillich sets forth his idea of knowledge of God in different contexts. Sometimes it is more Idealistic, at other times it comes closer to dialectical theology; sometimes it shows a pastoral concern for the skeptic and the seeker, at other times it is more systematic and more traditionally Lutheran. But Tillich always remains true to two basic principles: knowledge of God is possible through God alone, and God is present everywhere, even and especially in those who are skeptical or desperate.

Hence, Tillich's is a thinking of the *dedans* (Gilles Deleuze), not the *dehors*, based on the idea of being always already held by God, in contrast to an Other that always withdraws itself. Occasionally, with some reservation, Tillich could even call himself a 'panentheist'.[11] In the contemporary postmodern situation, his thinking offers a welcome move against the prevailing stream. It is an antidote both to a vague plurality and to attitudes of intellectual nihilism. The idea of being always already held by God could be the answer to the 'Prayers and Tears' (Jacques Derrida) of contemporary philosophers, because it presents a basic and comprehensive response to atheism: atheism, according to Tillich, is an impossible position, since a sense of the Unconditional is present in every human being.[12] God is not a hypothesis, which could be verified or falsified, but God is the thesis that is always already presupposed by every claim to truth and every statement about being or about the Unconditional. At the same time, an 'atheistic terminology' is present in every religious action, 'in the sense that all "names" of God are inadequate' (*MW/HW* IV, 297, 357ff.). If one seeks to overcome atheism on a large scale, it can be achieved only along these lines.

HOW TO SPEAK ABOUT GOD: NON-SYMBOLIC AND SYMBOLIC GOD-TALK

Authorial-discourse interpretation I: The origin of symbols

The origin of Tillich's theory of symbols is connected to the problem of the content and richness of religious language. The Unconditional must be related to concrete elements of ordinary experience, so that religion and theology can say more than merely pointing to the fact that many human actions presuppose truth, being and the Unconditional. Tillich, in a more developed fashion from the 1920s onwards, calls these elements symbols.[13] Symbolic language transcends the possibilities and rules of ordinary language:

> In the situation of revelation, language has a denotative power which points through the ordinary meanings of the words to their relation to us. In the situation of revelation, language has an expressive power which points through the ordinary expressive possibilities of language to the unexpressable and its relations to us.
> (*ST* I, 124)

In a brief phenomenological description, Tillich distinguishes two main features of a symbol:

(1) *Uneigentlichkeit* (its figurative character) and
(2) *Selbstmächtigkeit* (its imaginative potential).

With Nörenberg and Wenz, one can relate to these two main features of a symbol the other characteristics mentioned by Tillich:

(1) Concreteness, transparency, the ability to refer and the historical possibility to be replaced are related to the feature of *Uneigentlichkeit*, while
(2) Acknowledgement, authenticity, the impossibility to create or delete symbols arbitrarily, and the ability to elucidate deep dimensions of human beings and of reality are related to the feature of *Selbstmächtigkeit*.[14]

The two features are rooted in participation, which Tillich distinguishes from identity. Symbols participate in the Unconditional for which they are transparent, but they are not unconditional. Hence, religious symbols have to be paradoxical, that is, they negate themselves, as can be seen superbly in the symbol of the cross.

Authorial-discourse interpretation II: The application of Tillich's theory of symbols in different contexts

While Tillich's thinking on symbols remained fairly constant from the late 1920s onwards, he continually developed it in new contexts. Further, the theory of symbols allowed Tillich to interpret critically all religious propositions about God and transcendence in the entire history of religion. Symbols have to be living symbols, which refer to the Unconditional and do not attempt to replace it. If they claim for themselves the character of the Unconditional, they become demonic. One must examine everything finite within the context of religion, culture and politics, and ask whether it has become demonic and put itself into the place of the Unconditional.

Tillich's theory of symbols enables him, as early as 1928 and then more often in later essays, to comment on propositions of psychology of religion and sociology of religion:

> Religious symbols open up the experience of the dimension of this depth in the human soul.
>
> (*MW/HW* IV, 398)

Finally, the theory of symbols enables him to take a stand on the question of de-mythologizing. For Tillich, mythological language is symbolic language, which cannot be understood literally but must be interpreted as a symbolic expression of the Unconditional. In comparison with Bultmann's, Tillich's approach to mythological statements about God is much less reductionistic.

As a result of discussions in North America, Tillich was challenged to clarify his understanding of symbols.[15] The first important clarification regarding human speech about God occurred in the discussion about the non-symbolic statement. Wilbur M. Urban and Edwin Aubrey pointed out in 1940–1 that Tillich's proposition 'All knowledge of God has symbolic character' leads to the question whether 'God' is also a symbol.[16] If God, as a symbol, is not somehow related to reality, the entire religion hangs in the balance, as it were. In order to show that religious symbols possess a relation to reality, Tillich takes up an idea by Urban and integrates the idea of *analogia entis* into his understanding of religion.[17]

> The symbolic, affirmative concepts about God, his qualities and his actions, express the concrete form in which the mysterious ground and abyss of being has become manifest to a being as his ultimate concern.
>
> (*MW/HW* IV, 274)

Moreover, he sets forth an idea that is reminiscent of Ian Ramsey's theory of religious language. The statement that human speech about God is symbolic, like other religious statements, is paradoxical:

> Again it would be completely wrong to ask: So God is nothing but a symbol? Because the next question has to be: a symbol for what? And then the answer would be: For God! God is symbol for God. This means that in the notion of God we must distinguish two elements: the element of ultimacy, which is a matter of immediate experience and not symbolic in itself, and the element of concreteness, which is taken from our ordinary experience and symbolically applied to God.
>
> (252)

Subsequently, Tillich resolves the paradox by introducing a non-symbolic proposition as the basis of all statements about God: God is being-itself. 'We must say that there is a nonsymbolic element in our image of God – namely that he is ultimate reality, being-itself, ground of being, power of being and the other, that he is the highest being in which everything that we have does exist in the most perfect way' (399). Likewise, he says in his *Systematic Theology*, 'The statement that God is being-itself is a nonsymbolic statement. It does not point beyond itself. It means what it says directly and properly . . . Other assertions about God can be made theologically only on this basis' (*ST* I, 238–9). Werner Schüßler rightly emphasizes that Tillich was aware that the concept of God as being 'also is a symbol, with which one likes to associate various contents taken from the realm of finite reality'.[18] But unlike such concepts as person or love, with which we qualify something conditioned, 'God' or 'being-itself' in ordinary language does not signify something conditioned. Evidently, Tillich aims to reintroduce the paradox over against a simple and risk-free identification of God and being.[19] In his restatement before the third part of his *Systematic Theology* he says:

> this is the point at which we must speak non-symbolically about God, but in terms of a quest for him. In the moment, however, in which we describe the character of this point or in which we try to formulate that for which we ask, a combination of symbolic with non-symbolic elements occurs. If we say that God is the infinite, or the unconditional, or being-itself, we speak rationally and ecstatically at the same time. These terms precisely designate the boundary line at which the symbolic and the non-symbolic coincide.
>
> (*ST* II, 9–10)

Here, we notice a proximity to the crossed-out mode of discourse about being in the thought of the late Heidegger and Jean-Luc Marion.[20]

Performance interpretation

Tillich's theory of symbols possesses a great productivity. It allows an appreciation of traditional metaphors of God and, at the same time, a critical insight into their ambivalence, particularly in the case of literalist interpretations. It also allows the critique of symbols that are fascinating, like an idol, and do not open up, like an icon, the space for an infinite transparency of interpretation.[21] From today's perspective, one must also add critically that Tillich underestimated the power of narrative as an element of myth and that, in the end, he did not arrive at a satisfying description of the identity of God and being-itself. We will return to this problem in the next section.

HOW TO THINK ABOUT GOD: TILLICH'S DOCTRINE OF GOD AND GOD'S ATTRIBUTES

Authorial-discourse interpretations I and II: Meaning, origin and development of Tillich's predicates of God

Tillich's statements about God have to be interpreted against the background of his theory of symbols. Every proposition about God must be understood symbolically, except certain non-symbolic statements that we consider first.

In the earliest texts, the idea of God as the Absolute is dominant. In his student fraternity *Wingolf* Tillich even had the nick-name 'the Absolute'.[22] His enthusiasm for the term stemmed from the influence of German Idealism, with Hegel probably playing the biggest role. In his *Systematische Theologie* from 1913–14, Tillich sets forth a philosophy of spirit in which 'the opposites of ideal and real, abstract and concrete, formal and material' are superseded by the 'absolute truth' (*MW/HW* VI, 66). In this system, God appears as the 'absolute that has become personal' (67). A few years later, in a letter to Emanuel Hirsch from December 1917, Tillich dissociates himself from the term: 'I accept [Martin] Kähler's claim that "the absolute is an idol", when the religious function is grounded in the completion of a theoretical concept of God' (*ENGW* VI, 99).

After this letter, the idea of the Absolute to a large extent disappears from Tillich's writings. Instead, the idea of the Unconditional becomes prevalent. Tillich's early texts define it in the context of a theory of meaning (*Sinn*): '"The Unconditional" is a meaning, but not a single meaning, since every single meaning is subject to doubt and could not justify the person who doubts. The Unconditional is meaning itself, it is the expression that there exists meaning, the constitution of the sphere of meaning' (*ENGW* X, 169). Notwithstanding this *sinntheoretische* interpretation, Tillich's idea of the Unconditional is a prime example of the complexity of his statements. On the one hand, it seeks to summarize the fundamental religious act, as it is expressed in the first commandment; on the other hand, it is influenced by German Idealism, and finally it is also developed phenomenologically:

> The term 'unconditional' . . . points to that element in every religious experience which makes it religious. In every symbol of the divine an unconditional claim is expressed, most powerfully in the command: 'Thou shalt love the Lord thy God with all thy heart and with all thy soul and with all thy mind.' No partial, restricted, conditioned love of God is admitted. The term 'unconditioned' or the adjective made into the substantive 'the unconditional' is an abstraction from such sayings which abound in the Bible and in great religious literature.
>
> (*MW/HW* IV, 327 n. 1)[23]

Tillich's concept of the Unconditional (*Unbedingte*) alludes to the linguistic connection between *Ding* and *be-dingen*.[24] The Unconditional itself is not a *Ding* (thing), but it can *bedingen* (condition) everything else. This means, expressed in the phenomenological terminology of Max Scheler, that the Unconditional is 'a qualification of all values, i.e., of the whole human existence' (III, 231). In a further development, Tillich underlined the grasp of the subject by the Unconditional, when he spoke not merely of *the* Unconditional but of what *our* ultimate concern is.[25] In accordance with the development from subject to being, in his later works the concept of the Unconditional is preserved but complemented by the idea of being-itself. The concept of being as the single non-symbolic statement about God plays a major role especially in the *Systematic Theology*, and it is rooted in the attempt to combine theology and ontology. The concept of being-itself had long been embedded in the theological-philosophical tradition and was used again by Schelling, among others.[26] At the same time, this concept emphasizes that God is not a being among other beings. Another term for being-itself is 'ground of being'. In a dialogue about the latter expression, Tillich said: 'I would prefer to say "being-itself". But I know that this term is even more disliked. I speak of the ground of being. I actually mean, with the classical theologians, being-itself' (*UC*, 46). Still another expression for the Unconditional in our relation to God is the concept of 'God above God':

> The courage to take meaninglessness into itself presupposes a relation to the ground of being which we have called "absolute faith". It is without a special content, yet it is not without content. The content of absolute faith is the "God above God". Absolute faith and its consequence, the courage that takes radical doubt, the doubt about God, into itself, transcends the theistic idea of God.
>
> (*CB*, 176)

In this context, Tillich seems to be influenced by reflections about the phenomenon of courage and the critique of theism, which also began to emerge in North American process theology. Moreover, there are connections with Plato, neo-Platonism, German Idealism and, above all, mysticism.[27]

After the non-symbolic statements, we turn to the avowedly symbolic statements about God. While the metaphor of 'depth' comes close to non-symbolic language, Tillich makes clear that it is a symbolic expression, while he can also translate it as 'what your ultimate concern is':

> And if that word has not much meaning for you, translate it, and speak of the depths of your life, of the source of your being, of your

ultimate concern, of whatever you take seriously without any reservation.

(*SF*, 63–4)

By contrast, the concept of God's life more clearly belongs to the realm of symbolic-figurative speech: 'Life is the actuality of being, or, more exactly, it is the process in which potential being becomes actual being. But in God as God there is no distinction between potentiality and actuality. Therefore, we cannot speak of God in the proper or nonsymbolic sense of the word "life"' (*ST* I, 242). Despite its figurative character, the symbol participates in God's reality. Religious language would not be possible without anthropomorphic symbols: 'theology should not weaken the concrete symbols, but it must analyze them and interpret them in abstract ontological terms' (242). Since God is the ground of being and being is the actuality of potentiality, we can speak symbolically of God's life.

In order to describe God's life, Tillich uses the bipolar terminology that he expounded in his ontological analysis of being as human experience.[28] They are the polarities of individualization and participation, dynamics and form, and freedom and destiny. These elements are symbols of the divine life, which is distinguished from human life by the following characteristic: 'Within the divine life, every ontological element includes its polar element completely, without tension and without the threat of dissolution, for God is being-itself' (243). Whereas Fichte criticized the idea of a personal God, since persons are by definition limited, Tillich says that the personality of God does not describe an individual existence without universal participation: '"Personal God" does not mean that God is a person. It means that God is the ground of everything personal and that he carries within himself the ontological power of personality' (245). Tillich regards the expression that God is Spirit as a comprehensive, inclusive symbol: 'Spirit is the unity of the ontological elements.' At the same time, it is the unity of 'the abyss of the divine (the element of power) and the fullness of its content (the element of meaning)' (250). Tillich associates the abyss in God with God the Father and the element of meaning with God the Son or Logos. The Spirit provides the unity between them. In regard to the symbolization of the divine life as Spirit, Tillich thus speaks of Trinitarian principles (249–52).

A new level of symbolic description of God is achieved when Tillich considers God's relation to the world. On the one hand, it is an easier topic, since the 'correlate of man's finitude' is presented: 'The doctrine of creation is not the story of an event which took place "once upon a time". It is the basic description of the relation between God and the world. It is the correlate to the analysis of man's finitude' (252). On the other hand, these statements possess a two-fold symbolism, as it were, since the respective divine attributes as well as the relationship between God and humankind must be understood symbolically: 'If God is said to be in relation, this statement is as symbolic as the statement of God as a living God' (271). The doctrine of creation provides the basis of this symbolism. It expresses the victory of the power of being over non-being. All statements about God's omnipotence and omnipresence, about the trinity of divine holiness, power and love, as well as the metaphors related to the basic symbols of God as Lord and Father, must be understood on this basis. In relation to the world, symbols always imply the critical and healing participation of God in everything that happens, which overcomes non-being.

Performance interpretation: The productivity of Tillich's attributes of God

Tillich's doctrine of God as being-itself and its manifold symbolic expressions has been widely criticized. The claim that being, not life, is the one non-symbolic statement about God seems to be rooted in the ontological philosophy of ancient Greece rather than in the biblical idea of a personal God. Eventually, the systematic and conceptual construction seems to gain the upper hand over against the phenomenology of revelation. However, the formulations of God as the unity of act and potency, the renewal of the doctrine of the immanent trinity as Trinitarian principles, the *analogia entis*, the idea of participation and the claim that God is beyond the opposition of essence and existence demonstrate that Tillich's doctrine of God remains remarkably traditional. In contrast to his North American conversation partners and their tendency towards process theology, Tillich sets forth a theology that is shaped significantly, from his earlier writings onwards, by patristic and medieval traditions. Admittedly, he undercuts certain medieval discussions because his theology lacks important differentiations, like the clear distinction between God's being and created being. Nevertheless, his integration of German Idealism (for example, the Hegelian refusal to describe God as sheer infinity, separated from the finite realm) and the consistent development of his basic principles result in a very creative doctrine of God.

The attributes of God that are more prevalent in other writings besides the *Systematic Theology* ('the Unconditional' or 'God above

God') are more productive when it comes to the descriptions of religious or semi-religious phenomena, as a brief reference to African theology illustrates. To a certain extent, the importance of Tillich's theology in Africa stems from his metaphorical language of God as depth, which is perceived as liberating, since the attribute of God as depth also appears in the theology of many native tribes, for example in Congo and Angola, who speak of *Kalunga* (depth) or *Kalunga wa Kalunga* (depth of depth). Christian missionaries, however, often associated depth with hell or the devil. Hence, Tillich's theology can contribute to the rediscovery of the concept of depth as a legitimate expression for God.[29]

Finally, the analytic power of Tillich's idea of the demonic as the pseudo-Unconditional is still relevant for the understanding of political, economic and personal phenomena.[30]

CONCLUSION

In conclusion, the greatest achievement of Tillich's doctrine of God seems to me the positive assessment and integration of atheism, and his insight into the problematic nature of the concept of God's existence:

> It is as atheistic to affirm the existence of God as it is to deny it. God is being-itself, not a being.
>
> (*ST* I, 237)

Notes

This chapter was translated by Matthias Gockel.

1 SeeWolterstorff (1995), 130–82.

2 Wenz (1979), 13.

3 See the evidence presented by Schüßler (1989), 31–55. See also Foerster (1965) and Re Manning (2006).

4 Werner Schüßler cites an unpublished letter of Tillich's from September 1921, where he writes that he has had 'many grand illuminations about issues pertaining to the philosophy of religion', which he wanted to express in his essay 'Die Überwindung des Religionsbegriffs in der Philosophie'.

5 See U. Barth (2003), 89–123.

6 Tillich's renunciation of the idea of the Absolute and his turning to the idea of the Unconditional are closely related to this turn. One should not over-estimate the turn, however, since Tillich could always identify the Uncon-ditonal and God with truth. See for example, *ST* I, 206: 'The unconditional element appears in the theoretical (receiving) functions of reason as *verum ipsum*, the true-itself as the norm of all approximations to truth.'

7 Irenaeus (2004), 4.6.3f., with references to several passages from the Gospel of John.

8 In regard to Tillich's different arguments for his rejection of the proofs for the existence of God, see Seigfried (1978).

9 See Scharf (1999). Scharf portrays the rise of the concept of breakthrough in Tillich's writings between 1919 and 1924, the writings in which break-through and paradox are dominant concepts of his theology between 1925 and 1936, and the decline of the concept of breakthrough after 1951. He con-cludes, however, that the concept of breakthrough is not simply abandoned in the later years.

10 See Dumas (1993), especially 35ff.

11 See Repp (1986), 308, citing an unpublished lecture by Tillich from 1956.

12 See, for example, Caputo (1997).

13 Tillich's first systematic consideration of symbols appeared in 1928 with the essay 'The Religious Symbol' ('Das religiöse Symbol', *MW/HW* IV, 213–28). The essay marks the end of a development that began in 1919, when Tillich used the concept of the symbol probably for the first time, in 'Justification and Doubt' ('Rechtfertigung und Zweifel'). This led to a more intense con-sideration of the concept of the symbol in the context of a *sinntheoretische* reconstruction of religion from 1922 and finally to the above-mentioned essay. For the development of Tillich's concept of the symbol and its origins in the idea of the paradox, see Danz (2006a), 59–75.

14 See Nörenberg (1966) and Wenz (1979), 163–5.

15 After the Second World War, Tillich explained his understanding of symbols in numerous writings, which are quite different in conceptual precision. A full discussion is not yet available.

16 See *MW/HW* IV, 269–77, including Tillich's response.

17 For the later integration of the *analogia entis* in Tillich's theory of symbols, see Schüßler (2006), 135–53, especially 150–2. Schüßler shows that Tillich distances himself from an understanding of the *analogia entis* that is either static or connected to natural theology.

18 Schüßler (1989), 163.

19 For a critique of this reading, see Leiner (2007).

20 See Marion (1991).

21 The thinking of Jean-Luc Marion and Emmanuel Levinas can be connected easily with Tillich's understanding of symbols.

22 See Albrecht and Schüßler (1993), 27, citing a letter by Friedrich Büchsel, 'The "Absolute" has given a brilliant speech. Of course, it was not easy, but it possessed an enviable strength and steady intellectual self-confidence.'

23 For Barth's trenchant critique of Tillich's use of this term, see their 1923–4 exchange (with Gogarten) in the *Theologische Blätter*, in Robinson (1968), 131–62, especially Barth's upbraiding of Tillich: 'You have spoken a great word [unconditioned] . . . ! Is it not God that is spoken of here? Why this hide-and-seek with the frosty monster, "the unconditioned"? . . . why not then with all good and bad Christians name God "God"? Is not the old simple word "God" in the mouth of a theologian who does not want to be anything else but a theologian safer in the end against dialectic, in the face of which I do not regard "the unconditioned" as weatherproof either?' Ibid., 147.

24 Cf. Novalis' aphorism in 'Blütenstaub': 'Wir suchen stets das Unbedingte und finden stets nur Dinge' ('Everywhere we seek the Absolute and always find only things').

25 In many English texts, however, Tillich simply speaks of 'the ultimate concern', not 'our ultimate concern'.

26 See Schelling (1977), 108: 'The starting-point of this science is our statement that we are not interested in being but strive only for the αὐτό ὤν [being-itself].'

27 The major references and connections can be found in Schüßler (1986), 152–76.

28 See *ST* I, 174–86. For the anthropological foundation, cf. also ibid., 243.

29 See Khal-Tambwe (in press). For Mark C. Taylor's postmodern critique of Tillich's idea of depth, see Re Manning (2005), 180.

30 See Schweiker (2005) and M. L. Taylor (2005).

Further reading

Bulman, Raymond F. and Frederick J. Parrella eds. (2001). *Religion in the New Millennium: Theology in the Spirit of Paul Tillich*. Macon, Ga.: Mercer University Press.

Jahr, H. (1989). *Theologie als Gestaltmetaphysik. Die Vermittlung von Gott und Welt im Frühwerk P. Tillichs*. Berlin, New York: Walter de Gruyter.

Kegley, Charles W. and Robert W. Bretall eds. (1956). *The Theology of Paul Tillich*. New York: Macmillan.

Leiner, Martin (2007). '"Kein Gott, der den Menschen Fragen stellt?" Jüdische und literarische Anfragen zur theologischen Methode und zur Gotteslehre Paul Tillichs'. *Tillich Preview* 2007. Berlin: Lit. 3–20.

Nörenberg, K.-D. (1966). *Analogia Imaginis. Der Symbolbegriff in der Theologie Paul Tillichs*. Gütersloh: Gütersloher Verlagshaus.

Scharlemann, Robert P. (1984). *The Being of God: Theology and the Experience of Truth*. San Francisco, Calif.: HarperSanFrancisco.

Schüßler, Werner (1986). *Der philosophische Gottesgedanke im Frühwerk Paul Tillichs (1910–1933). Darstellung und Interpretation seiner Gedanken und Quellen*. Würzburg: Königshausen und Neumann.

Seigfried, A. (1978). *Gott über Gott. Die Gottesbeweise als Ausdruck der Gottesfrage in der philosophisch-theologischen Tradition und im Denken Paul Tillichs*. Essen: Lugerus Verlag.

4 Tillich's Christology

ANNE MARIE REIJNEN

INTRODUCTION: 1957

Throughout his life Tillich grappled with the problem of history. Very early on he cleared a speculative space by asserting that there need be no historical certainty concerning the actual life of Jesus of Nazareth. Later he wrote: 'faith does guarantee the factual transformation of reality in that personal life which the New Testament expresses in its picture of Jesus as the Christ' (*ST* II, 107). If there is indeed a dividing line in Western theology between those who ask the modern or 'liberal' question of Jesus' place in our story and other theologians – postmodern or pre-modern– who choose to enquire only 'into our place in his', Tillich certainly belongs to the former.[1] Another aspect of Tillich's engagement with history is his keen sense of theologians' double allegiance: to their own time and to the 'eternal' message. Finally, history is intimately bound up with theology because the New Being was received in 'preparatory' events. From the death of Jesus and the birth of Christians, 'history is transformed and you and I are no more, and should not be any more, what we were before' (*NB*, 179).

When English-speaking readers of Tillich look for a complete account of his Christology, many will reach for the third part of the *Systematic Theology*, 'Existence and the Christ', which constitutes the second of three volumes. Simultaneously with the academic Christology of the mature theologian, a narrative and poetic version came into being, namely the second volume of Tillich's American sermons, *The New Being*. A third group of texts is the (much) earlier writings of the German period, starting from 1911.

By the time he published the second volume of *Systematic Theology* in 1957, Tillich had already spent twenty-four years on American soil, yet the memories of the German debacle were still vivid. In June 1944 he was himself one of the 'ten millions of exiles from practically all nations [who were] trying fervently to penetrate into the darkness of their unknown future'.[2] But Tillich's contemporaries were looking forward and outward to a 'last frontier'. The year 1957 is a watershed in the history of aeronautics: the Soviets launched Sputnik I and II and, for the first time, organic life was carried into space. As Hannah Arendt writes in the Prologue to *The Human Condition*, an 'event second in importance to no other, not even the splitting of the atom', for according to *communis opinio* it represents 'the first step toward escape from men's imprisonment to the earth'.[3] Yet, as Arendt points out, 'the earth is the very quintessence of the human condition, and earthly nature, for all we know, may be unique in the universe in providing human beings with a habitat in which they can breathe without effort and without artifice'.[4] Now I suggest that Tillich too is responding to speculations that are characteristic of the age of the Sputnik when he raises a question that:

> has been carefully avoided by many traditional theologians
> even though it is consciously or unconsciously alive for most
> contemporary people. It is the problem of how to understand the
> meaning of the symbol "Christ" in the light of the immensity of
> the universe, the heliocentric system of planets, the infinitely
> small part of the universe which man and his history constitute,
> and the possibility of other "worlds" in which divine
> self-manifestations may appear and be received.
>
> (*ST* II, 96)

Tillich's answer is dialectical. Christ is the central event of the history of humankind; he creates the meaning of that history and, in that sense, the event is unique. But Tillich modifies the familiar heliocentric and anthropocentric view by affirming that 'Man cannot claim to occupy the only possible place for Incarnation' (96). Put positively, 'if there are non-human "worlds" in which existential estrangement is not only real – as it is in the whole universe – but in which there is also a type of awareness of this estrangement, such worlds cannot be without the operation of saving power within them' (96).

Space ships and astronomy bring home the truth of the vastness in which the 'lonely planet' is a mere speck; nuclear technology, on the other hand, confronts human beings with the possibility of the self-annihilation of humanity. Under Eisenhower and Khrushchev, the United States and the Soviet Union competed for nuclear supremacy. In 1957, in the middle of the Cold War – familiar, like his fellow Americans, with such terms as 'thermonuclear holocaust', 'atomic apocalypse' and 'overkill', and steeped in a popular culture replete with images of mushroom clouds – Tillich interprets his contemporaries' acute consciousness of their finitude and the implications for Christology. 'It could be imagined – and today more easily than ever – that the historical tradition in which Jesus appears as the centre would break down completely . . . After mankind has gained the power to extinguish itself, this question cannot be repressed. Would the suicide of mankind be a refutation of the Christian message?' (99). If one of the two *conditions* of that message – namely the community that receives the Christ – disappeared, would that not imply that the message must also disappear?

Tillich's solution here is analogous to the one he gave regarding the plurality of 'worlds' in space. 'In faith it is certain that for historical mankind in its unique, continuous development, as experienced here and now, Christ is the centre . . . This existential limitation does not qualitatively limit his significance, but it leaves open other ways of divine self-manifestation before and after our historical continuum' (101).

By the time he published the middle volume of his *Systematic Theology*, Tillich had already received widespread attention. It is most of all his method that had come under attack; it is his method, therefore, that he feels impelled to defend and explain in the opening chapters. Tillich's starting-point is that 'Existentialism is the good luck of Christian theology' (27). In existentialist philosophy but also in the visual arts, in psychology, in literature and drama, there is an 'immense amount of material which the theologian can use and organize in the attempt to present Christ as the answer to the questions implied within existence' (27). This premise justifies, I believe, this brief reminder of the *situation*, keeping in mind Tillich's method: 'The situation to which theology must respond is the totality of man's creative self-interpretation in a special period' (*ST* I, 4).[5]

THEOLOGY AS POIESIS

For we which now behold these present days
Have eyes to wonder, but lack tongues to praise[6]

The second remarkable feature of Tillich's approach, also fiercely contested, is the freedom he claims for the theologian to discard established terms and thoroughly to revise the language of faith, forging novel word-creations where necessary. He offers no apologies for his 'apologetic' variety of theology, asserting that 'Theology must be free from and for the concepts it uses. It must be free from a confusion of its conceptual form with its substance, and it must be free to express this substance with every tool which proves to be more adequate than those given by the ecclesiastical tradition' (*ST* II, 142).

While Tillich affirms the right (the duty) of theology to emancipate itself from authoritarian dogmatism, his solutions are in fact quite faithful to what has been taught by the church 'always and everywhere'. Like Mondrian, whose only colours, for a time, were red, blue and yellow, the theologian resorts to three colours to create the picture of Jesus as the Christ:

> In all cases, the substance is untouched. It shines through as the power of the New Being in a threefold color: first and decisively, as the undisrupted unity of his being with God; second, as the serenity and majesty of him who preserves this unity against all the attacks coming from estranged existence; and third, as the self-surrendering love which represents and actualizes the divine love as taking the existential self-destruction upon himself.
>
> (138)

The main tenets of this Christology are classical: Jesus as the Christ is 'one with the Father'; he knows temptations and overcomes them; he knows he 'must' suffer on the cross. Tillich, for all his proclaimed freedom to reformulate the substance of the creed, never goes far astray from the *communio sanctorum*. He expresses a fundamental trust in the reliability of the Christian tradition. This, I suggest, ensures that the believer, at a loss for words, is not deluded into adoring some idolatrous distortion of Jesus as the Christ: 'And if the right words fail us in the absence of God, we may look without words at the image of him in whom the Spirit and Life are manifest without limits' ('Spiritual Presence' in *EN*, 91).

It is words, more than vision, that are problematic. Tillich might have called his own time one where 'we have eyes to wonder, but lack tongues to praise'. Certainly, this constitutes the most stimulating aspect of Tillich's Christology: readers encounter traditional notions that are deemed indispensable – the Christ, sin, healing. Such familiar coinages appear alongside notions that are imported from (existentialist) philosophy such as essence, existence and estrangement. Finally, idiosyncratic creations like 'New Being' or the 'picture' of Christ play a prominent role.

The following example serves to illustrate the mechanism of *redditio*, of the 'return' of a notion back into the Christian tradition after a passage through secular spheres: the Christ-like figure of

Che Guevara, a famous icon of contemporary culture, was borrowed back by the Church Advertising Network in 1999. In their campaign, the figure of Christ, now shown in the likeness of Che Guevara, dispels the notion that Jesus was 'a wimp in a nightie'.[7] Scholars might say with good reason that this insight could readily have been found in the Bible. But for some Christians, the popular icon of the revolutionary has become the vehicle to reclaim this forgotten aspect of an old truth.

Sometimes Tillich's *poiesis* seeks to create images by drawing expressive 'word-pictures'. In a sermon preached at the time of the writing of *Existence and the Christ*, Tillich recalls the woman of Bethany who poured ointment over the head of Jesus. He introduces an overarching new category that warrants close attention: *holy waste*. The apparent oxymoron qualifies both an 'ecstatic' relation to God and an attribute of Godself, as shown in the exuberance of creation (the Leviathan). Tillich goes on to exhort his listeners: 'Keep yourselves open for the creative moment which may appear in the midst of what seemed to be waste.' What greater waste than the execution of an innocent! According to Tillich:

> the Cross does not disavow the sacred waste, the ecstatic
> surrender. It is the most complete and the most holy waste. Yet the
> Cross does not disavow the purposeful act, the reasonable service.
> It is the fulfilment of all wisdom within the plan of salvation. In
> the self-surrendering love of the Cross, reason and ecstasy, moral
> obedience and sacred waste are united.
>
> ('Holy Waste' in *NB*, 47ff.)

Here the *correlation* between the quest for meaning and the reality of fulfilment becomes manifest.

EXISTENCE AND THE CHRIST: ABOUT CORRELATION

In the volume containing the Christology, the word 'Christ' is hardly mentioned until almost half-way, a tangible proof of Tillich's deeply held opinion about the nature of apologetic theology as *answering* theology: 'it answers the questions implied in the "situation" in the power of the eternal message and with the means provided by the situation whose questions it answers' (*ST* I, 6). The human predicament and the quest for the New Being must be described and understood as thoroughly as possible in order for the 'reality' of the New Being to be grasped. Thus, Tillich's position is diametrically opposed to accounts that refuse to consider the quest for salvation and the reality of Christ separately. Such theologies of the Word of God reject the independent treatment of theological anthropology ('sin'): the human predicament ('sinfulness') is only disclosed where redemption, in the figure of the Crucified, is already revealed.

For Tillich, there is no simple *diastasis*, rather a simultaneous dependence and independence of the questions and answer. The dependence is expressed by the *circle*. In plain words: 'Man cannot receive an answer to a question he has not asked' (*ST* II, 13). There is an aspect of this circularity that, I suggest, is akin to the classic notion of 'prevenient grace'. Tillich affirms: 'The question of salvation can be asked only if salvation is already at work, no matter how fragmentarily . . . The quest for the New Being presupposes the presence of the New Being as the search for truth presupposes the presence of truth' (*ST* III, 80). Here one remembers the *Confessions*: God 'who art with me even before I am with Thee'.[8]

Are religious experiences and religious expectations, then, simply homogeneous? Would humanity in its quest for meaning necessarily have discovered the figure of some christ or other? It is a fair question. 'Cheap' correlation rests on the assumption of dependence, but Tillich's correlation is the *unity* of dependence and independence. Therefore an equally strong affirmation of *independence* is needed: 'it should be reaffirmed that the answers cannot be derived from the questions, that the substance of the answers – the revelatory experience – is independent of the questions . . . The question does not create the answer' (16). The next step, securing that *hiatus* between what is expected and what is given – in other words, in defending God's sovereign initiative – involves a strong understanding of paradox:

> That is paradoxical which contradicts the *doxa*, the opinion which is based on the whole of ordinary human experience, including the empirical and the rational . . . The appearance of the New Being under the conditions of existence . . . is paradoxical, that is, against man's self-understanding and expectations.
>
> (*ST* II, 92)

Schleiermacher's concept of the 'God-consciousness of man', inchoately present in every human being and supremely realized by Jesus as the Christ, was *anthropological*, as opposed to Tillich's view of the 'essential unity between God and man', which is *ontological* (150). At the very end of the Christology, when he analyzes 'the reality of the Christ', Tillich proposes his interpretation of the doctrine of 'justification through faith by grace':

There is nothing in man which enables God to accept him. But man must accept just this. He must accept that he is accepted; he must accept acceptance . . . It means that one is drawn into the power of the New Being in Christ, which makes faith possible; that it is the state of unity between God and man, no matter how fragmentarily realized.

(179)

A *simple* correlation would require only the pole of subjectivity – the human (God-given) desire for wholeness – and its corresponding theological pole – the assurance of redemption as restoring wholeness. But Tillich's rendering of correlation is more complex, since the central paradox runs against the grain of human expectations. Also, the process of salvation is not merely subjective but also ontological: there is a positivity or *facticity* pertaining to the power of the New Being. In the words of the 1963 Earl lecture, Tillich explains the relevance of the 'new creation':

What we see is the astonishing fact – the paradoxical fact – that in the midst of human existence we find an image of essential humanity. It is not an 'ideal', something merely hoped for or prophetically announced, as in the Old Testament (and, in fact, in the whole history of religion). Here it is seen as a *reality* which radiates through Jesus' image, as that was remembered by the disciples when they received it.

(*IR*, 53)

It has not arisen out of our human deliberations, rather it grasps us as a reality that is outside ourselves. 'We may not comprehend, but we *are* comprehended. We may not grasp anything in the depth of our uncertainty, but that we are grasped by something ultimate, which keeps us in its grasp and from which we strive in vain to escape, remains absolutely certain' ('Faith and Uncertainty' in *NB*, 77). Yet again, the power and the reality of the New Being are not 'thrown at' the seeker, nor do they suppose a *tabula rasa* on the receiving side. 'The question about the manifestation of the New Being is asked both on the basis of the human predicament and in the light of the answer which is accepted as *the* answer of Christianity' (*ST* II, 93).

Tillich's use of correlation is a *leitmotiv* that runs through his entire work, not only in the *magnum opus* which is our starting-point but already from the earliest smaller texts and until the very end. Schelling's interpretation of the coincidence of opposites is a lasting influence on

Tillich's thought, as David Hopper has shown in his *Theological Portrait*: 'No matter how sharp the antithesis between two things, a more fundamental moment of identity between the two is always presupposed because no contrast can be observed or stated apart from some common ground of comparison.'[9] Although the relationship of the Unconditional to the conditional is determined by negation, there is also an even more basic point of *affirmation*, of a fundamental identity between the two, as expressed in the term 'ground of being'. Hopper points out that Tillich uses two kinds of paradox, a critical one and a positive one; the assertion above is an instance of the latter kind. Another way of approaching the positive *root* of the critical paradox is to say that because of the 'ground of being' creation is oriented towards redemption, and redemption is accomplished within creation; in faith, the two are apprehended together.[10] Correlation is what allows the transition from estrangement to the life in the Spiritual Presence, through the acceptance of acceptance, that is, through grace by faith. When Tillich describes the ambiguities of human life, the promises of the unambiguous life are already present.

Estrangement manifests itself in the human predicament with its procession of ills and of suffering: the symbols of the Bible speak of the expulsion from 'paradise', the 'hostility' between human beings and nature, the deadly rancour of brother against brother, the estrangement between the nations through the confusion of language and alienation in its multifarious forms. The Apostle describes 'man against himself', powerless in the face of his distorted desires.[11] Yet for Tillich, the bleak catalogue of human frailty does not obliterate human dignity, for several reasons. Against determinism, which reduces human beings to passive recipients of a tragic fate, 'the unity of destiny and freedom must be preserved in the description of every condition of man'.[12] The second argument belongs to the realm of faith: it is a confession of God's enduring presence. 'Man's hostility to God proves indisputably that he belongs to Him.'[13] This is the mark of human freedom: it is finite, but it still is freedom. 'Only man, because he is finite freedom, is open to the compulsions of existential estrangement.'[14] Tillich affirms the power of freedom, and he may be said to defend a Christian humanism. But he is quick to point out the limits of human power: he or she is 'unable to achieve the reunion with God'. Against Pelagian accounts of meliorism and moral 'synergy', Tillich defends the classical Lutheran doctrine of *sola gratia*. In Tillich's vocabulary, human beings 'must receive in order to act. New being precedes new acting.'[15]

THE NEW BEING: CHRIST AS POWER
AND PICTURE

For our sake, what we can see of God's grace is shown to us in the improbable shape of the unseemly:

> There is something surprising, unexpected about the appearance of salvation, something which contradicts pious opinions and intellectual demands. *The mystery of salvation is the mystery of a child.* So it was anticipated by Isaiah, by the ecstatic vision of the sibyl and the poetic vision of Virgil, by the doctrines of mysteries and by the rites of those who celebrated the birth of a new eon.
> ('Has the Messiah Come?' in *NB*, 95 (the emphasis is Tillich's))

The new-born child represents the precedence of 'being' over 'acting'. Also, the child, insofar as it is vulnerable, is a reminder of the contingent nature of all historical existence. It is in history and not yet historical. We are mindful of the story of the massacre of all children under the age of two in and around Bethlehem, in chilling proximity to the Nativity in the Gospel according to Matthew. To be a child is indeed to be defenceless and utterly dependent on others. We may compare this with the unpredictability and the power of promise as shown by Hannah Arendt. She crafted a word for it: *natality* – the opposite, I suggest, of fatality.

> The miracle that saves the world, the realm of human affairs, from its normal 'natural' ruin is ultimately the fact of natality, in which the faculty of action is ontologically rooted. It is, in other words, the birth of new men and the new beginning, the action they are capable of by virtue of being born . . . It is this faith and this hope for the world that found perhaps its most glorious and most succinct expression in the few words with which the Gospels announced their glad tidings: 'A child has been born unto us'.[16]

Salvation has the nature of a child, although it runs counter to common wisdom to affirm that strength can derive from such weakness, that suffering can signify victory. My commentary is of course coloured by Martin Luther's theology of the cross, as contrasted to the theology of glory. This Lutheran filiation is important, because both Luther and Tillich are adamant about the centrality of the paradox. For Luther, grasping this is synonymous with the gift of authentic faith. It is not optional, for all other ways of doing theology are worthless; in fact, blasphemous. And it is this indispensable experience of the paradox that 'makes' the theologian.[17] Standing in the tradition of this theology of the cross, Tillich admonishes his audience: 'He who wants a salvation which is *only* visible cannot see the divine child in the Manger as he cannot see the divinity of the Man on the Cross as the paradoxical way of all divine acting' (*NB*, 95). In words also borrowed from the Lutheran vocabulary, only the *deus absconditus* has the power to redeem.

This reminder is important, I believe, in order to avoid a misunderstanding that might arise from the frequent use by Tillich of the terms *picture* and *power*. If Jesus as the Christ is the faithful 'picture' of the overwhelming power of the New Being, then the rejection by his kin and by the authorities, the ridicule, his loneliness and ultimately his execution cannot be understood. We must listen closely to do justice to the dialectical nature of Tillich's rhetoric about Jesus as the Christ who is the 'picture' of the power of the New Being. Tillich warns repeatedly against the monophysitic mistake of portraying Jesus the Christ as a semi-god, impervious to frailty or only pretending to enter the human condition: 'the New Being participates in existence and conquers it' (*ST* II, 150). More explicitly, Tillich writes that this conquest of existence and of the estrangement that is a part of it does not 'remove finitude and anxiety, ambiguity and tragedy; but it does have the character of taking the negativities of existence into unbroken unity with God' (134). The New Being can be properly understood only as that *movement* of living through completely the pain of existence without being destroyed by it.

Another question, related to the problem of the power and the weakness, is the following: is Jesus as the Christ (only) the bearer of the New Being or does he 'create' it? Is his function comparable to that of a prophet, announcing the divine judgement and the coming Kingdom, or is he 'personally' the (co)creator of a decisive change in the history of humankind? Tillich's answers fluctuate, as do the biblical portraits of Jesus as the Christ. They oscillate between the Kingdom-centred narratives, mostly encountered in the Synoptic Gospels, and the 'Christ'- or Logos-centred pericopes of the fourth Gospel. When Tillich writes that Jesus as the Christ brings the New Being, he means that in Him, the New Being is *actualized* through the work of the Spirit of God. One may say that in Him the New Being is manifest, provided one take the term 'manifest' in a 'high' or strong sense. For we must remember that in Tillich's epistemology, manifestations – like symbols – are effective expressions, not mere communications (175).

On the other hand, this New Being is by no means restricted to the narrow span of time of the mortal life of Jesus of Nazareth. In all history, before the birth of Jesus and also after his death, among the innumerable beings who have not heard the Good News, processes of salvation are at work. He is not unique, although he is of ultimate or eschatological import. About the cross, Tillich says: 'It is not the only actualization but it is the central one, the criterion of all other manifestations of God's participation in the suffering of the world' (175).

How does liberal Protestant theology describe Jesus' power to save and heal? Is it fair to consider, with David Kelsey, that Tillich's model likens the redemptive power of Jesus as the Christ to 'the impersonal power that drives life itself'?[18] That expression is an adequate rendering of the 'God above God', beyond or before Trinitarian differentiation, as encountered in the conclusion of *The Courage to Be*: being-itself, or the ground and the power of being (10). But Tillich's New Being is not impersonal, since it comes about as the community between God and the centre of a *personal* life.

We must now address the complex matter of 'picture-talk' in Tillichian Christology. Obviously, it has a biblical precedent in Paul's words: 'the image of the invisible God, the firstborn of every creature' (Colossians 1:15). What Tillich finds wanting in Schleiermacher's category of *Urbild* is *participation*, since the notion of an 'archetype' or a 'primordial image' favours the idealistic transcendence of 'true' or essential humanity over human existence (150). In a seminal essay, 'On the Idea of a Theology of Culture', Tillich in 1919 proposed a three-pronged approach to art, which I believe to be implicit in his thoughts about the power and the picture in Christology. Every interpretation of culture should encompass three elements: form; content; and, less conventionally, the *Gehalt* – 'substance', 'depth-content' and 'import' are all imperfect translations. The *Gehalt* of any work of art is grasped in the content, by means of the form. In Expressionism, the shapes of people are distorted as a way of expressing a power that manifests itself precisely by the very way in which it breaks through the form and the content of objects. This 'shattering' power is the 'deeper meaning' or *Gehalt* of expressionist pictures. The critical or prophetic principle is similar to the shattering power described above; it is at work even in the heart of that most sublime of religious symbols, Jesus (as the) Christ.

The critical principle underlies the enigmatic affirmation that the Christ is both Jesus and the negation of Jesus: 'By dying on the cross, Jesus Christ, who is the basic symbol of being-itself in Christianity, underlined the fact that symbols have their significance not in themselves but as manifesting the Ultimate.'[19] Within this symbol two opposing forces are continually at work: representation and self-effacement. According to Tillich, Protestant theology has best perceived this dynamic of 'yes' and 'no': Jesus as the Christ both is, and is not, the New Being. 'For this is the greatness of Protestantism: that it points beyond the teaching of Jesus and beyond the doctrines of the Church to the being of Him whose being is the truth' ('What is Truth?' in *NB*, 71).

Between the painter, the sitter, the picture and the viewer there must be some common language, but it cannot be the language of 'plain' figurative art. In fact, more often than not the gaze of the faithful should be directed *away* from the picture! Tillich challenges his hearers as follows:

> Do we always make it clear that believing in Him does not mean believing in *Him*? If not, are we not working for destruction more than for salvation? . . . When in our time Jesus became an object of biographical and psychological essays and was portrayed as a fanatic or pious sufferer, or as a social benefactor, or as a religious teacher, or as a mass leader – He ceased to be the one in whom we can believe, for He ceased to be the one in whom we do not believe, if we believe in Him. He was no longer the Jesus who was the Christ.
>
> ('He Who Believes in Me' in *NB*, 99)

The name 'Jesus', then, is like the outstretched finger of John the Baptist pointing away from himself to the Lamb of God. Like the prodrome, Jesus says of *himself*: 'He must increase, but I must decrease' (John 3:30). Becoming totally translucent in relation to the coming Kingdom of the Father is the self-emptying ('kenotic') way of Jesus the Christ. That, and only that, is truly new in him rather than his teaching – since almost all his sayings have parallels in contemporary rabbinical literature – or his 'miracles' – fairly commonplace at the time of the Second Temple. The picture has to be broken; Jesus has to negate himself, in order to be true to God's intention. The followers of Jesus resented this, accustomed as they were to 'seeing' in him the power of the New Being:

> And when He sacrificed Himself, they looked away in despair like those whose image and idol is destroyed. But He was too strong; he drew their eyes back to Him, but now to Him crucified. And they could stand it, for they saw with Him and through Him the God who is really God. He who has seen Him has seen the Father: this is true only of the Crucified. But of Him it *is* true.
>
> ('Seeing and Hearing' in *NB*, 133)

For his contemporaries, Jesus of Nazareth was not 'the Christ', even if they marvelled at his words and his 'signs'. Only after his passion and death did he become the Christ, by virtue of the combination of a symbol available within the religious culture of the era of the Second Temple with an event – the New Being overcoming existence under the conditions of existence (*ST* II, 154). The birth of a community of believers is testimony to the fact that 'the death of Jesus of Nazareth was not able to separate the New Being from the picture of his bearer' (158).

Jesus as the Christ is the most complete 'picture' of God's power of being. As a picture, it is outside myself, so I can contemplate it, and it is also a mental image. Robert Scharlemann observes that:

> the New Being in Jesus as the Christ does not take the place of my own act of existing, but makes it possible for me to get beyond the impasse of despair at which existence ends, not as someone else's act in my place, but by something which empowers my own act, even though in the first place I meet it outside of myself.[20]

I submit a *tertium* besides the usual opposition of Christology from above and from below: Tillich's is a Christology from *between*. His main emphasis is the movement between interiority –the inner experience of the encounter – and exteriority, that is the New Being in history. And I would suggest that it is because of this character of 'between' that Tillich's Christology cannot give an unequivocal answer to the question raised in the next section.

IS JESUS AS THE CHRIST FOUND IN HISTORY?

Tillich's Christology goes against the grain of most contemporary portrayals 'from below' in one important aspect: his project started with an audacious declaration of freedom regarding historical fact. As Peter McEnhill and George Newlands point out, 'His willingness to concede at least the possibility that Jesus of Nazareth never lived dismayed many who might otherwise have been attracted to his position.'[21]

This is not to be mistaken for indifference to the dimension of history. Looking back on his beginnings, Tillich portrays a 'turn' or conversion to history – similar, I would suggest, to the 'conversion' of German Jewish thinkers both to history and to the faith of their people between the world wars. According to Mircea Eliade, the pursuit of history was *Geschichte*, not *Historie*: Tillich was not an historian of religions, nor, strictly speaking, an historian at all; rather, 'he was interested in the existential meaning of history'.[22]

As early as 1911, in the '128 Theses' presented at the 'Whitsun Conference' in Kassel, and time and again up to his last lectures more than fifty years later, Tillich asserted that faith in 'Christ' cannot rest on historical information, nor can it be undermined by the lack of such data. Even in the – rather improbable – eventuality that all the stories about Jesus of Nazareth could be proved to be without a basis in history, this would not alter the image or 'picture' of Jesus as the Christ, which has grasped and continues to grasp countless restless hearts and minds. Let us understand that this eventuality is the most extreme consequence of Tillich's radical proposal, not its main thrust. The point is that a gap remains even between the most plausible historical evidence and the inner experience of the 'picture'.[23]

This epistemological move is the young theologian's attempt to free himself from the constraints of both the liberal and the (neo-)orthodox defences against the growing demands of the historical-critical research. To use a simile from the world of chess, one might say that they find themselves in the predicament of being forced to play to counter an opponent's move (*Zugzwang*). This is what Tillich counteracts when he asserts the indispensable incertitude (*Ungewissheit*) regarding the historical Jesus. This insight in turn liberates Christology from having to play to heteronomous physical categories and provides a foundation that is no more, but also no less, than the certitude of the spirit itself, which, because it is in history, is truly autonomous.[24] Through his radical skepticism Tillich – not unlike Kant with his criticism – is *de facto* defining the limits within which the 'Christian certitude' can unfold. But the question arises how one can love a dogma or become a disciple of a dogma. In Tillich's later work the concrete life of Jesus as interpreted by the authors of the Gospels is given greater importance. Compared with the terseness of the '128 Theses', the mature Christology is rendered with great warmth and evocative strokes of the brush: 'It was just this concreteness and incomparable uniqueness of the "real picture" which gave Christianity its superiority over mystery cults and Gnostic visions. A real, individual life shines through all his utterances and actions' (*ST* II, 151).

'Christian certitude' is the belief that in Jesus who is believed to be the Christ something of inordinate importance has happened. In his life and henceforth in the 'now' of our own lives, Eternity has broken through. Renewal, reconciliation and resurrection follow in the wake of this event of cosmic importance. But how do we know this?

It is the certainty of one's own victory over the death of existential
estrangement which creates the certainty of the Resurrection of
the Christ as event and symbol; but it is not historical conviction
or the acceptance of biblical authority which creates this certainty.

(155)

Tillich's position is questionable – but then, he would have said *Si
fallor, sum*. We must agree with his critics that the combination of
the principle of the historical 'unknowability' in matters of faith and
the importance of the concrete 'picture' is disconcerting. For if we are
to believe that the New Being 'shines through' every trait of the man
Jesus of Nazareth, should we then not be able to look for a relatively
trustworthy 'picture' of him? In a critical assessment, Michael Palmer
queries: 'if, following Tillich, the quest for an historical Jesus behind the
Christological meaning of his being is truly irrelevant to theology, how
can it be then maintained that the New Testament portrait of that man
is not a fiction?'[25]

In Tillich's Christology, formal rationality is present in *semantic* enquiry that analyses the biblical records of Jesus as the Christ.
The records contain historical, legendary and mythical elements, corresponding to three ways of looking at reality. Although the elements tend
to overlap, Tillich attributes the highest importance to the third dimension. Historical reports produce the 'anecdotal' character of the Gospels;
they were chosen according to their value in answering the questions of
human existence in general and of the early congregations in particular.
The legendary form emphasizes the universal quality of particular stories. Finally, myths express the universal meaning of the overall event
of Jesus who is said to be the Christ (151). To illustrate this triple 'take',
let us reflect on the figure of Rosa Parks.[26] She is remembered for a well-
documented action in the struggle for civil rights in the South of the
United States; that is the kernel of 'hard', factual history, and it situates
her action as a response to the questions of her African American community. While she was still alive, she had already acquired legendary
stature; children would ask her whether she had known Sojourner Truth
and Harriet Tubman, the 'Black Moses'. This emphasizes the universal
meaning of some of the narratives of the struggle for civil rights. Finally,
the government of the United States, by placing her body in the Rotunda
of the Capitol, invested her with a quasi-mythical status. Using Tillich's
categories, Rosa Park's person and work may be interpreted as the sub-
jection to existential estrangement – the racist segregation that was
sanctioned by the customs and the laws of the South; her trial and
punishment within that framework – and as the conquest over that

estrangement, the successful boycott of the local public transport system that led to a revision of 'Jim Crow' regulations.

To some extent, Jesus as the Christ is found in history, for the Christ-event is not the only breakthrough of New Being; there have been and there will be many other breakthroughs. 'Christ is not an isolated event which happened "once upon a time"; he is the power of the New Being preparing his decisive manifestation in Jesus as the Christ in all preceding history and actualizing himself as the Christ in all subsequent history' (180). Jesus as the Christ is found in history because of the history of the Spiritual Community and because of the historical changes brought about by those who expect the Kingdom 'on earth as it is in heaven'.

CHRISTOLOGY WITHIN THE *GESTALT* OF THE SYSTEMATIC THEOLOGY

To start and to complete an enterprise like a systematic theology must be considered an expression of the 'courage to be'. The enterprise is undergirded by an assumption that to my mind belongs more to the nineteenth century than to ours – a fundamental trust in the intelligibility of reality, for 'the world is the world of the *Logos*'.[27] Such trust warrants the belief that 'No fair question has an unknowable answer.'[28]

That *Existence and the Christ* is separated from the sections *Life and the Spirit* and *History and the Kingdom of God* is for merely practical reasons; organically they belong together. 'Our statement that the Christ is not the Christ without the church makes the doctrines of the Spirit and of the Kingdom integral parts of the Christological work' (*ST* II, 180). Indeed there *is* no Christ without the community of persons who 'give birth' to him by receiving him, as did Mary, the mother of Jesus, the 'mother of all believers' in Calvin's words.

Christology is at the centre of Tillich's *Systematic Theology*; by depicting the quest and the reality of the New Being it serves as the most expressive illustration of the method of correlation. Yet Tillich's system is not truly Christocentric because of its open-endedness, which he defined as 'eschatological panentheism'. Accordingly, the conclusion of this chapter on Tillich's Christology must be the unfolding of a new beginning:

The paramount image is the eternal and temporal Spiritual Presence who mediates and consummates the work of the creative ground and the Reconciling Christ.

(IR, xxviii)

Notes

This chapter is dedicated to Will Storrer and the Center of Theological Inquiry (Princeton).

1 Jenson (1997), 34.
2 'The God of History' in *Christianity and Crisis,* 1 June 1944, in Cowan (1966), 18.
3 Arendt (1958), 3.
4 Ibid.
5 If the threat of nuclear destruction is the theme, the 'situation' is better expressed, for instance, by a Las Vegas showgirl in 1957, called 'Miss Atomic Bomb', who donned a pert mushroom costume, than by the papers of the War Office, since the former is already a creative interpretation, not unlike the responses to the all pervading thought of impending death by a death-defying burlesque, the 'dance with Death' shown by Huizinga for the period of the Middle Ages.
6 Shakespeare (2002), CVI.
7 See www.churchads.org.uk/past/1999.html
8 Augustine (2000), X, 6.
9 Hopper (1968), 41.
10 Ibid., 44. Hopper refers to an article by Tillich from November 1923 (he was 'Privat-Dozent' at the time) in the *Theologische Blätter* published in Leipzig, 'Kritisches und Positives Paradox. Eine Auseinandersetzung mit Karl Barth und Friedrich Gogarten', 265. This text is now in *MW/HW* IV, 90–8.
11 Hopper (1968), 45.
12 Ibid., 56.
13 Ibid., 45.
14 Ibid., 79.
15 Ibid.
16 Arendt (1958), 122–3.
17 An expression attributed to Martin Luther: *Sola experientia facit theologum.*
18 Kelsey (2005), 34.
19 Alston (1972 (1967)), VII, 125.
20 Scharlemann (1969), 96.
21 McEnhill and Newlands (2004), 260.
22 Braaten (1967), xvi.
23 'Die christliche Gewissheit und der historische Jesus', Vortrag auf der Kasseler Pfingstkonferenz 1911, in *ENGW* VI, 53. This is the text of Tillich's conference, not found in *MW/HW* VI. It is Tillich's commentary on the '128 Thesen' which are reproduced in *MW/HW* VI with rigorous text-critical notes on the different versions.
24 'Die christliche Gewissheit . . .' Die 128 Thesen, These 12, 34.
25 Palmer (1984), 199.
26 Born Rosa McCauley in 1913, she died on 24 October 2005.
27 Royce (1982 (1892)), 471.
28 Ibid., 365.

Further reading

Bulman, Raymond F. and Frederick J. Parrella eds. (2001). *Religion in the New Millennium: Theology in the Spirit of Paul Tillich*. Macon, Ga.: Mercer University Press.

Foster, A. Durwood (2007). 'Tillich and the Historical Jesus'. *Bulletin of the North American Paul Tillich Society* 33:1, 6–14.

Hopper, David (1968). *Tillich: A Theological Portrait*. Philadelphia, Pa.: JB Lippencott.

Re Manning, Russell (2006). 'The Place of Christ in Tillich's Theology of Culture' in *Christus Jesus – Mitte der Geschichte!?/Christ Jesus – Center of History!?* Tillich-Studien, vol. XIII, ed. Peter Haigis, Gert Hummel (†) and Doris Lax, 34–53. Münster: LIT Verlag.

5 Tillich's theology of the concrete spirit
FREDERICK J. PARRELLA

For Paul Tillich, the Holy Spirit is no 'forgotten God' but the reality of 'God present to our spirit', the one who makes the New Being of the Christ alive in life and history (*EN*, 84). Tillich's theology of Spirit, comprising the largest section of the five-part *Systematic Theology*, is the constitutive element of his understanding of God and the human person, and completes the Trinitarian structure of his system. The last volume on the Spirit is the least examined and discussed of the *Systematic Theology*, but it is vital to an interpretation of the whole. Langdon Gilkey, one of his finest interpreters, reminds us that 'Tillich is in truth a theologian of being; but what he means by being is often misunderstood if he is not also seen as a theologian of the Spirit.'[1] This chapter will explore Tillich's idea of the Holy Spirit or what he calls the 'Spiritual Presence' – its correlative relationship to 'life', its place in the Trinity, its relationship to ecclesiology and what Tillich calls theonomy in morality, culture and religion. It will conclude with some reflections on Tillich's pneumatology and his call for the 'Religion of the Concrete Spirit' and a brief application of Tillich's interpretation of Spirit to 'spirituality'.

Tillich considered in brief fashion the divine Spirit in the first and second volumes of his *Systematic Theology*: in volume I, when spirit was described as 'the most embracing, direct, and unrestricted symbol for the divine life', in volume II, when the divine Spirit became the Spirit of Jesus the Christ, constituting him as the Christ and making the power of the New Being effective (*ST* I, 249; *ST* II, 156–7). While Tillich also considers the Spirit in a number of his sermons, it is only in the third volume of his system that a full picture of the divine Spirit can be found. Like the other parts of the system, Tillich's approach is primarily ontological, not biblical; speculative, not doctrinal; experiential and practical, not abstract or deductive (though some may view this last point differently). Tillich's concept of the Spirit is central to his entire theological system, linking his ontology with his theology of culture and his synthesis of culture, morality and religion; it serves as a window onto his theology of the church and the relationship between Christianity and other religious traditions, and is an essential part of his interpretation of history, the Kingdom of God and eternal life.

TILLICH'S PHILOSOPHICAL HERITAGE

Tillich's theology is indebted to the thought of many philosophers and theologians, most notably Nicholas of Cusa, Luther, Böhme, Schleiermacher, Hegel, Schelling and Nietzsche. But Tillich's special contribution to theology does not lie in the unusual fact that, as a Protestant, he was a metaphysician and 'ontologist par excellence'; rather, his significance lies in the *kind* of ontology he fashioned.[2] By creating his theology within the Platonic-Augustinian ontology of participation, Tillich retrieves the ontological perspective found in the classical mystics and mystical theologians in which God is immediately knowable and the ground of one's self-knowledge. This theological perspective, which receded in formal theology from the late thirteenth century onwards, to be replaced by Aristotelian Thomism, nominalism and subsequent philosophies, reaffirms the paradox of God's transcendence and immanence and re-establishes the immediacy of God in human experience. Tillich's understanding of the Spirit must first be seen in this ontological context, to which one must add Schelling's positive philosophy of his second period, where a turn to the existential replaced Schelling's earlier idealism. Both these elements – the ontological and the existential – are particularly visible in Tillich's theology of Spirit.

THE MEANING OF LIFE AND THE QUEST FOR THE SPIRIT

Tillich's theological method of correlation links the ontological and the existential: transcendent theological answers correlate with human existential questions (*ST* I, 59–66). As God is the answer to the question of being and Jesus the Christ to the question of existence, the divine Spirit answers the question of life. In order to comprehend Tillich's theology of the Spirit, a thorough examination of his treatment of life is important, because life is the actualization of being, the concrete expression of being-itself and the New Being of the Christ. At its core, human life opens up a deep yearning for the unambiguous, the life of the New Being, that only the divine Spirit or Spiritual Presence can make actual in every concrete situation (*ST* III, 286). Spirit overcomes, although in a fragmentary, temporary and fleeting way, the ambiguities of life.

The multidimensional unity of life and the fundamental elements of the actualization of being

The distinction between essence and existence, between what ought to be and what is, underlies Tillich's entire theological system (*ST* III, 11–12). Life inevitably actualizes both essential and existential being; it is from essence-estranged existence that the ambiguities of life spring. For Tillich, life possesses a 'multidimensional unity'. Rejecting the hierarchical term 'levels' to describe different aspects and forms of life, Tillich instead uses the metaphors of 'dimension' and 'realm'. In one dimension of life, therefore, all dimensions are potentially present, while some may be actualized; they cut through each other and do not interfere with each other. For example, the dimension of the inorganic interpenetrates the dimension of the spiritual and vice versa (12–17).[3] As Tillich says, 'what happens to man happens implicitly to all realms of life, for in man all levels of being are present . . . man [is] the "microcosmos"' (*ST* II, 120–1). As Schelling remarks of the unity of spirit and nature in the Fall, 'Nature also longs for a lost good' (*SF*, 82). Each dimension of life possesses its own degree or power of being, and the evolution of one dimension to a more complex one – for example, the inorganic to the organic – depends on a constellation of conditions (*ST* III, 17–20). Here, Tillich reveals the influence of modern naturalism on his thinking (*ST* I, 261).[4] Likewise, Tillich's attractiveness today to the field of eco-theology (which he could never have imagined in his day) developed from his insistence on the multidimensional unity of life.[5]

According to Tillich, three basic movements are present in everything alive: self-identity, self-alteration and a return to oneself. These movements, which create the pattern of going out from one's self-identity and returning to oneself, take place in life's three functions: self-integration, self-creation and self-transcendence. While even the inorganic dimension of life shares in these functions, in the dimension of the spirit they have particular import and application. *Self-integration* is a circular quest for centredness; it actualizes the polarity in all beings (which Tillich develops in the first volume of *Systematic Theology*) between individualization and participation; in the realm of the spirit, it is morality. *Self-creation* is a horizontal quest for growth; it actualizes the polarity between dynamics and form; in the realm of the spirit, it is culture. Finally, *self-transcendence* is a vertical quest for the sublime; it actualizes the polarity between freedom and destiny; in the realm of the spirit, it is religion. The basic movement of life – self-identity, self-alteration and a return to oneself – share in t.e distortions of existence: disintegration in the moral order, destruction in the cultural order, and profanization and demonization in the sphere of religion. Thus, life is always ambiguous, because in each of its three functions it is a mixture of the essential and the existential, the positive and the negative elements within being (*ST* III, 32).

First function: self-integration and ambiguity in the moral sphere

Through self-integration, the actualization of individualization and participation within every being, life maintains its centredness. Everything alive has a centre, a point that cannot be divided, only destroyed. In the inorganic realm, it is a process of concentration and expansion; in the organic realm, the tension between integration and disintegration. A profound ambiguity exists in the process of self-integration in every dimension. Expanding from one's centre may mean a scattering of the centre and its ultimate loss; this is the death of self-alteration. Remaining in one's centre may result in an immobility that destroys the force of life; this is the death of self-identity (*ST* III, 32–8). Self-integration in the dimension of the spirit is the function of morality, 'in which the centred self constitutes itself as a person; it is the totality of those acts in which a potentially personal life process becomes an actual person' (39). Since a person not only has an environment but also a world, he or she is a completely centred individual and free to decide and deliberate in terms of the moral act through freedom. A person discovers the norms determining the moral act through freedom in an encounter with another, in an I–Thou relation, where the Thou becomes the unconditional limit to an individual's drive to assimilate the world. In the other, the person experiences the ought-to-be of his or her own self-integration; in other words, self-integration takes place in a community where centred self encounters centred self (38–41).

Second function: self-creativity and ambiguity in the cultural sphere

Through self-creativity, the actualization of dynamics and form, life grows and re-creates itself. Growth is the creation of a new form, positing a moment of 'chaos between the not-yet-form and the no-longer-form'. Hence, all creation reveals an element of destructiveness. In the inorganic realm, the concept of growth is metaphorical; in the organic realm, tension is present in the constant struggle for life and the inevitability of death. The awareness of life's exhaustibility and the dialectic of the life instinct and the death instinct exemplify the profound ambiguities in the function of self-creation (*ST* III, 50–7). Self-creativity in the

dimension of the spirit is the cultural act. In culture, the inherent ambiguity is reduced to the same pattern: a separation or split of subject from
object. This separation from subject and object occurs both in *theoria*,
the grasping function of reason in cognitive and aesthetic acts, and in
praxis, the shaping function of reason in personal and communal acts
(*ST* I, 76–9). Both the theoretical split, which makes truth and beauty
possible, and the practical split, which makes the question of humanity
and justice possible, are simultaneously the conditions that make their
unambiguous attainment existentially impossible.

Third function: self-transcendence and ambiguity in the religious sphere

Through self-transcendence, the religious act uniting freedom and
destiny, life is 'freed from itself' and liberated from bondage to its own
finitude. It is 'a striving in the vertical direction toward ultimate and
infinite being' (*ST* III, 86). Properly speaking, self-transcendence is not
a function beside the other two functions of the spirit, but a quality
of all of them; if it were a separate function, it itself would have to
be transcended, and life cannot genuinely transcend itself in one of
its own functions. Self-transcendence is the source of unity between
morality, culture and religion because religion is the element of the
self-transcendence of the spirit found in the other functions of life (96).
Religion gives morality its ultimate seriousness, and it gives culture
its ultimate depth. In their essential nature, religion, morality and culture interpenetrate one another, but this unity is one of 'transhistorical
remembrance' and 'utopian anticipation'. In actual life, the essential is
mixed with the existential and the three functions separate, each with
their own particular ambiguities.

The ambiguities in religion take two forms: the profane, which
resists transcendence, and the demonic, which distorts it. Profanization is an ambiguity within the religious function itself, such as the
failure of religious institutions properly to face the transcendent, or the
reduction of the transcendent element by society to culture or morality. Demonization involves the elevation of something conditional to
unconditional validity; in every case, it identifies the bearer of the holy
with the holy itself. All religious life reveals the presence of both these
distortions to a greater or lesser degree, whether openly or in secret (98–
102). The ambiguities of religion are doubly profound because religion
claims to be the answer to ambiguities in the other functions of life; yet
it itself is subject to ambiguity and therefore distorts the unambiguous
answer that it receives in revelation (98–104). As Tillich says, 'Religion

as the self-transcendence of life needs the religions and needs to deny them' (97–8).

THE SPIRITUAL PRESENCE

Since life is the actualization of being, the anxiety and longing of finitude and the sting of estrangement become real and concrete *only* in life; put differently, the ambiguity of life emerges from the actualization of estrangement and fallenness. This ambiguity poses the question: can life be actualized where estrangement is vanquished, where individuals and society live in harmony and creative justice, where religion and culture manifest the depth of being in perfect form and where religion itself is transparent for one's ultimate concern and the ultimate itself? The answer is yes, and for Tillich this happens in the presence of the Holy Spirit or the Spiritual Presence.

The Spirit is the unity of power (God as being in the second section of the *Systematic Theology*) and meaning (the Christ as the New Being in the third section). This unity is made actual, real and concrete *in* life *as* Spirit. Tillich's emphasis on the Spirit as 'God with us' and the Spirit as the most direct and unrestricted symbol of the divine life is most significant for the restorative principle of his system. The Spiritual Presence makes God as creator and redeemer actual and effective; the Spirit presupposes both creation and salvation and is the fulfilment of both. Put differently, only the Spirit makes the transcendent union of the human with the divine in unambiguous life possible. Without the 'ecstatic transformation' of the Spirit, God as 'creative power' and 'saving love' would remain unactualized and incomplete (*ST* III, 283).

The divine Spirit grasps the human spirit in a process called ecstasy, in which the human spirit 'goes out of itself under the impact of the divine Spirit'. In the same way that reason was ecstatic in response to the miracle of revelation, ecstasy, according to Tillich, 'describes the human situation under the Spiritual Presence exactly' (*ST* I, 111–14). The human spirit cannot grasp the divine Spirit because the finite cannot comprehend the infinite; it must be grasped by the Spirit as unconditional and ultimate (*ST* III, 112). In this ecstatic process, the centred self or reason is not destroyed. Instead, the divine Spirit creates unambiguous life within the spirit's centre; it elevates the human spirit into the realm beyond the distinction of subject–object.

The divine Spirit is not one dimension in the unity of life among others but rather 'the ground of being of them all and the aim toward which they are self-transcendent'. How is the human spirit touched by the Spiritual Presence? Tillich affirms no direct correlation but a 'mutual immanence' between them. Since the finite is essentially 'an element in the divine life, everything finite is qualified by this essential relation' (112–13). Anthropologically, the human spirit possesses an 'antecedent Godlikeness', so that, in spite of human sinfulness, the divine and the human are not strangers, but estranged.[6] This is evident in the Pauline teaching on prayer (Romans 8:26–7) that God, as Spirit, prays when we pray. The paradox of prayer reveals 'the identity and non-identity of him who prays and Him who is prayed to: God as Spirit' (192). In prayer, 'we talk to someone who is not somebody else, but who is nearer to us than we ourselves are' (*NB*, 137). Hence, the Spiritual Presence grasps the human spirit not as an object, but as the ground of subject and object; to be grasped by the Spirit is that ecstatic movement of the spirit to transcend the subject–object distinction, or participate in the transcendent union of unambiguous life. As Tillich says, 'there is no place to which man can withdraw from the divine Thou, because it includes the ego and is nearer to the ego than the ego is to itself' (*ST* I, 271). In the same way, Buber states that the eternal Thou 'embraces my self without being it'.[7] When unambiguous life appears through the Spirit, actual being becomes the authentic expression of potential or essential being, and the Spirit moves to create theonomy where culture, morality and religion are united.

This actualization of essential being is not a return to essential being 'before the fall' or dreaming innocence. The New Being, revealed in the Christ and made present in the Spirit, is new *in* history, new with respect to not only estranged being but also to potential essential being (*ST* II, 119). Since the Spiritual Presence creates the transcendent union or makes life unambiguous in existence, it is fragmentary, that is, 'appearing under the conditions of finitude but conquering both estrangement and finitude', in history (*ST* III, 150). 'Unambiguous' is primarily an ontological concept, signifying the transcendent union in life; 'fragmentary', an eschatological concept, anticipating the eschatologically fulfilled transcendent union in the Kingdom of God (140).

Word and sacrament

The Spiritual Presence is manifested in word and sacrament. Because the Spiritual Presence is universal, everything in the finite order can be a sacrament or vessel of the Spirit. In fact, the 'Spiritual Presence cannot be received without a sacramental element, however hidden the latter may be' (*ST* III, 122). Sacrament is more than one of the church sacraments and much broader than something culturally religious. Unless all of reality could be a sacrament of Spiritual Presence, no specific sacrament would be possible – 'if the whole universe is not seen sacramentally, the partial sacraments die off' (*IR*, 62). Sacraments form what Tillich calls a '*Gestalt* of grace', a grace that is 'actual in objects, not as an object but as the transcendent meaning of an object' ('Protestantism as a Critical and Creative Principle' in *PolE*, 25). These forms of grace 'are finite forms pointing beyond themselves. They are forms that, so to speak, are selected by grace, that it may appear through them' (*ProtE*, 212). As examples of such sacramental forms, Tillich cites private prayer or meditation, exchanges with others about spiritual experiences, secular conversations with friends, the experience of creativity, the insights that occur in private counselling or the presence of the transcendent in church services. Experiencing the Spiritual Presence is 'like the breathing in of another air' whenever the Spirit is visible in sacramental times, places and persons (*ST* III, 236).

Since the basic expression of Spirit is language, the word becomes the other (and more important) medium of Spiritual Presence. Whenever human words 'become vehicles for the Spiritual Presence' they are called the Word of God, regardless of their specific religious content. The Bible is unique as the Word of God because it is the document of the central revelation of the Christ. Its uniqueness lies not in itself but in the universality of the Spiritual Presence, whose concrete and central historical manifestation it describes (124). For Tillich, the Bible is one of the sources of revelation, but not the only one (*ST* I, 34–6). While Tillich rejects the unmediated presence of the Spirit to spirit, as well as the concept of the 'inner word', he emphasizes that 'God is not bound to any of his manifestations' (*ST* III, 124–6). The Spirit is free from any of the ambiguous forms in which it is received in religion or culture; more important, no particular manifestation of the Spiritual Presence can exclude another in validity and transformative power.

Content of the Spiritual Presence: faith and love

When the Spirit is present, the human spirit in ecstasy is first grasped by the transcendent union in a process called faith and then taken into the life of that union, which is love (*ST* III, 129). Faith is the state of being grasped by that 'toward which self-transcendence aspires, the ultimate in being and meaning' (130). Faith, the 'most centred act of the human mind', is the movement of the whole being towards the Spiritual Presence as one's ultimate concern. Anything less than the whole self and authentic ultimate concern would be idolatrous or demonic. Since the Spiritual Presence is universal, faith is likewise universal.[8] Thus, to speak of a 'community of faith' would mean to speak, in the broadest sense, of universal humanity.

Love, the second element of the Spiritual Presence, is the ontological principle operative in all the processes of life. Being is not actual without love, 'that drives everything that is towards everything else that is'.[9] No life exists without love, the drive towards the reunion of the separated at every level of being. While all love is one, Tillich distinguishes love as *epithymia*, *philia* and *eros*. Each form of love seeks to transcend the ambiguities of its actualization; it seeks out *agape*, the unambiguous love of God. Through *agape*, the finite spirit participates ecstatically in the transcendent unity of the divine Spirit. Love is also universal, that is, all people participate in *agape* to some degree, or they would have no life and no being (*ST* II, 167). To speak of a 'community of love', therefore, is to speak of universal humanity.

THE SPIRITUAL COMMUNITY

The Spiritual Presence must be received by community, the Spiritual Community. As there is no revelation without reception, there is no Spiritual Presence without a Spiritual Community, a term Tillich employs only in the *Systematic Theology* for the essential or ideal church (*ST* III, 152–4). The divine Spirit touches the human spirit not in isolation, but in social groups: 'all the functions of the human spirit – moral self-integration, cultural self-creativity, and religious self-transcendence – are conditioned by the social context of the ego–thou encounter' (139). No personal life exists without encounter with other persons in a community, and community itself has no meaning without the historical dimensions of past and future (135). The Spiritual Community describes the ideal community of those who are grasped by the Spiritual Presence and participate through faith and love in the transcendent union of the Spirit; it is the community of the New Being, the place 'where the New Reality which is Christ . . . moves into us and is continued by us' (*TC*, 212–13). The church's nature is ontological: it should 'stand for the power of being-itself'. Its function is soteriological: it should 'mediate a courage which takes doubt and meaninglessness into itself' (*CB*, 178). It is the place where the 'reunion of man to man is pronounced and confessed and realized', where this reunion becomes an 'actual event' in space and time (*NB*, 24). Healing, the process of participating in the transcendent union, was pre-formed in a person's essential nature, disrupted in existential estrangement, and re-created and made actual in the Spiritual Community by the power of the Spiritual Presence (*ST* III, 157).

For Tillich, the two biblical symbols of the Spiritual Community are the *ekklesia* (church), or assembled people of God, and the body of Christ. *Ekklesia* as the 'assembly of God' is composed of individuals from all nations, called out of the bondage of estrangement to share in the unambiguous, though fragmentary, life of the Spirit (*HCT*, 19). The body of Christ is, for Tillich, a 'strictly theonomous symbol' representing the community of people participating in the transcendent unity of the Spiritual Presence (*ProtE*, 62). The body of Christ is the Spiritual Community, the essential church 'as it should be' (*ST* I, 148).

The Spiritual Community as both latent and manifest

In one of the most complex aspects of his ecclesiology, Tillich distinguishes between a latent and manifest Spiritual Community. The latent Spiritual Community was derived from his experience of humanist groups in the 1920s, people who could hardly be designated 'unchurched' or untouched by the Spiritual Presence simply because of their alienation from the formal creedal denominations (*IH*, 48–9). These people reflected 'the quest for the eternal and the unconditional, an absolute devotion to justice and love, a hope that lies beyond any utopia, an appreciation of Christian values' – all qualities of the Spirit's Presence. Tillich realized that this category could have a much broader application to the entire history of religion and culture. Whenever the power of the Spiritual Presence is at work in communities outside the organized church, Tillich describes this as the latent Spiritual Community 'in which the unexpressed church would be a living reality'. Thus, he created a double form (*Doppelgestalt*) of the church, latent and manifest, not to be confused with the invisible and visible church.[10] Latent Spiritual Communities are invisible whenever the Spiritual Presence grasps the hearts of human beings; and visible when the Spiritual Presence is at work in temples and cults and movements of all kinds, and especially in the great religions of the world (*ST* III, 162). Manifest Spiritual Communities are usually visible, but they can also be invisible, such as persons who explicitly accept Christ as the New Being, but who reject involvement in the visible symbol structure of any of the churches. This takes into account the situation in which many people find themselves today.

The Spiritual Community and the historical churches

Manifest Spiritual Communities must not be identified with the historical churches because, while they participate in the unambiguous life of the Spiritual Community, they also exist *in* time and space under the conditions of estrangement (*ST* III, 376, 168). The Spiritual Community is the 'inner *telos*', the dynamic essence, of the churches and the 'source of everything that makes them churches' (162–4). Churches share in all the ambiguities of life, and of religion in particular. The churches live in the 'yes and no' of the world: they reveal the Spiritual Presence that creates their essence; they also conceal and distort this essence through the profanization and demonization of religious life (165). There are not two churches but *two* aspects of *one* church (*Doppelgestalt*), of 'essentiality determining existence and being resisted by existence' (163).

In addition to the Spiritual Community as symbol of the unambiguous life, Tillich also uses the historical symbol of the Kingdom of God. The same 'yes and no' pattern within the churches exists in the symbol of the Kingdom. The churches in history 'share actively . . . in the running of historical time toward the aim of history'. The churches are 'tools of the Kingdom of God' and should become 'vehicles of history's movement toward its aim' (376).[11] At the same time, the churches are part of the scandal of history, for in existence they are often poor tools and inadequate vehicles for God's Kingdom. The Spirit is alive in the churches, but it transcends any historical expression while being present in all of them. The Spirit, following Hegel, is the 'concrete-universal', at once the source of fulfilment of every concrete human spirit and of universal life itself, and the norm and destiny towards which every dimension of life inexorably moves.

THE SPIRIT AND THEONOMY

Theonomy, the final gift of the Spirit, is culture under the impact of the Spiritual Presence, where God is the *nomos*, or the law (Tillich first considered calling theonomy the 'Spirituality of culture', because theonomy is culture that is Spirit-determined and Spirit-directed) (*ST* III, 250). In a theonomous culture, everything finite is perfectly transparent to the infinite; theonomy 'communicates the experience of holiness, something ultimate in being and meaning, in all of its creations' (251). Theonomy creates an unambiguous, though fragmentary, state of self-integration in the moral sphere, self-creativity in the cultural sphere and self-transcendence in the religious sphere. In a theonomous culture, religion and culture essentially belong together, where 'religion is the depth of culture' and 'culture the form of religion', not as what *ought to be* but what *is*. In a theonomous culture, the Spirit fulfils and frees, rather than intrudes upon or possesses the human spirit. Growth in theonomy is the Spirit's work towards the actualization and essential-ization of everything that has being.

In theonomous morality, love as *agape* is the driving and motivating power, not as a law but a reality, 'not a matter of ought to be . . . but a matter of being'. Love as a gift of the Spirit is the unambiguous cri-terion of every moral decision, uniting the unconditional character of the moral imperative with the conditional nature of all moral content. *Agape* alone is 'by its very nature open to everything particular while remaining universal in its claim' (272–3). In a theonomous morality, 'Spirit, love, and grace are one and the same reality in different aspects. Spirit is the creative power; love is its creation; grace is the effective presence of love' in every person (274). Of course, in ambiguous life the theonomous unity of religion, culture and morality is visible only in anticipatory form. In some eras, cultures and societies, theonomy is more visible or more hidden than in others. In every culture, in every period of history, 'Theonomy can never be completely victorious, as it can never be completely defeated. Its victory is always fragmentary because of the existential estrangement underlying human history, and its defeat always limited by the fact that human nature is essentially theonomous' (250).

THE SPIRIT AND THE TRINITY

In placing the doctrine of the Trinity at the conclusion of the fourth section of his *Systematic Theology*, after he has explored the mystery of God, the New Being and the Spiritual Presence, Tillich reaffirms both the ontological nature and the existential importance of the Trinitarian doctrine.[12] Tillich (unlike Barth) could not consider the Trinitarian sym-bols until late in his system, because he was faithful to his method of correlation; as John Dourley points out, 'he must show in man's human and religious experience some basis which asks for and receives the specifically Christian revelation of the trinitarian God'.[13] For Tillich, the original purpose of the Trinitarian doctrine was 'to express in three symbols the self-manifestation of God to man, opening up the depth of the divine abyss and giving answers to the question of the meaning of existence' (*ST* III, 291). Likewise, the Trinitarian symbols 'become empty if they are separated from their experiential roots' (*ST* II, 143–4).

This is especially true of the doctrine of the Spirit, which makes God present, real and concrete in life and within the complexities of human experience. The Trinity is grounded in the human experience of the divine as 'creative power, as saving love, and as ecstatic transformation' (*ST* III, 283; *ST* I, 248–9).

Tillich insists that the Trinitarian structures present in the mind are not simply the result of subjective perception or projection but are the 'reflections of something real in the nature of the divine . . . [they] have a *fundamentum in re*, a foundation in reality, however much the subjective side of man's experience may contribute' (*ST* III, 283). The Trinity is the goal of theonomy, overcoming the split between subject and object. In the Trinitarian life, the abyss of power and the fullness of meaning are united in life as Spirit, serving as the ground and model of all of life, particularly the life of the human spirit. Ontologically, the Spirit unites power and meaning within being-itself. The Spirit is universal, since being-itself is universal; it is concrete, because it is the ground, ideal and destiny of every concrete life. God as ground, form and act – what Tillich calls a 'pre-Trinitarian formula' – makes Trinitarian thinking possible (284). Here, Tillich is indebted to the German Idealism of Hegel, and especially to Schelling.

RELIGION OF THE CONCRETE SPIRIT

The Spirit is both universal and concrete. While it is the unity of power and form in the divine life – as the actualization that makes God a real God – the Spirit also makes God present in the concrete finite order. This sheds significant light on Tillich's understanding of other religions. Many scholars have pointed out that an important transformation of his thought had begun to take place in relation to his ideas in *Systematic Theology* in the last decade of Tillich's life (*ST* III, 6).[14]

In a famous final lecture, 'The Significance of the History of Religions for the Systematic Theologian', Tillich sought to develop what he called the 'religion of the concrete Spirit', which he states cannot be identified with any particular religion, even Christianity (*FR*, 88). After his dialogue with Buddhist and Shinto monks beginning in the 1950s and his trip to Japan in 1960, he became aware of the limitations of his *Systematic Theology*, fearing that his work would be relegated to the 'dust heap of the past' even before his death.[15] In this lecture, he develops a dynamic-typological approach to the history of religions, analysing the sacramental, mystical and prophetic elements in the universal human experience of the Holy (86–7). In stating that the religion

of the concrete Spirit is his 'hope for the future of theology', several questions arise: firstly, has Tillich abandoned the Christocentric structure
of his *Systematic Theology* for a kind of relativism where there '*may
be*' a central event in the history of religions that 'makes possible a concrete theology that has universalistic significance?' (81). This approach
appears to stand in contrast to the uniqueness and the universality of
the Christ-event in his second volume and the reality of Jesus the Christ
as the final revelation in the first volume (*ST* I, 150ff.; 133ff.). Secondly,
what is the relationship of his treatment of the divine Spirit in volume
III to volumes I and II, and to the religion of the concrete Spirit?

No clear answers exist, but it would be helpful to remember Langdon Gilkey's words on Tillich: 'The main role of [Tillich's] thought has
been to provide a point – on a surprising number of different axes –
where seemingly opposite positions come into a tense, comprehensible
relation.'[16] It seems that Tillich did not abandon the basic tenets of his
Systematic Theology, but he wanted to see it in a new and more expansive context, one that included more than the encounter of the Christian
message with the scientific and secular world. He sought to place his
system in the context of a theology of the history of religions, to explore
the inner *telos* of such a history, which he describes as the religion of
the concrete Spirit (*FR*, 88). His goal, according to Mircea Eliade, who
shared his final seminar, was not a theology of the history of religions
but 'a *renewal of his own Systematic Theology*'.[17]

Tillich's concept of the cross, characterized as the perfect symbol
because it rejects any claim for itself and surrenders its particularity
to the universal, may be understood in this more expansive and inclusive understanding of Spirit. While the cross is a symbol for Christians
and provides the criterion for every religious symbol, it may be one
kairos, regardless of its world-wide significance, among many *kairoi*.
What happens in the event of the cross 'also happens fragmentarily
in other places, in other moments, has happened and will happen even
though they are not historically or empirically connected with the cross'
(88).[18]

Similarly, theonomy, the inner meaning of the religion of the concrete Spirit, is not confined to Christian symbols (90). When God shall
be all in all, as Paul tells us in his own explanation of theonomy
(1 Corinthians 15:28), the Spirit that makes God present will speak
in many tongues. Both Paul and Tillich know that such theonomous
moments are only fragmentary in time. Thomas O'Meara's words to
describe Catholicism are apt for all cultures and religions grasped by
the Spiritual Presence in a fragmentary manner: 'a tangle of tangible

presences of grace'.[19] But it will not always be this way: 'Only in eternal fulfillment does the subject (and consequently the object) disappear completely. Historical man can only anticipate in a fragmentary way the ultimate fulfillment in which subject ceases to be subject and object ceases to be object' (*ST* III, 253). Or as St Paul tells us: 'At present we see indistinctly, as in a mirror, but then face to face. At present I know partially; then I shall know fully, as I am fully known' (1 Corinthians 13:12).

SPIRIT AND SPIRITUALITY

No word has recently expanded so much in its meaning and use, as well as in its misappropriations, as spirituality. Spiritual Presence or the religion of the concrete Spirit is not about intellectual assent and doctrinal formulations but the experience of being grasped by the Spirit, and the gift of *agape* in human lives and cultures. Hence, one might argue that much of Tillich's treatment of the divine Spirit is in itself spirituality as well as theology.

How might we apply Tillich's ideas to 'spirituality' today? First, as Tillich reminds us, St Paul uses the term 'spiritual' not to mean a soul distinct from a body, but the inner core of the whole person, both body and soul, alive and filled with the Spirit of God. It is a profoundly personal but never individual affair, because it must always be grounded in a community in which such a response can be heard, received and sustained.

In estranged existence, the unity of power and meaning within being has been fragmented. On one side, power without meaning leads to an unbridled and heteronomous use of power or a frenzied search for meaning of any kind. Tillich's student, the psychologist Rollo May, described this loss of meaning as the crisis of intentionality, that is, the loss of an horizon of meaning against which our own individual actions can make sense.[20] Loss of meaning causes confusion and anxiety, and becomes one of the sources of violence. Likewise, meaning without power avoids the self-transcending dimension of being and confines meaning in a finite expression; this confinement makes an idol of any finite form, be it a sacred book, a doctrine, a church, political theory or life-style. Meaning without power provides security, but the price is the limitation of freedom and the creation of a fanatic and defensive world-view. The goal of the spiritual life, expressed in any cultural or religious terminology, is to rediscover and grow into the unity and harmony of power and meaning, to grow into one's essential self as the image of God as Spirit.

Finally, spirituality is a movement of the spirit to theonomy, or what Tillich has called the religion of the concrete Spirit. A theonomous spirituality would see the presence of the divine Spirit as essentially possible everywhere, not just in the confines of church or doctrine. This spirituality would establish a relationship between spirit and Spirit in human communities whose communal forms and structures reflect a freedom and a transparency to grace.[21]

CONCLUSION

Paul Tillich's doctrine of the divine Spirit unlocks the mystery of life in all of its expressions and the power of God as being-itself present to all of divine creation. It unites and connects his understanding of revelation, God and the Christ, but it also goes beyond God and the Christ as theological concepts to make them concrete *in* life *as* Spirit. Without his doctrine of the Spirit, his fundamental theology would be incomplete and his theology of culture, so central to his thought, would lie on infertile ground. God and the Christ are fulfilled and completed in the Spirit, the face of being-itself in all of its mysterious and abysmal depths, turned towards us, alive within us not only as judgement but also as grace and promise.

Notes

1　Gilkey (1990), 164.
2　Braaten (1967), xxv, xxxii.
3　See also 'The Idea of God as Affected by Modern Knowledge' in Bixler (1961), 105.
4　See Stiernotte (1964), 132–3.
5　For example, see Drummy (2000).
6　See Paul Tillich, 'What is Wrong with Dialectical Theology?' *Journal of Religion* 15, 2 (1935), 141–2.
7　Buber (1979), 148.
8　See *DF*, Chs. 1 and 2.
9　See *LPJ*.
10　'Kirche und humanistische Gesellschaft' in *GW* IX, 60–1. Original: *Neuwerk* (Kassel), XIII, 1 (April–May, 1931), 4–18.
11　See also 'What is Wrong with Dialectical Theology?' 134–5 (n. 6 above).
12　See Parrella (2004).
13　Dourley (1974), 132.
14　See, for example, Thomas (1995) and (1999); Palapathwala (2001). Interestingly, this coincides with the Second Vatican Coucil (1962–5); see the documents, The Pastoral Constitution on the Church in the Modern Word (*Gaudium et Spes*) and The Declaration on the Relationship of the Church to Non-Christian Religions (*Nostra Aetate*).

15   Pauck and Pauck (1976), 244.
16   Gilkey (1982), 26–7.
17   Mircea Eliade, 'Paul Tillich and the History of Religions', in *FR*, 33.
18   See Stenger and Stone (2002), 8–34.
19   O'Meara (1985), 296.
20   May (1969).
21   See Parrella (1994).

Further reading

Parrella, Frederick J. (1994). 'Tillich and Contemporary Spirituality' in *Paul Tillich: A New Catholic Perspective*, ed. Raymond F. Bulman and Frederick J. Parrella. Collegeville, Minn.: The Liturgical Press.
(2004). 'Paul Tillich and the Doctrine of the Trinity: A Catholic Perspective' in *Trinität und/oder Quaternität – Tillichs Neuerschließung der trinitarischen Problematik/Trinity and/or Quaternity – Tillich's Reopening of the Trinitarian Problem*, Tillich-Studien, vol. X, ed. Gert Hummel and Doris Lax, 280–98. Münster: LIT Verlag.
Wenz, Gunter (1979). *Subjekt und Sein. Die Entwicklung der Theologie Paul Tillichs*. Munich: Chr. Kaiser Verlag.

6 Faith (and religion)

MARY ANN STENGER

In his introduction to *Dynamics of Faith*, Paul Tillich states: 'There is hardly a word in the religious language, both theological and popular, which is subject to more misunderstandings, distortions, and questionable definitions than the word "faith"' (*DF*, ix). In his most widely read work, *The Courage to Be*, Tillich reinterprets the idea of faith, both to correct misconceptions and to enable readers to experience the underlying power and meaning of faith. Because he grounds faith ontologically and existentially, his analysis of faith connects to all functions of human spiritual life and to everyday living. His existential analysis includes psychological aspects of faith and recognizes great diversity in the contents of people's faith, as well as destructive and sometimes pathological forms of faith. Moreover, Tillich's theological understanding of faith and his critique of forms and contents of faith, while rooted in Christian tradition, extends outside Christianity to include other religions and even secular forms of faith. Discussion of faith for Tillich includes ontological, existential and psychological aspects, with these connecting further to epistemological and ethical dimensions.

FAITH AS ULTIMATE CONCERN: ONTOLOGICAL, EXISTENTIAL AND PSYCHOLOGICAL DYNAMICS

'Faith is the state of being ultimately concerned', Tillich asserts in *Dynamics of Faith* (*DF*, 1).[1] This formal definition of faith focuses on a person's state of being (ontological), his or her individual connection to ultimacy (ontological, existential and psychological) and the experience of concern (subjective: existential and psychological). 'Faith as ultimate concern is an act of the total personality', Tillich argues, providing an understanding so much deeper, broader and more existentially significant than the view of faith as belief, especially when that belief is understood to have a low degree of evidence (*DF*, 4; *ST* II, 47). Nor is faith acceptance of creeds or church practices and authorities, although people may find their existential experience of faith confirmed and celebrated in such creeds and institutional authorities ('Realism and Faith' in *ProtE*, 78).[2]

Tillich's ontological analysis focuses on persons of faith experiencing their ontological connection to ultimacy (power of being, ground of being, being-itself, God), a connection he sees as universal.[3] He describes this experience as 'the state of being grasped by the power of being-itself', offering that description as a definition of faith (as well as of religion) (*CB*, 172). The power of being-itself is present in people's everyday life experiences of affirming being and life in the face of threats of non-being, such as death, doubt and guilt. For Tillich, everyone participates in the power of being and the power of being in them. That participation is the ontological ground of faith, the ontological basis for 'being grasped by the power of being which transcends everything that is and in which everything that is participates' (173).

People may not consciously recognize this presence, but when they do, they are experiencing faith. They accept that experience of 'being grasped', of being accepted by the power of being. Tillich argues that everyone 'has some awareness' of that acceptance, of participation in the power of being, 'especially in the moments in which he experiences the threat of nonbeing' (156, 177, 181). The ontological root of faith is the activity of being-itself or the power of being affirming being over non-being. The participation of all beings in being-itself empowers beings to face threats of non-being. Specifically for humans, facing threats of non-being means affirming one's own being, experiencing and expressing the courage to be.

The experience of the power of being in the face of threats of possible non-being is an existential experience that offers courage, meaning, hope and love in spite of the experiences of insecurity, doubt, guilt and/or rejection in life. To be grasped by even a momentary sense of security, meaning, forgiveness and love is, for Tillich, to be grasped by the power of being-itself. He does not see the threats of non-being conquered, as they still continue as part of finite life; rather, he sees the experience of faith as enabling and empowering people to face the threats to their security and to meaning and goodness in their everyday lives.

With this understanding of faith as ultimate concern, Tillich emphasizes that all people experience something as ultimate that engenders their commitment (even if that something is not truly ultimate). The source of this experience is the human 'awareness of the infinite' to which all humans belong. This is not just a casual awareness but involves participation, Tillich emphasizes: 'There is no faith without participation!' (*DF*, 100). Tillich speaks of humans as 'driven toward faith' by this awareness of the infinite to which we belong (9). That connection to the infinite or ultimate is the basis of the courage to face the challenges of everyday life.

This ontological, existential understanding of faith connects to Tillich's psychological analysis of faith. Tillich argues that faith includes both the unconscious and conscious elements in the personality. If faith were only an unconscious act, it would be a compulsion. But faith is free, even though faith can involve unconscious strivings that affect the type of faith and choice of symbols a person responds to. On the conscious level, faith as one's ultimate commitment provides a uniting centre that influences and even regulates daily life. Faith deepens all aspects of one's life, including artistic creativity, scientific knowing, forming of ethics, organizing of politics, setting of personal discipline and contemplation (107).

In *The Courage to Be,* Tillich offers an ontological understanding of anxiety as 'the state in which a being is aware of its possible non-being'. He argues that anxiety is a natural aspect of human finitude. Awareness of one's own finitude, in the forms of fate and death, doubt and meaninglessness, guilt and condemnation, is a normal part of life experienced by all humans (*CB*, 35). Although people often deal with anxiety by turning it into fear of something specific, anxiety is at the root of every fear, anxiety about 'ultimate nonbeing' (38). One does not eliminate anxiety because it belongs to existence; rather, one faces it in courage which is rooted in faith as 'the state of being grasped by the power of being-itself' (39, 172).

When one faces anxiety, affirming one's self in spite of the threats to one's being, one exhibits courage (32). People normally affirm them-selves through various groups to which they belong or as individuals somewhat separated from others (86–9). But underlying those forms of courage is faith, the experience of the connection to (being grasped by) the power of being, in spite of threats to one's own being.

THE RISK OF FAITH: DISTORTIONS

Although Tillich's ontological analysis of faith, anxiety and courage emphasizes the integrating, positive qualities of faith, he is well aware of the distortions of faith, both in the understandings of what faith is and in the contents of faith. On the subjective side, faith is the experience of ultimacy, but one must evaluate whether that experience is holistic and integrated or partial and perhaps pathological and destructive. On the objective side of faith is the element of ultimacy itself, where distortions involve the content of what one holds as ultimate. Holding as ultimate that which is not ultimate (idolatry) can be existentially disappointing, disrupting and destructive (*DF*, 12).

Distortions on the subjective side relate to epistemology and psychology. A common misrepresentation of faith is to see it as belief with little evidence or as trust in authorities. But such acceptance and trust in authorities is not 'faith' by Tillich's definition; rather, that trust and acceptance are part of the broader process of humans seeking, testing and judging knowledge about themselves and their world (31–3). Such knowledge has varying degrees of probability, ranging from the 'certainty' of empirical experience and mathematical rules to claims far removed from empirical observation. But faith as ultimate concern is not subject to verification or disproving through varying degrees of evidence; because faith involves the whole human personality, the certainty of faith is 'existential' (34). One can centre one's faith in something less than ultimate, leading to existential disappointment and destructive results. Tillich sees this on a deeper level than experiences of certainty or uncertainty with respect to empirical or theoretical judgements.

Psychological distortions of faith include focus on the will (voluntarist) or focus on the emotions. The misrepresentation of faith as the will to believe connects to understanding faith as belief with little evidence. If there is insufficient evidence to compel belief, then an act of faith must be an act of the will over against one's normal doubt or questioning. Even if one understands this act of the will as given by God's grace, the context for so moving one's will is usually a structure of authority. Over against such a view, Tillich argues that faith as ultimate concern is primary, with obedience stemming from the commitment of one's ultimate concern rather than the will enacting or originating the faith. 'No command to believe and no will to believe can create faith' (38). Human action (or will) cannot produce ultimate concern or the existential certainty of faith. Similarly, faith is more than subjective emotions or feeling, although emotion can be part of faith and people can express their faith commitment emotionally. Faith includes cognitive, voluntarist and emotional aspects, but reducing faith to any one of these distorts the fact that in faith the whole person is grasped (39).

On the objective side of faith, it is the ultimate that is given specific content in people's particular forms of faith and in different types of courage. Faith has a content towards which people direct their commitments and ultimate concern. Many contents of faith can be false ultimacies or forms of idolatry, elevating a finite preliminary reality to ultimacy (11–12). Idolatrous faith is still faith, still ultimate concern experienced as free, ecstatic and promising fulfilment, but Tillich argues that idolatrous faith will disappoint a person existentially, disrupting rather than centring and uniting the personality (12). Both sides of faith – the subjective and the objective – are subject to distortion, some-times with disastrous consequences for individuals (or occasionally, even for groups).

Sometimes, the distortions can be pathological, reflecting neurosis rather than existential courage. Tillich sees the neurotic person, the per-son with pathological anxiety, as more sensitive than the average person to the threats of non-being. 'The difference between the neurotic and the healthy (although potentially neurotic) personality is the following: the neurotic personality, on the basis of his greater sensitivity to nonbeing and consequently of his profounder anxiety, has settled down to a fixed, though limited and unrealistic, self-affirmation' (68). The key difference relates to the unrealistic character of the self-affirmation of the neurotic, while the healthy individual is more realistic.[4] Yet the ordinary person can become neurotic if the forms of courage that have worked no longer work, where the anxieties overwhelm the person and the person turns to an imaginary or false world as the source of courage (*CB*, 69–70). Tillich distinguishes a fanatic who may defend the current order (or a vision of a past order) from the neurotic defending an imaginary order, but if the fanatic's defence cannot cope with the depth of anxiety stemming from reality, the fanatic can become neurotic (70).

Faith, then, involves a risk – a risk that the content of faith is not truly ultimate (idolatry) or even that what one affirms as real is not real (neurosis). But such risk does not and cannot keep people from faith, although the risks can lead people to deep questioning of traditional contents and even forms of faith. Because Tillich's analysis is open to secular as well as traditionally religious contents, deep questioning may lead to different forms of faith but, in his view, not to a state of no faith.

DOUBT AND ABSOLUTE FAITH

For Tillich, faith involves a more fundamental risk: doubt. 'Courage does not deny that there is doubt, but it takes the doubt into itself as an expression of its own finitude and affirms the content of an ulti-mate concern' (*CB*, 101). Courage in faith does not repress doubt but includes it as an awareness of the risk of faith, the element of 'in spite of', taking seriously the experience of doubt. Recognizing that such a view counters a traditional view of faith as without doubt or tensions, Tillich argues that the traditional view is non-dynamic, even 'dead', but that it can become alive again through the power of the symbols of faith (102). Symbols hold the tension between transcendence and concrete reality, a tension that Tillich sees as an essential dimension of faith. In an early discussion of faith and realism, Tillich argues for holding the tension between a realistic attitude that often questions faith as utopian or romantic (doubt) and faith that involves ecstatic transcendence of reality.[5]

The element of doubt in faith is balanced by the experience of 'immediate certainty' in faith that stems from the Unconditional itself, that grounds one's ultimate concern. That experience of the Unconditional always connects to concrete content that can be doubted, asking whether the content is truly ultimate (*DF*, 102–4). The possibility of idolatry exists, as people can easily take something finite as ultimate or use the bearer of the ultimate for finite purposes, a possibility that Tillich counters with the criterion against idolatry: the cross of the Christ (97, 104). But not only does the cross critique any absolutizing of the finite, it also affirms God's connection to humans. God acts and gives in faith, rather than humans giving to God; Tillich calls this 'the only absolute content of faith, namely, that in relation to the ultimate we are always receiving and never giving' (105).

The faith that accepts not just doubt but meaninglessness into itself is a meaningful act of faith, rooted in what Tillich terms 'absolute faith'. He analyses three elements in absolute faith: 1) the experience of the power of being even in the midst of radical manifestation of non-being, such as meaninglessness; 2) 'the dependence of the experience of nonbeing on the experience of being and the dependence of the experience of meaninglessness on the experience of meaning'; 3) the 'acceptance of being accepted' (*CB*, 177). Conscious acceptance of this experience of being/meaning is absolute faith, a faith without content, as all contents have been removed in doubt. This absolute faith grounds courage; or one can reverse it and say that the courage to be in the face of non-being reveals the nature of being, that being resists non-being, that 'being affirms itself against nonbeing' (179). This active resistance makes courage and faith dynamic elements of life.[6] The character of being-itself, affirming being over against non-being, makes courage possible. And when people consciously affirm that power of being, they are aware of faith. But Tillich argues that even if people do not consciously accept acceptance by that power of being, they 'nevertheless accept it and participate in it' in their experiences of courage (181).

Tillich's analysis here applies the Pauline or Lutheran idea of justification, usually applied to moral awareness of sin (i.e. at the same time justified, at the same time a sinner), to the experience of doubt, to spiritual anxiety. Doubt of concrete contents is not answered with proof of concrete contents; rather, doubt and meaninglessness of concrete contents are accepted. Yet meaning itself rooted in the power of being-itself is experienced as the ground of all meaning. The person as doubter is accepted in spite of doubt.[7]

Absolute faith is neither an event nor a momentary experience; rather, absolute faith undergirds all forms of faith that do have concrete content. Absolute faith 'is always a movement in, with, and under other states of the mind . . . It is not a place where one can live, it is without the safety of words and concepts, it is without a name, a church, a cult, a theology. But it is moving in the depth of all of them' (188–9). Forms of faith with concrete content depend on absolute faith, but humans move from the boundary experience of absolute faith to faith with concrete forms and contents. They can recognize them as non-absolute and yet experience absolute power or the power of being-itself *through* them, always knowing that the concrete content is not absolute in itself. One becomes aware of absolute faith when one recognizes that ordinary symbols and meanings no longer have power; yet one is able to say yes to being, affirming being even though nothing concrete can overcome the non-being or conquer the anxieties (189).

The paradoxical element in absolute faith, as Tillich discusses it in *The Courage to Be*, also penetrates his early German writings as well as his later American works. In his 1919 'Rechtfertigung und Zweifel', Tillich calls this unity of the Unconditioned and the conditioned the absolute paradox (*ENGW* X, 127ff.). In 'The Conquest of the Concept of Religion in the Philosophy of Religion' (1922), Tillich calls the paradox of encountering the Unconditional ontological and rational (*WR*, 123). In 'Kairos und Logos' (1926), Tillich sees this religious paradox of the Unconditioned intersecting the conditioned as a guardian or limit standpoint for knowledge (*GW* IV, 74–5).[8] In that essay and in many later works, Tillich expresses this paradox of ultimacy and finite reality through the criterion of 'the Protestant principle' that rejects all absolutization of the finite but allows for ultimacy breaking into the finite. That is precisely the paradoxical point expressed in absolute faith, that no concrete symbol or concept can hold absolute meaning; yet one can affirm and experience the affirmation of the power of being and meaning as ultimate in spite of radical doubt of all concrete contents.

CONCRETE FAITH: ONTOLOGICAL AND MORAL TYPES

Tillich distinguishes two basic types of faith that are interdependent and rooted in human experiences of ultimacy or 'the holy' (*DF*, 56). In ontological faith, the experience of the presence of the holy breaking into ordinary reality, the experience of the 'holiness of being' dominates. In the moral type of faith, a person is more aware of the judgement of the holy over everything, experiencing the 'holiness of what ought to be' as predominant.

Within the ontological type of faith Tillich includes sacramental faith, where one experiences something as holy, i.e. where one is grasped by holiness through the medium of something concrete (58). In contrast, mystical faith emphasizes the finite quality of all concrete forms and encourages experience beyond concreteness in the 'abyss of pure divinity'. This experience of faith turns inward to the 'depth of the human soul', to the 'point' of encounter of finite and infinite, a point of emptiness of all concrete forms and preliminary concerns, to a depth that goes beyond subject and object to a point where the ultimate overcomes that duality (60–1). Yet another form of ontological faith does not transcend humanity or the human world, instead focusing on the ideals of humanity. Humanism is an ontological, secular form of faith, experiencing ultimacy in ideals or essential qualities of humanity that move beyond the distortions of our actual world but are seen as possible within the human world (63).

Shifting to the moral types of faith, Tillich distinguishes juristic, conventional and ethical types in a discussion that tends towards stereotyping the approaches of non-Christian faith traditions. He identifies Talmudic Judaism and Islam as following juristic approaches, Confucian China as conventional and Jewish prophetic faith as ethical. Although these types of faith may reflect ontological forms, such as the mystical or sacramental, in Tillich's view they emphasize analysis of laws and obedience because the laws express 'what ought to be', experienced in Judaism and Islam both as God's gift and God's command (65–6).

Tillich's typology reflects emphases in varying forms of faith, not a complete divergence of type. Ontological forms usually include some moral elements, just as moral forms include some experience of ultimacy. In fact, Tillich concludes that both ontological and moral elements are essential to faith, even though they often split, conflict and may try to destroy the other type (69). But he argues that the history of faith also shows the convergence of these types, a convergence he sees as necessary in the ongoing dynamics of faith, allowing for blends of the various forms of faith, as well as varying approaches and contents (70, 73).

THE TRUTH OF FAITH

With such multiplicity, the question of the truth of faith arises, along with other epistemological issues. One such issue is the relationship of reason and faith. Arguing against views that contrast reason and faith, Tillich posits instead that reason is central to human identity, serving as the basis of creativity, language, knowledge, art and morality; reason makes possible a centred personal life, as well as a community of centred persons. Ultimate concern assumes rationality understood as the basic ontological structure of reason in the human mind and in reality as a whole. In this view, reason is necessary to faith, as well as to knowledge of the finite world. But in faith 'reason reaches ecstatically beyond itself', fulfilling reason in ecstasy but not destroying reason (*DF*, 75–6).

Such ecstatic experience is often called revelation within religious communities. Tillich describes revelation as an event that grounds a person's and/or a community's ultimate concern, often shaking and transforming their present situation in religion and culture (78–9). On an essential level, such experience does not create conflict between faith and reason, but in ordinary, estranged life the relationship between faith and reason can be distorted.

With respect to scientific reasoning, Tillich opts for a 'two-dimensions' approach to science and faith, where he sees the role of science as discovering and describing 'the structural laws which determine reality', with the descriptions verifiable through repeated experiments (81). He applies this not only to the natural sciences but also to psychology and notes that conflicts arise when one dimension interferes with the other. If science forgets the preliminary and non-absolute character of its statements and claims of truth, it shifts to the dimension of faith, making ultimate claims. Similarly, if faith attempts to make scientific claims in the name of its ultimate concern, it shifts to the dimension of science, using a basis that does not conform to scientific verifiability. Tillich argues, 'science can conflict only with science, and faith only with faith; science which remains science cannot conflict with faith which remains faith' (82). Psychological studies cannot give answers about ultimate meanings for humans, although psychology can inform people about aspects of the human mind and personality. On the reverse side, Tillich thinks it is problematic to use recent science to confirm the truth of faith, as that moves the discussion from the dimension of science to the dimension of faith (83–5).

Historical truth differs from scientific truth in that history cannot be subjected to repeatable experiments (85). Yet, like science, history presents factual truth, where the facts must be backed up by documents, artefacts and testimonies of people present at events or during the time period. Faith cannot provide or guarantee such factual historical truth. But because history involves interpretation of facts as well as description, historical truth and the truth of faith become intertwined; faith 'can and must interpret the meaning of facts from the point of view of man's ultimate concern' (86). But interpreting facts is quite different from basing faith on history, as history offers degrees of probability of truth. For Tillich, what faith can claim is 'that something of ultimate concern has happened in history', as such a claim involves ultimacy. But faith should not move from that faith claim to claims about historical conditions or details about an event (87–9).[9] The faith claim rests on the transformation of people of faith, who experience history and life as transformed, not on whether scholars of history can prove a particular event. As with faith and science, claims of truth in faith and in history do not interfere unless history makes ultimate claims or faith makes historical claims.

With philosophical truth, Tillich employs a basic 'pre-philosophical' understanding that philosophy tries to find or develop universal categories that present the basic structure of being that humans experience. Because both one's ultimate concern and philosophical truth claims seek to express the nature of ultimate reality, ultimate reality is a point of identity in the two cognitive enterprises (90–1). Tillich distinguishes these two disciplines by arguing that philosophy is more detached, expressing its understandings in concepts, while faith is a more 'involved expression of concern about the meaning of the ultimate for the faithful', usually expressed in symbols (91).[10] While this separation works theoretically, it often breaks down in actuality, as the same person often engages in both enterprises, and for Tillich, all humans, including philosophers, have an ultimate concern, and all people of faith can think and often seek conceptual understanding, a mix that Tillich sees throughout the history of philosophy and of theology. In fact, Tillich acknowledges that a similar mix may show up in science and in history, as scientists and historians also have ultimate concerns and also often engage in some philosophical discussion (91–3). Tillich leaves us with the interconnection of philosophical truth and the truth of faith: 'There is truth of faith in philosophical truth. And there is philosophical truth in the truth of faith' (94). Put differently, every religious symbol can be connected to concepts, but faith does not determine a specific philosophy. In the end, he concludes that 'the truth of faith and the truth of philosophy have no authority over each other' (95).

In analysing the truth of faith, Tillich distinguishes truth on the subjective side of faith and truth on the objective side of faith. Subjectively, faith is true for someone if it 'adequately expresses an ultimate concern'. Objectively, 'faith is true if its content is the really ultimate'. For a symbol adequately to express an ultimate concern, it must create 'reply, action, communication' (96). Symbols live and die, expressing a group's ultimate concern for a time but then becoming inadequate and part of the history of the group. So subjectively, faith is true if it is alive for people, if it works, if it evokes a response in them. The history of faith traditions focuses on this subjective side, expressing what people have found to be an adequate expression of their ultimate concern. The more challenging test of faith addresses the objective side.

In *Dynamics of Faith*, Tillich uses the symbol of the cross as the criterion of the truth of faith on the content or 'objective' side. The cross of the Christ expresses Jesus' self-sacrifice that simultaneously affirms and negates Jesus as the Christ. The criterion of the truth of faith, then, is self-negation, that the ultimate itself can be manifest but no human or finite thing can hold that ultimacy. 'That symbol is most adequate which expresses not only the ultimate but also its own lack of ultimacy' (97). Thus, faith holds the tension of doubt and risk, and faith requires courage.

But one moves beyond the paradox to accept concrete contents of faith even while recognizing their non-absoluteness and finite qualities. As discussed above, faith as ultimate concern connects to the whole of a person's life, not only to intellectual and cognitive dimensions, discussed at length here, but also to moral and communal aspects of life. And the moral and communal aspects relate to the healing and integrating power of faith. Always aware of the disintegrating, destructive forces in life as well as the creative powers, Tillich recognizes that integration of the human personality is always partial, occurring along with experiences of disintegration and disease; yet 'the integrating power of faith has healing power' (108). The extent of healing will depend on how open a person is to the power of faith and 'how strong and passionate is his ultimate concern' – the subjective factor in the integrating power of faith (109).

Tillich connects faith to love because he sees the underlying direction of faith as reuniting the separated, reuniting humans with the ultimate, with other humans and with themselves – a reunion enacted through love (112).[11] Love, then, is not separate from faith or even external to it but rather belongs to ultimate concern itself. Once again, Tillich takes account of the ambiguities of human life, recognizing that distorted faith can produce the opposite of love. He particularly notes that faith understood as strong affirmation and defence of a set of doctrines does not lead to actions of love but often to 'crimes against love' (113). Although this is analysed more deeply in *Love, Power, and Justice*, Tillich does note that he is speaking of love not as an emotion but as the driving power in all reality to reunite with all beyond oneself, including the driving power of ultimacy itself to reunite with that which has separated from it (in estrangement) (114).

Because faith involves this desire to reunite the separated and actions of love, faith also implies connection to a community where those actions take place. Community does not preclude the inner life of faith in each member, but community brings together people with a shared content of faith, shared interests in actions rooted in faith (117–18). Within communities, people express faith symbolically through cult and myth. As with other aspects of faith, these elements can be distorted, such as seeing cultic activities as magic or taking the mythic aspects literally rather than symbolically (119–21). These elements often serve to define a particular community over against another, but they do not necessarily lead to intolerance of other communities.

Within any one nation and within the human world, communities of faith encounter each other. The challenge is to keep such encounters in a context and with attitudes of tolerance rather than intolerance. Here, Tillich connects intolerance and idolatry and once again asserts his criterion against idolatry: 'The criterion of every faith is the ultimacy of the ultimate which it tries to express. The self-criticism of every faith is the insight into the relative validity of the concrete symbols in which it appears' (123). Such a self-critical attitude can help retain tolerant, civil interactions between people of diverse faiths, even when secular faith encounters traditionally religious faith. Sometimes, the encounter of faith with faith can lead to the conversion of an individual, where the person sees a different set of values or beliefs as better expressing the ultimate concern. But even in the encounter with secular faith, one has to acknowledge that one cannot argue a person out of his or her ultimate concern, even though one can discuss the intellectual content of one's concern. Converting involves surrender by the individual to the ultimacy he or she experiences in the expressions of the new community (124–5). Even when people deny that they have faith, they express their ultimate concern (127). Thus, the challenge is to develop and maintain tolerance in spite of radical differences in forms of faith.

This broad approach to faith makes Tillich's analysis applicable to culture and politics, as well as to religious studies. One example of such past application was the United States Supreme Court decision in *United States* v. *Seeger* in 1965, when Tillich's idea of ultimate concern was used to support granting conscientious-objector status to a person who did not have specifically religious training but who did invoke ultimate pacifist commitment.[12] Tillich's analysis can help explain the religious dimension of conflict by recognizing the ultimacy people attach to their positions. And his awareness of the possibility of distortions of faith provides critical and analytical value, applicable to a variety of cultural areas. Today one may wish for an application of Tillich's criteria of faith, particularly his analysis of faith in false absolutes, to various forms of fundamentalism, especially in their intersections with politics. Tillich's own experience of individuals and communities placing ultimate concern in utopias, Nazism and nationalism influenced his emphasis on the existential risk of faith and the disruptive results of idolatry. Tillich's ontological, existential analysis of faith provides insight into both individual experiences of faith and broader encounters between communities of faith.

Notes

1 Tillich often interchanges faith and religion and sometimes offers the same definition for each word. In *CB*, Tillich argues for a religious root in 'every courage to be', justifying this by his definition of religion as 'the state of being grasped by the power of being-itself' (156). A few pages later, he offers the same definition for faith (172).

2 This essay was originally published in *RV*. Tillich expresses the same argument in *ST* II, 85.

3 Tillich asserts the participation of the power of being in everything that is as a basic ontological claim throughout his writings (although sometimes he uses the 'Unconditioned' in place of the 'power of being'). For examples, see *SD*, 6 and *LPJ*, 63.

4 What is accepted as 'real' varies by historical, social and cultural context.

5 See also *ProtE*, 67–8. In his early writings, Tillich discussed this tension in faith in terms of 'belief-ful' or 'self-transcending realism' to emphasize the rejection of absolutes on the ordinary level of reality and yet the acceptance of ultimacy penetrating or breaking through the ordinary level. See Paul Tillich, 'The Formative Power of Protestantism' in *ProtE*, 215.

6 Moreover, this activity of affirming being over against non-being shows God
   as a living God, as in a dynamic process of saying yes and overcoming the
   no (*CB*, 180).
7 See also Paul Tillich, 'The Protestant Message and the Man of Today' in
   ProtE, 201.
8 See also *ProtE*, 77 and 'The Protestant Principle and the Proletarian Situation' in *ProtE*, 163. The latter essay was originally published in 1931 as the
   brochure, *PP*.
9 See *ST* II, 101–7.
10 See also his discussion in *BR*.
11 See also *ST* III, 129.
12 *United States* v. *Seeger*, 380, U.S. 163, 1965.

Further reading

Gilkey, Langdon (1990). *Gilkey on Tillich*. New York: Crossroad.
Kegley, Charles W. and Robert W. Bretall eds. (1956). *The Theology of Paul
   Tillich*. New York: Macmillan.
Scharf, Uwe-Carsten (1999). *The Paradoxical Breakthrough of Revelation: Inter-
   preting the Divine–Human Interplay in Paul Tillich's Work 1913–1964*.
   Berlin/New York: Walter de Gruyter.
Scharlemann, Robert (1969). *Reflection and Doubt in the Thought of Paul
   Tillich*. New Haven: Yale University Press.
   (2006). *Religion and Reflection: Essays on Paul Tillich's Theology*, ed. Erd-
   mann Sturm. Münster: LIT Verlag, 2006.
Schüßler, Werner (1989). *Jenseits von Religion und Nicht-Religion. Der Reli-
   gionsbegriff im Werk Paul Tillichs*. Frankfurt am Main: Athenaeum.
Wenz, Gunter (1979). *Subjekt und Sein. Die Entwicklung der Theologie Paul
   Tillichs*. Munich: Chr. Kaiser Verlag.

7 'First, read my sermons!' Tillich as preacher

ERDMANN STURM

TILLICH'S THEORY OF HOMILETICS

When they appeared in German translation, Tillich's American sermons – *The Shaking of the Foundations*, *The New Being* and *The Eternal Now* – were given the revealing subtitle *Religiöse Reden*, or 'religious speeches'. In his 1923 *System of the Sciences*, Tillich placed preaching ('religious speech') within rhetoric as a part of practical theology: 'rhetoric on theonomous ground' (*GW* I, 188). Tillich's homiletic theory is firmly embedded in his understanding of systematic theology; even as a preacher, Tillich remained above all a systematic theologian. His sermons, in much the same way as his famous method of correlation, are determined by his insistence upon posing with all seriousness the question of the relevance of the Christian message to his contemporary society.

Tillich did not immediately arrive at this 'cultural-theological' understanding of the task of preaching. In his *Kirchliche Apologetik* of 1912–13 Tillich challenged apologetic theology to be conscious of the contemporary religious situation, characterized as the dominance of autonomous spiritual forms that had become foreign to the churches and to Christianity. By contrast, he characterized sermons as the presentation (*Darlegung*) of Christian teachings to the conscious members of that community (*GW* XIII, 44). However, in the course of the 1920s Tillich abandoned this dualism between apologetics and sermons. In his 1928 lecture 'The Protestant Message and the Man of Today' Tillich characterized his contemporaries as living in a situation of an uncertain autonomy (*GW* VII, 70–83; *ProtE*, 192–205). Humanity, Tillich claimed, 'has built an autonomous culture and lives in it, influencing it and being influenced by it'. At the same time, however, 'autonomous man . . . has become insecure in his autonomy' (*ProtE*, 192):

Modern man is without a world view, and just because of this he
has the feeling of having come closer to reality and of having
confronted the problematic aspects of his existence more
profoundly than is possible for the man who conceals these
problematic aspects of life by means of a world view.

(193)

It is this present state of humanity, whose spiritual possibilities are
absolutely at an end, to whom the Protestant proclamation (gospel) must
be addressed. This gospel is the proclamation of justification. However,
it should not simply be tied to the Reformation but must 'discover anew
the reality which was apprehended in that earlier day and which is the
same today, and then present it in new terms to the man of today' (196).
The situation of humanity before God, which the Reformers saw, Tillich
describes as a 'boundary-situation': human-being is more than simply
unmediated being-there (*Dasein*) but involves the 'transcending of vital
existence' and 'the freedom from himself, the freedom to say "Yes" or
"No" to his vital existence' (197). Humans cannot extract themselves
from this situation; they stand under the absolute requirement 'to realize
the true and to actualize the good' (198). When this requirement is not
fulfilled, then our existence is driven by a conflict and an agony from
which it cannot free itself with its own strength, not even through death.

In this way, the human situation is grasped as a boundary-situation.
Also Tillich stresses that the church stands in this boundary-situation;
it does not possess the truth but stands in truthlessness. The doctrine
of justification thus refers not just to the moral sphere ('good works')
but also to the question of truth. Where the church no longer questions
itself, it is 'questioned . . . radically and destructively' by autonomous
culture (200). For Tillich, this is now the situation: '[the Church's] task
is not the defense of a religious domain but the proclamation of the
boundary-situation in which every secular and religious domain is put
into question' (200).

The Protestant church must place under judgement and promise
everything that raises an ultimate concern, be it cultural or religious.
The Protestant proclamation therefore cannot demand that humanity
first accept the traditional religious contents of faith, e.g. the contents of
'God' or 'Christ'. The 'no' and 'yes' applies to mankind ultimately, not
under the condition of the acceptance of particular religious contents. If
it were so, it would create a legalism that would place men under a burden that is heavier even than the moralistic legalism that the Reformers
spoke so passionately against:

The profoundest aspect of justification, in our situation and for the man of today, is that we can discern God at the very moment when all known assertions about "God" have lost their power.

(203)

The Protestant proclamation must be three-fold. Firstly, it has to preach to the human situation – in its no and in its yes. It must thereby strike down every 'secret reservation' to which humanity can flee, even the most refined and spiritual of consolations. Secondly, it must:

proclaim the judgment that brings assurance by depriving us of all security; the judgment that declares us whole in the disintegration and cleavage of soul and community; the judgment that affirms our having truth in the very absence of truth (even of religious truth); the judgment that reveals the meaning of our life in the situation in which all the meaning of life has disappeared.

(204)

This 'yes' is, as Tillich stresses:

the pith and essence of the Protestant message, and it must be guarded as such . . . It must remain the depth and background of all our pronouncements; it must be the quality that gives to the message its truth and power.

(204)

Tillich adds a third element to the Protestant proclamation: the New Being that for Christians has become visible in Jesus as the Christ. Only from this New Being can Protestantism preach to the human boundary-situation in its no and its yes. It is remarkable how seriously Tillich takes this understanding of the human situation as a boundary-situation. To gloss over this human situation in its unconditionality would be to destroy the Protestant proclamation with its genuinely dialectical embrace of judgement and promise.

In his mature thinking, however, Tillich gives a completely different account of the nature of the homiletic task. In his 1963 lecture series *The Irrelevance and Relevance of the Christian Message*, given in Berkeley, California (by which time he had already published his three volumes of sermons), we no longer find the human situation defined as a boundary-situation. Instead, Tillich describes the spirit of modernity, using the symbol of space travel, as 'forwardism': as a horizontal forward movement that proceeds without knowing or asking why and for what. Reason is now technical reason, which wants to calculate and control everything. It is this against which existentialism revolts. Tillich is convinced that Christianity can give an answer to the spirit of the modern age and to the existentialist revolt. He begins, therefore, with an 'event that is experienced, an event that consists of two parts: the fact of a personal life and the reception of this life through a group known as disciples or followers' (*IR*, 46). Everything else, according to Tillich, follows from this event.

For Tillich, it is crucial that Christianity is based on an event in space and time, on a man, Jesus, whom his followers considered the anticipated Christ. 'Now this means that Christianity is not based on an idea or a set of symbols' (46). This event-character is unique among religions. The churches retained it and made it into tradition; however, paradoxically they also concealed and destroyed it. They represented the Kingdom of God or the spiritual community, but at the same time they betrayed and concealed their true nature. This is the paradox of the churches. Tillich also calls it 'the Protestant principle'.

The Protestant principle has its basis in the paradox of the dying and self-sacrificing Messiah. Its consequence is a Christianity that understands itself as the self-interpretation of humanity in the vertical direction towards the Unconditioned but also at the same time is able to take up into itself the horizontal line with which we all concerned. It can also take up the other religions into itself. But it may not set itself up absolutely: it must negate itself. However, the self-negation alone is no saving power: 'It is only saving if it is based on something positive, on the highest form of self-affirmation' (52). This positivity is the event of Jesus as the Christ, the New Being. From him comes a saving power: the acceptance of our selves in spite of our being unacceptable. Grace or justification or salvation is healing, overcoming of negativity. Tillich is convinced that in this way the Christian faith can overcome all forms of meaninglessness, such as those both diagnosed and perpetuated by existentialism. As bearer of the New Being, the church must bring this New Being to expression; this, however, is for Tillich always a risky venture:

> This risk the church must take! The minister who simply preaches in traditional ways, without risking error and controversy, should not have become a minister. Ministry means service, and he or she does not serve, does not heal, but rather prevents healing.

(59)

In this way Tillich describes the task and the risk of preaching, against which his own sermons can be measured. In addition, he names the themes and contents of his sermons in the 1963 lectures. It is interesting to compare these two reflections upon the nature of preaching. For both it is clear that the task of a sermon is the proclamation of justification. However, in his later view Tillich emphasizes much more strongly than in his earlier one that this is embodied in the event of the New Being, in Jesus as the Christ and the church. The proclamation of the no and yes in Tillich's early formulation remains abstract and formal; in his later writing it becomes concrete. Above all else, however, it is his characterization of the doctrine of justification as 'healing' that is most decisive for his mature theory of homiletics. Having considered Tillich's theoretical statements on the nature of the task of preaching, we can now turn to look at his own contributions to this form of practical theology.

Tillich's sermons can be divided into three distinct periods: his early parish sermons; his sermons delivered as an army chaplain during the First World War; and his American sermons. As will be seen, there are some considerable differences between the sermons from these different periods, largely determined by the contexts of their delivery, as well as by Tillich's own shifting assessment of the task of the preacher. The early (pre-war) sermons, preached from 1909 to 1914, were delivered in various parishes in what were then suburbs of Berlin. They belong to his ministerial training and reflect his early ecclesial understanding of preaching as the reiteration of the Christian message to self-confessed members of the Christian congregation – preaching, as it were, to the converted. By contrast, his battlefield sermons, delivered between 1914 and 1918 throughout the long duration of the First World War, show him addressing himself to a very different audience: his fellow men in the midst of the terrible existential and spiritual crisis of trench warfare. Finally, in his American sermons, delivered primarily as an invited preacher to church services in an academic setting, the split between apologetics and homiletics is overcome. In these sermons, Tillich is most clearly speaking as a theologian – from within the theological circle – to the new situation of the 'sacred void', characteristic of mid-twentieth-century humanity. In spite of these differences, certain characteristically Tillichian features can been found throughout his sermons. Consistently, Tillich's sermons are not expositions of particular biblical passages, but they are dedicated to certain themes, to which Tillich then attaches a short biblical text (characteristically, he also selects various translations, according to his intentions). In this way, Tillich does not adhere to the prescribed texts for respective Sundays; rather, he chooses freely his topic and his text. As for the themes themselves, in the early sermons as much as in the later, they are always strongly pastoral as well as apologetic.

THE EARLY SERMONS

The early sermons (from 1909 to 1918) have only recently been published and remain relatively unexamined by scholars (*ENGW* VII).[1] They consist of 67 parish sermons preached from 1909 until 1914 and 106 battlefield sermons preached from 1914 until 1918. In contrast to the famous American-era sermons, Tillich formulated these in his mother tongue. They are also much more strongly oriented around the liturgical year and Christian festivals than his later addresses.

The Berlin parish sermons

In the early parish sermons, Tillich's themes included: 'Evil, a Tool in God's Hand', 'We Must Learn to Wait', 'Christ and Joy', 'Of the Drunkenness and Sobriety of the Soul', 'The Mystery of the Crowd', 'Of the Suffering of Isolation' and 'Of Eternal Peace in the Midst of Time' (delivered on 6 September 1914!).

While it is impossible to give a comprehensive account of these sermons, a typical example, in terms of its contents and style, is a sermon on melancholy that he delivered as curate in Nauen in autumn 1911, accompanied by a text from Psalm 90 (*ENGW* VII, 184–90). In the sermon, Tillich enters into a dialogue with the Psalmist about the origins of the melancholy of his song. The Psalmist answers him: 'I stood on the bridge and looked down there into the rushing river, where wave pushed upon wave' (185). All waves go to the ocean. The eternal song of futility! An endless ebb and flow, a continual rising and falling. 'There the first sadness fell upon my heart' (185). This sadness in nature and history increases: the poet sees the twitching bodies on the battlegrounds, the desperate faces in the prisons, the beggars, the diseased. He looks into the heart of men and sees one final image: the crucified God, God himself suffering. 'There I sank down before God and grew silent, and as I rose, I wrote the Psalm of melancholy' (189). For Tillich, our melancholy has its deepest ground not in our transitoriness, but in God, who, suffering and dying, bears the suffering, death and guilt of the whole world.

The battlefield sermons

The battlefield sermons cover almost the whole duration of the war, from October 1914 to summer 1918, and reflect the inner experience of

the war on the Western front – above all, the attrition of static trench
warfare and the big 'pushes' of 1916. In a report to the army provost,
Tillich distinguished between two forms of sermon: the contemplative (*Quietiv*) and the motivational (*Motiv*). The contemplative adopts a
mystical and comforting tone. These sermons are directed to the troops
at the front, who are in grave danger. Through the sermons the word of
Christ calls to them: 'you are my friends' (John 15:14). By contrast, to
the soldiers behind the front line, who have forgotten the seriousness
of their situation and have become accustomed to the peace and quiet,
the sermon acts as a motivation, concerned with their inner moral
struggle. Tillich reports that for him the first kind of preaching predominates because of his audience and also because of his own personal
disposition.

Within the surviving material, we find examples of both kinds
of sermon, such that Tillich's battlefield sermons constitute a highly
developed war theology. Primarily, it is biblically grounded (mostly Old
Testament): many of Tillich's sermons are calls to hold out against 'complaints' (*Murren*), which are understood against the background of the
Old Testament 'complaints' as complaints against God (Exodus 15:24).
The soldiers are exhorted again and again to self-sacrifice; they are to
become Christ-like, or something similar, through their heroic deaths
(*ENGW* VII, 399, 620, 636). These sermons present the holy, true, perfect
sacrifice as the hero's death. Like the Lord's servant in deutero-Isaiah,
Germany must suffer for the sins of other people (492, 494). At the same
time, all suffering is reflected in the heart of God. God himself suffers.
There is a 'holy necessity' and 'law: through suffering to joy, through
death to life', and this 'holy necessity' is also in God (582). God reveals
himself in this war as the suffering God.

Alongside the themes of sacrifice, judgement and suffering, Tillich's
war theology is also determined by eschatology. All his sermons are
centred upon the thought of the eternal, who stands above all time and
nevertheless in the midst of it, able to pull us from out of this time into
eternity. The soldiers are to rise above immanence and 'with unveiled
eyes look towards the eternal, which is revealed as so majestically above
time and human life' ('Report to Provost' (1915) in *GW* XIII, 79). 'I am
a pure eschatologue', Tillich wrote in 1916 to Maria Klein, 'I preach
almost exclusively about the end' (*ENGW* V, 119).

In his sermons, Tillich wants to strengthen and console; indeed, at
the risk of becoming an apologist for the war, he seeks to strengthen
and to comfort at the limits of the humanly and theologically permitted
and also beyond. Above all, these sermons are intended as pastoral care

or spiritual welfare (*Seelsorge*). By transcending the realm of nature and history into the sphere of the spirit and from there to the sphere of the divine and the eternal, the situation of doubt is correlated with the certainty of God, understood as certainty of eternal life and eternal love in time and over all time. The distinction between law and gospel, of categorical importance for Lutheran theology, is reflected in this distinction between the situation of uncertainty and doubt on the one hand and the certainty of God and eternity on the other.

THE AMERICAN SERMONS

It is interesting to match up the three volumes of sermons, *The Shaking of the Foundations* (1948), *The New Being* (1955) and *The Eternal Now* (1963), with their nearly contemporaneous three volumes of *Systematic Theology* (1951–63). Together, these constitute the theological heart of Tillich's mature thought. Translated into numerous languages, they have made Tillich famous as a preacher, and one should not underestimate their subsequent influence on the theory and practice of Christian homiletics in America and Europe.

The Shaking of the Foundations
The title of the first collection, *The Shaking of the Foundations*, is derived from the first sermon. The actual 'text' is the dropping of the atomic bombs on Hiroshima and Nagasaki at the beginning of August 1945. Tillich selected in addition words from the prophets Jeremiah (4:23–30) and deutero-Isaiah (54:10; 24:18–20), who speak on the one hand of the destruction of the earth and the passing away of the world and on the other of the grace, judgement and salvation of God. Tillich asks: how could the prophets paint such terrible pictures of destruction and downfall? His answer is clear: 'beyond the sphere of destruction, they saw the sphere of salvation . . . in the doom of the temporal, they saw the manifestation of the Eternal' (*SF*, 20). The experience of the downfall corresponds to the judgement of God upon the world, the demonstration by the eternal one of his promise or covenant. Significantly, there is no mention of the New Being in the sermon: the 'yes' appears as demand, as the prophets looked through the disintegrating world to 'the rock of eternity and the salvation that has no end'.

In 'On the Transitoriness of Life', Tillich returns to Psalm 90. As in 1911, Tillich speaks of the tragedy of the human situation. In 1911 courage has its ultimate and deepest ground in the crucified and the suffering God, who is 'the eternal, infinite triumph over melancholy'

(*ENGW* VII, 189). In the later sermon, Tillich applies the human tragedy also to history:

> Whenever history seems to come near to its fulfilment, it is thrown back and is further from its fulfilment than ever before. That is what we experience so inescapably in our time. And so we ask, as all generations of men have asked: is tragedy stronger than hope? . . . We are driven to and fro between melancholy and expectation – from tragedy to hope, from hope to tragedy.
>
> (*SF*, 80–1)

This is the description of the human situation. As he had done already in the 1911 sermon, Tillich now confronts the situation with the message of 'God subjecting Himself to transitoriness and wrath, in order to be with us' (81). Tillich knows that in Psalm 90 this answer is not yet given. The Psalmist leaves the questions, which are decided in the human situation, unanswered. The answer comes from the message of the New Being in Christ. However, 'We must know that it is a real answer only if we understand it permanently in the light of our human situation, in which tragedy and hope fight each other without victory. The victory is above them. The victory came only when the prayer of the psalmist was answered' (81).

We remain here in the correlation of situation and message. Tragedy and hope struggle with one another. Only in the *Eschaton* will a victory of the New Being over the tragedy of the human situation emerge from the struggle. In contrast to the 1911 sermon, Tillich now develops a transcendental argument from reflection: we can notice our misery and tragedy as such only because we look out to what is beyond them. Even for modern pessimists, 'hidden – often to themselves – is a criterion by which they measure and condemn human existence. It is something beyond man' (74).

Probably the best-known of Tillich's sermons is 'You Are Accepted', accompanied by the text from Romans 5:20: 'Moreover the law entered, that the offence might abound. But where sin multiplied, grace did much more abound.' The sermon is an example of the risk of translation (expression or manifestation) that Tillich would speak about in his 1963 lecture referred to above. In this sermon, he describes sin as the 'splitting' of life and grace as 'the *reunion* of life with life, the *reconciliation* of the self with itself. Grace is the acceptance of that which is rejected. Grace transforms fate into meaningful destiny; it changes guilt into confidence and courage. There is something triumphant about the word "grace"' (158).

Tillich describes how in individuals a fight takes places between estrangement and reunification – in our relationship with ourselves, with others and with the ground and goal of our being. In very concrete terms, Tillich identifies our experiences of estrangement: the enmity deep within our souls, the tremendous power of self-destruction within society and within ourselves. We feel, he claims, 'that something radical, total, and unconditioned is demanded of us' and nevertheless we evade it (161).[2] However, this 'something' is the ground of our being, to which we are bound and from which we cannot become split, even though we are separated from it.

The words of St Paul testify to the 'most overwhelming and determining experience of his life': 'In the picture of Jesus as the Christ, which appeared to him at the moment of his greatest separation from other men, from himself and God, he found himself accepted in spite of his being rejected. And when he found that he was accepted, he was able to accept himself and be reconciled to others' (162). For Tillich, grace depends on this overwhelming experience, not on faith in the existence of God. 'To believe that something *is*, is almost contrary to the meaning of grace' (162). Rather, grace meets us:

> when we walk through the dark valley of a meaningless and empty life . . . when our disgust at our own being, our indifference, our weakness, our hostility, and our lack of direction and composure have become intolerable to us . . . when year after year, the longed-for perfection of life does not appear, when the old compulsions reign within us as they have for decades, when despair destroys all joy and courage.
>
> (163)

In such a moment, light breaks into our darkness, and it is as if a voice speaks to us:

> "You are accepted. *You are accepted*, accepted by that which is greater than you, and the name of which you do not know. Do not ask for the name now; perhaps you will find it later. Do not try to do anything now; perhaps later you will do much. Do not seek for anything; do not perform anything; do not intend anything. *Simply accept the fact that you are accepted!*"
>
> (163)

The New Being

The title of Tillich's second volume of sermons, published in 1955, suggests a new accent in his preaching, which comes particularly to the

fore in the title sermon, 'The New Being'. Here the correspondence with
the second volume of Tillich's *Systematic Theology* (1957) is clear, both
in terms of content and method. In the preface to his second volume
of sermons, Tillich notes that the first volume, *The Shaking of the
Foundations*, left questions open which are now to be answered. 'The
New Being is, so to speak, the answer to the questions developed in
The Shaking of the Foundations' (*NB*, vii). In the first volume, it is the
situation that is emphasized more than the message, whereas in the
second volume this is reversed, and the message or soteriology comes
to expression and the situation withdraws.

The theme of this volume is therefore the New Being, which Tillich
describes in three-fold manner as love, freedom and fulfilment. The first
sermon, 'To Whom Much Is Forgiven . . .', speaks of forgiveness as an
experience of breakthrough:

> In the midst of our futile attempts to make ourselves worthy, in
> our despair about the inescapable failure of our attempts, we are
> suddenly grasped by the certainty that we are forgiven, and the fire
> of love begins to burn. That is the greatest experience anyone can
> have. It may not happen often, but when it does happen, it decides
> and transforms everything.
>
> (12–13)

This experience of forgiveness is identical with the experience of
being accepted by a power that is stronger than we ourselves, stronger
than our friends, advisors and ministers. Whosoever is accepted by this
power can also accept themselves. Forgiveness is unconditional acceptance. In a way that echoes Kierkegaard, Tillich claims that forgiveness
and acceptance almost suspend moral uprightness (*Rechtschaffenheit*).
Tillich asks why children turn away from honest parents, why women
turn away from honest men, why Christians turn away from honest
ministers. He asks why they turn to those who are not the just. His
answer is that they look for a love that is grounded in forgiveness. The
message of justification suspends every form of self-righteousness and
moralism. Tillich understands Jesus as a critic of a loveless and cold
moral uprightness and sets his message of justification against an American Christian moralism that he sees as a contemporary form of Phar-
isecism. Far from simply apologetic, time and time again Tillich uses
his sermons to mount a polemic against this narrow and self-righteous
Christian moralism.

For Tillich, Christianity is the message of the New Being, of the new
creation and the new reality, which has appeared in Jesus as the Christ.
This is the subject of the sermon that gives the collection its title,

accompanied by a text from Galatians 6:15. Reading the text Christologically, Tillich claims that the New Being is a reality, which is to be reconciled with neither the Jewish practice of circumcision nor with pagan uncircumcision. Tillich concludes from this that 'no religion matters – only a new state of things' (*NB*, 16). Therefore, we should not be worried 'about the state of the Churches, about membership and doctrines, about institutions and ministers, about sermons and sacraments' (18). For Tillich, all this belongs to 'circumcision'. Only the new creation is of ultimate significance: it is this that is our ultimate concern, and that alone should be our 'infinite passion'. The message of the New Being is thus combined with a radical criticism of the church. For Tillich, the question about the New Being is the all-decisive question: 'In comparison with it everything else, even religion or non-religion, even Christianity or non-Christianity, matters very little – and ultimately nothing' (19).

Tillich attaches great importance to the statement that the New Being is an unconditionally valid actuality. It is not an ideal or a task. The New Being really has appeared. In it we *are* reconciled – with God, with other people and with ourselves: 'But it does *not* mean to try to reconcile the others, as it does not mean try to reconcile yourselves. Try to reconcile God. You will fail. This is the message: A new reality has appeared in which you *are* reconciled' (21–2). We can only join into this New Being. It is already there, wholly without our effort. We can only accept it and let ourselves be grasped by it. Tillich describes the New Being as an overwhelming power in personal life and in history. It is the power of reconciliation and the reunification of the separated:

> The New Creation is the reality in which the separated is
> reconciled. The New Being is manifest in the Christ because in
> Him the separation never overcomes the unity between Him
> and God, between Him and mankind, between Him and Himself.
> This gives His picture in the Gospels its overwhelming and
> inexhaustible power. In Him we look at a human life that
> maintained the union in spite of everything that drove Him into
> separation. He represents and mediates the power of the New Being
> because he represents and mediates the power of an undisrupted
> union. Where the New Reality appears, one feels united with God,
> the ground and meaning of one's existence. One has what has been
> called the love of one's destiny, and what, today, we might call the
> courage to take upon ourselves our own anxiety. Then one has the

astonishing experience of feeling reunited with oneself, not in pride and false self-satisfaction, but in a deep self-acceptance.

(22)

Along with the second volume of his *Systematic Theology*, these sermons present a powerful account of Tillich's Christology. As a preacher (perhaps more so than as a theologian?), Tillich is clearly seeking the comfort of a firm certainty, such that he risks proclaiming something of a 'positivism of being' analogous to the kind of revelatory positivism that he was so critical of. Such is the force of his proclamation of the New Being in its undestroyed unity that our broken experience even of that which heals our estrangement – the paradox of justification that Tillich previously insisted upon – is perhaps occluded. Just as with his systematic theology, so with his sermons, Tillich's method of correlation – of existential questions and theological answers – itself needs to be completed by a third moment, that of the ambiguities of life and spirit.

The Eternal Now

The third volume contains sermons from 1955 to 1963, and its contents should be seen in the context of the third volume of *Systematic Theology* and Tillich's doctrine of the Holy Spirit. In the preface Tillich relates that he gave the volume the title *The Eternal Now* because the experience of the presence of the eternal is the basis for most of the sermons. He rejected an alternative title, *Spiritual Presence* (the title of one of the sermons), because of the many negative connotations of the term 'spiritual'. Tillich divides the seventeen sermons in the book into three groups: those describing the human situation, e.g. 'Loneliness and Solitude' and 'The Riddle of Inequality'; those in which the presence of the divine Spirit is foregrounded, e.g. 'God's Pursuit of Man' and 'The Eternal Now'; and admonishments, e.g. 'Do Not Be Conformed', 'Be Strong', 'In Thinking Be Mature' and 'In Everything Give Thanks'.

I shall consider a characteristic sermon from each group. The human situation is described and interpreted in the light of the message. In this way, for example, Tillich describes concretely and vividly 'the riddle of inequality'. At the very beginning, he clarifies that we cannot expect that the biggest and perhaps most agonizing mystery of our lives – the mystery of the inequality of all organisms – can be solved. Neither the Bible nor religion contains solutions. Tillich wants to find only one way we can live with this unresolved mystery.

There is no solution as long as we speak not of the fate of all but of the fate of individuals: 'Only in the unity of all beings in time and eternity can there be a humanly possible answer to the riddle of inequality' (*EN*, 26). However, there is such an ultimate unity of all beings. It is based in the divine life. If we become conscious of this unity, then we participate in the divine life and in one another, 'in each other's having and in each other's not having' (26). However, how are we freed from our own narrowness? This happens by being seized by the power of the eternal, 'which is present in everyone and everything – the eternal, from which we come and to which we go' (26).

Tillich considers this divine reality in the sermon 'Spiritual Presence' under the text of 2 Corinthians 3:5–6. Tillich interprets the expression 'Holy Spirit' as the power *in* us which is not *from* us which makes us capable of the service of the New Being. We all have the task to be priests to one another and to mediate the New Being. However, who is intended by this 'we'? Who is not meant? We are inclined to consider ourselves as incompetent or incapable of helping each other as priests. Tillich reminds us of the 'action of a person whose life we know was disrupted, had a priestly awakening, and healing effect upon us' (54).

In such a man the Spirit of God is at work, the power that drives the human spirit out from itself to that which it cannot attain through its own power. Tillich names many indications or signs through which the divine Spirit reveals itself to us, e.g. the longing to overcome an empty and meaningless life or the power to take on the angst that belongs to all life. The question remains of how the presence of the divine Spirit can be united with the experience of the absence of God. Tillich's answer is that 'the final answer to the question as to who makes God absent is God himself!': 'in knowing God as the absent God, we *know* of him' (58). 'The divine spirit can hide itself, it can hide God: Then the Spirit shows us nothing except the absent God, and the empty space within us which is *his* space' (58).

Even if we experience God as absent, it is always the divine Spirit that works within us. Even the experience of the absence of God is to be interpreted as the work of God.

Paul's demand 'In Thinking Be Mature' (1 Corinthians 14:20) is the subject of one of the last of Tillich's sermons. To become mature in thought is, according to Tillich, to be open to the divine foolishness, of which Paul also speaks. Characteristically, Tillich translates the Pauline concepts into his own terminology. Divine foolishness and the final maturity of our thinking – as Tillich translates them – come together in the experience of something of ultimate validity: the holy, eternal and divine. If we want to speak of it, then we speak of an inexpressible one:

'Such experience is the most human of all experiences. One can cover it up, one can repress it, but never totally' (*EN*, 114).

Tillich asks: how can we produce this experience? The person who has the meaninglessness of their existence forced upon them is at the same time one who is grasped by divine foolishness. Here again we encounter the argument that the experience of the absence of God is an effect of his presence. To be mature in thought does not ultimately mean to abandon thought completely. In the symbols of Christmas and Good Friday (God present in a child and as crucified) Tillich sees the divine foolishness and the ground of all human maturity.

THE PREACHER AS THEOLOGIAN

In his contribution to the Tillich-Festschrift of 1959, *Preaching: Genuine and Secularized*, Rudolf Bultmann defined true Christian preaching as 'the call of God though the mouth of man [which] as the word of authority, demands belief'.[3] The preacher passes the word on as authoritative Word. This is a formal interpretation of the nature of preaching, which Tillich would not accept. For him, faith cannot be required by an authority. Also for him, the preacher is less a prophet than a priest. For Tillich, we all have the duty to serve each other as priests of the New Being 'from the strength of the New Being'. The paradox of the Word of God and the word of humanity, as Bultmann expresses it, corresponds for Tillich to the paradox of the Unconditioned. In order to be able to state it as Unconditioned, we need to overcome (*aufheben*) it as hypostatized, thus as Unconditioned. Religion, for him, is only justified 'where its dialectic is seen through and the glory is given to the unconditioned alone' (*GW* I, 382).

Karl Barth, in his famous lecture 'The Word of God and the Task of Theology' from 1922, offers what many see as a corrective to Tillich: 'As ministers (*Theologen*) we ought to speak of God. We are human, however, and so cannot speak of God. We ought therefore to recognise both our *obligation and our inability* and by that very recognition give God the glory.'[4]

For Bultmann, the paradox of preaching is revealed 'when it, as human speech, speaks God's forgiveness'.[5] Tillich would agree with this definition of preaching in terms of its contents, even if he himself would speak of the proclamation of the New Being and the acceptance of that which is unacceptable instead of the forgiveness of God and the strength of grace. In spite of their different terminologies, Bultmann and Tillich are united in their association of sermons with soteriology.

I conclude with a fascinating series of three short sermons from *The Shaking of the Foundations* ('The Theologian'), in which Tillich spoke directly about the nature of preaching as theological existence. For him, theological existence is church existence; it is existence of one 'who is grasped, within the Church, by the Divine Spirit, and who has received the word of wisdom and knowledge' (*SF*, 124). Its basis is the paradoxical statement 'Jesus is the Christ' (124). However, Tillich also asks to whom this applies: 'who can decide to become a theologian?' (124) His answer is three-fold. Firstly, if someone were to come to ask with full seriousness the question about that which concerns them ultimately and about Jesus as the Christ, then Tillich would call them a theologian. Secondly, the theologian must, like the Apostle Paul, 'become all things to all men' (Tillich's text in this second address is 1 Corinthians 9:19–23) in his theology (126). Tillich considers the most profound of Paul's statements that 'to the weak I have become weak myself in order to gain the weak' (128). As theologians, we must free ourselves from all theological self-assertion and participate in the 'weakness of all those to whom we speak as theologians' (128). Thirdly, the theologian must be an answering theologian. Although he participates in the weakness and in the errors of all men, he must be capable of answering their questions: 'For true theological existence is the witnessing to Him whose yoke is easy and whose burden is light, to Him who is the true paradox' (132). As theologians, we may not defend false stumbling-blocks or false paradoxes 'but interpret that paradox, and not throw paradoxical phrases at the minds of the people' (132).

Notes

This chapter was translated by Russell Re Manning.
1   For an initial analysis, see Sturm (1995).
2   Ibid., 161.
3   Bultmann (1959), 237.
4   K. Barth (1957), 186.
5   Bultmann (1959), 239.

Further reading

Gisel, Pierre (2002). 'Première guerre mondiale et apories de la modernité' in *Mutations religieuses de la modernité tardive*, ed. M. Boss, D. Lax and J. Richard, 50–77, Tillich-Studien 7. Münster, LIT Verlag.

Sturm, E. (1995). '"Holy Love Claims Life and Limb": Paul Tillich's War Theology'. *Zeitschrift für neuere Theologiegeschichte* 2: 60–84.

Part II

Theology of culture

8 Tillich's analysis of the spiritual situation of his time(s)

JEAN RICHARD

The reader of a philosophical theologian like Paul Tillich is inclined to understand his main ideas – for instance, the concepts of religion and culture – as fully universal and valid for all times. Of course, this is not so; all ideas and concepts bear the imprint of their time. As a modern thinker, Tillich is entirely aware of this and developed his own theory of the relationship between the universal, the concrete-historical and the normative. For him, the most universal concepts, like religion and culture, are normative concepts which are answers to the questions arising out of the concrete present situation. Moreover, Tillich offered two detailed descriptions of his situation: in Germany, *Die religiöse Lage der Gegenwart* (1926) and in the United States, *The World Situation* (1945). This chapter will consider these cultural-theological analyses after an exploration of the philosophical and theological background to Tillich's constructions.

THE THEORETICAL BACKGROUND

In his programmatic essay, 'On the Idea of a Theology of Culture' (1919), Tillich makes a sharp distinction between the objective empirical sciences, like the natural sciences, and 'the systematic sciences of culture', where 'the standpoint of the systematic thinker belongs to the thing itself' (*OITC*, 19 (orginal in *MW/HW* II, 70)). Cultural realizations – a concrete historical religion, a concrete historical society – are creations of the human spirit. This implies a general idea of a religion or a society, which depends on what is usually acknowledged as a religion or a society in the course of history. But it includes also a normative vision of what an authentic religion or a fair society should be. Hence, the three forms of the sciences of culture:

philosophy of culture, which attends to the universal forms, the
a priori of all culture; philosophy of the history (*Geschichts-philosophie*) of the cultural values, which, through the fullness of
the concrete [realizations] forms the transition from the universal
forms to its own individual standpoint, which it thereby justifies;
and finally normative science of culture, which brings the concrete
standpoint to a systematic expression.

(20 (translation modified) (71))

Thus, the spiritual or cultural situation refers to the meaning, to the
historical orientation of the present world. Such a meaning, however, is
not the result of a purely objective consideration of what is given. It is
determined according to the standpoint of the subject who contemplates
the flow of history. This is 'the standpoint of the systematic thinker'. It
'belongs to the thing itself', since the meaning of the current situation
is at the same time seen and determined by such a systematic thinker,
by his own way of correlating the present situation with the past and
with the expected future. Here is the normative moment in Tillich's
epistemological stand.

The second part of the lecture is about 'Culture and Religion'. Here
we dive into the thing itself, which was to be Tillich's main concern
his whole life long: the future of religion in our secularized culture.
The problem arises from the autonomous claim of such a culture which
allows for no religious heteronomy: no dogma against science, no theological ethics above philosophical ethics, no religious community, no
church alongside society or state. Tillich fully agrees with such a claim,
not only in the name of the autonomous culture but also on account of
religion itself, that is, according to the unconditionality of religion:

The religious principle is not one principle besides others in the
life of the spirit. The absolute character of every religious
consciousness would break through such limitations. But religion
is actual in every spiritual domain.

(23–4 (73))

In this way, religious heteronomy is kept away and the autonomy of
culture is fully honoured. This should not mean, however, that religion
is rejected altogether. From this point on, Tillich's endeavour will be
to show how religion may be consistent with autonomous, secular culture. A new concept of religion is needed at this point, that is, a deeper
understanding of the essence of religion with regard to culture. Tillich
holds that, beyond every particular realm of the culture or function of

the spirit, religion is essentially and fundamentally 'a certain quality of consciousness', determined through its relation to the unconditioned (23 (73)):

> Religion is the experience of the unconditioned, and this means the experience of absolute reality founded on the experience of absolute nothingness. One experiences the nothingness of entities, the nothingness of values, the nothingness of the personal life. Wherever this experience has brought one to the nothingness of an absolute radical No, there it is transformed into an experience, no less absolute, of reality, into a radical Yes.
>
> (24 (74))

Thus, religion is no longer considered a special sphere of culture that might be contrary to others, for instance, dogma as opposed to science. This is so because religion is no longer understood as a special function of the spirit, oriented to a divine reality alongside the world, but as the experience of the Unconditioned, not besides but through our cultural world, as the abysmal and infinite ground of such a finite world. In this way, the autonomy of culture is no longer opposed to the heteronomy of religion but can be internally inspired by religion and so become theonomous: 'The autonomy of science is preserved entire, religious heteronomy in any shape or form is made impossible. Instead, the whole of science is put under the "theonomy" of the religious basic experience' (25 (74)).

This does not mean, however, that any given culture is necessarily theonomous; nor is this another way of enforcing religion upon culture. A concrete historical culture may be more or less theonomous, more or less religious, or even not religious at all. Hence Tillich's next question: how to test the religious (or theonomous) weight of an actual culture? His answer is in terms of the distinction between the *Gehalt* (usually translated as 'content', 'substance' or 'import') and the 'form' of culture:

> I should like to propose that the autonomy of the cultural functions is grounded in their form, in the laws that govern their employment; theonomy, on the other hand, is grounded in their substance (*Gehalt*), the reality that is represented or conveyed by means of these laws. It is now possible to state the law: the more form, the more autonomy; the more substance, the more theonomy.
>
> (25–6 (translation modified) (75))

Such a distinction between *Gehalt* and *Form* corresponds to the first task of the normative sciences of culture, which is here, in the theology of culture, formulated as 'a general [i.e. theoretical] religious analysis of culture' (27 (76)). It consists in analysing the different relationships that can be found between *Gehalt* and *Form*. Here we look especially to 'the power in which each [i.e. *Gehalt* and *Form*] comes to expression' (27 (76)). The overpowering form produces autonomy with a liberating effect against religious heteronomy, while the overwhelming power of the *Gehalt* breaks through the cultural form, giving birth thereby to a new theonomy.

At this point, we reach the concept of *kairos*, which Tillich formulated in 1922 as 'the irruption of a new theonomy on the soil of a culture loosened (*gelösten*) or dissolved (*auflösten*) by autonomy' ('Kairos' (1922) in *MW/HW* IV, 66). The dialectics of history then become manifest from Tillich's philosophical and religious point of view. The rational-critical principle moves history forwards, towards autonomy, away from the ties of the origins. But the movement of culture is thereby carried away also from the wellspring of life. Hence the irruption of the *Gehalt* on behalf of a new theonomy:

> Since there is no history without autonomy, one can say that the sense of history is the realization of a theonomous spiritual situation (*Geisteslagen*) on a soil loosened by autonomy. So, the orientation toward the unconditioned comprises always two moments: the autonomous consciousness of the creative power forming history and the surrender of that autonomous power to the filling of the unconditioned *Gehalt*. The actualization of the autonomy is the preparation of the *kairos*; the irruption of the theonomy is its achievement.
>
> (67)

Indeed, Tillich's religious and theological analysis of culture will focus on the dynamics of religious heteronomy, cultural autonomy and irrupting theonomy, in order to state where we are coming from, where we stand and where we are going. Of course, his main concern is normative: not only to know where we stand and where we are going, but where we should go.

THE SPIRITUAL SITUATION IN 1926

In his first best-seller, *Die religiöse Lage der Gegenwart* (1926) (*The Religious Situation of the Present Time*), Tillich, from the beginning, clearly states both his intention and his own position. What he intends to investigate is not first and foremost the present situation of the churches. He is, rather, mainly concerned here with the whole of our – let us specify, occidental – modern culture, 'for there is nothing that is not in some way the expression of the religious situation' (*RS*, 40).[1] Obviously, religion is not conceived here as a particular sphere of culture. As indicated above, it is meant as a quality of consciousness, as its relation to the Unconditioned which may be found in every sphere of culture. Therefore, to analyse the present situation from a religious point of view is 'to contemplate things from the point of view of eternity'. So, the relation of the conditioned forms of culture to the Unconditioned *Gehalt* is translated here as 'the relation of our time to eternity' (25).

Such an analysis does not proceed from a purely objective observation. It is a normative investigation which implies the vital commitment of the investigator. Tillich openly states his own position as 'a responsible and creative criticism of [his] own time', a time characterized by 'the spirit of capitalist society'. The dynamic involvement of the author makes such a criticism possible: 'If the book succeeds in bearing effective testimony of the shaking of this spirit and hence to the shaking of our time by eternity it will have fulfilled its purpose.' The spirit of capitalist society means 'a fundamental attitude toward the world', which is the attitude of self-sufficient autonomy, while the shaking of such a spirit indicates a new *kairos*, the in-breaking of a new theonomy (27).[2]

Having set the scene, Tillich turns to consider the present time in relation to the future: 'To understand the present means to see it in its inner tension toward the future', that is, 'the direction from that which is to that which ought to be'. With Tillich, let us specify that the 'ought to be' is not only an idea in the mind of the observer: it is the 'apprehension of the growing form' of that which is 'creatively new and pregnant with the future'. Such an apprehension is necessarily 'the outlook of a creative will, not merely of indifferent observation', since 'one is enabled to speak of that which is more vital in the present, of that which makes the present a generative force, only insofar as one immerses oneself in the creative process which brings the future forth out of the past' (33–4).

Yet a further step is required: to consider the relation of time to eternity. This is the true meaning of the *religious situation*, since 'religion deals with a relation of man to the eternal' (36). There is indeed something eternal in the present. It is not only a flowing reality which is here today and gone tomorrow: 'it has an unconditioned meaning, an unconditioned depth, an unconditioned reality'. Of course, this is not 'a matter of proof or disproof but only of faith in the unconditioned meaning of life' (35). Faith, then, is something different from and deeper than belief: 'It refers to an unconscious, self-evident faith which lies at a deeper level than the apparent antithesis of the belief and unbelief which both arise out of it and are both equally rooted in it' (40).

Moreover, the relation of time to eternity implies the dialectics of the self-sufficiency and the self-transcendence of time. On the one hand, the eternal is concretely realized in time and history; it is 'taken up into the forms of time, it becomes an existential form, temporal and contemporary'. This is the ground for 'the self-sufficiency of time, the secularization of the holy' (38–9). On the other hand, 'it is not possible for any time to be self-sufficient. Because it is time there is something within it which drives it beyond itself at every moment . . . toward something which is no longer time.' This is most conspicuous 'in the profound, catastrophic movements in reality, where that which is really creative is at work' (37–8). Here is, no doubt, an allusion to the catastrophes of 1918: the end of the war and the German revolution. For most people of his time and his country, this period was interpreted as a disaster, as the collapse of the prevailing German culture. For Tillich, however, such apocalyptical events are but the pains of a new birth, prodrome to a new creation. They are irruptions of the eternal *Gehalt* through the cultural forms of time.

Tillich next deals with the concrete and characteristic elements of the 'bürgerliche Gesellschaft', that is, modern secular society. There are three of these: the physical sciences, technique and economy. However, everything is oriented towards economy as the first value and the ultimate end of all endeavour: 'for science is a servant of technique in which it also celebrates its greatest triumphs while technique is a servant of the economy and makes possible the development of a world-embracing economic system' (42).

Tillich shows how that same spirit of capitalist society pervades the different aspects of the modern world. In the theoretical field of the sciences, the result of it is positivism, psychologism and historicism. In political life, 'the nation state [is] drawn externally and internally into the service of economics'. Ethics itself 'becomes more and more subservient to the economic end'. With implicit reference to Max Weber, Tillich goes on: 'the fundamental virtues in the ethics of capitalist society are economic efficiency, developed to the utmost degree of ruthless activity' (42–4).

With regard to the dialectics of time and eternity, of self-sufficiency and self-transcendence, the meaning of such a spiritual situation is clear: 'it is an extreme example of a self-assertive, self-sufficient type of existence'. Indeed, 'all phases of life which are subject to the spirit of rationalistic science, technique and economy bear witness to the time as one which is self-sufficient, which affirms itself and its finitude' (47–8). This applies to mathematical physical science, 'which pursues the goal of demonstrating that reality is governed wholly by its own laws and is rationally intelligible'. It applies also to technique, 'with its will to conquer space, time and nature and to make the earth a well-furnished dwelling of man'. It applies finally to capitalist economy, 'which seeks to provide the greatest possible number of men with the greatest possible amount of economic goods, which seeks to arouse and to satisfy ever increasing demands' (47).

It is significant that this section is entitled 'The Religious Situation of Capitalist Society in the Nineteenth Century'. This is not exactly Tillich's situation; however, it is of the utmost importance, since it is 'that period on which our own lives are founded', even if 'we are moving away from it'. Indeed, Tillich writes that 'we come out of a time in which existence was directed toward itself, in which the forms of life were self-sufficient and closed against invasions of the eternal . . . Capitalist society rested undisturbed in its finite form' (50–1).

By 1926, however, Tillich is able to assert that 'that situation has been destroyed. The time has experienced shocks which it could not resist, the effects of which it could neither reject nor secularize.' Of course, the war (1914–18) and the German revolution (November 1918) were crucial, but the general movement away from the former situation was more profound: 'Not only war and revolution brought about these shocks. Even before these occurred internal revolts against the spirit of capitalist society had begun all along the line and had led, in the younger generation, to decisive transformation.' The study of the spiritual situation of the present time should therefore comprise also the first decades of the new century: 'Hence we may include the entire first quarter of the twentieth century in our study' (51).

Towards the end of the introduction, Tillich indicates why the religious analysis of the present time should begin with the non-ecclesiastical aspects of the social life and only afterwards consider the specifically religious movements: 'For just as it was the non-ecclesiastical culture which had almost exclusively held the leadership in the previous century so also it was out of this culture that the revolutionary movements of the twentieth century arose. The churches

followed very slowly and contributed creative power at very few points'
(51–2).

There is also a more fundamental reason. The specifically church
religion 'is only a part of the total phenomenon; it is that part which
testifies to the ultimate meaning and which has been especially called to
do so since by nature it seeks to be in relation to the eternal' (37). This is
more explicitly expounded in the 1919 lecture, where Tillich specifies
the correlation between the theology of culture (*Kulturtheologie*) and
the theology of the church (*Kirchentheologie*):

> In order to experience religious values in culture, to develop a
> theology of culture, to distinguish and name the elements of
> religion, a specifically religious culture must have preceded. In
> order to conceive the state as church or art as cultus or science as
> the doctrine of faith, church, cultus, dogma must have preceded,
> and not only preceded. In order to experience the sacred as
> somehow distinct from the secular, we must lift it out and set it in
> a special sphere of cognition, prayer, love, and organization.
>   (*OITC*, 35 (translation modified) (81–2))

Here we see the difference between Tillich and most theologians of
his time – the 'young Turks' of 'dialectical theology', Karl Barth, Eduard
Thurneysen, Emil Brunner, Friedrich Gogarten and Rudolph Bultmann.
They held that the First World War meant a rupture which put an end to a
former liberal and optimistic theology and gave birth to a new theology
centred on the crisis of this world and the transcendence of God as
wholly other. Liberal theology was criticized because of its synthesis (i.e.
equation) between the Christian idea and the highest values of modern
culture. This gave rise to what was rejected by dialectical theology under
the pejorative title of *Kulturprotestantismus*.[3]

In many respects, Tillich shares in that new theology. In a 1922
lecture, he writes: 'In this regard, it is on the basis of the religious
reality itself that I indicate my spiritual affinity in the following ideas
with men like Barth and Gogarten whose concern is the religious Word'
('The Conquest of the Concept of Religion in the Philosophy of Religion'
in *WR*, 123). Indeed, at that time Tillich feels reluctant to be called a
liberal theologian, and in the years following 1919 he very seldom uses
the phrase 'theology of culture', most probably to avoid being identified
with *Kulturprotestantismus*.[4]

Nevertheless, Tillich is no neo-orthodox theologian. According to
Tillich, criticism of the modern world does not come first from on high,
from the divine Word or Judgement: it comes from the heart of culture

itself, from the irruption of the spiritual *Gehalt* of culture, thus giving birth to a new *kairos*. Accordingly, what matters is not a new wave in theology, which would make a stand against the world; what really matters is a new wave in culture itself. What is required is not a new church theology that would now say 'no' to the world; what is most needed is a theology of culture that would see and conceive what has been going on in culture since the turn of the century.

THE WORLD SITUATION IN 1945

About twenty years later, in the United States, Tillich had the opportunity to write on the same subject: 'The World Situation'.[5] Once again the discussion is centered on the 'bürgerliche Gesellschaft', now translated literally as 'bourgeois society'. The general evolution of that modern society is now sketched in three phases: the rise, the triumph and the crisis.

The first period was marked by the great bourgeois revolutions in all spheres of culture, from politics to economics. These revolutions are meant as movements of liberation, as emancipations from all kinds of heteronomy, political as well as religious. Autonomy then is conceived as the absence of every authoritarian control. It is the economy of *laissez-faire*, with its implicit belief in a pre-established harmony: 'it was believed that the welfare of all would be best served by the unrestrained pursuit by each individual of his own economic interests; the common good would be safeguarded by the "laws of the market" and their automatic functioning'. Likewise, in the political order, democracy is grounded on the same belief: 'it was supposed that the political judgement of each citizen would lead automatically to right political decisions by a majority of citizens; community of interest would assure democratic procedures' (*MW/HW* II, 167).

The second period is that of the 'victorious bourgeoisie', and it is marked by 'the loss of control by human reason over man's historical existence'. Owing to his newly acquired control over physical nature, man 'created a world-wide mechanism of large-scale production and competitive economy'. But 'he was swallowed up by his own creation. Step by step the whole of human life was subordinated to the demands of the new world-wide economy. Men became units of working power. The profit of the few and the poverty of the many were driving forces of the system' (168).

The third period is characterized by the crisis of that bourgeois society and its conception of life: 'The foundation of bourgeois society has broken down: namely, the conviction of automatic harmony between individual interest and the general interest' (169). The two world wars are witnesses to such a collapse. And the void that followed has been filled with two demonic figures: the Fascist and the Soviet systems. In both cases 'absolutism returned, but without the social, cultural, and religious tradition which furnished solid foundations for the earlier absolute systems' (170).

Let us note immediately two differences with regard to the analysis of 1926. First, a small one: three phases are indicated now (the rise, the triumph and the crisis), whereas previously only two had been mentioned: the prevailing culture and the irruption of the new. Much more significant, however, is the description of the crisis. 'The foundation of bourgeois society has broken down' not under the irruption of a new *kairos*, but out of dissolution. The consequence is not a new spiritual substance, a new theonomy, but a 'void' that has been filled with two demonic figures: the Fascist and the Soviet systems. On the whole, then, an *anti-kairos*. This is clearly and dramatically stated, a year later, in an article in which Tillich acknowledges the collapse of his first idea of a theology of culture:

> The *kairos* which we believed to be at hand was the coming of a new theonomous age, conquering the destructive gap between religion and culture, in which we are living. But history took another path, and the question of religion and culture cannot be answered simply in those terms. A new element has come into the picture, the experience of the 'end' . . . While after the First World War the mood of a new beginning prevailed, after the Second World War a mood of the end prevails. A present theology of culture is, above all, a theology of the end of culture, not in general terms, but in a concrete analysis of the inner void of most of our cultural expressions.
>
> ('Religion and Secular Culture' (1946) in *MW/HW* II, 201–2)[6]

Another characteristic feature of this new analysis of the cultural situation is that it revolves round the notion of reason. In the first period the guiding principle was the belief in reason: 'Reason was the very principle of humanity which gives man dignity and liberates him from the slaveries of religious and political absolutisms' (*MW/HW* II, 166; cf. 184). This is 'revolutionary reason', which is 'concerned with ends beyond the existing order'. Soon however, revolutionary reason was put aside and replaced by technical reason, which 'became concerned with means to stabilize the existing order'. So, 'the transformation of revolutionary reason into technical reason was the decisive feature of the transition from the first to the second period of modern society' (168; cf. 184–5). The third period, then, would be characterized by 'planning reason', which would attempt 'to bring the incalculable mechanism of world economy back under the control of man'. This is the direct opposite of 'the principle of automatic harmony epitomized in *laissez-faire* liberalism in economics' (170).

The most significant change with respect to the 1926 analysis, however, occurs in the final section of the 1945 article. The question is no longer about 'The Religious Situation of the Present Time in the Realm of Religion', as indicated in the title of the third and last part of the 1926 book. In 1945 the matter is about 'Christianity in the Present World Situation', that is, the relation of Christianity to our modern culture, 'as one of both adaptation to, and transcendence over, the present world situation' (189). What is called for, then, is a more explicitly theological consideration, to show not only the actual situation of the different churches and religious groups in the modern world, but how Christianity specifically should behave towards the world in the present situation.

The analysis begins with an account of the problem. The history of the relations between Christianity and modernity goes back to the origin of the secular, autonomous world: 'Indeed, in the later Middle Ages and at the Reformation, religion itself helped to prepare the soil for the growth of autonomy in all realms of life.' Autonomy, then, means secularity, that is, emancipation from religion. Hence the problematic situation of religion in the modern world: 'so doing, religion helped to create alongside itself a secular sphere that step by step invaded and mastered the religious sphere. Thus religion itself became secularized and was drawn into the conflicts and contradictions of the new society' (189). Here we see clearly how the distinction between religion and culture is historically marked. It appears with the autonomy of the spirit, with the emancipation of all the functions of the human spirit from the bonds of its origins.

This is especially manifest in the realm of knowledge: 'The triumph of autonomous knowledge, particularly in the natural sciences, has pushed aside religious knowledge', leading to the opposition of dogma and science. But something still more insidious happens: religious knowledge 'is transformed by secular interpretations'. Religious knowledge itself is drawn into the turmoil of secularization. It is rationalized, objectified: 'God comes to be thought of as one being alongside other beings, even though the highest.' So 'religious knowledge loses its authority' (191). It is no longer theonomous knowledge; it is brought back to the level of technical, rational knowledge, where it does not belong, from where it is expelled.

In recent centuries, three types of theology occurred to solve the problem of Christianity in the modern world. Traditional-orthodox theology has preserved the treasures of the past, but it escapes the situation, since it is satisfied with the adaptation of the structure, leaving untouched its content. Dialectical theology fully comes to grips with the present situation, relating to each other in radical criticism both the contents of Christian tradition and those of modern culture: 'In this sense, it is dialectical. It delights to declare "No" and "Yes" in the same breath.' However, 'when this type of theological thinking tried to become constructive, it simply relapsed into the mere reiteration of tradition. It became "neo-orthodoxy"' (193–4).

Without doubt, Tillich now gives liberal theology preference over the two other types. The challenge any Christian theology must face is clearly stated: 'the relation of Christianity to any culture can never be adequately interpreted merely in terms of adaptation. By the very nature of its message, it must seek to transcend every particular historical situation' (189).[7] The same statement is also expressed in the title itself: 'Christian Acceptance and Transcendence of Reason' (193). Actually, liberal theology 'has accepted unreservedly the reign of reason, not only as a factor in the secular world to which it must seek adjustment, but also as an agency of its own regeneration'. For instance, historical criticism was applied to the study of the Bible and to the whole history of the church: 'The honest radicalism of this work of Christian self-criticism is something new in church history and brought values never before recognized or accepted.' On the other hand, liberal theologians 'are distinguished from humanism by their refusal to adapt Christianity entirely to the demands of current vogues' (193). So, not only did they fully accept the demands of reason, they also tried to transcend autonomous reason towards an authentic theonomy.

The relationship between Christianity and the modern world is conceived now as the Christian answer to the world situation. More precisely, the Christian message is meant as the answer to the questions that rise out of the present situation.

At the very outset, Tillich expresses his intention 'to seek to discover the inner logic and meaning of that [world] situation, and to ask what message Christianity has to offer it' (166). Dealing with the present crisis in civilization, he writes that 'Christianity must give its message to a world in which Leviathan in its different aspects threatens all human existence to its very roots' (171). At the end of the section on person-ality, community and education, we read: 'The Christian answer to the educational problem must be given in unity with the answer to the prob-lems of personality and community' (178). With regard to the problem of existential truth – how to relate the concrete-existential truth of the new community of faith to the universal truth of Greek rationality – Christianity formerly 'found an answer in its Logos doctrine . . . In this brief formula [Jesus the Christ is the Logos], early Christianity united, at least in principle, existential and rational truth.' Since the present world situation raises a similar problem, Christianity 'must give essen-tially the same answer, though in different terms and with different intellectual tools' (188).

Tillich concludes his article with 'Guideposts for the Christian Answer'. First, the Christian answer should not be brought to the situ-ation from on high, that is, from a supranatural revelation: 'The Chris-tian message to the contemporary world will be a true, convincing, and transforming message only insofar as it is born out of the depths of our present historical situation' (195). Those are the depths of suffering, of contradictions and aberrations that demand answers. But the world sit-uation does not offer only negative features: it comprises also positive ones, such as the elevation of reason as the principle of truth and justice. So, 'the answers themselves must acknowledge and accept the positive contributions of the modern period' (196). This is especially the case as Christianity 'affirms that the influences of divine grace are never absent from each historical situation. It relates them directly or indirectly to the history of divine revelation and especially its central reality – Jesus Christ' (196).

Thus, the world situation is not to be seen just as the reign of evil. Conversely, the actual Christian answer is not to be meant as a pure expression of the reign of God, since it is embodied in the culture of our time: 'Insofar as Christianity has adjusted itself to the character of modern society, it is able to bring only a very incomplete answer to its problems, for Christianity, as it has been drawn into the destructive contradictions of the present stage of history, is itself a part of the prob-lem' (189). The same must be said of the church, which is the concrete, historical figure of Christianity: 'The Christian church should furnish the answers thrust forth by the present situation in the economic, politi-cal, and international orders. But the churches largely lack that power because they themselves have become instruments of state, nation and economy' (192). The case of the church is especially significant here, since it is the concrete, practical and symbolic representation of the

Christian answer. These are indeed the final words of Tillich's article: 'Lastly, the Christian answer must be at the same time both theoretical and practical . . . Despite the measure of their bondage to the present world situation, the Christian churches are the historical group through which the answer must be given' (196).

Here we have a first glimpse of the method of correlation that will be the distinguishing mark of his mature theology:

> The method of correlation explains the contents of the Christian faith through existential questions and theological answers in mutual interdependence . . . In using the method of correlation, systematic theology proceeds in the following way: it makes an analysis of the human situation out of which the existential questions arise, and it demonstrates that the symbols used in the Christian message are the answers to these questions.
>
> (*ST* I, 60–2)

These passages enable us to have a fuller understanding of the meaning of correlation for Tillich. It certainly does not mean that the Christian answers will fill the gaps of the human situation. The interdependence of questions and answers is much deeper. The correlation is to be found between 'pregnant questions' and 'fragmentary answers': the questions are pregnant with answers, while the answers are but fragmentary or incomplete, since they are caught in the turmoil of the situation. Therefore, the Christian answers have to be interpreted by every new generation of believers to show their relevance, their living meaning for them at the present time. That is the risky hermeneutical task of theology that Tillich leaves to us in our present situation.[8]

Notes

1   See also: 'Yet it must be conceded at the outset that this attempt is subject to certain essential limitations. Not every situation, not every society, can be understood from the point of view of another situation or society; but only that one which is vitally related to the one from which it is observed. Hence the present about which we can speak is the life of our Western society. Even this society is divided and is cut across by creedal and national walls which it is difficult for individuals to surmount. To concede this does not mean that we are limiting ourselves intentionally but that there are actual limitations which can never be wholly transcended and of which one must remain conscious, particularly when one's point of view is located in the midst of deeply shaken mid-European society' (*RS*, 40). This long quotation shows clearly how Tillich is fully aware of the relativity of his point of view. He did not realize his own provinciality only when he first came to the United States.

2   Note that 'der Geist der bürgerlichen Gesellschaft' is translated by Niebuhr as 'the spirit of capitalist society' to avoid the morally pejorative overtones of the English phrase 'bourgeois society'.

3   See Gisel (2002), 50–1.

4   See 'Troeltsch does not conceive any more the possibility of a dogmatics. It must be said to its credit that he has cleaned the table. He got rid of the remains left by liberal theology' (*Dogmatik-Vorlesung (Dresden 1925– 1927)* in *ENGW* XIV, 2). Here, 'liberal theology' refers to a specific trend in the theology of the nineteenth century. In the United States, Tillich will feel more distant from Barth and closer to Troeltsch. Then he will side with 'liberal theology' in a broader sense.

5   References are given to *MW/HW* II, 165–96. The text was first published as a chapter of the book edited by van Dusen (1945). The book gathered papers from the members of the Theological Discussion Group of which Tillich was a member.

6   The same mood of deception comes to the fore as early as 1926: 'Die geistige Welt im Jahre 1926' in *GW* X, 94–9; *MW/HW* II, 115–20, as well as 1930: 'Die Geisteslage der Gegenwart: Rückblick und Ausblick' in *GW* X, 108–20.

7   Cf. 193: 'Christianity is not only a part of the contemporary world; it is also a protest against it and an effort to transform it by the power of Christian faith.'

8   This chapter has taken into account Tillich's situation in Germany (1926) and in the United States at Union Theological Seminary (1945). We might consider, however, that he experienced a new situation in Harvard (1955–62), a situation characterized by the encounter of world religions, which would ask for a new kind of correlation between history of religions and theology. For his part, Langdon Gilkey has written an excellent chapter on 'The Religious Situation at the End of the Twentieth Century', according to Tillich's mind, in Gilkey (2001), 7–18.

Further reading

Adams, James Luther (1965). *Paul Tillich's Philosophy of Culture, Science, and Religion*. New York: Harper & Row.

Bulman, Raymond F. (1981). *A Blueprint for Humanity: Paul Tillich's Theology of Culture*. Lewisburg, Pa.: Bucknell University Press.

Carey, John J., ed. (1978). *Kairos and Logos: Studies in the Roots and Implications of Tillich's Theology*. Macon, Ga.: Mercer University Press.

Despland, M., J.-C. Petit and J. Richard eds., (1987). *Religion et Culture*. Quebec: Presses de l'Université Laval/Éditions du Cerf.

Gilkey, Langdon (2001). 'The Religious Situation at the End of the Twentieth Century' in *Religion in the New Millennium: Theology in the Spirit of Paul Tillich*, ed. R. F. Bulman and F. J. Parrella, 7–18. Macon, Ga.: Mercer University Press, 2001.

Haigis, Peter (1998). *Im Horizont der Zeit. Paul Tillich Project einer Theologie der Kultur*. Marburg: N. G. Elwert Verlag.

Moxter, M. (2000). *Kultur als Lebenswelt. Studien zum Problem einer Kultur-theologie*. Tübingen: Mohr Siebeck.

9 Theology of culture and its future

WILLIAM SCHWEIKER

In order to rejuvenate Christian theology after the First World War, Paul Tillich, Karl Barth, Rudolf Bultmann and others insisted that theology reclaim as its proper object the reality of God. They sought to overcome the failure of cultural Protestantism and nineteenth-century liberal theologians to clarify the relation of Christian faith to cultural and social values. Among his contemporaries, Tillich conceived of the theological task in a distinctive way. The object of theological reflection is the depth, import or substance of human cultural activities. A theology of culture is thereby distinct from, if still related to, forms of theology in which the object of reflection is the God of the Bible within the faith of the church formulated in dogmas.

This chapter explores Tillich's theology of culture mindful of the enduring task of Christian theology and his conception of religion and human spirit. The constructive claim advanced is that theology of culture must be reconceived in light of contemporary global dynamics. More pointedly, the connection between theology of culture, ethics and what Tillich called 'ecstatic humanism' will be developed. The position proposed advances the agenda of the theology of culture in a new way for a new age; it can be called 'theological humanism'.[1] In a time when religions are shaping world-wide realities, sometimes violently and sometimes peacefully, it is important that they be given humane expression. Similarly, in an age of expanding human power, some ethical direction and limit to that power are needed in order to protect present and future life. These challenges define the future of theology of culture.

OVERVIEW, LEGACIES AND CRITICISMS

Tillich believed that theological reflection on culture was both possible and necessary in order to disclose the religious meaning of an increasingly secular world and also in order to clarify the relevance of

Christian faith to contemporary life. He worried that other attempts to rejuvenate theology might too easily return to a quasi-supernaturalism because of their appeals to biblical revelation and would thereby be inadequate for the modern age. Tillich also believed that a theology of culture was a new type of ethical reflection. The shift from ethics to the theology of culture was needed to avoid the possibility of a double ethics, one for believers (theological ethics) and another for secular society (philosophical ethics). Further, an adequate ethics must escape the dual threat of graceless moralism and normless relativism.[2] His theology of culture, then, entailed a specific conception of the theological task, sought to speak to the religious situation of modern cultures and, further, laboured to clarify the connection between faith and morality with respect to social and cultural activities. Theology of culture links the theoretical and the practical, the scientific and the moral, by articulating the meaning-giving power of human activities.

Tillich's conception exceeded reflection on the nature of theology and its various tasks. Any attempt to grasp the religious import, those matters of ultimate concern or meaningful depth, must be carried out with respect to an analysis of actual cultural forms. Tillich engaged an astonishing range of cultural expressions and their religious meanings, including painting, the plastic arts, poetry, architecture and even cultural movements.[3] He held, for instance, that the anxiety of post-Second World War Europe found expression in poetry and drama but also abstract painting. Cultural forms are the self-interpretation of human life in a particular age and, systematically understood, an expression of human spirit. Therefore, to analyse cultural forms is actually to probe the particular shape in which human spirit manifests itself in an age. Theology of culture thus aligns itself with the normative sciences of spirit or the human sciences, as he called them in his 1923 *The System of the Sciences*.[4] Tillich's position thereby creatively weaves together a conception of theology, an account of human spirit, a historically minded analysis of culture and a theory of religion in relation to spirit and culture. Armed with this agenda, Tillich sought to illuminate the modern situation.

For all of its brilliance, Tillich's conception of the theology of culture has roots deep within Christian thought. He acknowledged that 'theology of culture' continued what others, especially Friedrich Schleiermacher and Richard Rothe, called 'theological ethics'. His work also continued historical reflection by Ernst Troeltsch on the embeddedness of Christianity in Western civilization. Tillich engaged the philosopher Friedrich Schelling and, like him, affirmed the categorical difference between the Unconditioned and human conditioned reality. As a kind of existentialist, Tillich sought to situate reflection within the limits and ambiguities of human existence.[5] With greater historical perspective, the enterprise of theology of culture reaches back to the apologists of the early church. St Augustine's magisterial *The City of God* engaged the wider culture with respect to Christian beliefs about the divine and the highest good. Augustine did so, much like Tillich, in order to clarify a specifically Christian conception of God and Good thereby answering human longings. Theology finds expression through social and cultural reflection.

Tillich insisted that his task was to apply the Lutheran and Protestant idea of justification by faith and the theology of the cross as convictions not just about salvation but also the shape of theological reflection. Grace is not subject to human whim or control, and it often appears under its opposite, the cross. The religious experience of ultimate reality can and does appear in the shattering of the cultural experience of nothingness. There is, further, a divine and human protest against any absolute claim made for a relative conditioned religious or cultural reality. He called this the Protestant principle. Most importantly for theology of culture, Tillich held as a principle Luther's claim that the 'finite is capable of the infinite' (*finitum capax infiniti*). Finite reality, including human existence, while under its own autonomous rule and power can nevertheless mediate and disclose the divine ground and power of all things. Reflection under this conviction is 'theonomous', that is, 'a turning towards the Unconditioned for the sake of the Unconditioned'. 'Theonomy', he clarifies, 'is directed toward being as pure import (*Gehalt*), as the abyss of every thought form' (*SS*, 203). All domains of reality fall within the scope of theological reflection, especially the domains of culture and history. While there were some revisions in this thought, these ideas basic to theology of culture remained a touchstone throughout Tillich's long career.

Tillich's work inspired theologians to probe religious meanings in culture and to articulate the relevance of theological claims. In the 1960s thinkers like Langdon Gilkey drew inspiration from Tillich to address the 'death of God' in secular culture. Later, Robert Scharlemann and others, in different ways, sought to use the resources of postmodernism and deconstructionism in ways informed by Tillich's thought. Creative Roman Catholic theologians, like David Tracy, used and revised Tillich's method.[6] Additionally, Tillich's attention to specific cultural forms flowered into sustained reflection by many thinkers on the connection between religion, the arts and literature. And today too there are thinkers who reclaim, revise and extend the direction of theology of culture, and even cross-cultural reflection.[7]

However, it must be noted that virtually every aspect of Tillich's theology of culture, or any enterprise like it, has come under harsh criticism over recent decades. Some church theologians, as Tillich would call them, insist that any theology of culture will formulate Christian beliefs in non-Christian terms. In contrast, the theological task, they believe, is to reflect on the reality of the church and the story of Christ.[8] Others revise the dogmatic enterprise associated with the work of Karl Barth in terms of the culture of the Christian community.[9] Another version of church theology is so-called Radical Orthodoxy. Theonomous culture, as Tillich calls it, is supposedly inconceivable to such thinkers because it grants validity to the secular world distinct from the church. The theologian must 're-theologize' the world.[10]

Still other postmodern thinkers challenge Tillich's ideas about 'spirit', 'depth', 'being' and 'religion'. These ideas betray their Western origin in the undue priority given to a specific conception of reason, language and being that too easily enfolds all reality within their reach and thereby effaces what is other, different. Appeal to the 'depth' of culture may be seen as problematic when any one culture is in fact internally diverse and contentious, and also when contemporary cultural life is focused on the play of media forms rather than anxiety about 'meaning'.[11] Tillich's definition of religion as 'ultimate concern' and the 'substance' of culture is also overly abstract and lacking in historical and social precision; by sheer definition it makes every human being and every culture 'religious'. Finally, liberation as well as ecological theologians find the theology of culture too anthropocentric and lacking sustained attention to praxis, race, gender and liberation.[12]

With this brief overview of the task, legacies and also criticisms of theology of culture, we can now turn to explore Tillich's actual conception of it and the responses to his critics.

THE IDEA OF THEOLOGY OF CULTURE

Tillich's idea of theology of culture centres on a distinctive conception of the relation between religion and culture. He puts it thus:

Religion as ultimate concern is the meaning-giving substance of culture, and culture is the totality of forms in which the basic concern of religion expresses itself. In abbreviation: religion is the substance of culture, culture is the form of religion. Such a consideration definitely prevents the establishment of a dualism of religion and culture. Every religious act, not only in organized religion, but also in the most intimate movement of the soul, is culturally formed.

('Aspects of a Religious Analysis of Culture' in *TC*, 42)

In order to grasp Tillich's conception, one must clarify form and 'substance', the concern of religion and also how religion can express itself through cultural forms.[13]

Tillich's initial formulation of the 'idea' of a theology of culture was given in a lecture before the Kant Society in Berlin in 1919. It was his first publication after four years of service as a chaplain in the German army in the First World War, during which he experienced the devastation of war. In this lecture, Tillich insisted that religion, as the experience of the Unconditioned, is 'actual in all domains of spirit' (*OITC*, 24 (translation modified)). By 'spirit' Tillich does not mean a ghostly figure; it is not a reality opposed to 'matter': spirit 'is the self-determination of thought within being'. Further, 'spirit is neither a mode of thought nor a mode of being. In spite of its dependence upon both of these elements, it is an irreducible mode. Spirit is the mode of existing thought' (*SS*, 137). Further, every domain of human spirit (e.g. science, art, law, ethics, community, religion etc.) manifests the power of a radical yes to its being in spite of the experience of the no, radical nothingness. The 'basic concern of religion' is this yes to reality in the face of nothingness. And that is the meaning of Tillich's definition of religion as ultimate concern, namely, that what concerns human beings ultimately is being or non-being. Religion is an activity or conduct of spirit ('ein Verhalten des Geistes') as a *quality* of consciousness (*Bewußtsein*) not reducible just to consciousness. How then is one to examine religion as the specific object of theology of culture?

Tillich notes that theology of culture must consider the relation of form and import ('Form und Gehalt'). Import, or 'substance' (*Gehalt*), is different from content (*Inhalt*).[14] Form is the shape or media for expressing content and import; it might be a painting, or a social movement, or an organization or an entire culture. Cultural content (*Inhalt*) is the objective meaning raised into expression by a specific form, like the subject of a painting or the ideals of a social movement. Import (*Gehalt*), while brought to expression by form, is the sense (*Sinn*), the spiritual substantiality, which gives form its meaning (*Bedeutung*). Import is meaning-giving power. The distinction between import and content is crucial, Tillich insisted. Content cannot exhaust or exceed its form; the content of a particular painting is presented in the form of the painting. Without form, the content of the painting is not conveyed. With respect to import, the specific 'form' can become more and more inadequate to meaning-giving power such that it is shattered by *Gehalt*. The form is broken open to the power that endows it and its content with meaning. Yet this shattering, Tillich claims, itself is, paradoxically, a form, a kind of form-denying form. He thought that the artists of his time were attempting to express the paradox of form that shatters form, say, in Expressionist painting or some kinds of architecture and, paradigmatically, in Picasso's *Guernica*. The task of theology of culture, he says, 'is to trace this process in every sphere and creation of culture and to bring it to expression' (*OITC*, 26). The enterprise is distinctly theological, insofar as the standpoint of reflection is import rather than form; cultural sciences and the arts, conversely, adopt the standpoint of form. Thinking within this shattering of form by import is theology, properly conceived.

Theology of culture articulates the unity of domains of spirit in terms of the power of meaning that both conditions and shatters them. Here too it has a unique standpoint, but now in contrast to philosophy. In philosophical reflection, the unity of culture is found in the categories of thought and being. For the theologian, this unity is conceived with respect to import (*Gehalt*). More precisely, the theologian articulates the religious depth of culture, its import, expressed through cultural forms and the categories of thought and being. A theology of culture explores the shattering of cultural forms by the excess of import, insofar as this expresses the basic religious concern. Yet theological reflection is scientific; it is a form of knowledge, because religious import, the meaning-giving power, is the ground of the categories of thought and being and thus the unity of culture. Theology is an act of spirit, the mode of existing thought. These distinctions allow the theology of culture to clarify its standpoint, method and claim to truth. In terms of Tillich's later work, the power of being and the courage to be in spite of the threat of non-being are available in all domains of human spirit.

In the 1919 lecture Tillich designates as 'theonomy' the appearance of meaning-giving power, the import, through the shattering of forms of culture that discloses the depth of culture. All domains of spirit and forms of culture retain their characteristics and autonomy, they are not under the domination of a religious institution or other heteronomous authority, and yet they also can manifest the basic religious experience. What is more, he contends, 'the more form, the more autonomy; the more import, the more theonomy' (26). The modern

world, as Max Weber and Ernst Troeltsch had argued, is that social condition in which the social spheres function by their own logics, values
and norms free from religious domination. Granting autonomous social
domains, Tillich's point is that every domain can express the religious
import and in so doing can become theonomous, can manifest the depth
of meaning-giving power in culture.

FINITE MEDIATION AND CRITICISMS

Throughout the remainder of the 1919 lecture Tillich develops the
idea of theology of culture with respect to specific cultural analyses (art,
ethics, politics) even as he relates and distinguishes theology of culture (*Kulturtheologie*) and a theology of the church (*Kirchentheologie*).
Tillich addresses the question dear to current church theologians: 'What
is to become of specifically religious culture, of dogma, cultus, sanctification, community, church?' (*OITC*, 35). There are, he suggests, three
possible attitudes of church theologians towards culture, attitudes found
among contemporary thinkers too: opposition to culture in the name of
the church and the Kingdom of God; a return to supernatural revelation; the attempt to draw a distinction between the normative religious
principle and the actual religious culture, the church. The theologian of
culture is not bound by these options. Rather, such a theologian 'stands
freely within the living cultural movement, open not only to every
other form but also to every new spirit' (37). The church is a spiritual
community, as he calls it in the *Systematic Theology*, namely, a type
of the 'church within the church' (*ecclesiola in ecclesia*). The task of
the church is to gather and concentrate the religious elements of culture in order to make them the most powerful (*kraftvollsten*) cultural
factor.

Unlike church theologians, past and present, Tillich rightly sees
that the distinction between church and culture is a sign of brokenness,
even sin. What is sought is not to vitalize the church against culture, but,
rather, to enact theonomous culture in which the religious community
is one element. Further, the 'world' is not to be absorbed into the church,
as some think, nor is the theologian's job to 're-theologize' the world
and thereby deny autonomous cultural forms. The task is to show the
relation of autonomy and theonomy, and thereby not only to appreciate
the domain of worldly activity but also to grasp its depth and power
of meaning in the divine manifest in and through finite form. When
the 'secular' is open to its depth of meaning, it is secular, but it is also
theonomous.

Tillich was also at pains to distinguish theology, as a concrete nor-mative science of religion, from metaphysics and also supernatural ideas about revelation. Import, meaning-giving power, is not to be conceived as some being beyond the world, like a supernatural god, nor is it the totality of being, as in classical metaphysics. It is 'an actuality of mean-ing (*Sinnwirklichkeit*) and, indeed, the ultimate and deepest actuality of meaning that shakes everything and constructs everything anew' (25 (translation modified)). On this point, just like the question of the church, some current criticisms of theology of culture seem wide of the mark. Tillich, like many postmoderns, believed that classical ideas about 'being' and metaphysics are no longer tenable. Being is not to be conceived as analogous to 'substance' or 'thing-ness', and unaided human reason cannot grasp the structure and whole of reality. As he wrote, 'rational metaphysics attempts to abolish the theonomous inten-tion and to replace it with the autonomous one – an attempt that necessarily fails' (*SS*, 210). In contemporary terms, any closed system of thought, a complete rational metaphysics, fails, insofar as it disal-lows one to think within the appearance of 'otherness', the in-breaking of meaning-giving *Gehalt* of culture, under the power of that appear-ance. The point of disagreement, then, turns, much like the criticism of the church theologians, on how the appearance of 'otherness' is con-ceived and mediated. Tillich insists *finitum capax infiniti* even as import shatters cultural form. Thinkers who deny theonomous thinking, who question the 'depth' of culture, reject this claim, just like church theologians reject finite human culture as a domain of theonomous power.

However, matters are not quite so simple. Scholars discern shifts within Tillich's thought, even if they disagree about their number and the reasons for them.[15] The most obvious shift was due to his shock at the horrible crisis brought by Nazism, whose forces and ideas he opposed earlier than many theologians. After the Second World War, Tillich described the cultural situation as nothing less then a 'sacred void'. In an essay written in 1946 Tillich held that a 'present theology of culture is, above all, a theology of the end of culture, not in gen-eral terms but in a concrete analysis of the inner void of most of our cultural expressions' ('Religion and Secular Culture' in *ProtE*, 60). Ten years later, in a piece ultimately published in his 1959 book *Theology of Culture*, Tillich contends: 'Theology must use the immense and pro-found material of existential analysis in all cultural realms . . . But the-ology cannot use it by simply accepting it. Theology must confront it with the answer implied in the Christian message' (*TC*, 49). Theological analysis of culture no longer seems to be able to answer the religious question from within the *Gehalt* of culture.

The revision can helpfully be conceived in terms of how one understands the capacity of the finite to bear the infinite: the idea of mediation. Tillich's original 1919 account of theology of culture held that the realms of spirit can be transparent to their ground and power, their religious content, and in this respect answer the religious problem, that is, a quest for a yes to reality in the face of the threat of nothingness. Following the rise of Nazism and the Second World War, Tillich increasingly conceived the theological enterprise as the apologetic task of correlating the answer of the Christian message with questions of human existence. The answer cannot be derived from the question, he said. At best, the domains of human activity that usually conceal their meaning-giving power might become translucent to that import.

Given this shift, the analysis of domains of cultural activity cannot provide the necessary and sufficient normative answer to the quest for the power to be in the face of non-being. That is given only in the message of Jesus as the Christ as the power of New Being. The theological standpoint is conceived not in terms of a concrete normative science of religion, as it was in 1919. The theological standpoint is properly within what he calls the 'circle of faith', that is, the faith of the Christian church. Theology of culture seemingly isolates the human questions, as well as anticipations of the Christian answer, but it cannot validly grasp an answer from within culture. The appearance of the power of New Being in the Christ is not in terms of a shattering of cultural forms, an excess of meaning and power that fragments the limitations of form. '*It is the power of being conquering non-being*. It is eternity conquering temporality. It is grace conquering sin. It is ultimate reality conquering doubt . . . And out of this ground we can get the courage to affirm being, even in a state of doubt, even in anxiety and despair' ('Communicating the Christian Message: A Question to Christian Ministers and Teachers' in *TC*, 213). Tillich still seeks an answer to the religious problem. 'God' is not a being alongside other beings; the symbol 'God' points to the ground and power of being. Theonomy is the deepest truth of existence. Yet the force of the shift is that, in the face of evil and sin, the finite can indeed 'mediate' the infinite, but finitude itself, in its brokenness and doubt and anxiety, must be *conquered* by the power of new being.[16] Theology is decisively God-centred. What then of theology of culture and human spirit?

ETHICS AND ECSTATIC HUMANISM

In 1958 Tillich delivered a lecture, 'Humanität und Religion', on receiving the Hanse-Goethe Award for services to humanity. He wrote: 'Where reverence of God is purchased with the degradation of the human, there in truth is God's name disgraced' ('Humanität und Religion' in *GW* IX, 114). Tillich insisted, then, that regard for the dignity and worth of human beings, a human-centred perspective, cannot be opposed by a God-centred theological outlook. Further, throughout his theological career Tillich sought to engage the legacy of humanism. The encounter between early Christianity and the Greek and Roman world, he mused, did not create Hellenism so much as 'Christian humanism'. 'In Christian humanism the fate of Christianity and the fate of philosophy are bound together' ('Fate and Philosophy' in *ProtE*, 9). Yet Tillich also knew that various forms of humanism, especially since the Renaissance, believe in the self-sufficiency of human spirit. As he noted in the *Systematic Theology*, these kinds of humanism derive 'the Christian message from man's natural state'. But this means that 'everything was said by man, nothing to man'. In contrast, the theologian must insist on revelation that 'is "spoken" to man, not by man to himself' (*ST* I, 65). The shift we have discerned in Tillich's theology of culture is found in his engagement with humanism. He both continues to insist on the humanistic outlook, forcefully stated in the Hanse-Goethe lecture, while also denying a purely secular or naturalistic humanism. The possibility of this double stance is found in his idea of 'ecstatic humanism', an idea crucial to the future of theology of culture.

'Ecstatic humanism' means human existence grasped by a power beyond itself, a word spoken to it, which nevertheless does not violate the dignity and free self-determination of human beings in community with others. It is the event of theonomous human existence and is, furthermore, best defined in terms of love (*agape*). Theonomous existence is both the fulfilment of the moral aim, which Tillich defined as becoming a person in community with persons, and also the overcoming of human estrangement from our own most unconditioned depths, from the divine. *Agape*, he notes, 'points to the transcendent source of the content of the moral imperative' and thereby reunites human actual existence with its essential being (*MB*, 40). *Agape* shatters the forms of human love (*eros*, *philia*) as itself a form of love. This love draws within itself justice, the proper acknowledgement of the other as a person and also the power to act, human freedom. *Agape* is, thereby, an answer to graceless morality and also normless relativism. Insofar as theology of culture must examine the domains of human spirit, then, properly speaking, it must do so not just in terms of cultural forms or the theological circle defined by Christian faith, but also with respect to this human ecstatic possibility. Only in this way will the reality of religion as the import of culture not be purchased at the cost of human dignity. Stated otherwise, the religious question, the search for a yes to reality in the face of its negation, is answered in the domain of culture in terms of ecstatic humanism.

The idea of ecstatic humanism is important to make sense of Tillich's convictions, but also in order to address another criticism. Recall that Tillich believed theology of culture was the continuation of theological ethics. Yet as his thought developed the ethical force of theology of culture became eclipsed. The effect was to blunt the critical edge of reflection on culture in the face of those forces, including religious forces, which denigrate human and non-human life. We live in a time when, horrifically, human power endangers all forms of life on this planet and in which the return of virulent religious fundamentalism means the 'religious' and the 'demonic' too easily cohere one with the other. This age also demands a viable norm or standard by which to orient human power and to judge the moral acceptability of religious appeals and religious authorities. To be sure, Tillich decried forces of disintegration and destruction and was often much more aware of their reality than other theologians of his time. He was mindful that religion can become demonic. Nevertheless, the ethical intentionality of theology of culture must be reclaimed in light of world-wide endangerments to life and demonic impulses in every religion. Three options are then possible to develop a normative theological ethical stance on culture: (1) return to the 1919 formulation of theology of culture in an attempt to derive norms directly from domains of human spirit; (2) shift with Tillich to the norm and answer disclosed in the Christian message alone; or (3) extend the insight about ecstatic humanism as the 'aim', rather than ground or message, of thinking about culture and thereby formulate a norm for cultural and religious realities.

Theology of culture, I submit, is most readily and powerfully revised in and through a robust theological account of humanism which situates human worth, responsibility and dignity not against but within the wider realms of life on this planet. On this account, a theology of culture would not only reassert the ethical demand on all theological thinking, but would also widen the scope of reflection beyond culture and the church to the patterns and processes of life and the interactions among the world's religions. This new agenda, what we can call theological humanism, stands in alliance with the intention of Tillich's project. Its possibility is grasped in the realization that for our time the import, the meaning-giving power, of human aspiration, cultural forms and the wider reach of existence that is the true ethical aim and standard is best conceived as the integrity of life.[17]

THEOLOGICAL HUMANISM AND THE FUTURE FOR THEOLOGY OF CULTURE

Most of the critics of Tillich's theology of culture seem to deny what he judged one must affirm and formulate in the idea of theonomy. On this point, the spade is turned: either one believes that finite, fallible human and non-human realities can mediate unconditioned divine power and meaning while not themselves being the source and norm of that import, or one denies that conviction. This is a matter of fundamental theological orientation and religious sensibility, and, as noted, much contemporary theology denies this conviction and thereby risks a veiled supernaturalism or a linguistic idealism in which religious language is to suffice for the divine, or it becomes ardently secularist. However, any purchase of the divine at the cost of the dignity of finite life is a denigration of God even as the celebration of the secular at the cost of the transcendent ultimately demeans finite life. Granting this point of continuity with Tillich's stance on the capacity of the finite for the infinite, theology of culture must take a new direction from within itself.

That new direction is the enterprise of theological humanism focused on the integrity of life. The quest to overcome estrangement, the problem of religion, as Tillich called it, must be conceived in terms wider than human and cultural ones. What is sought is the power to respect and enhance the integrity – the right integration – of forms of life against forces that demean and destroy existing life. Yet the integrity of life as norm and aim is not a predicate of any one form of life or a condition that only some beings, human or non-human, can enjoy. It is also a concept for the import, the power and meaning, that respects and enhances finite life in its various realms. Because human and non-human life is now vulnerable to human power, what is needed is a humanistic outlook that places responsibility for the fate of life squarely on human beings and yet also transforms the aim of human life to a good that includes but exceeds the human kingdom, that is, the integrity of life. That outlook is captured in the idea of *theological* humanism, insofar as it can link theological reflection on cultural domains with the ethical aim of the integrity of life.

The argument works in the other direction as well. Our age is not only endangered by the rampant extension of human power, what can be called the over-humanization of the world. It is also threatened by the return of virulent religion in demonic form which threatens finite life with promises of supernatural rewards. Thus, not only is a theological transformation of humanism needed but also a *humanization* of religion and thus of theology. If theology of culture is to remain a normative science of religion, granting all the ambiguities in the conception of both science and religion, then it must articulate its proper norm. And for our age that norm can only be conceived as the integrity of life invigorating the humane transformation of the world's religions. From this perspective, the theologian not only analyses and decodes the power of the integrity of life within various cultural domains, but the theologian also works to articulate and transform religious existence within specific communities before that very same power and import. Thus, theological humanism, much more than the original conception of theology of culture, works at the interface of cultural forms and religious traditions as crucial forces that endanger life but also, surprisingly, mediate the power to respect and enhance the integrity of life. In this way, one extends the legacy of theology of culture in an age in which global realities pose grave and frightening dangers but also further the deepest longings of the human adventure. If theological thinking is to remain a search for truth and relevant to the world we now inhabit, it must continue in some form the brilliant, faithful and humane enterprise of Paul Tillich's theology of culture.

Notes

1   On this idea, see Schweiker (2005). On Tillich's connection to humanism, see Bulman (1981).
2   See *MB*.
3   See Palmer (1984).
4   *SS*, esp. Part 3, 137–216.
5   It should also be noted that Tillich dedicated his *System of the Sciences* to Troeltsch. For an exploration and extension of Tillich's thought, see Re Manning (2005).
6   See Gilkey (1984), Scharlemann (1984) and Tracy (1987).
7   For examples, see Schweiker (1998), Crockett (2001), Klemm and Klink (2003), Ihuoma (2004), Klemm (2004), Cobb (2005) and Re Manning (2005).
8   Hauerwas and Willimon (1989).
9   See Tanner (1997).

10 See Milbank, Pickstock and Ward (1999).
11 See M. C. Taylor (1987).
12 See Gustafson (1992) and Hopkins (2005).
13 For a detailed treatment of the triads that structure Tillich's thought (form-content-import; culture-religion-religiosity; autonomy-heteronomy-theonomy), see Haigis (1998).
14 The translation of *Gehalt* as 'substance', while found in earlier English renderings of his work, is misleading, insofar as Tillich never conceived of the divine or the power of being as 'thing-like', the impression given by the word 'substance'. Recent translations use the term 'import' and, additionally, I will also render *Gehalt* as 'meaning-giving power'.
15 On this, see Clayton (1980), Richard (1986), Scharlemann (1987), Palmer (1990) and Cobb (1995). Cobb provides a fine discussion.
16 See Gilkey (1990).
17 See Schweiker (1995).

Further reading

Adams, James Luther (1965). *Paul Tillich's Philosophy of Culture, Science, and Religion*. New York: Harper & Row.
Bulman, Raymond F. (1981). *A Blueprint for Humanity: Paul Tillich's Theology of Culture*. Lewisburg, Pa.: Bucknell University Press.
Clayton, John P. (1980). *The Concept of Correlation: Paul Tillich and the Possibility of a Mediating Theology*. Berlin: Walter de Gruyter.
Despland, M., J.-C. Petit and J. Richard eds. (1987). *Religion et Culture*. Quebec: Presses de l'Université Laval/Éditions du Cerf.
Haigis, Peter (1998). *Im Horizont der Zeit. Paul Tillich Project einer Theologie der Kultur*. Marburg: N. G. Elwert Verlag.
Ihuoma, Sylvester I. (2004). *Paul Tillich's Theology of Culture in Dialogue with African Theology: A Contextual Analysis*, Tillich-Studien vol. XI. Münster: LIT Verlag.
Klemm, David E. (2004). 'Introduction: Theology of Culture as Theological Humanism'. *Literature and Theology* 18:3, 239–50.
Klemm, David E. and William Schweiker (2008). *Religion and the Human Future: An Essay on Theological Humanism*. Oxford: Wiley-Blackwell.
Moxter, M. (2000). *Kultur als Lebenswelt. Studien zum Problem einer Kulturtheologie*. Tübingen: Mohr Siebeck.
Re Manning, Russell (2005). *Theology at the End of Culture: Paul Tillich's Theology of Culture and Art*. Leuven: Peeters.
Schweiker, William (2005). *Theological Ethics and Global Dynamics: In the Time of Many Worlds*. Oxford: Blackwell.

10 Tillich's theology of art

RUSSELL RE MANNING

INTRODUCTION

It is widely acknowledged that Paul Tillich's engagement with the arts was the most sustained of any theologian of his generation. Indeed, more than that of any other theologian of the twentieth century, it is Tillich's theological encounter with art that has been the most profound, creative and influential (albeit often indirectly). Moreover, Tillich's reflections on the relationship between theology and art were crucial, indeed in many ways formative, for his wider project of a theology of culture, itself fundamental to his reformulation of theology as correlative to the concerns of his contemporaries. From our perspective, it is perhaps all too easy to overlook the dramatic – and profoundly unsettling – transformations that took place in the artistic spheres in Tillich's lifetime. Among other factors, new movements (e.g. impressionism, expressionism and modernism), new media (e.g. photography and film) and new estimations of the role of the artist (e.g. art for art's sake, readymades and popular art) all led to a need for a new theological engagement, one deeply rooted in the Christian tradition, inspired by the German Idealist tradition of art theory, and immersed within the new art of the *avant garde*. It is to Tillich's great credit that he took up this challenge and it is his great achievement that he gave to theologians and religious people a means of engaging with the new artistic situation of the twentieth century. Drawing on theological, philosophical and cultural analyses, Tillich gave his contemporaries a language with which they could enter into a genuine dialogue with the arts, both in terms of theological interpretation of art and of theological development through art.

This chapter has four sections. In an opening section I will consider Tillich's formative place within the now widely established field of 'theology and the arts', emphasizing the extent to which Tillich can be considered the unacknowledged theoretician of the mainstream of this significant development in theological studies. Secondly, I will reconstruct Tillich's own writings on theology and art. As is well known, Tillich never developed a systematic account of the relations between theology and art; it was, however, a constant concern for him, and references as well as more sustained discussions can be found in every period of his writing. Tillich's earliest proposals for and exercises in a theology of culture, his work in systematic and doctrinal theology, his occasional lectures and addresses on art in the 1950s and 1960s, as well as his late engagements with non-Christian religions, all contain reflections upon the relation between theology and art, as well as Tillich's own theological analyses of specific works of art. In tracing Tillich's thought on the relations between theology and art, I will highlight his reliance upon an Idealist metaphysics of the identity of meaning and being, his analysis of the structural contents of culture as *Form*, *Inhalt* and *Gehalt*, and his essentially Platonic theory of participatory symbols. In the third section, I will consider some of the critiques of Tillich's writings on the relations between theology and art in response to the widespread consensus that while Tillich's writings have been justifiably influential and laudable in their insistence that theologians take seriously the requirement to engage meaningfully with art, Tillich's own engagements are profoundly problematic. Finally, this chapter will place Tillich in our own contemporary situation and consider the possibilities for a Tillichian engagement between theology and art in postmodernity. Drawing on Tillich's discernment of a 'metaphysical dizziness' and contemporary postmetaphysical (a/)theologians of culture, such as Mark C. Taylor, the chapter will conclude that in spite of the very real difficulties with Tillich's theological encounter with art it nonetheless remains rightly formative and a rich resource for the ongoing – and risky – venture of apologetic theology.

TILLICH AS THE UNACKNOWLEDGED
THEORETICIAN OF 'THEOLOGY AND THE ARTS'

While Tillich's methodological proposals for the nature of systematic theology, summarized for many in the 'question-and-answer dialectic' of the 'method of correlation', have on the whole met with a frosty reception among systematic theologians of the second half of the twentieth century, their impact can clearly be discerned in the growth of interdisciplinary approaches to theology, nowhere more so than in the rise of 'theology and the arts' as a recognized sub-discipline of academic theology. Theological reflection on art in general, on particular themes such as beauty or harmony, or on specific artists is, of course, as old as theology itself, and yet a remarkable shift in the contours of this engagement has occurred with the establishment of a designated area of study under the heading 'theology and the arts', now considered an indispensable component of most undergraduate courses in theology (alongside that other 'correlational' area of study, 'science and religion'). It is perhaps here, rather than in systematic theology *sensu stricto*, that the influence of Tillich's correlational methodology is most apparent in characterizing the theological task as one of engagement, rather than of commentary or critique. The theologian recognizes the arts as dialogue partners with whom to enter into an open-ended conversation. Thanks to Tillich, such an encounter is no longer restricted to certain predetermincd, theologically relevant themes or subject matters: art itself is the subject of theological interest, in all its disparate manifestations, from Botticelli to Warhol, from Dante to science fiction, from Shakespeare to *The Sopranos*.

A good example of Tillich's subterranean influence here is the now firmly established area of 'theology and film'. In their seminal edited volume, *Explorations in Theology and Film* (1997), Gaye W. Ortiz and Clive Marsh explicitly refer to Tillich's paradigms for relating theology and the arts.[1] They consider that Tillich's own approach is too restrictive for their new venture into the medium of film, and yet they and their fellow contributors clearly apply Tillich's methodology of correlation. Theirs is not a 'theology of film' in which they 'read' films through the lens of theology; particular films do not simply offer illustrations of pre-determined theological themes; nor is the range of films considered limited to those with obvious (or obviously implicit) religious subject matter. Like Tillich, the emergent discipline of 'theology and film' aims to engage theologically with film, that is to say, to correlate the forms of cultural productions that are always, inasmuch as they are creative human productions, substantially religious with the explicit religious substance, or *kerygma*, that is itself always expressed in cultural forms.

TILLICH'S THEOLOGY OF ART

Tillich's theological engagement with art must be located within the framework of his wider project of a theology of culture. This revolutionary undertaking, first explicitly proposed in his 1919 lecture 'On the Idea of a Theology of Culture', consists in nothing less than a call for a new type of theological thinking.[2] As revisionary (and equally as orthodox) as Karl Barth's contemporary 'theology of crisis', Tillich's programme for a theology of culture is an attempt to overcome the bankruptcy of pre-First World War Protestant theology. For Tillich, the war had exposed the catastrophic error of late nineteenth-century theology: religion had become separated from culture and had been reduced to a 'particular sphere' of concern. Ironically, the *Kulturprotestantismus* of the theological heirs to Schleiermacher had responded to the rejection of religion by its 'cultured despisers' not by reinvigorating the vital relation between theology and culture but by isolating religion, either as an area held apart (immune from cultural critique or engagement) or as simply an area within a particular cultural arena (and hence to be reduced to a detachable epiphenomenon of a more fundamental cultural movement). Accordingly, for Ritschl and Herrmann as much as for Troeltsch and von Harnack, the crucial reciprocal engagement between religion and culture had been lost, replaced by a theological positivism on the one hand and a scientific (historical) reductionism on the other. It was in this situation that Tillich declared that the 'intolerable gap' between religion and culture must be overcome and that the way to do so lay in the development of a theology of culture.[3]

'One moment of beauty': art and revelation

To the extent that Tillich's greatest legacy to subsequent theologians has been his encouragement to engage with twentieth-century art that does not address an explicitly religious subject matter (prompting them, for example, to take abstraction seriously), it is perhaps surprising that Tillich's own impetus to a recognition of the importance of art for his theological project came in his encounter with a piece of explicitly religious Renaissance art, namely the *Raczinski Tondo* or *Madonna with Singing Angels* (1477) by Sandro Botticelli. Tillich recalls that while on leave as an army chaplain in 1918, inspired by the cheap reproductions of old masters that he had used as comfort and escape in the trenches, he visited the Kaiser Friedrich Museum in Berlin and found himself transfixed by the beauty of the painting:

> Gazing up at it, I felt a state approaching ecstasy. In the beauty of the painting there was Beauty itself. It shone through the colors of the paint as the light of day shines through the stained-glass windows of a medieval church. As I stood there, bathed in the beauty its painter had envisioned so long ago, something of the divine source of all things came through to me. I turned away shaken. That moment has affected my whole life, given me the

keys for the interpretation of human existence, brought vital joy
and spiritual truth. I compare it with what is usually called
revelation in the language of religion.

(*OAA*, 235)

Tillich's admission that he found in this moment 'keys' for the interpretation of human existence and his awareness of a feeling of joy that
he can only compare to 'that which in religious language is normally
designated by the name revelation' are crucial for an understanding
of the role that art plays in his subsequent theology. For Tillich, art
'expresses meaning' and 'indicates what the character of a spiritual situation is' (*RS*, 85). In other words, art is the clearest indicator of the
self-interpretation of a particular situation; if culture as a whole is the
expression of the totality of humanity's creative self-interpretation, it is
in art that the character of this self-interpretative activity becomes most
clearly visible. Further, because human self-interpretation, for Tillich,
inevitably embodies a response to the existential predicament of finitude, art expresses the meaning of its particular culture or situation.
Never 'simply aesthetic' nor 'merely formal', art, in this interpretation, is indeed revelatory of its era, and as such revelatory of that which
enables existential meaningfulness to be grasped, that which Tillich will
later designate as 'ultimate concern'. Here the category of revelation is
already destabilized; no longer to be associated primarily with the dis-
crete ('concrete') contents of religious traditions, it is now principally
understood as a 'fundamental revelation' (*Grundoffenbarung*) that 'is
altogether indifferent with regard to its content. Man has no knowledge,
no content to show. The divine is the ground and the abyss of meaning,
the beginning and the end of every possible content . . . This is the hour
of [the] birth of religion in every man' (*GW* VII, 92). For Tillich, just
as all concrete religions are grounded in this immediate non-objective
and non-symbolic apprehension of the ground of meaning and being
('the Unconditional' or 'God'), so all art, inasmuch as it is genuine art,
expresses a particular moment of human self-interpretation because it
too is grounded in this 'gift' or 'breakthrough' of ultimacy and as such,
therefore, itself expresses something – formally and symbolically – of
that 'presence of God prior to any knowledge of God'.[4]

The engagement between theology and art, therefore, is correlational, but not in the simple sense of providing theological answers to
cultural questions, but in the more robust sense of the reciprocal relation of religious and cultural expressions of the fundamental revelation
of meaningfulness and ultimate concern. This Idealist metaphysics of

identity, essentially a Christian Platonic dialectic of participation, lies behind both Tillich's theology of art and his related theory of symbols.[5] Just as Tillich is able to liberate the category of the symbolic from mere signs towards an ecstatic participation, so art is no longer determined by representation or form but can once again become truly iconic.

The decisiveness of style

Tillich declares in his 1919 lecture 'On the Idea of a Theology of Culture' that any such project will have three tasks: firstly a 'general religious analysis of culture', secondly a 'religious typology and philosophy of cultural history', and finally a 'doctrine of the religious norms of culture'. As should be clear by now, this third stage will not consist in a heteronomous imposition of religious norms upon culture, but will rather be what Tillich calls the theonomous science (normative theology) of culture itself. As such the first two tasks are of crucial importance to his project – and indeed Tillich himself devotes considerable attention to the religio-cultural analysis of cultural productions, especially art. The first task of Tillich's theology of art – a 'religious analysis of art' – has characterized art as expressing meaning and hence as 'revelatory' (in Tillich's revised sense of the term). The second task corresponds to Tillich's identification of an interpretative principle according to which the 'religious history of art' can be undertaken, that is to say a hermeneutic mechanism by which Tillich is able to answer the question: what is it that makes art religious?

The short answer to this question is that art is religious on account of its 'style'. Referring to Tillich's distinction between *Form* (form), *Inhalt* (content) and *Gehalt* (depth, import or substance), Victor Nuovo summarizes:

> Not form, or better, not form by itself, rather through the mediation of form or of a formative or compositional technique, an unfathomable depth is disclosed that may be taken to be the source of religious insight and meaning. The principle of this disclosure is the style of an artwork. It is by virtue of its style, and not of its form or content, that an artwork is religious.[6]

For Tillich, artworks, as any cultural artefacts, are constituted by the three structural elements of *Form*, *Inhalt* and *Gehalt*, and it is the organization of these elements that he refers to as 'style'. As a particular expression of culture, a work of art has a certain shape or organization – it has *Form*. Tillich is clear that the *Form* of a work of art is both a reflection of the situation from which it is derived (different media and techniques of composition predominate at different times) and the result of the artist's free choice: an artwork's *Form* is nothing less than its aesthetic quality as an autonomous artistic creation. The *Inhalt* on the other hand is the 'content' or 'subject matter' of which a work of art is constituted; it designates the material substance out of which the artwork is crafted – both in the sense of the marble that makes up the sculpture and the subject (David or the Pietà) that is depicted. It is, as it were, the mute materiality of art and as such, though an essential ingredient of art, it is the least significant culturally or theologically of the constituent elements. By contrast, the third element, *Gehalt*, is clearly of most interest to Tillich. An artwork's *Gehalt* is its meaning or significance; it is that which the artwork expresses; it is its truth. In 1919 Tillich makes a clear identification of *Gehalt* and theonomy: 'the more *Form*, the more autonomy; the more *Gehalt*, the more theonomy' (*OITC*, 26). This is not to say, however, that an artwork is religious on the basis of its *Gehalt* alone – an artwork's *Gehalt* is its revelatory content. What makes it religious is the manner in which its *Gehalt* comes to expression in the artwork, the way it is 'enformed', that is to say, its style.

Two important, and not unexpected, conclusions result from this initial analysis of the constituent elements of art: artworks are religious on the basis of their style, not on the basis of their subject matter; and it is the element of *Gehalt* that predominates in the identification of an artwork's 'religious style', just as it is the element of *Form* that predominates in the identification of 'aesthetic' styles. The first conclusion clearly frees religious art from the constraints of a religious subject matter and enables the intuitive sense that, as Tillich famously puts it, 'it is not an exaggeration to ascribe more of the quality of sacredness to a still-life by Cézanne or a tree by van Gogh than to a picture of Jesus by Uhde' (*RS*, 88–9). Similarly, it is on this basis that Tillich is scathingly dismissive of 'religious kitsch', in which the religious *Inhalt* masks the absence of a religious style. A famous example of this (and of the difficulties of translating the German term *Kitsch*!) is Tillich's dismissal of Salvador Dalí's *The Sacrament of the Last Supper*, as reported (with some relish) by *Time* magazine in 1956:

Harvard Theologian Paul Tillich last week dealt a resounding uppercut to a piece of art that had invaded his preserve. Tillich's target: the new, vista-domed painting of The Last Supper by antenna-mustached Surrealist Salvador Dali. The big picture is now the public favorite at Washington's National Gallery of Art, where it has pushed Pierre Renoir's dear little Girl with a Watering Can into the mud as a runner-up. Declaiming before the Institute of Contemporary Arts, Dr. Tillich deplored Dali's work as a sample of the very worst in "what is called the religious revival of today." The depiction of Jesus did not fool Tillich: "A sentimental but very good athlete on an American baseball team . . . The technique is beautifying naturalism of the worst kind. I am horrified by it!" Theologian Tillich added it all up: "Simply junk!" In Spain, Artist Dali seethed under the misimpression that Tillich had said "drunk." Retorted he, with mustaches atremble: "I have been drinking mineral water exclusively for more than ten years!"[7]

The second conclusion has the important consequence that the styles employed by the theologian of art in his or her discernment of the religious character of artworks will not necessarily correspond to those used by art theorists or historians of art, whose judgement is made under the 'sovereignty of *Form*' (*GW* IX, 318). Of course, this is not to say that these categories may not coincide, and indeed the aesthetic classifications may well be of use to the theologian, but they should not be identified. Hence, the range of the 'expressionistic' religious style, for example, extends well beyond those works identified by the aesthetic style 'Expressionism'. Equally, this consideration should make it clear that, on Tillich's view, the religious character of an artwork is not necessarily a reflection of its aesthetic 'value'. However defined (in terms of 'beauty', its place within a tradition, its 'formal qualities', its emotional expressiveness etc.), aesthetic value must never be identified with the religious value of a work of art.

It is on the basis of his analysis of the constituent elements of art that Tillich proceeds to a typology of religious styles that is itself determined by the organization of these elements. Accordingly:

> three fundamental types of style are revealed: the *Form*-dominated style (impressionism-realism), the *Gehalt*-dominated style (romanticism-expressionism), the balanced style (idealism-classicism).
>
> (319)

Tillich's logic is correlational: 'pure *Form*' and 'pure *Gehalt*' are impossible, just as culture and religion stand in a necessarily reciprocal relation to each other. As a result, Tillich is adamant that the most religious style is that in which *Gehalt* predominates, but without wholly subverting *Form*. Tillich names this style 'expressionistic' and characterizes it by its dynamic predominance of *Gehalt* in the paradoxical shattering of *Form*. By contrast, for example, in the impressionistic style the artist is determined by 'a formal problem' such that she:

> sees all that is between heaven and earth; but not in its essence. It is present as a study of light, colour or movement, it is present as a piece of the surface of nature. What is shown is a new impression or momentary vision, interesting and striking, but fundamentally a landscape, in which the form is captured anew . . . The form is everything, the form, which is the high point of technique and rationality has become light and cold, despite all the surface fireworks of colour.

(*GW* II, 38–9)

It is on the basis of this initial classification of styles that Tillich goes on to develop his fragmentary and even idiosyncratic analysis of particular artworks, an analysis that is never intended to pass aesthetic judgement on the works but, in accordance with the third task of the theology of art (within theology of culture), to produce a 'concrete religious system-atization of art'. Tillich, accordingly, identifies individual artworks and movements as exemplars of the different styles, as shown here in tabu-lated form.

Type	Religious style	Aesthetic exemplars
Form-dominated, subjective	impressionism	Nineteenth-century Impressionism (Monet, Degas)
Form-dominated, objective	realism	Dutch and German late Gothic/early Renaissance Realism; nineteenth-century Naturalism
Balanced, subjective	idealism	Renaissance Humanism (Raphael, Rubens)
Balanced, objective	classicism	Classicism
Gehalt-dominated, subjective	romanticism	Nineteenth-century Romanticism; twentieth-century Expressionism
Gehalt-dominated, objective	expressionism	Twentieth-century Expressionism; twentieth-century Neo-Realism ('die neue Sachlichkeit')

It is here that Tillich is at his most intriguing (and frustrating) for those trained in both the autonomous discipline of art criticism and the heteronomous discipline of theological aesthetics: Tillich's interpreta-tions of particular artworks are hence often surprising and provocative, freed from (some may say ignorant of) the conventions of art theory and the orthodoxies of determinate theological traditions. Once, however, his classification is understood, his interpretations become more explicable, indeed even predictable. Take, for example, his contrasting interpretations of Cézanne and van Gogh, *Starry Night*:

> With Cézanne, landscape is all important; everything less than landscape – the still-lifes, for instance – become landscape in his work. There is no *nature morte* in Cézanne – although he calls almost half his pictures just that. On the other hand, his groups and portraits too become landscapes. His great self-portraits are views of "the fullness of being," not of a formed personality. And furthermore, the pictures are beautiful, and that is the main thing.
>
> (*MTD*, 107 [19 June 1936])

> Or, consider another artist, Van Gogh, and, for instance, his *Starry Night*. Here . . . we have the character of going below the surface. It is a description of the creative powers of nature. It goes into the depths of reality where the forms are dynamically created. He does not accept the surface alone. Therefore he goes into those depths in which the tension of the forces creates nature.
>
> (*OAA*, 95)

Expressionism: the style of *kairos*

As has already been adverted, Tillich's classification and the subsequent interpretations of artworks, artists and movements are not intended primarily as an exercise in cataloguing or assigning works to their appropriate religious style, rather his intention throughout is to articulate a normative theology of art in keeping with his energetic proclamation of the *kairos*. It is for this reason that Tillich's greatest attention is devoted to that art with the greatest revelatory power: the pair of *Gehalt*-dominated styles, romanticism and expressionism.

The religious style of expressionism consistently occupies the central place in Tillich's theology of art, from his earliest outline to his frequent subsequent reformulations. In his 1919 Berlin lecture, Tillich opens his cultural-theological analyses with a description of the expressionistic style, and in his 1922 piece, *Masse und Geist*, in which he considers the artistic depiction of crowds as indicative of the cultural estimation of the masses, he writes that in expressionism:

> the outer form of things is still dissolved, as it was in the case of Impressionism, but not, however, in order to reaffirm it, but in order to pass to the ground of all things, of the world. In this way a

new mysticism of the inner life of things is awakened and a new
style created. There are many Expressionist pictures of crowds in
which the landscape is no longer the significant feature. It has been
replaced by the spirit of the faces of the people – not in their
naturalistic appearance, but in their metaphysical significance.

(*GW* II, 29)

Thirty-two years later, in his article 'Theology and Architecture' he
makes it clear that 'all specifically religious art is expressionistic
throughout the history of mankind . . . expressing not just the subjectivity of the artist but the ground of being itself' (*OAA*, 190–1). In
the course of his writings Tillich identifies Grünewald, Dürer, Bosch,
Breughel, Goya and Michelangelo as expressionistic painters, but it is to
the artists of the early twentieth-century movement of German Expressionism that Tillich most frequently refers. Heckel, Nolde, Schmidt-
Rottluff, Munch and Marc are all cited as exemplars of the expressionistic style, and Tillich even admits that his definitions of the constituent
elements of art themselves 'bear the impress' of the movement, which
was, of course, contemporary with Tillich's own programmatic work in
the theology of culture. Indeed, his project can, with some justification,
be described itself as an expressionistic one: German Expressionism
is perhaps better thought of as wider than the artistic movements of
Der Blaue Reiter or *Die Brücke*, as a cultural *Zeitgeist* that informed
and characterized art, literature, architecture, philosophy, politics and,
of course, theology.[8] It is interesting that for all his obvious proclivity
for the works of the *Expressionismus*, in his most sustained cultural-
theological analysis in the 1926 book *The Religious Situation* Tillich
identified not Expressionism but its successor movement 'New Realism'
('die neue Sachlichkeit') as the clearest manifestation of the expressionistic style:

> The empirical reality of things is once again sought after. However,
> not for itself but as the expression of the objective *Gehalt* that is
> the inner power of things . . . Expressionism broke through the
> outer forms of things in order to express their *Gehalt*; the new
> Realism turns quite deliberately to the outer form in order to show
> the inner power of things in and through their outer form. In this
> way their works have a strange, often unsettling suspension
> between experience and transcendence . . . Ultimately, their
> success depends upon the extent to which they do not begrudge
> our situation and grasp the transcendent, not only in abstraction

and paradox but in the power of life and with creative
symbols.

(*MW/HW* IV, 194)

Finally, if there is any one particular artwork that Tillich identifies as
exemplary of the expressionistic religious style of art, it is Picasso's
Guernica. For Tillich, Picasso's protest against the bombing of the spiritual capital of the Basque country, first displayed in the 1937 Paris
Exposition in the Spanish pavilion, itself dwarfed by Albert Speer's mon-
umental *Deutsches Haus* alongside it, was quite simply 'the classical
work of the contemporaneous expressive style' (*OAA*, 136). *Guernica*
is 'the artistic expression of the human predicament in our period' that
'shows the human situation without any cover' (120; 95–6). Far from the
calming beauty of Botticelli's *Madonna*, Picasso paints 'this immense
horror – the pieces of reality, men and animals and unorganic pieces of
houses all together – in a way in which the "piece" character of our
reality is perhaps more horribly visible than in any other of the modern
pictures' (95).

New frontiers in Tillich's theology of art

Later in life, Tillich came to understand his emigration in 1933 as
'the conquest of theological provincialism', in which he recognized the
narrowness of having 'identified the history of theology in the last four
centuries with the history of German theology'.[9] However, it was perhaps in the cultural sphere that this provincialism was most keenly
felt; he famously confessed that he always felt Shakespeare sounded
better in German, and he clearly struggled to engage with the cultural
environment of post-Second World War America. Coupled with his dis-
location was Tillich's profound sense of disappointment in the failure
of his kairotic expectations: the promise of the Weimar Republic had
resulted in the demonic distortions of Nazism and the catastrophe of
a divided Europe. No longer inspired by the cultural prophets of the
kairos, Tillich struggled to embrace the theological significance of the
avant-garde artists of the mid-century (with their interests in formal-
ism, abstraction and popular culture). Never wholly negative, however,
Tillich turned instead to the apophaticism of the 'sacred void' of a culture of the 'death of God'. He concludes a 1965 address on 'Honesty and
Consecration in Art and Architecture' with the stark demand that:

> 'Sacred emptiness' should remain the predominant attitude for the
> next foreseeable time. One should express our experience which
> has been called the experience of 'the absent God.' This does not

mean a negation of God but it does mean: God who has withdrawn in order to show us that our religious forms in all dimensions were largely lacking both in honesty and consecration.

(*OAA*, 228)

In his numerous typological surveys of the 1950s and 1960s, most of which consist of short lectures, Tillich applies his analysis of the religious styles of art in a variety of different ways.[10] While these addresses invariably contain some startling observations on particular artworks and are consistent with Tillich's wider project of theology of culture, they lack the penetration and, dare I say, vision, of his earlier writings on art. One has the impression here that Tillich is struggling to express himself in this changed situation. His analysis was born out of his close engagement with the art and artists of German Expressionism, and its theonomous potency comes from Tillich's theological participation within the cultural life of the Weimar Republic; it seems stretched – even heteronomous – when taken out of context and reformulated (again and again) for an American audience. John Dillenberger reports that while Tillich knew Willem de Kooning and praised 'the fullness of reality without a concrete subject matter' of Jackson Pollock's *Number 1, 1948*, 'he makes no reference that I know of to Mark Rothko or Barnett Newman, though Hannah Tillich informed me that he was fascinated by Rothko's paintings' (*OAA*, xx). This is disappointing, not simply because of Tillich's failure to engage with his situation, but also because this is a style of art crying out for precisely the kind of theological engagement that Tillich could, but does not, provide!

CRITICAL ISSUES IN THE RECEPTION OF TILLICH'S THEOLOGY OF ART

Theological seeing

Even his most sympathetic commentators are led to conclude, in John Dillenberg's words, that:

Tillich made the visual vital for many of us (theologians) precisely because of his dazzling theological interpretations. But therein was also the major problem, for a theological interpretation that is grounded in theological seeing without faithfulness to the artworks themselves is unconvincing to critics and art historians.[11]

That Tillich's theological vision of art may be unconvincing to the methodologically secular approach of art history and criticism is, on its own, not particularly damaging to the strength of Tillich's proposals.

To a certain extent such a divergence of views is to be expected and, moreover, is precisely illustrative of the need for a theological engagement with art. Surely, we cannot be satisfied with a purely autonomous account of the nature and history of art; indeed the failure of much twentieth-century aesthetics lies in its tendency to reduce the meaning of art to its formal components alone. That Tillich could be better informed about some of the artworks he discusses is beyond dispute, and it is clear that he simply did not understand some of the most exciting developments in mid-century art. However, at their best – and his discussion of Picasso's *Guernica* is a case in point – Tillich's theological engagements with specific artworks, artists or movements are profoundly illuminating.

A more problematic acknowledgement, however, is that Tillich identifies two spheres of value in his analysis of art: religious and aesthetic.[12] Of course, the danger here is that Tillich might be seen to be re-inscribing the kind of separation between religion and culture that his project of a theology of culture intends to overcome, and that the 'religiosity' of an artwork can be said to reside in a specific and separable element – its religious style. Far from a genuine correlational engagement between theology and art, then, Tillich seems to present us with the religious interpretation of artworks alongside an aesthetic interpretation, such that in spite of his own very genuine attempts to engage correlationally with art, in the end he cannot avoid imposing a heteronomous set of theological convictions upon the works under consideration. The crux of this critique, however, lies not so much in Tillich's theological engagements with art, as in his risky project of theological engagement *per se*. The unstable dialectic of theonomy – the dynamic interaction between the theological and the cultural – all too easily slips into a destructive and competitive estrangement. Hence the importance to Tillich's theology of art of the *kairos*: without it, all theological engagement with art can only be fragmentary and ambiguous, and the vital element of normative theonomous religious style is fractured into two – heteronomous religious style and autonomous aesthetic style.

Tillich's limited horizons

Like his former student and friend Theodor W. Adorno, Tillich shared 'the unique blend of mandarin tastes and Marxist social critique' that characterized the Frankfurt School's vehement rejection of mass culture in favour of the disruptive *avant garde*.[13] While we may concur with Tillich's dismissal of 'beautifying sentimentalism' (in particular religious kitsch), it is perhaps unfortunate that Tillich effectively restricts his theological engagement with art to the established classics of European high culture and those developments in early twentieth-century art 'that are the most alienating . . . and incomprehensible . . . to even moderately literate people' (*OAA*, 132).[14] It is not enough to note with Jane Dillenberger that Tillich's knowledge of art was largely restricted to the museum collections he knew well; we must, rather, acknowledge with Kelton Cobb that Tillich's failure to engage with popular culture is not simply a political contradiction, but also a theological limitation:

> much can be learned about the total situation of a culture's deeper allegiances from an examination of its magazines, television viewing habits, popular novels, fashions, lawncare, broadcast news media, car industry, billboard hits, cinema, favorite leisure destinations, and state-of-the-art technologies.[15]

That Tillich did not rise to this challenge is undeniable; that his theology of art is incapable of such an expansion is far less clear.[16] At the same time, however, it is important to note that Tillich's understanding of culture is not necessarily as elitist as Cobb's analysis indicates and may provide for a critical alternative to the predominantly anthropological models of culture that have dominated 'cultural studies' since Clifford Geertz's semiotic definition of culture.[17] As is widely acknowledged, the risk of such an approach is of an undifferentiating relativism, able to include popular culture but unable to pass judgement upon it. More work needs to be done here, but perhaps Tillich's alternative model of culture as the participatory 'totality of man's creative self-interpretation in a special period' may be a fruitful corrective to the relativistic tendencies of contemporary cultural analysis without resorting to a mandarin elitism.

Religious art is expressionistic

A common critique is that Tillich's theology of art is over-determined by his appreciation of the particular aesthetic movement of German Expressionism. Here, rather than a theological imposition upon the autonomy of art, Tillich is accused of falling into the liberal trap of accommodation: if religious art is expressionistic, then it is Expressionism that becomes the arbiter of the religious value of art, not theology. Tillich frequently refers to the importance of German Expressionism for the development of his theology of art (and culture more generally) and even confesses that certain of his key terms (in particular the notion of

Durchbruch or 'breakthrough') are derived from his experience of this artistic movement. Tillich interprets *Expressionismus* as the conscious attempt to break through the superficialities of the technical bourgeois European culture to express its ecstatic, chaotic and vibrant depths. It is this violent, disruptive protest characteristic of German Expressionism that Tillich baptizes as the religious 'expressionistic' style of art.

Two important consequences follow: Tillich was unable to articulate the positive religious value in other aesthetic styles (in spite of his own admission of the revelatory significance of Botticelli's *Madonna*). Hence 'expressive' elements of other styles, such as Byzantine art, are misinterpreted and entire artistic movements (not just sentimental kitsch) are dismissed as lacking in any genuine religious expression; for example, Tillich claims that 'the Renaissance, in its religious pictures, has ceased to be religious in any Christian sense' (*OAA*, 106).[18] We might well agree with Tillich's characterization of Renaissance religious art as 'Christian humanism', but is not such a celebration of the created autonomy equally as religious as Picasso's depiction of the '"piece" character of reality' (95)? More importantly, perhaps, Tillich's privileging of German Expressionism and its disruptive character makes it extremely difficult for him to affirm the positive value of traditional Christian iconography, or indeed the possibility of a renewal of distinctively Christian symbols in contemporary art.[19] Again, Tillich correctly discerns that the religious value of an artwork cannot lie in its subject matter alone and finds a means of articulating this through Expressionism's distaste for representation. However, perhaps the iconoclasm of the Expressionistic rejection of objective symbolism is more powerful than Tillich reckoned, such that no traditional symbols – even the self-transcending symbols of Christianity – can survive such a purging.

The key here might lie in Tillich's mistaken (and indeed superficially self-serving) interpretation of Expressionism as an implicitly Christian movement. As Michael Palmer contends, Tillich's understanding of Expressionism is simplistic and inadequate to the subjectivist, even Nietzschean, character of the artworks themselves:

> Where there is destruction of natural form . . . this was done not to reveal the dimension of depth but to *prevent any interpretation other than that intended by the artist*. Thus, when Kandinsky speaks of the spiritual in art, he is not, as Tillich might suppose, speaking of a specific religious concern but of a desire to connect the visual material in art to the inner life of the artist.[20]

The point here is not so much that Tillich's interpretation does not coincide with that of the artists, it is rather that the artworks themselves simply cannot support the theological weight that Tillich gives to them. Tillich's error here is profound: rather than discerning the future of religious art in the expressionistic style, he has been taken in by Expressionism as the Trojan Horse of a secular and nihilistic aesthetic alternative to religion. Tillich is justified in his later equivocation: expressionism cannot reinvigorate traditional Christian symbols. The best he can hope for is a '"waiting" for the return of the hidden God who has withdrawn and for whom we must wait again' (*OAA*, 228).

Romanticism, idealism and the re-enchantment of art

The reason that Tillich's theology of art may be said to fail to be true to the artworks themselves, to the full range of cultural productions, and to the requirements of a specifically Christian art with particular identifiable symbols and representations, beyond the fundamental revelation of the ground of meaning and being in a culture's ultimate concern, might lie deeper than his misunderstanding of the religious value of German Expressionism in his acceptance of a fundamentally Romantic conception of art. As Nietzsche, in his perceptive diagnosis of Romantic idealism put it, 'Art raises its head where religions decline.'[21] The idea that art will replace religion as the site of enchantment is a commonplace of Romantic theories of art and is nicely illustrated in the paintings of Caspar David Friedrich, in which the sublime landscapes all but overwhelm the mute remnants of religious symbolism.[22]

Tillich was influenced by this tradition through his theological affinity to Schleiermacher and his philosophical dependence on Schelling, as well as by his contemporaries Eckart von Sydow, Georg Simmel and Wilhelm Worringer, and embraced this Romantic-Idealist conception of art as the pinnacle of human expression and the experience of enchantment. Not any art, however: only that art in which the original *Kunstwollen* or 'artistic volition' is allowed free rein through the abstraction away from naturalistic forms to 'transcend nature by denying space in representation'.[23] As Morgan notes, through the example of Franz Marc's 'struggle for the Absolute', this Romantic-Idealist desire to see through the outer forms of nature to 'see things "as they really are," shorn of the categories of human knowledge' leads not to the pure abstraction of geometric forms and colours (such as might be associated with Kandinsky and the later Abstract Expressionism) but to the expression of the inner vitality of nature.[24] Beyond both naturalistic mimesis and wholly non-representational abstraction, Marc's expressionism is the desire to 'seek beneath the veil of appearances the hidden things in nature' in a new breakthrough of the abstract *Kunstwollen* in artists who 'depend *no longer on the image of nature*, but *destroy* it, in order to show the powerful laws which reign behind beautiful appearances'.[25] Two further passages from Marc's writings from 1912 to 1913 confirm this Romantic-Idealist (indeed Platonist) faith in the enchantment of art:

> What we understand by 'abstract' art . . . It is the attempt {and yearning to see and depict the world no longer with the human eye but} to bring the world itself to speaking . . . Art is, will be, metaphysical; it can be today for the first time. Art will free itself from human purposes and human will. We no longer paint the forest or the horse as they please us or appear to us, but as they really *are*, as the forest or horse feels itself, its {abstract} absolute essence lives behind the phenomenon, which we only see.[26]

> The yearning for immutable being, for liberation from the sensory deceptions of our ephemeral life is the fundamental disposition of all art. Its great aim is to dissolve the entire system of our incomplete sensations, to manifest an unearthly being that lives behind everything, to break the mirror of life [in order] that we gaze into being.[27]

It is clear that Tillich shares in this high Romantic estimation of art; what is less certain is the extent to which this view is compatible with a Christian theology of art or whether it leads to an alternative aesthetic transcendence in which the re-enchantment of art coincides with the eclipse of religion. As Morgan concludes, 'by violently perforating the outer shell of phenomena, abstract painting promised to unveil the abso-lute . . . Gripped by the need to glimpse what was invisible, to embrace what was transcendent, the artist–shaman cast a spell that bewitched whosoever shared his urgency.'[28] Perhaps Tillich was one of those who fell under such a spell.

TOWARDS A POSTMODERN TILLICHIAN THEOLOGY OF ART

In conclusion, I want to suggest with Wessel Stoker that in spite of its difficulties, Tillich's theology of art does indeed have a future and that this lies in a critical encounter with contemporary postmodern

radical theologies, such as that of Mark C. Taylor.[29] Like Tillich's theology of culture, Taylor's project of a/theology is an attempt to think
'about religion' and 'after God'; to articulate the displaced presence of
the religious other within and through culture.[30] Through his critical
reception of postmodern philosophy, Taylor provides the possibilities
for a contemporary Tillichian theology of art. Tillich's 'sacred void' can
thus serve as the 'dis-figuring' of the unconditioned – not of the experience or knowledge of the absence of God, but of the absence of the
experience and knowledge of God that is the characteristic of all true
Christian philosophical mysticism and that Tillich himself refers to as
the *Grundoffenbarung*.[31] Similar to Marc's understanding of vision as a
Weltdurchschauung or 'looking-through-the-world', such a theological
seeing of art transcends the mystical enchantment of the aesthetic in its
endless deferral and refusal to settle for what Tillich called the 'whole
cemetery of dead categories' that are the legacy of the nineteenth century (*OAA*, 182).

Tillich consistently closed his late surveys of the relations between
art and religion with the pressing question of the future of religious art.
While he remained committed to the priority of the expressive style, he
nonetheless realized that the future of religious art lay elsewhere. When
he admonished his audience at the end of his last ever lecture in the
theology of art, 'Religious Dimensions of Contemporary Art' (1965), not
to look 'back to the wonderful fixed world of the years before 1900 in
which everything felt familiar', he perhaps included himself and his own
Romantic-Idealist embrace of the Expressionistic *avant garde*. Instead
he points forward to a situation of 'nonart', theology 'without God',
psychology without soul, philosophy without *philia* and music without
the muses:

> And this certainly is a situation which makes us dizzy: A kind of
> metaphysical dizziness grasps us. Yet we must encounter it.
>
> (182)

Notes

1   Ortiz (1997).
2   *OITC*.
3   For a fuller discussion of the theological and philosophical roots of Tillich's
    project of a theology of culture, see Re Manning (2005).
4   Schüßler (1987), 161.
5   See Kegley (1960) and Dixon, Jr (1963).
6   Nuovo (1987), 394.

7   *Time*, 19 November 1956. For an interesting consideration of Tillich's 'mis-interpretation' of the painting, see Novak (2007).

8   See Peter Steinacker (1989) for a defence of the claim that 'inhaltlich stimmt Tillich mit dem expressionistischen Verständnis der Geschichte und Kultur überein' ('in terms of content, Tillich belongs in the Expressionistic inter-pretation of history and culture').

9   Rex Crawford (1953), 139.

10 Scharlemann identifies four different typologies, with three, four, five and six types respectively. All are, however, fundamentally consistent with the basic typology outlined above. See Scharlemann (1985), 173.

11 Dillenberger (1987), 221. This criticism is also echoed in Begbie (1987), 103f., Nuovo (1987), 400–2 and Baumgarten (1994), 214. See also Henel (1981), 59.

12 Nuovo (1987), 398.

13 Cobb (1995), 72–3.

14 Ibid., 73. All of which make his failure to engage with mid-century develop-ments even more frustrating.

15 Ibid., 78. For Dillenberger's comment, see *OAA*, xxiii.

16 Cobb (2005).

17 Geertz (1973).

18 Thomas Matthews remarks that 'styles which "disrupt the naturally given appearance of things" cannot be grouped together and interpreted as expres-sionist, for within different styles the so-called "distortions" have widely different meanings. The elongated figures and exaggerated curves of Art Nouveau, for example, do not betray a concern for the ground of being itself but rather a concern for a never-never land of sensual fantasy. Moreover, even when we are sure that the artist is profoundly interested in the religious, as in Byzantine art (to use Tillich's example), the so-called "distortions" are often conventional rather than expressionist in intention. Thus the awk-ward poses, the angular patterning of lights and shadows, the irrational per-spective – Byzantine traits which might be mistaken for expressionistic – these are characteristics of a thousand-year tradition of learning to draw from copying manuscripts instead of from copying live models.' Matthews (1967), 17.

19 See, for example, *OAA*, 98–9.

20 Palmer (1990), 23.

21 Nietzsche (1984), 105.

22 For example, *Monk by the Sea* (1819).

23 Morgan (1996), 324.

24 Ibid., 326f., 352 citing Marc (1978), 112.

25 Marc (1978), 102, 108 in Morgan (1996), 327, 329.

26 Marc (1978), 112 (brackets enclose original text which Marc crossed out; emphasis in original) in Morgan (1996), 327.

27 Marc (1978), 169 in Morgan (1996), 332.

28 Morgan (1996), 341.

29 Stoker (2006).

30 M. C. Taylor (1987) and (1992).

31 M. C. Taylor (1992). The contrast between experiential and ecstatic mysti-cism is drawn from Turner (1995).

Further reading

Adams, James Luther (1965). *Paul Tillich's Philosophy of Culture, Science, and Religion*. New York: Harper & Row.

Baumgarten, Barbara Dee (1994). *Visual Art as Theology*. New York: Peter Lang.

Dillenberger, John (1987). *A Theology of Artistic Sensibilities: The Visual Arts and the Church*. London: SCM.

Palmer, Michael (1984). *Paul Tillich's Philosophy of Art*. Berlin/New York: Walter de Gruyter.

Re Manning, Russell (2005). *Theology at the End of Culture: Paul Tillich's Theology of Culture and Art*. Leuven: Peeters.

Thiessen, Gesa (1993). 'Religious Art is Expressionistic. A Critical Appreciation of Paul Tillich's Theology of Art'. *Irish Theological Quarterly* 59:4, 301–11.

11 Tillich's philosophy
CHRISTIAN DANZ

In his autobiographical sketch, *On the Boundary*, Paul Tillich offers a striking account of his passionate interest in philosophy, which began in his final years at school and which would last throughout his life. This interest is shown not only in his numerous writings up to and including his main systematic work, the three-volume *Systematic Theology*, but also in his prolific academic teaching. As a young *Privatdozent*, Tillich lectured on the religious content of Western philosophy at the University of Berlin; in 1929 he was appointed the successor to Max Scheler at the University of Frankfurt am Main and held a chair in philosophy and sociology; and in 1940 he accepted a chair in philosophical theology in New York, which he held until his retirement in 1955. Tillich's theology is permeated by philosophical reflection that should never be reduced simply to philosophy of religion. Tillich not only accurately describes his own relationship to philosophy using the metaphor of a border, but also defines his philosophical thought with this same metaphor.

Broadly speaking, there are three phases in Tillich's philosophical thinking. Firstly, there is his enthusiastic reception of the speculative idealism of Fichte and Schelling. This phase began in his student days and continued up to the First World War. The second phase, which began shortly before the end of the war, is characterized by a reshaping of the speculative philosophy of his pre-1914 theology and philosophy in terms of a new theory of meaning. The decisive characteristic of this phase can be seen in Tillich's employment of the concept of meaning as the basic category for the concept of religion. The third and last phase of his philosophical thinking is characterized by a concern with ontological questions. This third phase extends back as far as the late 1920s and reaches its culmination in the *Systematic Theology*. These three phases of Tillich's philosophical thinking are nevertheless characterized by a high degree of continuity, and the theory of meaning that is central to his earlier thinking never fully recedes.[1]

This chapter will set out the philosophical bases for these three phases of Tillich's own philosophy, showing both how Tillich forms his philosophy in dialogue with contemporary trends in philosophy and how he develops his own distinctive perspective. After situating Tillich's philosophical foundations in the revival of Idealism of the early years of the twentieth century, this chapter will consider in more detail Tillich's assimilation of these Idealist assumptions with a neo-Kantian theory of meaning. It is the development of this Idealist/neo-Kantian framework that is Tillich's most significant philosophical achievement and that forms the basis for his subsequent – and better-known – turn to ontology. Indeed, it is only on the grounds of this crucial second phase of Tillich's philosophical development that his later contributions to philosophical theology can be fully understood. Accordingly, before turning to his third phase, this chapter will explore Tillich's application of his Idealist/neo-Kantian theory of meaning to three crucial areas: the philosophy of religion, the philosophy of culture and epistemology.

TILLICH'S FIRST PHASE: THE RENAISSANCE OF IDEALISM AND THE CRISIS OF HISTORICISM

Fritz Medicus (1876–1956), the *Privatdozent* in philosophy at Halle during Tillich's student years, had an important influence on the shape of Tillich's understanding of philosophy.[2] Medicus, whose philosophical roots were in south-west German neo-Kantianism, was a forerunner of the early twentieth-century renewal of interest in Fichte.[3] At Halle, Tillich began an intensive study of Fichte's philosophy; he gave a seminar paper on the theme of 'Fichte's Philosophy of Religion in its Relation to John's Gospel' ('Fichtes Religionsphilosophie in ihrem Verhältnis zum Johannesevangelium'); engaged in prolonged debates with his friend Friedrich Büchsel; and defended his Breslau thesis on 'Freedom as a Philosophical Principle in Fichte' ('Die Freiheit als philosophisches Prinzip bei Fichte') (*ENGW* IX, 4–19; *ENGW* VI, 14–27, 62–74; *ENGW* X, 55–62).[4]

Tillich's understanding of philosophy took shape as part of the early twentieth-century renaissance of Idealism, the context of which is the 'Crisis of Historicism' (Ernst Troeltsch): in order to check the consequences of historicism, various different authors from diverse philosophical movements turned to Idealism. Tillich's most significant contribution to this Idealism-renaissance, following his interest in Fichte, is his work on Schelling (*CHR; MGC*; 'Gott und das Absolute bei Schelling' in *ENGW* X, 9–54). In his 1910 draft of 'God and the Absolute in Schelling', Tillich makes his turn to Idealism quite explicit:

> In order to explain the world, the philosopher must raise God above the absolute. In order to explain the world, the theologian must make the absolute on the basis of the Godhead. It is clear that this problem is at the same time the most concentrated expression of the problem of theology and philosophy or, in other words, the problem of the "absoluteness of Christianity".
>
> (*ENGW* X, 11)[5]

Tillich joins Troeltsch and Schelling in understanding history as the process of the self-inclusion (*Selbsterfassung*) of spirit in its inner structure. However, against Troeltsch (but following Schelling) Tillich understood history not as an externally unfolding process but rather as a history of self-consciousness, in which self-consciousness grasps itself in its inner historicity. For Tillich, the end point of history lies in the self-awareness of spirit in its relation to itself. According to Tillich, this takes place in Christianity, or, more precisely, the revelation of God in Christ marks the decisive stage on spirit's way to its self-transparency, in which it becomes evident to itself in its historicity and as knowledge about history.

Tillich construes the concept of God as the ground of self-relatedness such that an inner antinomy is assimilated into the identity of self-relatedness:

> Only when God can really be distinguished as positing and posited can aseity become actual and living and God become spirit and personality. But this is only possible when the distinction itself is posited by God, when nature in God is his will. The process of self-positing is living when it enters into contradiction. The divine self cannot posit itself in a living way unless it opposes itself, and it cannot attain perfect freedom unless it posits itself in a living way, and it cannot be a spiritual personality unless it attains perfect freedom.
>
> (*CHR*, 56)

The concrete, posited as non-derived by God, is at once both the necessary and contradictory representation of God's self-relatedness. The concrete is in unity with God when it is assimilated into the identity of His self-relatedness. The concept of history results from the irrational opposition of the individual against the essence, and the reaction of the essence against the opposition of the individual (56). This history is a history of self-consciousness, in which consciousness grasps itself in its own inner reflexivity and historicity. The internal structuring of history in mythology and revelation is interpreted by Tillich, again following Schelling, as a growth in reflection in self-relatedness. Whereas mythological consciousness has not become transparent to itself in the historicity of its self-relatedness proper to itself, in revelation self-consciousness grasps itself in the inner reflexivity of its self-relatedness (139f.). Revelation was understood by Tillich as the event in which a concrete particular brings to expression that reflexivity constitutive of spirit in its relation to itself. In this way, and from as early as 1910, Tillich regards religion not as a function of culture but as the site where self-relatedness becomes evident to itself in its historicity (122f.).

In his philosophical dissertation Tillich assimilates Schelling's late religio-historical philosophy of history, in which Schelling justifies the absoluteness of Christianity in an historico-philosophical manner. The conceptual medium for this is Tillich's Schelling-inspired identity philosophy of spirit ['identitätstheoretische Geistphilosophie']. Tillich's first independent draft of a philosophy of history, his programmatic 1911 Kassel theses 'Christian Certainty and the Historical Jesus' ('Die christliche Gewißheit und der historische Jesus') draws upon this construal of history (*ENGW* VI, 31–50).[6] The basic principle of this philosophy of history is a concept of truth, according to which the concrete determinations of self-relatedness are the means of representing the identity of self-relatedness (41).[7] The concretely real posited by spirit is true when it is assimilated into the synthesis of self-relatedness and thereby becomes the means for representing self-relatedness. The resulting philosophy of history claims to go beyond both rationalism and historicism: while rationalist philosophy of history orients itself to the universality of self-relatedness and excludes the concreteness of truth, a historicist philosophy of history rejects the 'universal in the historical in favour of the universal validity of each individual' (42). By contrast, Tillich's philosophy of history links both aspects in the concept of the simultaneously necessary and contradictory concreteness of historical truth (42). The certainty of spirit lies exclusively in the becoming-evident of self-relatedness in its inner historicity. For Tillich, this finds expression in Christology, which he understands as expressing the event of the comprehension of self-relatedness in its contradictory relation to itself.

This philosophy of history, as it was elaborated under the clear influence of Fichte and Schelling, was further developed in his 1912 dissertation, 'Mysticism and Self-Consciousness in Schelling's Philosophical

Development', as well as in his 'Systematische Theologie' of 1913 (*GW* I, 278–434). Both texts aim to provide an historico-philosophical justification of the absoluteness of contemporary Christian certainty, and both texts understand history as a process of the self-awareness of self-relatedness in its inner reflexivity and historicity.[8]

TILLICH'S SECOND PHASE: TOWARDS AN IDEALIST/NEO-KANTIAN THEORY OF MEANING

Tillich's historico-philosophical foundation of theology and philosophy of religion underwent a transformation during the course of the First World War. This transformation – which is documented in his correspondence with his friend Emanuel Hirsch between November 1917 and July 1918 – was induced by two things: Hirsch's criticism of his construal of the concept of God and Tillich's own appropriation of discussions in contemporary neo-Kantianism and phenomenology ('Emanuel Hirsch, Die große religionsphilosophische Debatte' in *ENGW* VI, 95–136).[9]

Tillich wrote to Hirsch in December 1917 to say that he had begun 'to fill great gaps' in his thought, insofar as he had 'energetically made an assault on modern philosophy . . . The questions we spoke about have given my "System of the Sciences" a decisive start; now I am already so far along that the literature has become clear to me, the direction is more or less plain and the central problem is intelligible' (98ff.). The authors whom Tillich names in this letter – Edmund Husserl, Heinrich Rickert, Hermann Lotze, Christoph von Sigwart, Wilhelm Windelband, Emil Lask, Eduard von Hartmann, Hans Lipps, Hermann Ebbinghaus – represent the main contributors to the contemporary debates about theories of meaning.[10]

In the same letter to Hirsch, Tillich informed his friend of a revision in the foundation of his theology and philosophy of religion. Tillich explained not only the 'central problem' of his most recent thinking, which consisted in knowing how 'certainty can be united with theoretical doubt to constitute the essence of faith', but he also explicitly subjected his earlier conception to criticism, which had aimed at an 'intellectual overcoming' of doubt 'through the "scientific concept of God"' (99). The changes in Tillich's conception of system receive their most striking expression in his redefinition of spirit following Hirsch's criticism of his previous version of the concept of God. Tillich assimilated Hirsch's construal of the concept of God through a double-experience, by grasping it as a polarity of the life of spirit itself (105ff., 117, 119). The concept of God was not to be identified with the becoming-evident-to-itself of spirit, but rather the life of spirit was itself already characterized

through the double-consciousness of infinity and of value. In this way
Tillich tried to assimilate Hirsch's 'becoming aware of the "other," the
"stranger" as the Divine' into spirit itself (106). 'God as stranger is nothing other than the expression of the original paradox of the existence
of spirit' (122). Tillich included this revised version of spirit as an inner
polarity of consciousness of infinity and value in his concept of meaning:
'spiritual life is life in meaning or incessant creative meaningfulness'
(125).

In this way, the concept of meaning became the explanatory framework within which the concept of religion was construed. By 'religion'
Tillich now understood not a function of spirit, but rather reflexivity working through cultural forms. The religious act is the becoming-
evident-to-itself of self-consciousness in its historicity. However, Tillich
no longer understands truth as determined by its content as a contradiction against which essence prevails, as in the theses of 1911, but
rather the concretely real represents the simultaneously contradictory
and appropriate form of the representation of the self-relatedness of
spirit. Insofar as consciousness becomes transparent to itself in religion
in the inner reflexivity and antinomy of its self-relatedness, it understands its determinations of content as historically changeable forms
of expression of the dimension of indetermination, which is the self-
understanding of spirit. Tillich's concept of God therefore contains the
form of expression of spirit which has become transparent to itself in the
inner reflexivity of its self-relatedness and historical determinateness.
In his post-1918 theology Tillich thus connects philosophy of history
with the concept of God and relocates the former into the religious act
itself.

Thus, Tillich was able not only to define the relationship between
religion and culture more exactly than was possible in the pre-1914
writings, but in addition he made the concept of spirit, understood in
terms of meaning, the basis of his philosophy of religion and culture, as
well as his epistemology.[11]

Philosophy of religion

Following his indications of a neo-Kantian foundation for philosophy of religion in his correspondence with Hirsch, in his crucial 1919
Berlin lecture 'On the Idea of a Theology of Culture' Tillich characterized religion as experience of the Unconditioned:

> Religion is the experience of [directedness towards] the
> unconditioned, and this means the experience of absolute reality

founded on the experience of absolute nothingness. One experiences the nothingness of entities, of values, the nothingness of the personal life. Wherever this experience has brought one to the nothingness of an absolute radical No, there it is transformed into an experience, no less absolute, of reality, into a radical Yes.

(*OITC*, 24)

This conception of religion as experience of the Unconditioned is expressed in various forms in his writings from the beginning of the 1920s as 'experience of unconditionality' (*Unbedingtheitserlebnis*), and 'relation to reality' (*Realitätsbeziehung*), and in the course of the systematic elaboration of his theory of meaning is assimilated into the formula – also prevalent in his later period – 'religion is that which concerns us unconditionally' ('Religion ist das, was uns unbedingt angeht'), otherwise put: 'religion is our ultimate concern' (*ENGW* XII, 405). This theory is of central importance to Tillich and was intended as a solution to the much disputed problem in contemporary religio-philosophical debates about the correlation of religion and culture.

Tillich's philosophy of religion in terms of a theory of consciousness is linked with a critique of transcendental conceptions of religion. That is to say, the site of religion should not be sought at the level of the transcendental functions of consciousness, such as logic, ethics or aesthetics, but rather, as Tillich puts it in the 1919 *Kulturvortrag* (in allusion to Schleiermacher's phrase), religion is 'actual in every spiritual domain' (*MW/HW* II, 73).[12] If this were not the case, for Tillich, one could neither retain a distinction between religion and the cultural functions of consciousness nor maintain the independence of either religion or the autonomy of cultural functions ('Das Christentum und die Gesellschaftsprobleme der Gegenwart' in *ENGW* XII, 71). Equally it would also be wrong to isolate religion from the other functions of consciousness, as this would undermine the unity of consciousness, a critique that Tillich brought to Rudolf Otto's theory of religion ('Die Kategorie des "Heiligen" bei Rudolf Otto' in *GW* XII, 184–6; 'Religionsphilosophie' in *ENGW* XII, 438f.). Both aspects – firstly, the distinction between religion and the cultural functions of consciousness and, secondly, the relation of religion to the cultural functions – are assimilated into Tillich's construal of the concept of religion in terms of a theory of consciousness.

Tillich understands religion as the event of reflexivity upon the cultural functions of consciousness and thus as the becoming-transparent-to-itself of self-relatedness in its inner reflexivity and historicity.

Religion is thus understood as the contingent comprehension of the individual spirit in its relation to itself through the concrete forms posited by spirit. This version of the place of religion in a theory of consciousness shows why religion is both distinguished from but also related to cultural consciousness: religion can only realize itself through assimilation by, and therefore through, the cultural forms posited by spirit, in such a way that it simultaneously both uses and negates these forms. In this actual event of the becoming-reflexive of self-relatedness, the concrete forms posited by spirit become the medium for the representation of self-relatedness (*ENGW* XII, 402). The dimension of the Unconditioned does not therefore indicate a substance-like quantity to which consciousness directs itself in the religious act, but rather is the Unconditional that is constitutive for self-relatedness in its relationship to itself (372f.).

Tillich's distinction between 'narrow' and 'broad' concepts of religion, which pervades his work, derives from this understanding of religion as the contingent event of spirit's becoming-reflexive in its relation to itself. This understanding of religion is assimilated into Tillich's broad concept of religion, namely, the formula that religion is 'das, was uns unbedingt angeht' or 'our ultimate concern' ('Religion als eine Funktion des Geistes?' in *GW* V, 40). The narrower concept of religion results from the fact that religion can only realize itself through the concretely determined forms of self-relatedness. It designates, as it were, a self-relatedness of a kind that has not become transparent in its inner structure, namely the depth dimension of spirit. Hence the narrower concept of religion stands for a conception of religion as one cultural form among others, in which the true meaning of religion has been lost (41).[13]

Philosophy of culture

Tillich's philosophy of culture, already discernible in his two dissertations on Schelling and further developed in the 1920s, has its conceptual basis in his philosophy of spirit. For Tillich, spirit is, in its antinomian relation to itself, the basis of both religion and culture (*MGC*, 114).[14] The unconditionality contained in self-relatedness can only determine itself as concretely real in its self-determination and is always already concretely determined in this same act of self-determination. Tillich defines religion as the contingent intuition of the reflexive structure of spirit in its relation to itself, which can only take place through the concrete forms posited by spirit. Thus, for Tillich, religion, with respect both to knowledge and to action, relates to a reflexive knowledge of spirit in its theoretical and practical activities, with the result that these functions can themselves be considered culture. This correlation of religion and culture is encapsulated in Tillich's formula, 'culture is the form of expression of religion, religion is the content of culture' ('die Kultur ist die Ausdrucksform der Religion, und die Religion ist Inhalt der Kultur'), which expresses his intention to overcome the conflict between heteronomous religion and autonomous culture (*GW* I, 329 and, more famously, *TC*, 43).

The distinction between culture and religion is that between *intentio obliqua* (oblique intention) and *intentio recta* (direct intention). Tillich assimilates these different levels of reflexive knowledge into his two semantic categories 'content' and 'form', which are fundamentally constitutive for his neo-Kantian-influenced explication of philosophy of spirit in the 1920s.[15] The category of content was thus made to stand for spirit's knowledge in the reflexivity of its cultural activity, and the category of form for the object- and action-related autonomous activities of spirit, that is to say, the transcendental functions of spirit. Due to this inner relatedness of the two semantic categories 'content' and 'form', both categories coexist in both the religious and the cultural. Furthermore, the reflexive self-understanding of spirit in its theoretical and practical functions can only occur through the concrete determinations of spirit, namely (in Tillich's apt metaphor), as 'breakthrough' (*Durchbruch*).[16] In religion, spirit grasps itself in its reflexive structure and therein as the deep structure that lies at the basis of the cultural activity of spirit (*GW* I, 320). In its cultural activity, spirit is unconscious with respect to its own reflexive constitution and activity, although that same self-relatedness of spirit also constitutes the basis of cultural activity.

The conceptual basis of Tillich's philosophy of culture represents a modified philosophy of spirit, which enables him to defend both the autonomy of religion and culture as well as their necessary relatedness to one another. Therefore, it is the task of theology 'to bring to expression' the becoming-reflexive of spirit 'in every domain and creation of culture' (*OITC*, 24). Religion is the site where spirit becomes transparent in its cultural activity and in the concreteness of its actions. It is here that Tillich's theory of symbols has its basis.[17] This theory is not concerned with the representation of some sort of substantial transcendent being, but rather with the fact that spirit can create symbols of its own self-transparency in its activity.[18]

Tillich's conception of religious socialism also resulted from the interplay of philosophy of religion, philosophy of history and philosophy of culture.[19] Religious socialism is nothing other than an historical-philosophical interpretative category for an historical consciousness that has become transparent to itself and stands for the historical realization of such a consciousness, in which the autonomous cultural forms are consciously experienced as historically changing forms of expression of human sense-making (*MW/HW* III, 129). It is not a cultural movement, a political party or a religious confession, but an attitude of consciousness. Religious socialism is 'a community that hears the call of the Kairos and understands itself in it' (128). The concept is therefore a normative and not a descriptive one.

Epistemology

Tillich's concern with system is a characteristic of his philosophy. 'The power and vitality of the spirit are manifest not in its extensive knowledge of the details, but in its ability to unify this knowledge' (*SS*, 31).[20] Even before 1914 Tillich had produced a comprehensive draft of a system in his 'Systematische Theologie' (1913), which is concerned throughout with epistemological questions.[21] In his works after the First World War he resumed these questions and worked on them with the conceptual means supplied by the neo-Kantian theory of meaning, which he combines, of course, with his Idealist presumptions. His early Berlin lectures are pervaded by epistemological reflections that can be seen as precursors of his 1923 *System of the Sciences*.[22] These writings and lectures together document the evolution of Tillich's semantic philosophy of spirit, which achieves a tentative final form in the 1923 *System*.[23]

In his article 'Theology as Science' ('Die Theologie als Wissenschaft'), published in 1921 in the *Vossische Zeitung*, Tillich sketched out a system of the sciences, which introduced the three-fold division that would become so significant for his later work. The article addresses the epistemological status of modern theology by correlating theology with the cultural sciences, which are characterized by both their concreteness and the relativity of their standpoint:

> When it deals with a question, in which the personal
> standpoint plays a role in the experience of the world, then
> theology is not simply a cultural science but is also critically and
> radically subjective. A cultural science without a standpoint is an
> impossibility because in spiritual matters, spirit does not stand at an
> objective distance but in close proximity to the experiencing subject,
> such that a cultural science is always also a cultural creation.
>
> (*TW*, 2)[24]

Within the cultural sciences, Tillich distinguishes philosophico-conceptual, historico-philosophical-typological and normative disciplines, and affirms a strict correlation between the philosophico-conceptual and the normative ones.[25] By means of this differentiation Tillich aims to justify methodically the standpoint-relative nature of every general concept and thereby the fact that spirit in its positing and determining is always already concretely determined by the other. Theology therefore presupposes a philosophy of religion but is nevertheless distinct from the general concept of religion, since it is concerned with the normativity of a particular religion (*TW*, 2).

Tillich incorporated a revised version of this epistemological framework in his 1923 *System*; however, he subjected it to a redefinition on the basis of his recently elaborated philosophy of spirit. Here the normative sciences are correlated with the human sciences and these in turn to the conceptual foundation of the system of sciences. Tillich thereby not only positioned himself within the epistemological debates of his time (especially within neo-Kantianism and phenomenology), but above all he was able to elaborate the constitutive function of theology within the system.[26] Since in each cognitive act both an identity and a difference of subject and object – i.e. of thought and being – coexist, Tillich distinguished three moments in the idea of knowledge: thought, being and spirit (*SS*, 33f.). This internal structuring of the concept of knowledge incorporates central definitions of his earlier philosophy of spirit indebted to German Idealism and redefines them in terms of his theory of meaning, and is at the same time a critique of neo-Kantian epistemology. The construction of a system of sciences follows from the three distinct and correlated moments contained in the concept of knowledge. Following the three moments of knowledge – thought, being and spirit – Tillich distinguishes between the sciences of thought or ideal-sciences, the sciences of being or real-sciences, and sciences of spirit or normative-sciences (43–56, 57–136, 137–216). Decisive for his system, however, are its Idealist foundations and the construal of theology as the place in the system of sciences in which the necessary concreteness and historicity of knowledge, as well as the normativity of its own standpoint, becomes known. Since theology, defined by Tillich in the system of sciences as 'theonomous systematics', is understood as reflexive description of the actual act of faith and of the self-transparency of the historical consciousness of meaning connected with this, it is through theology that the conflict between autonomy and heteronomy, and religion and culture, is overcome (206f.).

TILLICH'S THIRD PHASE: THE TURN
TO ONTOLOGY

In Tillich's later work, as it is elaborated in his American period and especially in the *Systematic Theology*, ontology comes more strongly into the foreground than in earlier periods.[27] Central to his later work is the ontological definition of God as 'Being-Itself' (*ST* I, 235). According to Tillich, it is philosophy's task to pose the 'question of reality as a whole . . . the question of the structure of being. And it answers in terms of categories, structural laws, and universal concepts' (20). Thus, for the later Tillich, philosophy virtually becomes ontology.

However, the concern with ontology does not begin with his emigration to America: as far back as his writings of the late 1920s ontological questions were increasingly becoming a focus of his thinking, particularly in terms of his engagement with neo-Kantianism and phenomenology, especially Martin Heidegger.[28] The ontology he sets out from the late 1920s onwards is not an ontology in the pre-Kantian or realist sense, but rather a component of his philosophy of spirit.[29] Rather, Tillich's ontology is essentially a transcendental philosophical description of the structures of self-relatedness. 'The truth of all ontological concepts is their power of expressing that which makes the subject-object structure possible. They constitute this structure; they are not controlled by it' (*ST* I, 169). This is evident from the very construction of the *Systematic Theology* and the relationship of its three volumes to each other. As Tillich himself remarks in the first volume of his *Systematic Theology*, 'A third part is based on the fact that the essential as well as the existential characteristics are abstractions and that in reality they appear in the complex and dynamic unity which is called "life"' (66–7).[30]

At the most basic level, Tillich's ontology represents an ontological description of self-relatedness and the relationship of the self–world relation this implies. Both moments of self-relatedness constitute an irreducible correlation, according to which no relation-to-self is possible without a relation-to-world and vice versa. Tillich calls the individual moments that constitute this structure 'ontological elements', which share the characteristic of the fundamental structure of self-relatedness, namely, that they also constitute polarities. Tillich distinguishes between individualization and participation, dynamics and form, as well as freedom und destiny (*ST* I, 174–8, 178–82, 182–6).[31] The concept of God constitutes the foundation of this structure, which Tillich defines, within the framework of an ontological description of self-relatedness, as being-itself (235ff.). Needless to say, this ontological definition of the concept of God is not meant in a substance-like, realist or 'ontotheological' sense, but rather the description of God as being-itself represents an ontological reformulation of the dimension of unconditionality (*Unbedingtheitsdimension*) which is constitutive of self-relatedness itself.

CONCLUSION

There is a high degree of continuity in Paul Tillich's philosophy throughout all the stages of its development. His starting-point is the critical reception of German Idealism in the context of the challenge of historicism. In the early 1920s Tillich's Idealist philosophy of spirit was turned to the philosophy of meaning, such that the concept of meaning became the organizational fulcrum of his philosophical and theological thought. This chapter has reconstructed these foundations, as well as Tillich's early philosophy of religion, culture and science that results from them. These foundations also undergird Tillich's later philosophy, and it is crucial that any reconstruction of Tillich's later ontology under-stands its relation to his earliest philosophical considerations and their context of neo-Idealism, neo-Kantianism and phenomenology. In this way, not only can we come to a clearer estimation of Tillich's philoso-phy itself, but we can also evaluate the structural similarities between Tillich's philosophy and that of Martin Heidegger and other so-called existentialist philosophers. Like Tillich, Heidegger worked out his phi-losophy through a critical reception of Husserl's phenomenology in the context of the debates within neo-Kantianism in the years either side of the First World War. Tillich and Heidegger (in their different ways) both focus their philosophies on the concrete individual relation of the self in its historical certainty in response to the crisis of historicism.

Tillich's philosophy, throughout his life, remains a philosophy of spirit, grounded in his interpretation of spirit and meaning. It is, how-ever, worked out in a variety of contexts and debates, which can some-times obscure the character of its foundation. In his later American work, for example, the philosophy of spirit appears to recede, to be replaced by an ontological formulation. It is largely in this ontological sense that Tillich's philosophy has been understood by his Anglophone American interpreters; and yet, however superficially compelling this interpretation may be, any characterization of Tillich's philosophical development as a journey 'from meaning to being' raises more ques-tions than it does solutions. Most importantly, such a view must be able to explain how it might be that a thinker trained in and so profoundly shaped by German Idealism, neo-Kantianism and phenomenology could, in his late work, fall into an uncritical pre-Kantian substance ontology! Similarly, such a view has to account for the increasingly clear recognition that the central elements of Tillich's early philosophy of spirit, as well as his philosophy of religion and culture, are equally constitutive for his later work, in both theology of culture and systematic theology (WR). In light of these difficulties, it seems to me no longer helpful to characterize Tillich's philosophical development as a movement from meaning to being.

It is only on the basis of this presentation of the intellectual background of Tillich's own philosophy in the early twentieth-century debates on how best critically to contain historicism, which was central to the development of all the significant philosophical tendencies in Germany at the turn of the century, that we can understand Tillich's later judgements on Anglo-American philosophy. For Tillich, pragmatism and positivism were interpreted and criticized from the perspective of a philosophy of spirit formed by Idealism, phenomenology and neo-Kantianism. Through his membership of New York's Philosophy Club and his earlier close acquaintance with the 'as if' philosophy of Hans Vaihinger, Tillich was well informed about philosophical pragmatism; however, he was never able to find his way into its inner core. In this, as with his ontology, Tillich remained above all an Idealist, a philosopher of spirit and meaning, and of the self-relation of the Unconditioned.

Notes

This chapter was translated by Alexandra Wörn, David Leech and Russell Re Manning.

1 The continuities in the development of Tillich's thought have consistently been shown in the scholarship. See Fischer (1992), 150–7.
2 Tillich's relationship to Fritz Medicus has barely been investigated in the literature. To date there is only Graf and Christophersen (2004), 52–78.
3 Medicus (1902), (1905) and Fichte (1908–12). Aside from editing Fichte's works, Medicus also wrote a biography and reception history.
4 For the history of 'Fichtes Religionsphilosophie in ihrem Verhältnis zum Johannesevangelium' see ENGW IX, 1–3. However, it must remain an open question whether Tillich wrote this Seminararbeit under Fritz Medicus, as the editors claim. See Graf and Christophersen (2004), 52 n. 2.
5 For the backround to Tillich's philosophical dissertation, see Neugebauer (2006).
6 Tillich himself always stressed the importance of these theses for his own intellectual development. See OB in BOB 320 (GW XII, 32). For an overview of the importance of this statement for Tillich's Christology, see Foster (2007).

7   See Wittekind (2004), 138–43.

8   Concerning Tillich's theological dissertation, see Neugebauer (2006). For the 'Systematische Theologie' of 1913, see Wittekind (2004), 143–7 and Danz (2005a), 102–28, in particular 104–17.

9   See Danz (2004a), especially 80–6, Schütte (2004) and Wittekind (2004), 148–52. See also Reimer (1988). On the historical background, see Barth (2003), 89–123.

10 Concerning Tillich's debate with Georg Simmel, see Sturm (2004).

11 See 'Religionsphilosophie (Sommersemester 1920)' in *ENGW* XII, 333–565, 'Die Überwindung des Religionsbegriffs in der Religionsphilosophie' in *GW* I, 367–88 and 'Religionsphilosophie' (1925) in *GW* I, 297–364.

12 This localizing of religion in the construction of consciousness is connected with a critique of Ernst Troeltsch's concept of religion. For Tillich's critique of Troeltsch's religious *a priori*, see 'Ernst Troeltsch. Versuch einer geistesgeschichtlichen Würdigung' in *GW* XII, 166–74, in particular 167–9. See further Danz (2005b).

13 A fundamental text in this connection is Paul Tillich, 'Die Überwindung des Religionsbegriffs' in *GW* I, 367–88.

14 This conception of Tillich's is outlined programmatically in *OITC*.

15 See *SS*, 203f. and 'Religionsphilosophie' in *GW* I, 313ff. See Moritz (1960), Heinrichs (1970), Jahr (1989) and Moxter (2000).

16 The metaphor of 'breakthrough' had been employed since the 1920s for the event of the becoming-reflexive of self-relatedness in the epistemological dimension. See Moxter (2000), 66ff. and Danz (2005c). See also Scharf (1999).

17 See here the essential text, Paul Tillich, 'Das religiöse Symbol' in *GW* V, 196–212. Tillich had already elaborated his theory of religious symbols from the beginning of the 1920s in a continuation of the philosophy of spirit of his pre-First World War theology. See Paul Tillich, 'Rechtfertigung und Zweifel' in *ENGW* IX, 172.

18 Thus Urban (1940), Simpson (1967), Ford (1970), Grigg (1985) and Moxter (2000), 24ff. See also Danz (2000a) and Wittekind (2005), in particular 144f.

19 See especially Paul Tillich, 'Der Sozialismus als Kirchenfrage' in *MW/HW* III, 31–42, 'Grundlinien des Religiös[en] Sozialismus. Ein systematischer Entwurf' in ibid., 103–30 and *SS*. Concerning Tillich's understanding of religious socialism, see Danz (2005d).

20 See also Schütte (2004), 3–22.

21 See Danz (2004a), 74–80.

22 Especially relevant here are Tillich's lectures from the winter semester of 1920, 'Enzyklopädie der Theologie und Religionswissenschaft' in *ENGW* XII, 259–95, as well as his lecture on philosophy of religion from the summer semester of 1920 (348–62). See also *TW* as well as 'Wissenschaft' in *MW/HW* I, 349–51.

23 See Ziche (2004). From the earlier literature, see Büchsel (1923), Leese (1926), Adams (1965), 116–82, Wenz (1979) and Wiebe (1984), 142–61.

24 See also *OITC* and *ENGW* XII, 264.

25 See *OITC* and *ENGW* XII, 264f. The later *ST* still orients itself to this architectonic of knowldege, as is clear from Tillich's doctrine of the theological circle, see *ST* I, 17.

26 See Ziche (2004).
27 See 'Sein und Sinn. Zwei Schriften zur Ontologie' in *GW* XI. Concerning Tillich's ontology, see Thatcher (1978) and Thompson (1981).
28 Thus for example in his draft 'Das System der religiösen Erkenntnis', written around 1927 in *ENGW* XI, 79–174. Concerning the history of the text, see 76–8. The philosophico-historical background to Tillich's turn to ontological questions can be perceived in the relevant discussions on neo-Kantianism and phenomenology. Concerning Tillich's engagement with the philosophy of Martin Heidegger, see Sturm (2001).
29 Especially relevant here is 'Religionsphilosophie' in *GW* I, 307. The maxim discussed in Tillich's letter correspondence with Hirsch – 'In den Geist kann nichts hinein, was nicht aus ihm kommt, denn er ist niemals leere Form, sondern immer lebendige Aktualität. Er ist in sich unendlich und zieht alles in sich hincin.' (Tillich's letter to Hirsch of 20 February 1918, *ENGW* VI, 116) – is equally applicable to Tillich's ontology.
30 See Danz (2000b).
31 See *ST* I, 174–8, 178–82, 182–6.

Further reading

Clayton, John P. (1980). *The Concept of Correlation: Paul Tillich and the Possibility of a Mediating Theology.* Berlin: Walter de Gruyter.
Danz, Christian (2000b). *Religion als Freiheitsbewußtsein. Eine Studie zur Theologie als Theorie der Konstitutionsbedingungen individueller Subjektivität bei Paul Tillich.* Berlin/New York: Walter de Gruyter.
Danz, Christian, ed. (2004b). *Theologie als Religionsphilosophie. Studien zu den problemgeschichtlichen und systematischen Voraussetzungen der Theologie Paul Tillichs*, Tillich-Studien, vol. IX. Vienna: LIT Verlag.
Henel, Ingeborg (1981). *Philosophie und Theologie im Werk Paul Tillichs.* Frankfurt am Main: Evangelisches Verlagswerk.
Repp, Martin (1986). *Die Transzendierung des Theismus in der Religionsphilosophie Paul Tillichs.* Frankfurt am Main: Peter Lang.
Seigfried, Adam (1978). *Gott über Gott. Die Gottesbeweise als Ausdruck der Gottesfrage in der philosophisch-theologischen Tradition und im Denken Paul Tillichs.* Essen: Lugerus Verlag.
Thatcher, Adrian (1978). *The Ontology of Paul Tillich.* Oxford: Oxford University Press.
Thompson, Ian E. (1981). *Being and Meaning: Paul Tillich's Theory of Meaning, Truth and Logic.* Edinburgh: Edinburgh University Press.

12 Tillich's ethics: between politics and ontology

MARK LEWIS TAYLOR

I am convinced that we shall overcome because the arc of the universe is long but it bends toward justice.

Martin Luther King, Jr

Justice is not an abstract ideal standing over existence; it is the fulfillment of primal being, the fulfillment of that which was intended by the origin.

Paul Tillich

The young Martin Luther King, Jr focused on Paul Tillich as one of the two major thinkers treated in his doctoral dissertation at Boston University in 1955. King displayed in that work little of the ethical concern with racism for which he later became so well known. Nevertheless, the oft-quoted words of 1968 in the epigraph above, taken from his later moral struggle in the civil rights movement and against the Vietnam War, offer an artful rendering of a key feature of Tillich's ethical vision.[1] Like Tillich, King presents justice here neither as precept of a demanding divinity nor as mandate of a table of commandments, nor, primarily, as the virtue of the good person. Instead, King presumes justice to be so etched into the order of things that the universe may be said to arc towards it. Moreover, King's words traced that arc towards justice to motivate a people. It was meant to inspire, and part of its capacity to inspire amid political struggle was an ontological presumption that the universe, in which we all already participate, is, in spite of every political corruption and systematic distortion, created from its origins with an arc that points and carries a struggling people towards justice.

BETWEEN POLITICS AND ONTOLOGY

Tillich's ethics emerges from a tension between his discursive treatments of political existence and ontology. The treatment of political existence was basically a horizontal move embracing the complexity and anguish of a situation, while his treatments of ontology were a more vertical discerning of the depths of political existence to find structures and elements that helped define the situation.

There is a notable difference between Tillich and King concerning their hopes amid the American racial conflict of the 1960s. While King struggled to the rhythms of 'We shall overcome', Tillich barely dared hope. In 1961, according to his personal secretary at Harvard University, Tillich was inspiring students to enter the movements against racism in South Africa and the United States, but he himself remained despondent about the capacity of America to counter the threats of that time, especially 'the racial trouble' and 'the nuclear arms development' that together made up what he called the nation's 'awful sickness'. He said he could feel this sickness in all his speaking engagements throughout the country.[2] His secretary recalls an exchange that she and some of his students had with him:

> "Is there any way of stopping it?"
> He sighed heavily. "I hope and pray so. But I'm afraid not. Today the self-destructive urges in man are so strong – individually and on the group level – that I doubt if they can be overcome."
> "Isn't there anything any of us can be doing to help reverse the trends?" asked Victor intently.
> His face filled with a deep sadness. "It is already so late. I feel it may be too far gone – especially the racial trouble."
> "But Paulus!" I protested. "Is there no hope?"
> He sensed our plea. "There is only one way. Everywhere, in every way possible, we as individuals must fight against the forces of destruction. First, in ourselves, then on a group level. We must work for anything that will bring people together – but in encounters where love and justice become creatively one."[3]

This is vintage Tillich, nearly (but not quite) overwhelmed amid political forces of human self-destruction, accepting a challenge to offer hope, both on individual and group levels, making the ontological presumption again and again, here, affirming encounters between beings 'where love and justice become creatively one'.

The ethics that Tillich produced in the liminal world between political trauma and ontological reflection will not fit neatly with many received notions of what is usually taken for ethics. This chapter introduces Tillich's ethics as disciplined reflection on the legal and communal areas of society, from which are generated a cultural interest in justice and love, respectively. Tillich finds the creative unity of justice and love emerging when individuals and groups attend to the depth dimension of society's legal and communal areas, where persons' and groups' orientation to the Unconditional, their ultimate concern, brings forth the encounters with love and justice. From this perspective, Tillich's ethics is not so much a 'science of morality', even though he used that phrase at points, as it is a 'science of ethos' or of culture in its many functions.[4] The next, second section of this chapter unfolds this view of ethics more fully. A third section sets forth the major features of Tillich's ethics as 'theonomous ethics', before the final section clarifies the question of how ethics, in Tillich's sense, is normative.

Twenty-first-century philosophy and ethics do not offer the most hospitable welcome for ontology, especially as political thinkers using liberationist, feminist, poststructuralist, process, postmodern and post-colonial theories have forged the philosophy and ethics of our time. Ontology as a resource for an ethicist facing troubled political times can seem like a retreat, a turn to hoary theories of being that set up *a priori* universal structures that avoid the messiness of historical and cultural processes, or, in the case of theology, seem the precursor for introducing 'God' as transcendental ground for a hierarchy of universal structures. There have, indeed, been many cases of such 'onto-theologies', and they have rightly been criticized by analytic philosophers as being obfuscating and imprecise, by process thinkers as being too static for theorizing life's becoming, by feminists and others as masking an hubristic patriarchal ordering and an essentialism of being(s) that usually subordinates some female essence to a male essence, by postmodernists as enshrining a master narrative that runs roughshod over particularity and difference, and by postcolonial theorists who see in the ontologies a controlling interest that underwrites empire and colonialism. Perhaps Emmanuel Levinas's 'Is Ontology Fundamental?' has been especially damning to ethicists' interests in ontology, holding as he does that the ethical cannot be derived from ontology's discourse about being, but from relationships.[5]

Tillich was aware of such criticisms and in fact developed his own early critiques of 'abstract fundamental ontology' and of essence language (*SD*, 155, nn. 6, 9–10). He stressed in *The Socialist Decision* that ontology was but a 'final and abstract version of the myth of origin' and as such would need to be broken by a philosophy of history. The ontology he saw congruent with his early socialist vision could not be one unrelated to history (166, n. 6). A correlate to this claim is Tillich's frequent reminder that no system of thought, especially in theology (whether empirical-inductive or metaphysical-deductive), can escape that 'point where individual experience, traditional valuation, and personal commitment must decide the issue. This point, often hidden to the authors . . . is obvious to those who look at them with other experiences and other commitments' (*ST* I, 8).

Tillich's ontology is a politically and existentially interested conceptual exercise, with all the limitations that Tillich knew to inhere in conceptual thinking. His ontology is perhaps akin to the turn to ontology that Michael Hardt and Antonio Negri have counselled in their works *Empire* and *Multitude*, in which the multitude of the world's peoples struggle to form a political project amid the vicissitudes of war and empire. For Hardt and Negri, ontology is not an abstract science, even if it is theoretically rigorous; it is a necessary reflection to discern the 'biopolitical' powers of life that can move a multitude with grievances forward to experience another world.[6] Or again, Tillich's turn to ontology is consonant with what some feminist philosophers have done in turning to Spinoza's ontology to forge less dualistic theories for challenging Western philosophies' harsh gender binarism.[7] Tillich's ontology amid political crisis could be read as also akin to that of Latin American philosophers such as Enrique Dussel who, though fiercely critical of Western ontologies, nevertheless do not eschew all ontological reflection on being *qua* being, especially as certain 'pre- or trans-ontologies' proceed from the reality of those victims who have been denied life.[8] Similarly, African thinkers have not relinquished ontology in their attempts to convey distinctive African understandings of the person as rooted in community and cosmos.[9]

Tillich's ontology also shares some notable features with the recent work in politics, ethics and ontology by contemporary French philosopher Alain Badiou. Badiou's ontology is radically different from Tillich's in its claim that 'mathematics = ontology'. Moreover, Badiou may view Tillich's ontology as all too 'poetic' (like Heidegger's).[10] Nevertheless, as one who takes seriously the ontological problematic of 'being as being' in his magisterial *Being and Event*, and makes the ontological move (and an ethical move) in response to political crises of Western culture, Badiou's project is reminiscent of Tillich's.[11] In the context of political existence Tillich explored a 'sacred void' and found in it an inseparability of being from non-being that is similar to Badiou's claim in *Being and Event* that being *qua* being only 'allows itself to be sutured in its void'.[12] Moreover, Tillich could affirm Badiou's call: 'The militant of a truth is not only the political militant working for the emancipation of humanity in its entirety. He or she is also the artist-creator, the scientist who opens up a new theoretical field, or the lover whose world is enchanted.'[13]

WHAT IS 'ETHICS' FOR TILLICH?

It is no simple matter to state what Tillich means by ethics or to locate its distinctive intellectual operations. In some of Tillich's latest works he proffers definitions of ethics that accommodate widely familiar definitions of ethics, while leaving in the background the distinctive traits of his own preferred ethical thinking, which, if more fully foregrounded, would yield a quite different statement of what ethics is. As we shall see, this quite different statement, to which Tillich gives less emphasis in his later works on ethics, was in fact pronounced and discussed by him in his early German works, particularly in his *System of the Sciences* (1923).

Tillich's accommodating definition

It is in the later books *Love, Power and Justice* (1954) and *Morality and Beyond* (1963) that Tillich accommodates the widely accepted view of ethics in English-speaking academies, which sees it as largely a branch of knowledge concerned with moral principles and action, with the term 'moral' denoting a concern with the right, the good. The *Oxford English Dictionary* sets out the terms in these ways, and most texts in ethics lay out the terms 'ethics' and 'morals' in a similar manner.[14]

Tillich accommodates to this when in *Love, Power and Justice* he states that 'Ethics is the science of man's [sic] moral existence', 'science' here meaning generally disciplined theory. Fifteen years later, in *Morality and Beyond*, Tillich makes a similar accommodation when he writes, 'I recommend that "ethical" be reserved for the theory of morals' (*MB*, 22).[15] Here, as in *Love, Power and Justice*, the subject matter on which ethics reflects is morals, morality or moral existence.

Tillich's tendency towards accommodation is also evident in the third volume of the *Systematic Theology* (1963). There, he again repeats that the subject matter of ethics is morality, i.e. ethics is 'the science of the moral act' (*ST* III, 66). His posture of accommodation is registered in his phrasing about these definitions as 'probably more expedient'. The notion of the expedient suggests convenience and practicality, but with an underlying sense that there may be something improper about the expedient way, that there might be an alternative way to define what ethics is.

Stretching the meaning of morality and ethics

In the tension between Tillich's expedient definition and the one he hints at as preferable, we can discern Tillich's broader understanding of ethics. This stretching activity can be noted clearly in the 1963 volume of his *Systematic Theology*, where in the same paragraph announcing the expedient definition ('ethics is the science of the moral act'), Tillich states that 'one could subsume the entire realm [of *praxis*] under the term "ethics" and distinguish between individual and social ethics' (*ST* III, 66). By *praxis* Tillich has in view the whole realm of culturally creative actions performed by persons and social groups in interaction (65–6). Ethics would pertain here because there are norms operative throughout cultural creativity, whether in social relations, politics, law, administration, or personal life and development. This diverse realm of *praxis*, with norms at work throughout these many cultural functions, would be the subject matter of ethics, not, primarily, 'morality'.

Morality is presented by Tillich as the integrating, centring function of human life, where person encounters person. Morality in this broader sense, and only in this broader sense, can have what Tillich calls 'a foundational position' in ethics (21). The notion of morality is stretched from actions by individuals or groups that are judged towards a function of 'the cultural self-creativity of life' (66). This point will be reinforced throughout the third volume of the *Systematic Theology*, as when he insists that the subject matter of ethics is a 'moral-cultural situation' and that 'the ethical content is a product of culture and shares all the relativities of cultural creativity' (160). Ultimately, in fact, by the end of volume III it is clear that there is really no self-constitution, no moral act without participation in culture, and then also without morality and culture participating together in religion, in Spiritual Community (159).

Ethics as 'the science of ethos'

To my knowledge, the notion of 'ethos' does not appear at all in the *Systematic Theology* (1951–63) or in later works on ethics such as *Love, Power and Justice* and *Morality and Beyond*. Nevertheless, this notion as it occurs in his 1923 *System of the Sciences* remains important for interpreting the later Tillich's perspective on ethics.

Tillich's notion of 'science' or 'the sciences' should not be taken in too technical a sense. He generally means, as noted by Wiebe, 'cognitive disciplines'. There are three major groups of these, the sciences of thought ('The Ideal Sciences': logic and mathematics), the sciences of being ('The Empirical Sciences': physics, and organic, technical and social sciences) and the sciences of spirit ('The human sciences'). These human sciences, in turn, are divided into two spheres: the theoretical and the practical. The theoretical sphere is represented by two functions, Science (in this case, concerned with the forms of human experience) and Art (concerned with the import or meaning in these human forms) (*SS*, 178). This theoretical sphere, whether as Science or Art, is also pervaded by a general directing function, a will to grasp 'the Unconditional', and it is the task of metaphysics to study and trace that directing function.

The Unconditional is a very complex notion in Tillich's thought. It is important, though, because it is what gives depth to Tillich's broadened understanding of ethics pertaining to culture. The Unconditional is human being's reach through all conditions to that which seems beyond all conditions; but it is a reach that fills those conditions with meaning. In other words, it is a reach towards mystery but through the mundane, by which reach the mundane becomes meaningful. The Unconditional would in later writings by Tillich be discussed more often as 'ultimate concern'. In Tillich's *System*, it is metaphysics' role to trace this meaning-giving orientation in the theoretical sphere, and, as we shall soon see, 'ethos' performs this task in the practical sphere.

The practical sphere of the human sciences has two functions that generally parallel the functions of science and art of the theoretical sphere: law and community.[16] Law or the legal order moves by the power of a 'rational, determinate form', which Tillich identifies as justice. Community has an 'import-determined form', which is love.

The two practical functions of law and community are also marked by a general directing function, again the movement or orientation to the Unconditional. 'Ethos' is 'directedness to the Unconditional in action' or 'the active realization of the Unconditioned' (*SS*, 64, 201). It is here that Tillich introduces the notion of 'ethics' as 'the science of ethos' (201). In this 1923 *System* he takes pains to differentiate how taking ethos as the subject matter of ethics makes it a much broader cognitive discipline than it is usually understood to be:

> *Ethics* is concerned with neither the good nor obligation, with neither the personal order nor the legal order. It is *not* moral philosophy; it is the science of ethos, that is, *the science of the realization of the Unconditioned within meaning-fulfilling existential relationships.*
>
> (203, emphasis added)

Because ethics shares with metaphysics in the theoretical sphere a concern with the Unconditional, ethics and metaphysics (again, as

Tillich defines these) cannot work apart from one another. As Tillich puts it, 'Every proposition of a creative metaphysics is an expression of an ethos; every ethos expresses a metaphysics. This is why a metaphysician like Spinoza called his metaphysics *Ethics*' (201).

Ethos is an orientation, an attitude, a directional movement that can be found in action, particularly in law's pursuit of justice and community's pursuit of love. This pervasive orientation, ethos, is expressed through symbols, these being various linguistic terms and phrases that mark the reach or drive towards the Unconditional but that are always inadequate to describe it or, surely, to encompass it. Ethics studies this ethos and its symbols as they occur in not only the broad areas of practice called law and community, but in all the various cultural realms and functions that make up those two broad areas. The subject matter of ethos, then, is a complex scaffolding of inter-relating cultural functions that make up the whole sphere of *praxis*.

What this means is that ethics, in Tillich's 1923 *System*, as a science of ethos, is analogous to a 'theory of culture'. Ethics for Tillich, in sum, is a cognitive discipline reflecting on ethos, i.e. reflecting on the orientation and attitude that seeks the unconditional operative in all cultural functions, primarily in the practical sphere but also in the theoretical one where ethics is conjoined with metaphysics because of their shared orientation to the Unconditional.

THEONOMOUS ETHICS

It is against the background of this expanded notion of ethics as science of ethos that we can best understand Tillich's notion of 'theonomous ethics'. Theonomous ethics is ethics directing its reflection towards identifying and studying the ethos of culture, the ways that the Unconditional and ultimate concern are at work in the conditions of all culture, filling them with meaning. This leads to a very complex intellectual enterprise: tracing the theonomous dimension in culture, doing ethics as a science of ethos in culture, involving a large number of distinctions in culture so that the understanding of the ultimate or Unconditional in culture can be more concretely discerned.

In undertaking this complex endeavour of theonomous ethics, it is clear that, for Tillich, the drive towards the Unconditional, the situation of theonomy, can be found at many sites of culture, and it can also be stimulated and provided for by diverse concrete religious traditions, and often by secular movements, forming something he called the 'latent church'. Within his whole system, however, and this is why Tillich remained a Christian theologian, Tillich affirmed that 'the Christian church understood as the community of the New Being is the place where the new theonomy is actual'. Moreover, he sought to show ways that the church could relate in mutually critical dialogue so as to be the place from which theonomy then 'pours into the whole of man's [*sic*] cultural life and gives a Spiritual center to . . . spiritual life' (*ST* I, 148).

The church becomes this kind of community of New Being because of the way that the sacred is manifest to the church in the figure of Jesus taken as 'the Christ', the fulfilling one, in Christians' cultural life. The Jesus who is pictured in biblical narratives and who lived as the Christ in Christian community is presented by Tillich as generating the Spiritual Presence that traces, fosters and strengthens the meaning-giving and empowering theonomy of culture (147).

Placing such emphasis on Christian spiritual community has many marks of Christian hubris, seeming to privilege Christianity as *the* unique, theonomy-bringing community amid the pluralism of human cultural and religious forms. Tillich always reminded readers, however, that if the community of the New Being was to remain new for nurturing the theonomous function and viewpoint, and if it was really to be *final* (all-fulfilling and eminent among other forms), it would be final, paradoxically, through its self-sacrificing character, its relinquishment of privilege, even opposing its own absolutism of faith, doctrine or morals. 'Final revelation', wrote Tillich, 'does not give us absolute ethics, absolute doctrines, or an absolute ideal of personal and communal life' (151). On the contrary, any revelation purporting to be 'final' is oriented by a continual prophetic, 'Protestant principle', a practice of exposing the inadequacy of all conditioned forms for being final or ultimate, even the forms of belief and practice in the community of Jesus as the Christ. This way of the prophetic principle radiates from the Christian community's 'biblical picture' of Jesus, where Jesus is displayed as a figure involved in continual self-surrender. For Tillich, Jesus as the Christ can be a 'final revelation' because 'he is the Christ as the one who sacrifices what is merely "Jesus" in him. The decisive trait in his picture is the continuous self-surrender of Jesus who is Jesus to Jesus who is the Christ' (134).

We may summarize his ethical formulation by turning to a final summation that he himself gave towards the end of the *Systematic Theology*:

> Theonomous ethics in the full sense of the phrase, therefore, is ethics in which, under the impact of the Spiritual Presence, the religious substance – the experience of an ultimate concern – is consciously expressed through the process of free arguing and not

through an attempt to determine it. Intentional theonomy is
heteronomy and must be rejected by ethical research. Actual
theonomy is autonomous ethics under the Spiritual Presence.

(*ST* III, 268)

BUT HOW IS TILLICH'S ETHICS NORMATIVE?

In what ways is Tillich's theology-of-culture approach to ethics
'normative', i.e. pertaining to standards, rules, laws or to some principles that might discriminate the good and the better from the bad and
the worse? How does the good emerge, and what are its features? In
this final section I identify five features of the normative in Tillich's
ethics.

The normative as *donative*

By 'donative' I refer here to the gift character of the good, the fact
that the desirable norm for being and action, whatever it may be, has
the character of a gift, and this in two senses.

Firstly, it is a surprise, having an unexpected character. The good,
for Tillich, comes in a way that resonates with certain expectations and
hopes, but the coming is also a surprise. The surprise is rooted in the
fact that, for Tillich, the human situation is so marked by brokenness,
alienation and estrangement (both personal and political), conflict and
oppression that the normative, insofar as it occurs, comes as a surprising
gift. It meets expectations but surpasses them.

The notion of a gift that surprises and exceeds expectations
points to a tension that was at the heart of all Tillich's thought, the
kairos. Tillich's thought – whether about ethics, philosophy, politics or
theology – was done out of a sense of something emerging, something
the structure and character of which *could* be partially anticipated, but
which was also uncontrollable and unknown. *Kairos* was both crisis
and opportunity, both resonant with lived historical time, yet full of
the surprising and unanticipated. He worked out of this sense amid
various forms of politico-existential trauma that constituted the 'world
situation' of his thinking: after the First World War, when he spoke
of a 'new mysticism of love now stirring everywhere', after the Second World War, when he identified the 'sacred void' in which spiritual
reconstruction must be born anew, and to the end of his *Systematic Theology*, when he emphasized the importance of the *kairos* presented by
the politico-existential contours of religious pluralism, liberal humanism, nationalism (German, Soviet, American) and socialism (*OITC*, 48;

'Religion and Secular Culture' in *ProtE*, 60–5; 'Spiritual Problems of Postwar Reconstruction' in *ProtE*, 266–7; *ST* III, 6, 369–72).

Secondly, experience of the normative is 'donative' not just because it is surprising, but because it is also given by another kind of presence, an 'other' that is beyond, more than, even though with and within, the worlds of moral-cultural situations. Hence, Tillich will refer to *Spiritual* Presence, or *Spiritual* Community, to name this other kind of presence. Time and again, however, Tillich would quickly qualify his claim here, reminding readers that this Spiritual Presence was not on some super-natural plane, to be contrasted with natural or cultural realms. On the contrary, the spiritual (or religious) was a *dimension of* the natural, the human, the cultural. In volume III of the *Systematic Theology* Tillich links the emergence of the spiritual to the birth of 'the underivable' amid many derivable conditions. He references the creation of Shakespeare's *Hamlet*, recalling that its 'material, particular form, its personal presuppositions, occasioning factors, and so on, are derivable'. But no sum of their parts can account for what resulted, *Hamlet*. That result attended the conditioning derivables from human, material life and society, but the result (the play, with its enduring and transformative impact) has a newness that marks it as 'underivable' (*ST* III, 324). Note again, there is something new breaking forth here, but remaining inseparable from cultural and natural structures and dynamics. Similarly, for Tillich the Unconditional is never forced upon culture, never imposed – it cannot really even be invited. Instead, it comes, it occurs, it is disclosed as a moral agent's or community's being-grasped by its depth and so borne up and borne along, as it were, towards realization of its ideal norms, towards restoration of the unity of 'the ought' with 'the is'.

The normative as *immanental*

I here deploy the spatial term 'immanental' to highlight the last point made in the previous section, i.e. that the locus of the norm that comes as a gift is not external to culture and nature but internal to it. In other words, to experience the normative, especially the good, is to experience a particular, qualitative configuration of culture and nature, not to opt out of them. Tillich writes of the otherness of Spiritual Presence, but he emphasizes that this otherness is at work *within* the structures of a complex nature and culture. He would thus be at home with Grace Jantzen's reminder that immanence and transcendence are not opposites, that one could write of a 'sensible transcendental', where 'transcendental' refers not to something external to sensibility but to 'the projected horizon of our (embodied) being'.[17]

Precisely here, in this taking of the normative as immanental, is where Tillich places Kant's 'moral imperative'. The moral imperative is not an external universal demand for the ethical agent; on the contrary, it is still demand, but it is 'the demand to become actually what one is essentially and therefore potentially. It is the power of man's being, given to him [*sic*] by nature, which he shall actualize in time and space. His true being shall become his actual being – this is the moral imperative' (*MB*, 20). By internal, again, Tillich does not mean the inner life of individuals but internal dynamics of historical life, especially its social processes. Tillich insists that one's 'true being' is only realizable 'in a community of persons'. He writes directly, 'The moral imperative is the command to become what one potentially is, a *person*, within a community of persons' (19). Tillich's terms here about 'essence' and 'true being' can strike twenty-first-century academic ears as an 'essentialism' that ignores the constructive, shaping work of social forces. Not only was Tillich directly critical himself of such essentialism in his early cultural analyses, his later work, as we see here on the person's experience of the moral imperative, consistently used essence language in conjunction with, and in dependence upon, communal forms and processes (*SD*, 9–10). He was no constructivist, but he certainly knew that social constructs mediated all experience.

The normative as *social*

Tillich's way of articulating the moral imperative as a normative experience of persons in community indicates the high regard he had for the social in all his ethics. Indeed, Tillich was highly mindful, and indeed well-known, for his thematizing the personal *angst* and existential crises of selves seeking courage for their despair, and for the moral conundrums faced by individuals. But these dynamics of the self are for Tillich never thinkable or actualized apart from world, or apart from the way selves become persons by participating in (as shapers of and being shaped by) the many social forms and cultural functions (*ST* I, 168–74). Even in the volume that displayed his genius regarding the existential plight of the self, *The Courage to Be*, Tillich stresses that the courage to be as oneself is integrally connected with a 'courage to be as a part' of some collective life. Indeed, the dynamics of collectivity are treated first by Tillich in that book (*CB*, 141, 86–112).

To stress that Tillich's sense of the normative is social is to set his ethics more within the approach discussed by Hegel as *Sittlichkeit* (theory of customs or mores) and less within a Kantian tradition of *Moralität* that emphasizes demand and duty.[18] There is demand and duty in Tillich (and it receives its due from Hegel also) but, again, within the unfolding of social being. Using words from religious ethicist Jeffrey Stout, we can say of Tillich as Stout said of Hegel the norms 'emerge out of the mutually recognitive activities through which a people comes to share a culture'.[19] The choice of words here is especially apt for treating Tillich, since Tillich's theorization of social life is developed as a 'theory of culture' (*ST* III, 66). For Tillich, the normative is social: the 'meaning-fulfilling existential relationships of the individual to things and to reality are always *socially conditioned* relationships within which the *socially formed and socially determined* personality acts' (*SS*, 188).

To understand better how the normative occurs in society, we need to return to those two important broad areas, 'law' and 'community'. What are law and community for Tillich? It is important to respond briefly to this question, because it helps give context to Tillich's life-long ethical emphases on justice and love.

Law (*Recht*) is that broad area of human socio-cultural life in which ultimate concern is expressed through the formed life that human existence requires. Human existence also requires vitality and dynamism, but that could only come to fruition for Tillich in tensive balance with form. As Tillich analyst O'Keefe stresses, 'Law has as its aim the positing of rational and enforceable structures in social relations. Every positing of law is the positing of a formal structure that has the power to compel.'[20]

The key concept of concern to Tillich here, with respect to law, and which carries a socio-cultural group's concern to nurture the legal function, is 'justice'. Justice is the key concept here that names the demanding and ideal experience of law in social life wherein one member must acknowledge the other 'as being a free personality' ('The Philosophy of Religion' in *WR*, 68; *MB*, 46). Justice is a way of relating wherein all members in a social group lay claim to their own and others' rights to be free and to become a person – to become not just entities in a system but persons with freedom in community. Justice has, as he stresses in *The Socialist Decision* (1933), a special character as 'demand', and thus, because as demand it presses beyond every social situation, justice can be enshrined in his *Systematic Theology* as 'the aim of all cultural actions which are directed toward the transformation of society' (*ST* III, 67). We might say, following a suggestive expression of Terence O'Keefe's, that justice is what is nurtured when the Unconditional 'radiates' into law, into the legal functions of a people's cultural experience, thus bringing a form to the dynamic struggle to create social systems that foster a comprehensive mutual respect between persons as persons. Ethics, again, will be the cognitive discipline that traces and clarifies how orientation to ultimate concern in social life (ethos) creates legal forms marked by such justice.

Social life in which the normative is experienced, however, is not only structured by the form-giving area of 'law' under the demands of justice. It is also structured by the unity-making area of 'community' (*Gemeinschaft*). For Tillich, 'community' here refers to society's achievement of an organic unity (as contrasted with technical and mechanical relations based on atomized individuals in a collective), modes of communal living marked more by moral, co-operative and joint bonding than by depersonalized interaction.[21] Regarding community, the normative concept that is analogous to law's concept of justice is love. Love is an import-conveying and uniting power for society's interest in community. In comparison, although justice is essential, love remains primary; justice is a 'secondary and derived principle', love the 'creative and basic principle' (*MB*, 94). Justice can become 'creative justice' but only through its relation to unity-making love. 'Creative justice is the form of reuniting love' (*LPJ*, 71).

Becoming a participant in this kind of social life is, in Tillich's view, what it means for a person to become good or virtuous, or for a group to be identifiable as good. Tillich has many more distinctions and categories for tracing how individuals might navigate participation in social life, and many more of them that apply to how groups generate distortions as well as opportunities to manifest the good (*ST* III, 245–82). Moreover, Tillich emphasizes that the good and the virtuous never appear except fragmentarily, and even then, only with a host of accompanying 'ambiguities', tensions and double-binds with which theorists of culture and ethicists must wrestle ('The Divine Life and the Ambiguity of Life' in *ST* III, 162–282).

The normative as *dynamically principled*

The fourth and fifth features characterizing Tillich's view of normativity in ethics flow from the way Tillich has set up the normative as social. In this section, I suggest that justice and love are principles, effective as powers coursing through social being, and that the normative as social is, in significant part, an experience of being 'dynamically principled' by justice and love, by their character as moving forces (*LPJ*, 71; *MB*, 94).[22] The term 'principle' carries a double meaning that enables better understandings of justice and love in Tillich's ethical thought. One meaning takes 'principle' as a rule of thought, a governing idea, a mandate. This is the meaning I have presumed when articulating justice and love thus far as key 'normative concepts' relating to law and community, respectively. The second meaning, though, is what I wish to highlight here, one that takes 'principle' as the source or power of something. In English, for example, it is often said that a certain vehicle works '*on the principle of* internal combustion', meaning that the vehicle moves according to a certain dynamic power, a mixing of burning fuel with air so that the hot gases produced do the work of driving a piston. Principle, here, concerns a complexly operating power that causes movement.

Justice and love are principles in an analogous way. Justice and love are dynamic principles that move social groups and individual agents in society towards a way of being that is ethical, i.e. towards a way of being that is formed so that persons mutually acknowledge one another as persons (justice) and towards experiencing a complex social unity strengthened by a sense of shared ultimate import or meaning (love). To say that the normative for Tillich is 'dynamically principled' is to say that to experience a norm (always social, recall) is to have as one's principle of motion the dynamism of justice's power to form being, and also the dynamism of love's power to unite being. We might recall here, again, Tillich's claim set in this chapter's epigraph: 'Justice is not an abstract ideal standing over existence; it is the fulfillment of primal being' (*SD*, 140).

Justice and love are names for moral principles, then, not primarily in the sense of precepts that moral agents and communities should aspire to and seek to implement, but more in the sense of currents, rivers, powerful forces of being that carry one along towards the good. The normative has a riverine quality, i.e. the social process of persons mutually recognizing one another as persons (justice) and the social uniting of these persons around ultimate meaningfulness (love) carry moral agents and groups towards realization of the norms. For Tillich, this is no mere capitulation to, or being swept away by, just any currents of the times. There is critical thinking, the persistence of prophetic critique, hard struggle for justice and labours of love, but these are rooted in the flow of being's dynamism, its principles.

Another way to see justice and love as principles is to say that they are for Tillich modes of the power of being. They are the forming power and uniting power of being, respectively. In *Love, Power and Justice* the very middle term of his title suggests that the other two terms are ways of expressing that power. Power is not the same kind of riverine, normative principle that love and justice are; it is more the vital strength of all being that then forms social life as justice and unites it as love. One of Tillich's great contributions to ethics is the attention he gives to power, not only in his later work, but dating also from his earlier writings where 'power' (*Kraft*) is related to all being as a form of 'might' (*Macht*), but then differentiated from might as 'might on the level of social existence' ('The Problem of Power: Attempt at a Philosophical Interpretation' in *IH*, 182–3). Might is a vital energy of being, in tension with non-being, pervading all of life; on the level of society, though, it is 'power' that flows, as we have seen, with the forming power of justice and the uniting power of love.

The normative as *sapiential*

This final feature of Tillich's ethics as normative can be presented also in summary of this entire chapter on his ethics. This is because all his ethical thought is a wisdom, a process of discernment that must take in the entire matrix of being and culture to evaluate actions.

In a lecture given on 'Ethical Principles of Moral Action' Tillich himself lists wisdom as a third 'consideration', after the two principles of justice and love. He even refers to this consideration as a 'norm' alongside justice and love.[23] The lecture plays on two notions of wisdom. There are, first, principles of wisdom, such as those carried in collections of religious commands, e.g. the Ten Commandments. These are important, Tillich argues, and they are ignored or opposed at great risk. They represent, as other lists of commands also might, the accumulated wisdom of humankind. There is also a risk, however, if one 'slavishly follows the Commandments'. At times, counselled Tillich, going against them must be risked, as situations demand various practices of justice and love. There is no way to avoid risk in moral decisions, whether the risk is going against commandments or being obedient to them.

This, however, opens up the second meaning of wisdom that his understanding of the normative entails. If there is risk in all moral decision-making, as he stresses in numerous places throughout his work,[24] there is a deeper process of discernment that weighs multiple risks, and in light of the various situations and their complexities. There is a 'wisdom in us', Tillich writes, one that precedes all law, and out of which the various lists of commandments and principles come.[25] Tillich thus cites the Hebrew scriptures' representation of Wisdom, often personified and given a place beside God, assisting the creator and then settling into the hearts of people in everyday life. The wisdom that is present in us for discerning the normative in social life is, from Tillich's religious perspective, 'a medium of the creation of the world'.[26]

Wisdom also names a much broader process of discernment that catches up almost all of Tillich's thought. Paul Tillich's ethics as a 'science of ethos' is a cognitive discipline that traces how human orientation to the Unconditional radiates normative power throughout the many realms of culture, especially law and community. This science of ethos requires several key interpretive acts, as we have seen throughout this chapter. Firstly, interpreting the state of the political situation is crucial. The politics of state power, on domestic and international scenes, and extending throughout the relations of the body politic into the most personal modes of anguish and alienation, is the context for Tillich's move to ontology. Then, secondly, there is the interpretive act of undertaking ontology, discerning in the situation the presupposed structures of being that enable assessment of being and action, discerning also the ways ultimate concern can be traced through many cultural conditions. This of course entails interpretations of those cultural realms, especially in the areas of law and community, through which the principles of justice and love flow when legal and communal life are oriented towards the Unconditional. Theologians and ethicists of different sorts will bring their many diverse interests into relation with these two major discerning interpretations, and thus a host of other interpretive strategies will develop and be applied to many subjects.

It is often noted about Tillich's ethics that it is difficult to find amid his ethical interpretation the finer-grained analyses of wisdom that we often need for grappling with the moral challenges of poverty, sexuality, technology, racism, environmental destruction and so on. This is largely lacking in Tillich, especially if we limit ourselves to reading the later writings, *Love, Power and Justice, Morality and Beyond* and the *Systematic Theology*. Indeed, those are the more important, because they give the distinctive patterns of Tillich's ethical thinking. Nevertheless, it may be part of the future challenge in the study of Tillich's ethics to trace those patterns at work across the many short articles of his collected works, where he treats such issues as totalitarianism, immigration, economic orders, democracy, war and peace, psychological counselling, higher education, social work, the nuclear threat and Zionism, among others.[27]

Tillich's ethics, then, is a complex and comprehensive effort in philosophical and cultural analysis. This makes ethics an intellectual process difficult to summarize and focus, and from one perspective this may seem another weakness in Tillich's ethical approach. On balance, though, Tillich's ethical approach provides an intellectual context, enabling diverse strands of thought and culture to be brought into the study of ethics and moral philosophy that are often left outside them. Tillich's ethics offers to contemporary ethicists the challenge of keeping the scope of ethical and moral concern open to disciplined scrutiny throughout the many categories of thought and realms of culture.

We may conclude by recalling this chapter's opening epigraphs about justice. If justice is a fulfilment of 'primal being' having to do with origins, as Tillich notes, justice will have to be analysed against the backdrop of a multidimensional, and at times sweeping, vista of being. And if King is right, that justice is that towards which bends a whole 'arc of the universe', we should not expect ethical reflection on the concern with justice, or on other major moral concerns, to take us anywhere but to the horizons of that universe's being and thought. Whatever be the failures and successes of Tillich's own discernments, he keeps ethics open, amid ever new political and existential trauma, towards these broadening and deepening horizons of being.

Notes

For critical commentary on earlier drafts of this chapter, I express appreciation to W. Anne Joh, Peter J. Paris and Rachel S. Baard.

1 King, Jr (1968).
2 Cali (1996), 92.
3 Ibid., 92–3.
4 'Culture' in Tillich is understood as the creative function of human life, working in many spheres and areas, and fraught with a host of ambiguities. See *ST* III, 57–84.
5 Levinas (1996).
6 Hardt and Negri (2000), 354–5 and (2004), 221, 348–9.
7 See Gatens on Spinoza's ontology and 'embodied difference', in Gatens (1998), 27–8.
8 Dussel (1998), 300.
9 Coetzee (2003).
10 Badiou (2005), 9–10. On the political context of Badiou's thought, see Barker (2002), 13–40.
11 Badiou (2001).
12 Badiou (2005), 10.
13 Ibid., xiii.
14 'Ethics' and 'moral' in *OED*, 490 and 925 respectively.
15 It is worth noting that several of these essays reach back to the 1940s.
16 'Law' and 'community' are renderings of the German *Recht* and *Gemeinschaft*. See O'Keefe (1987), 63–4.
17 Jantzen (1999), 271. See now, also, Hardt and Negri (2000).
18 On *Sittlichkeit* and *Moralität*, see Taylor (1975), 376–7.

19 Stout (2004), 273.

20 O'Keefe (1987), 99.

21 Tillich is not here taking firmly the side of *Gemeinschaft* over against *Gesellschaft*, as in Tönnies (1887), or the side of 'organic solidarity' versus 'mechanical solidarity', as Émile Durkheim put it soon afterward (1893) in Durkheim (1960). Even though he used the notion of *Gemeinschaft*, he did so not to set up a binary between the organic and the mechanical, but to accent the overall importance of unity, even in a highly technologized, 'mechanical' *Gesellschaft*.

22 See also 'Appendix: Ethical Principles of Moral Action' in Carey (1987), 205–17.

23 Ibid., 211–12.

24 For another example, see *ST* III, 47.

25 Carey (1987), 216.

26 Ibid.

27 On these themes, see, for example, the following essays: 'The Totalitarian State and the Claims of the Church' (1934), *GW* X, 121–45; 'Mind and Migration' (1937), *GW* XIII, 191–200; 'The Meaning of Anti-Semitism' (1938), *GW* XIII, 216–20; 'The European War and the Christian Churches' (1939), *GW* XIII, 269–74; 'The Philosophy of Social Work' (1962), *GW* XIII, 221–6; 'The Hydrogen-Cobalt Bomb' (1954), *GW* XIII, 454; 'Conformity' (1957), *GW* XIII, 459–65; 'My Changing Thoughts on Zionism' (1959), *GW* XIII, 403–8; and outside the *GW*, 'Has Higher Education an Obligation to Work for Democracy?' in *Radical Religion* 5:1 (1940), 12–15; 'The Church and the Economic Order' in *Universal Christian Council for Life and Work* (Geneva: Geneva Research Department, 1937); 'Approaches to World Peace' in Bryson (1944), 684–5, 816–17; and 'Nuclear Morality' in *Partisan Review* 29:2 (1962), 311–12. Numerous treatments on particular moral crises abound also in *SSTS*.

Further reading

Bulman, Raymond F. (1981). *A Blueprint for Humanity: Paul Tillich's Theology of Culture*. Lewisburg, Pa.: Bucknell University Press.

Carey, John J., ed. (1987). *Being and Doing: Paul Tillich as Ethicist*. Macon, Ga.: Mercer University Press.

Despland, M., J.-C. Petit and J. Richard, eds. (1987). *Religion et Culture*. Québec: Presses de l'Université Laval/Éditions du Cerf.

Klemm, David E. (2004). 'Introduction: Theology of Culture as Theological Humanism'. *Literature and Theology* 18:3, 239–50.

Schweiker, William (2005). *Theological Ethics and Global Dynamics: In the Time of Many Worlds*. Oxford: Blackwell.

13 On the boundary of utopia and politics

RONALD H. STONE

INTRODUCTION

Paul Tillich was one of the most significant political theologians of the twentieth century. Nonetheless, although he by no means abandoned politics after his emigration in 1933, he was clearly more comfortable with his activity in German politics than with his American political role. His politics, like his thought in general, was characterized by boldness and risk-taking. This boldness was partially due to the fact that he was more a person of theory than one of action, although his activity in politics was more considerable and sustained than most of his philosophical and theological contemporaries'. Tillich was not active in local politics, but he addressed politics at its highest levels in both countries.

In 1951 he returned to Germany to present four lectures at the *Deutsche Hochschule für Politik* in Berlin; characteristically, he chose to lecture on the topic of utopia (*PolE*, 123–80). This chapter will take the theme of these lectures – the meaning of utopia – as a helpful starting-place for an interpretation of Tillich's politics. Having set out the foundations of his political theory in terms of its simultaneous embrace and critique of the concept of utopia, this chapter will trace the development in Tillich's political commitment, from his youthful embrace of religious socialism following the First World War, his critical stance against National Socialism, his contributions to German politics from exile to his critical engagements with American political life in the 1950s and 1960s, to his mature reflections on the possibility of peace and the right to hope.

UTOPIA

Politics for Tillich is never merely *Realpolitik*: it must always be referred to the depth or essence of humanity. This human essence provides the first of Tillich's meanings of utopia. Humanity is in part utopian because it is essential to human nature to be so. This is one of the great differences between Tillich and his mentor in American politics, Reinhold Niebuhr; although they never spoke about it in their infrequent public dialogues, it remained one of their disagreements. Niebuhr polemicized against the utopias of Germany's Third Reich, against the Russian-Marxist utopia of the Soviet Union and against utopia in general. Tillich, by contrast, would express the weaknesses of utopia, but also its strengths. Tillich's life-long struggle to unite politics and utopia failed, as any such struggle must fail, but from this struggle came political courage and a fascinating political theory.

Perhaps Tillich's most important assertion about utopia is that it is characteristic of humanity's being. It is neither a fantastic delusion nor a temporary phenomenon, but expresses the situation of humanity as finite freedom. Freedom means the possibility to act as a whole, centred person; finitude means that in all actions the threat of non-being is discovered. Political existence is necessarily a threatened existence, and the systems that deny this threat (as both churches and political movements are tempted to with promises of eternity or non-fallibility) are shown by history to be subject to non-being. Political existence, like human existence, is a combination of anxiety and courage. Utopia expresses the ideal possibilities of human existence, but it is an ideal. Usually it has both a backward look to an imagined utopia, which really reflects the essence of humanity, and a forward look to the expression of a paradise or a new reality in the future. Most utopias show this triadic movement: the corrupt present, the essentially good past and the promise of a new, better future.

Tillich emphasizes that the original meaning of utopia is 'no place' and that the word is a symbol without location in either time or space. Hence, the first principle of utopia is that it is the *negation of the negative*; the elimination of the negative allows the symbol to express the ideal and to expose the negatives of the society in which it is articulated. In this sense, utopia functions primarily as social criticism. Tillich, however, extends the function of utopia beyond the social, indicating for example that the biblical social utopias involved not only the removal of social evils but the reconciliation of the human with nature, of men with women, of nature with nature. Within Western society, the most important forms of utopia express either an egalitarian-political agenda or an organic-political agenda. Both entail dangers, however: the first is in danger of anarchism and the second of reaction and conservatism. Tillich therefore prioritizes forms of utopia that hold together individual and social renewal and that contain elements of both historical and trans-historical thinking. For Tillich, the Kingdom of God is the traditional Christian utopia, a symbol that holds these different aspects together.

Tillich's final lecture deals with 'Critique and Justification of Utopia'. On the positive side, utopia expresses the truth of the human situation. It is fruitful in that it anticipates and encourages human fulfilment; it has the power to change reality. However, on the negative side of utopia, the symbol does not show how estranged humanity can overcome estranged humanity. Niebuhr, in criticizing Marx's failed utopia, said that it was as if Marx pulled the new society out of estrangement like a magician pulling a rabbit out of a hat. Utopia holds up possibilities, but it sometimes confuses possibilities with impossibilities. Equally, utopia may be impotent and lead to disillusionment. Tillich noted in 1951 how the affirmation of utopian goals without the power to change society could lead to terrorism and other demonic forces as an expression of the disillusioned and powerless.

In his political thought Tillich looked for a way to transcend the negativity of utopia. After the First World War he saw revolutionary socialism as the movement of utopia. However, he found this political optimism opposed by the transcendental critical utopianism of Lutheranism, to which he himself remained committed. In Berlin in the 1920s Tillich and other young religious and theological thinkers formed a discussion group, known as the Kairos Circle, concerned with overcoming the conflict between socialism and the church, and also with the problem of timing and utopian actions. They found the solution in the concept of *kairos*. *Kairos* expresses the idea of fulfilment at a particular time while still recognizing the problems of finitude and estrangement. Their hope was to affirm utopia, but without its illusions: *kairos* as a concrete utopia. By the time of his 1951 lectures – in the aftermath of another global conflict – Tillich had come to think that the right moment for action for the realization of something of the Kingdom of God was no longer close at hand but rather far in the future. His task was to express utopia in its truth, but to guard against its untruth. He concluded by saying, 'Or, as I could perhaps say in summation of all four lectures on utopia: *It is the spirit of utopia that conquers utopia*' (*PolE*, 180).

RELIGIOUS SOCIALISM

Tillich was in the army in Berlin in 1918 when the service fell apart and the revolution against the Emperor succeeded. He soon accepted a position as an urban pastor and lectured at the University of Berlin, among other things on 'The Church and the Social Question'. His political stance is perhaps best described as a rather uncritical utopianism. By the time he left Berlin in 1924, however, the ambiguities of the revolutionary success were all too apparent, and he had partially worked out his theological solution to utopia, which he continued to develop up until the final volume of his *Systematic Theology* (1963).

Two documents from this period reflect his revolutionary optimism. The first is the announcement of the New Church Alliance, which was published in December 1918 a few days after Emperor Wilhelm abdicated. The document was signed by Tillich and five others. The young revolutionaries pledged that the new church would support socialism and the new republic rather than the old order. Capitalist egoism was rejected, to be replaced by the recognition of the worth of each person. The new church would be aligned with the international peace movement rather than with nationalist forces. The new church would replace the old hierarchical form of the church, with a new parliamentary system. Women would have the right to vote in the church, and the announcement, signed by two women, was addressed to all Evangelical men and women in Germany. The new church was to be committed to the renewal of religious motifs in the general culture. In the event, the New Church Alliance soon merged with the religious socialists, and Tillich did not remain active with the organization for long. Considered from the perspective of his later interpretation of utopia, this was a utopian statement announcing a future but, rather than on possibilities, it was based on impossibilities in the German ecclesiastical context at that time.

His second utopian statement from this period was the result of Tillich's self-justification in the face of ecclesiastical disapproval of his radical political stance. In 1919 Tillich and his friend Richard Wegener spoke at an Independent Socialist Democratic Party rally. They were denounced by the President of the Consistory of Brandenburg, D. Steinhauser, and summoned to explain themselves. Tillich and Wegener entitled their statement to the consistory 'Socialism as a Question of the Church'. They emphasized the transcendence of God and of religious experience as a transcending of particular social orders. Nonetheless, they claimed that as Christianity desires to shape life in the social situation it must make choices or, as they put it, love has consequences. The Gospel is not really reconcilable with the egoism of capitalism and fits better with the social sharing of socialism. Capitalism had drifted towards militarism, which is antithetical to Christianity, and the church would be well advised to move into the new order of socialism rather than identify itself with the old feudalistic, capitalistic order. They argued that there is no essential conflict between socialism and the church, despite the atheism of some socialist leaders; instead, the social ethic of socialism is more in line with the church's agenda, as it expresses the perspective of the working class. Steinhauser reacted negatively to their report, reminding them of the dangers of amalgamating politics and religion, and ordered them not to speak at any more rallies. In the end, this prohibition was unnecessary, as in the years that followed both young pastors drifted away from active church life – Wegener going into government and Tillich into university life. In light of Tillich's mature theory, this statement participated in the negativity of utopia by committing oneself to an impossible vision rather than to a possible one.

Tillich's participation in the Kairos Circle deepened his theoretical understanding of politics and economics, as the group expanded to include political theorists and economists, as well as theologians and philosophers. Ernst Troeltsch attended once, but the group was too radical for him; nonetheless, later, as Minister of Education, it was he who invited Richard Wegener to join him in government. Although the group discussed the roots of religious socialism, its primary focus was on Marxist theory. One of the dividing issues among Marxists was whether or not activism could produce the revolution or whether the forces of history unaided would produce the revolution in the right time. Once again, Tillich's proposed solution was the concept of *kairos*: a realistic vision could only be realized through action when the forces of history were correctly aligned. The decision for the *kairos* is both a personal, existentialist decision and a decision based on an analysis of timing and the movement of significant historical forces. This solution remained a central part of his systematic thinking and theology until the end of his life.

THE SOCIALIST DECISION

In the period between the world wars Tillich continued to write on *kairos*, power, history and religious socialism. By the 1930s, however, as the political struggles became more ominous, he had rejected his earlier Berlin work as too utopian. After going into exile, he explicitly rejected utopianism in his 1936 book, *The Interpretation of History*. Although translated by none other than Niebuhr himself, his hard labour in bringing the volume's essays (most of them written between the 1920s and early 1930s) into English has not been regarded as successful, and the book failed to have the impact it deserved. In it Tillich explicitly rejects all forms of utopia as untenable within his Lutheran theology, but at the same time affirms that utopianism is the central problem of socialism. Once again he turns to the concept of *kairos* to express his conviction that at a particular time the demands of judgement and promise could be unusually present. The struggle for a new social order is not to be identified with the Kingdom of God, which is transcendent. Nonetheless, the Kingdom of God retains a political significance as judgement and norm for a new society. Tillich recognized that religious socialism could not be realized in Germany, but in 1936 he still felt it was a vision or a utopia that had possibilities elsewhere.

However, Tillich's writings about the failure of German religious socialism in the early 1930s were overshadowed by the emergence of another utopian vision in Germany. Tillich was unequivocal in his rejection of Nazism. His 1932 *Ten Theses* were one of the most powerful critiques of National Socialism published at the time:[1]

> Protestantism must prove its prophetic-Christian character by setting the Christianity of the cross against the paganism of the swastika. Protestantism must testify that the cross has broken and judged the "holiness" of nation, race, blood and power.[2]

In 1933 he published *The Socialist Decision*, in which he tackled once again the problem of utopianism through an analysis of the nature of humanity. He showed how the victory of Nazi barbarianism would bring chaos and war. Although the book was more realistic than the 1919 essays, it still had an element of utopianism, and it was not possible to deliver on its vision. Here he was a philosopher using the concepts of utopia to attack a false utopianism of the Third Reich. The Third Reich used music, poetry, power tactics, the naïveté of others, Teutonic myths, false history, false science and human resentment to attack the Weimar Republic's failures with a vision of a mythical past and a promise of a utopia in the future. Tillich diagnosed the problem, but he could not prevent it.

This critical analysis, which was condemned by Hitler's allies, along with his Founder's Day speech to the University of Frankfurt in which he celebrated the Jewish contribution to German culture, and his public condemnation of anti-Semitic acts at the University, led to his dismissal from the University by the Nazi government. In 1933 he witnessed socialist writings being publicly burnt in Frankfurt, and, fearful for his safety, he accepted Reinhold Niebuhr and Horace Friess' invitation to Union Seminary and Columbia University in New York City.

TO MY GERMAN FRIENDS

His emigration, however, did not bring Tillich's involvement in German politics to an end. During the Second World War, in addition to caring for and resettling refugees, as founder and chairman of the 'Self-help for German Émigrés' organization, Tillich's major work was the preparation of over a hundred radio broadcasts in German, which were transmitted into occupied Europe to give Europeans hope and to call for resistance to Nazism (*ATR*). Two other activities reflected his interpretation of *kairos* and utopia in the character of history. The first was his participation, with John Foster Dulles, Reinhold Niebuhr and others, in the Federal Council of Churches Commission for a Just and Durable Peace. As part of the process he helped encourage American churches to mobilize to promote the development of the United Nations. This commission's remarkable work helped bring the United States out of its post-First World War isolationism. Interestingly, Tillich's three lectures to the group encouraged them to work without self-righteousness or the prideful assumption that they could establish either a just or a durable peace. Secondly, and in close parallel to his earlier efforts as the positive expression of utopia, was his role in chairing the Council for a Democratic Germany. This attempt was not welcomed by the United States government, and after the State Department pressured Thomas Mann not to accept the presidency Tillich assumed the chair and guided the organization for its short life. It published a bulletin, held meetings and laid plans for post-war Germany.

The Council, composed of refugee Germans, counted socialists, communists and anti-communists among its members. It hoped to establish a democratic Germany that would restore the German people to health while punishing those guilty of war crimes or of leading the Nazi movement. However, when it became clear that the group's fear that the Allied nations would divide Germany among themselves was realized, the Council broke up. The emerging tendencies of the Cold War divided the Council too much for its members to continue to co-operate. This failure dispirited Tillich regarding actual political practice and may even indicate something about his vision of utopia: the members did not have a common view of the human essence or how they would express this in a post-war Germany, and the arrival of new world-historical forces split the group. It is not only the human essence that is contained in a vision of utopia, but many assumptions about the meaning of that essence and which political structures would promote that humanity's fulfilment.

Tillich's speeches for broadcast into Europe were dropped by the United States government in 1944; he was not permitted to return to Germany until 1948, and he had no official role in the denazification or re-education process. His socialism was too much for the Washington DC administrations, and ironically this most democratic of German philosophers was continuously investigated by the Federal Bureau of Investigation (FBI). It could be said the utopian elements of religious socialism in his mind and writings were too much for the real politics of the American Republic at this time.

'I AM AN AMERICAN!'

Although a participant in Niebuhr's Fellowship of Socialist Christians (a group that, while hopeful for a socialist future, rejected utopianism in favour of achieving a balance of power and justice within the ambiguituies of history), after 1945 Tillich did not see a *kairos* for the United States. By this time he had experienced the shattering of most of his early political aspirations. He had witnessed at first hand the calamity of the First World War and had buried the dead on the fields of Verdun. He had seen the German revolution's hopes turned into a demonic upsurge of mad German nationalism. Theological allies had turned into supporters of Hitler, and Jewish friends had committed suicide, fled Germany or been killed. His family and closest friends had suffered the hell of Allied urban terror bombardment. German and American science and Allied power had terminated the war with surprise nuclear bombings, incinerating cities that should not have been targets. As a result, Tillich often found himself in a negative role, attacking the policies of his adopted country.

Along with Niebuhr and other theologians, he condemned the bombing of the cities in Japan as he had previously condemned the bombing of German cities. Tillich criticized the use of nuclear weapons: he could reluctantly accept them as a deterrent, but in spite of sharp criticism he refused to agree to sanction the defence of Berlin with atomic weapons. He did not regard Berlin as an adequate price for nuclear war. He criticized the United States' policy of reserving the right to a first use of nuclear weapons. His major statement on nuclear weapons was quite remarkable in calling for creative resistance to nuclear weapons defence and American policy, as the following long extract shows:

> The increasing and apparently unlimited power of the means of
> self-destruction in human hands puts us before the question of the
> ultimate meaning of this development . . . everyone who is aware

of the possibility of mankind's self-destruction must resist this possibility to the utmost. For life and history have an eternal dimension and are worthy to be defended against suicidal instincts, which are as real socially as individually . . . the resistance against the suicidal instincts of the human race must be one on all levels, on the political level through negotiations between those who in a tragic involvement force each other into the production of ever stronger means of self-destruction; on the normal level through a reduction of propaganda and an increase in obedience to truth about oneself and the potential enemy; on the religious level through a sacred serenity and superiority over the preliminary concerns of life, and a new experience and a new expression of the ultimate concern which transcends as well as determines historical existence . . . the resistance against the self-destructive consequences of technical control of nature must be done in acts which unite the religious, moral, and political concern, and which are performed in imaginative wisdom and courage.

(*TP*, 158–9)

The Committee for a Sane Nuclear Policy often lobbied Tillich to endorse its positions. Although he could not sign up to many of their positions, despite the fact that his secretary at Harvard lobbied him to do so, he did, in contrast to Reinhold Niebuhr, sign one in 1957, along with Eleanor Roosevelt and John C. Bennett, calling for arms control and the abolition of nuclear testing.

POLITICAL EXPECTATIONS

During the presidency of Dwight D. Eisenhower (1953–60) Tillich was less politically active than before as he pushed to finish his *Systematic Theology*, which he regarded as his greatest gift to his adopted country. Nonetheless, he endorsed the candidacy of John F. Kennedy and was present at his inauguration. Indeed, Kennedy's election reawakened his interest in what could be accomplished politically in the United States. The news of Kennedy's assassination in November 1963 reached him while he was in Europe and saddened him deeply. In 1964 in the *Washington Post* he published his strongest public statement against any particular political candidate in the United States as he rejected Barry Goldwater, railing against the negativities of his campaign:

One should hesitate to reject a political candidate in the name of religion. For the political concern is preliminary and temporal, while religion is concerned with the ultimate and eternal meaning of life. Since, however, the eternal expresses itself in the temporal, e.g. in political ideas and since such expression can be a distortion, religion sometimes must take a political side. Utterances of the Republican candidate and even more of forces supporting him show traits of such distortion: a disregard for economic and racial justice, an easy use of the warthreat, a production of false accusations and the suppression of free speech through them, the nourishing of hate towards foreign nations and the abuse of religion for all this. Therefore I feel as a theologian, justified in calling for the defeat of the Republican ticket for the presidency.[3]

In these last years the concept of the Kingdom of God moved into the centre of Tillich's political thinking: not so much as the welcoming of a new era, but rather as something present wherever faith joined in the victory over evil forces. For Tillich, the Kingdom of God is a present reality and particularly so in the struggle against non-being. In spite of this renewed engagement, however, one of the more significant political acts resulting from Tillich's conceptual thinking was not of his own doing. In 1963 the Supreme Court quoted from Tillich's *Systematic Theology* when it ruled in favour of David Andrew Seger's petition for conscientious-objector status on the basis of his philosophy, even though he was not a conventional theist. Tillich's writing that an affirmation of meaning is a calling upon the 'God beyond God' even by those who did not use conventional names for belief in God proved determinative for the Court. So the non-pacifist Tillich's discussion of God became the basis for opening conscientious-objector status to pacifists upon broadly based philosophical reasoning, as well as the usual Christian belief in God! He also agreed to testify in a case brought by the American Civil Liberties Union to support broadly based but non-theistic pacifism. At the same time, his vision of socialism did not die: he had rejoined and paid dues to the Socialist Democratic Party of Germany under the leadership of Willy Brandt following the war and he kept urging the Fellowship of Socialist Christians to continue their work, even as the group retreated from its socialist convictions in the face of the lack of interest in the United States in socialism.

LAST HOPES

Tillich remained committed to the possibilities of hope despite his critique of religious utopianism, as can be seen in two writings from the final year of his life. Although the 'Great Society' of Lyndon Johnson did provide some help for the social security of the poor, Tillich's expressions of social hope were more muted in the post-Kennedy years. He affirmed the great movements towards racial justice and decolonization, and he endorsed particular projects for black empowerment. However, he remained stronger as an oppositional and theoretical thinker than as a social planner.

He spoke of Pope John XXIII's encyclical *Pacem in Terris* as an important moment in the history of ideas (*TP*, 174–81). He affirmed the document's foundation in justice as a common ground for Catholics, Protestants, Jews and humanists, but he then asked why it addressed itself only to Western culture: peace presupposes a wider audience. Tillich noted that the encyclical's call for resistance to the violation of human rights would in some situations call for armed resistance and raised the ambiguities of unavoidable injustice through the use of force. He claimed that more discussion of the ambiguities of the use of power was needed; authority requires power, and power implies the use of coercive force. Finally, he cautions that personal norms require translation before being applied to social groups. He concludes that there are realistic limits to hopes for 'peace on earth'.

The ambiguities regarding the hopes for peace are rooted in the differing expectations for personal and group life held by various groups and persons. For Tillich, the conflict between goodness and the ambiguities of historical life was a permanent feature of human life. He argued that any peace conference needed to clarify the distance between realistic hopes for peace and false utopian hopes for total world peace. The Old Testament could be read as a book of hope for Israel, but even here one finds judgement, destruction and failure, as well as hope. What, then, were the realistic grounds for peace? In 1965 he proposed five such grounds: (1) the threat of nuclear destruction; (2) technical unity of humanity through space exploration; (3) cross-national fields of co-operation in food, medicine, population and protection of nature; (4) growing legal structures uniting humanity; and (5) communal *eros* building towards human world-wide consensus. On these grounds hope for partial victories over particular historical evils was possible, even if no final stage of historical peace was to be expected:

His sermon 'The Right to Hope' rejected the devaluation of hope
that regards it as utopian fantasy (*TP*, 182–90). Humanity requires
hope to overcome despair; both the Old and New Testaments
expressed hope against destruction and loss. Tillich presents the
Christian vision as one of a new heaven and a new earth and for

individual entry into this new reality. He notes that gradually with the failure of Jesus to return the church grew accustomed to what it had and surrendered its expectation, often turning instead toward hopes of individual immortality. However, expanding knowledge of biological reality and the seriousness of death in the 20th century undercut hopes for individual immortality. The failure of history in the same century made it appear that Christ had not vanquished the demonic forces of history. So how was real hope to be distinguished from illusory hope? Day-dreaming expectations of the goal, hoping for that which is unrealizable or not at all present, are dismissed. Hope requires, at the very least, seeing the seeds of hope for the future in the present. Hopes for a seed to become a tree or a pregnancy a person are real, but waiting is required.

Tillich then turned towards hopes for human history. Israel from the Old Testament to the present day was seen as a sign of hope, yet at the same time he affirmed that Israel contains arrogance and the will to power, and it needs the critique of justice as much as the United States. The world is 'a cemetery of broken hopes', and yet there are partial fulfilments. Democratic forms of life, social welfare, the struggle for the oneness of the human race all drive towards fulfilment with partial victories.

Realistic goals are not towards final perfection, but towards historical manifestations of the good and partial victories over particular historical evils. The Kingdom of God, for Tillich, at this point in his thought, comes in acts of truth, love and religious experience. As we experience the eternal in us now, so we have a right to hope for eternal life. He believed the deeper the participation in the divine life in history, the more assurance for participation in eternal life was given. He did not affirm a belief in a continuation of finite life into eternity, but the hope for return to 'the eternal from which it comes' and which is with all of creation, even with those whose lives have been futile or destructive.

Tillich maintained a hope for reunion with God and all of creation. Historical or political hopes were fulfilled in partial, finite victories and in the continuation of the struggle against the negative forces threatening humanity. His is a testimony of personal religious solace grounded in love, action and moments of religious experience. His political theory was critical and restless: his critique of the pretensions of National Socialism drove him out of Germany, and his critique of American oligarchic rule, nuclear defence policies, foreign policy towards Germany and militarism gained him the enmity of the FBI and regressive forces in the United States. His political participation, more on the level of political philosophy than practical politics, consistently maintained its critical edge. He continued to believe in his vision of a moderate, democratic religious socialism, even after the Second World War. The critical edge for him was correlated with his theological perception of humanity as finite freedom in an eternal world.

Notes

1   In Klotz (1932) and Mark K. Taylor (1987), 116–18. J. Stark's reaction was typical of the National Socialist intelligentsia: 'The book in question affords a valuable commentary on the intellectual level of numerous "evangelical" academic theologians. Never have I seen such an accumulation of ignorance, superficiality, presumption and malicious enmity to the German Freedom Movement.' See Stone (1980), 84–5.
2   M. C. Taylor (1987), 117.
3   Paul Tillich, 'American Leaders Speak', *Washington Post*, 22 October 1964.

Further reading

Bulman, Raymond F. (1981). *A Blueprint for Humanity: Paul Tillich's Theology of Culture*. Lewisburg, Pa.: Bucknell University Press.
Despland, M., J.-C. Petit and J. Richard, eds. (1987). *Religion et Culture*. Quebec: Presses de l'Université Laval/Éditions du Cerf.
Reimer, A. James (1988). *Paul Tillich and Emanuel Hirsch: A Study of Theology and Politics*. Lewiston, Idaho: The Edwin Mellen Press.
Schütte, H.-W. (2004). 'Subjektivität und System. Zum Briefwechsel Emanuel Hirsch (1888–1972) und Paul Tillich (1886–1965)' in *Theologie als Religionsphilosophie. Studien zu den problemgeschichtlichen und systematischen Voraussetzungen der Theologie Paul Tillichs*. Tillich-Studien, vol. IX, ed. Christian Danz, 3–22. Vienna: LIT Verlag.
Stenger, Mary Ann and Ronald H. Stone (2002). *Dialogues of Paul Tillich*. Macon, Ga.: Mercer University Press.
Tillich, Paul (1998). *Against the Third Reich*, ed. Ronald H. Stone and Matthew Lon Weaver. Louisville, Ky.: Westminster/John Knox Press.

Part III

Tillich in dialogue

14 Tillich in dialogue with natural science
JOHN F. HAUGHT

Paul Tillich's theological method of correlation, along with much of the actual content of his theology, is indicative of his immersion in the modern cultural 'situation' in which reason is shaped principally by natural science. Tillich's way of doing theology is hardly conceivable apart from his belonging to the age of science and its requirement that enlightened theologians give their discipline not only religious relevance but also intellectual stature. If it expects to be credible in the contemporary period of history, theology must be fully aware of science and the respect scientific understanding commands. Above all, however, it must avoid ever giving the impression of standing in a competitive relationship with science, nor should it approve or reject any set of scientific ideas for purely theological reasons. 'The distinction between the truth of faith and the truth of science leads to a warning, directed to the theologians, not to use recent scientific discoveries to confirm the truth of faith' (DF, 85).

CORRELATING THEOLOGY AND SCIENCE

Science and theology are independent ways of arriving at truth, and so one cannot logically contradict the other (DF, 80–2). Theology may oppose scientism or scientific naturalism, since these are expressions of ultimate concern that rival those of Christian theism (82–5). However, science as such is preoccupied with natural or proximate causes, whereas theology seeks to understand the notion of God as ultimate concern and ground of being. To speak of God as a cause, even a first cause, would be to demote the ground of all causes to being part of a continuum of things in nature. In effect, all attempts to locate God as the 'cause' of anything amounts to a religiously objectionable 'naturalizing' of that which infinitely transcends nature (ST I, 209).

However, even though science and theology cannot in principle conflict with each other, the shape of theology today is deeply influenced by science. Even Tillich's theological method, which involves the correlation of existential questions with revelatory answers, requires that one acknowledge that the situation of potential receivers of revelation in the contemporary period is one in which reason has an empirical quality that in previous ages it did not. As in the case of theologian Rudolf Bultmann, his contemporary, Tillich is persuaded that any convincing correlation of revelation with the existential situation of those whose world-view has been fashioned within a scientific culture requires a process of 'demythologization' (ST II, 29, 37, 102). This means, firstly, that the symbolic, mythic and metaphorical language of Christian faith must not be confused in any way with the kind of claims that science makes. And, secondly, if theology is to avoid evacuating the substance of the symbolic and mythic language of revelation, demythologization in an age of science must be able to expose persons to a dimension of depth that science itself cannot reach (152).

Tillich's self-conscious encounter with natural science and its method of enquiry is also reflected in the overall structure of his *Systematic Theology*, and especially the first part, 'Reason and Revelation' (ST I, 3–159). Here and elsewhere Tillich emphasizes that the way in which human reason encounters the truth of revelation is radically distinct from the way in which scientific reason deals with its own subject matter. For science, reality is objectifiable, but since God cannot be one object among others in the world, any theological understanding of the truth of revelation must be of a different kind altogether from that of science, though in no way contradictory to it. Encountering revelation entails our *being grasped* by it, not a grasping or objectifying of it (DF, 76). Faith is an ecstatic form of knowing in which reason humbly allows itself to be apprehended by God, that is, by the depth, ground and power of being. By no means does faith entail a mastering of its subject matter in the manner of scientific knowing, since that would amount to idolatry. But faith does not vitiate or destroy reason, including scientific reason. Rather, it opens reason to the infinite depth and ground that underlie nature and make it possible for scientific enquiry to occur at all.

According to Tillich, it is through revelatory *symbols* that we are grasped by the depth and ground of being. Through symbols derived from our experience of nature and human history the power of being addresses us sacramentally and invites human reason to surrender to the ground, power and depth of being that is inaccessible to science and rational control (ST I, 156).[1] A decisively revelatory symbol must be one that is completely transparent to the divine, and it must be one that refuses to allow itself to be mistaken for the infinite power of being that it makes manifest. That is, a fully revelatory symbol must be one that sacrifices itself so as to conquer the narrowness of idolatry. For Tillich, as a Christian, such transparency to God is presented to faith in the picture of Jesus as the Christ (147–50).

However, for faith to become transparent to the depth and ground of being it must be open to criticism. 'The criterion of every faith is the ultimacy of the ultimate it tries to express. The self-criticism of every faith is the insight into the relative validity of the concrete symbols in which it appears' (*DF*, 123). The 'restlessness of the heart' that humans experience indicates that the human person 'is driven toward faith by his awareness of the infinite to which he belongs, but which he does not own like a possession' (9). And the measure of the truth of such faith is not whether its content corresponds to scientific reason, but how transparent it renders the ground of being and how powerfully and decisively it allows the power of being to grasp the centre of our own being.

Even scientists, therefore, have faith, insofar as they allow themselves to be grasped by and surrender to truth. Not only is there no real conflict between faith and science, but science is impossible without a certain kind of faith. 'Faith is the most centered act of the human mind. It is not a movement of a special section or a special function of man's total being' (4). Faith is not belief in what appears incredible, nor is it a gratuitous positing of supernatural beings that dwell out of the sight of science. Rather, 'faith is the state of being ultimately concerned' (1). What distinguishes humans from other animals is that each of us has the capacity to be concerned about something of ultimate importance, something whose loss would divest our lives of meaning and rob us of the courage to be. Whether our ultimate concern is truly ultimate, and not a mere idol instead, can be determined only by observing how adequately it functions to give us courage in the face of fate, death, guilt and the threat of meaninglessness. Only an ultimate concern that does not frustrate our need for courage in the face of non-being can appropriately be called 'God' (*CB*, 155–78).

Therefore, because science and faith are related to truth in such distinct ways, it makes no sense to speak of a conflict between them. In fact, any sincere and honest scientist is also a person of faith to the extent that he or she is grasped by the 'power of being' implicitly experienced whenever truth becomes an ultimate concern (*DF*, 126–7). The rigorous and uncompromising pursuit of truth by way of scientific method is impossible apart from the state of being in the grasp of truth, a transcendental value that is inseparable from being-itself. Even though, logically speaking, science is not religion, every scientist sincerely concerned about truth is a religious person.

CONFLICT?

Why then does there often seem to be warfare between theology and science? From a Tillichian point of view, there can be no real conflict, but there can be three other disputes that are often mistaken for such a conflict. Firstly, there is the opposition by *naturalism* to every affirmation of divine transcendence (*ST* II, 5–10). Secondly, there is the resistance to scientific method or well-established scientific discoveries by what Tillich calls *supranaturalism* (*ST* I, 64–5, 115–17). And, thirdly, there is an ongoing conflict *between naturalism and supranaturalism* that presents itself publicly in the deceptive guise of irresolvable contradictions between science and religion. These are *not* conflicts between science and theology, since in principle such conflicts are impossible. However, since they are usually mistaken for such conflicts, I shall spend the remainder of this chapter elaborating on each set and then summarizing Tillich's prescription for healing it.

THE NATURALISTIC OPPOSITION TO THEOLOGY

Theology claims that the universe has an infinite depth and ground known as 'God'. Without our positing the reality of God, theology has always maintained, the universe's existence is unintelligible. Naturalism, on the other hand, is the belief that the natural world is self-contained and self-sufficient. It is its own ground and explanation. Thus, there is no need to look beyond the physical world for a distinct source of its being. The universe 'just is'.[2] Nature by itself, therefore, is the ultimate source of everything that occurs in the universe, including the emergence of life and mind. To most naturalists today, moreover, there is no need to look any deeper than science itself in order to account ultimately for everything. In his own time Tillich observed that the aura of religious reverence that had formerly accompanied pantheistic forms of naturalism was already lost, 'especially among philosophizing scientists who understand nature in terms of materialism and mechanism' (*ST* II, 6). This distaste for transcendence is expressed today in what has come to be called 'scientific naturalism'.[3] When scientific naturalists express their aversion to theology, therefore, it is not because they lack faith – in the sense of ultimate concern. It is because they believe that science itself is the only reliable way to truth (a belief known as 'scientism') and that nature is ultimately sufficient to fulfil all human needs and desires (scientific naturalism).

According to Tillich, however, sound theology must reject naturalism:

> The main argument against naturalism in whatever form is that it denies the infinite distance between the whole of finite things and their infinite ground, with the consequence that the term 'God' becomes interchangeable with the universe and is therefore semantically superfluous. This semantic situation reveals the failure of naturalism to understand a decisive element in the experience of the holy, namely, the distance between finite man, on the one hand, and the holy in its numerous manifestations on the other. For this, naturalism cannot account.
>
> (*ST* II, 7)

Tillich's analysis of naturalism is of utmost significance in any attempt to draw out the relevance of his thought for contemporary conversations about the relationship of science to theology. The many contemporary intellectuals who claim that natural science rules out or renders superfluous the existence of God are speaking not from the perspective of science as such, but from that of a naturalistic *faith* that confuses nature itself with the ground of being. Scientific naturalists today are no more devoid of faith than are their theistic opponents. The difference is that they fail to acknowledge nature's radical finitude. They do not realize that a finite natural world, no matter how large and resourceful it may be, is ultimately incapable of conquering the threat of non-being.

To be finite, according to Tillich, means to be subject to the threat of non-being, a threat experienced by conscious and free human beings in the form of existential anxiety (*CB*, 32–9). It is not just human beings, however, but the totality of finite being (which includes the whole of nature) that is subject to non-being, a fact that can be clarified simply by looking carefully at the categories science uses to understand the world: space, time, causality and substance. In the second part of his *Systematic Theology* ('Being and God') Tillich undertakes a brilliant analysis of the structure of finite being in which he exposes the threat of non-being implied in the very concepts that science and philosophy employ in their own understanding of nature. 'Finite being is a question mark' that points beyond itself towards the ground of being, and 'God' is the answer to the questions that arise from any careful analysis of finite being (*ST* I, 209). So beneath the scientific naturalist's protest against theology there lurks a failure to look candidly at the finitude of nature.

However, Tillich's proposed theological alternative to naturalism is not *supranaturalism*. Supranaturalism, in his definition, 'separates God as a being, the highest being, from all other beings, alongside and above which he has his existence' (*ST* II, 6). Picturing God as *supra* (above) nature turns the depth, ground and power of being idolatrously into something finite and in doing so makes it also subject to the threat of non-being. Even if God is understood as the highest being, this being itself is reduced in effect to existing as *a* (finite) substance located in terms of space, time and causality, categories of finite being. This 'god' cannot be the depth and ground of nature, but instead becomes part of nature. The god of supranaturalism is not the power of being that conquers the threat of non-being. So it does not deserve our worship but needs to be rejected in the name of genuine faith:

> The main argument against [supranaturalism] is that it transforms the infinity of God into a finiteness which is merely an extension of the categories of finitude. This is done in respect to space by establishing a supranatural divine world alongside the natural human world; in respect to time by determining a beginning and an end of God's creativity; in respect to causality by making God a cause alongside other causes; in respect to substance by attributing individual substance to him. Against this kind of supranaturalism the arguments of naturalism are valid and, as such, represent the true concern of religion, the infinity of the infinite, and the inviolability of the created structures of the finite. Theology must accept the antisupranatural criticism of naturalism.
>
> (*ST* II, 6)

Hence Tillich wants to articulate a 'third way', one that takes religious thought 'beyond naturalism and supranaturalism' (5). He realizes that many scientists and philosophers have taken refuge in naturalism because supranaturalism, which is often the only theological alternative they know about, fails to offer them a God worthy of worship. A God who exists merely as one being among other beings, or as one cause among other causes, is too small to be worthy of religious trust. One of Tillich's most important contributions to the science–religion dialogue, therefore, is to have shown that supranaturalism deserves the harsh treatment it receives from naturalists and should not be mistaken for serious theology.

From Tillich's point of view, naturalistic claims that science contra-
dicts religious faith are themselves based in a misguided kind of faith,
but it is faith nonetheless. More than a few scientifically educated
thinkers in modern times have themselves surrendered (religiously)
to what they take to be the comprehensively explanatory and salvific
power of science itself. Correspondingly, the universe as made known by
science has become for them in effect a revelatory – though idolatrous –
symbol of the power and depth of being. Scientific naturalism exhibits
both the promise and demands of any ultimate concern, and it functions
to provide courage and confidence in the face of the very same threats
that give rise to all religions, namely, fate, death, guilt and meaninglessness. Many scientific naturalists have made a sincere faith-commitment
to the rigorous and indeed almost puritanical requirements of scientific
naturalism. To them the universe itself appears resourceful enough to
conquer the threat of non-being.[4]

Because of the success and achievements of natural science it is not
hard to understand why science can function so readily as one's ultimate
concern or why scientific naturalism would be so appealing a belief
system. Nevertheless, whether scientific naturalism is a truthful and
ultimately satisfying world-view can be determined only by observing
whether it allows nature to function symbolically in such a way as to
be *fully* transparent to being itself, or what Tillich alternatively calls
the power and depth of being. This means asking whether naturalism
can function to give one courage *sufficient* to conquer the threat of non-
being. If not, then Tillich's theology would consider it to be a species of
idolatry.

It is obvious to Tillich that scientific naturalism is religiously
inadequate. Granted that science is powerfully effective in the human
encounter with fate, it has not yet conquered death, and even were it to
do so, it would still not have addressed the threat of meaninglessness or
guilt (*CB*, 46–57). It may even be argued plausibly that instead of conquering fate, science has made human existence more subject to fate and
possible extinction than ever. The threats to our existence by potential
nuclear disaster and environmental pollution are unprecedented, and
these have become possible because of science. Through medicine science may help alleviate disease and even pathological states of guilt,
but it can never abolish the gap between one's actual and ideal states
of moral being. Science, one must agree, is a good, but it is not an
ultimate good. Nature too is resourceful, but its finitude keeps it from
being able to deliver us from the threat of non-being. As cosmologists
agree today, even the entire Big Bang universe is destined to perish

eventually. Therefore, naturalism cannot adequately satisfy the human need for either courage or truth.

At this point the naturalist may respond that the existence of a personal God is incompatible with natural science. Albert Einstein, for example, wrote that a responsive God, one who can answer prayers and intervene in nature (the God of the Bible, in other words), would violate or suspend the universal laws of nature that make science and scientific prediction possible. If the laws of science can be broken by miraculous divine intervention, even if only occasionally, this would be enough to undermine science's credibility altogether. Einstein considered himself to be a religious person, in the sense of being ultimately concerned – to use Tillich's terminology – about ethical values, beauty, truth and the deep mystery that the universe is comprehensible at all. But he remained convinced that belief in a personal God is the main source of conflict between science and religion today. He hoped that religious teachers would have the honesty and integrity to give up this doctrine once and for all.[5]

In some ways Tillich shares Einstein's concern about attributing personality to God. A personalistic theism can easily decay into the idolatry of supranaturalism by turning God into *a* being, *a* substance or *a* cause existing alongside nature and occasionally intruding into it. This kind of theism deserves Einstein's criticism. However, Einstein's naturalistic refusal to think of the depth, ground and power of being as *at least* personal is also religiously unsatisfying. The danger in Einstein's religious naturalism is that it posits as ultimate what is fundamentally an impersonal universe, an 'It' rather than a 'Thou'. But human persons, Tillich replies to Einstein, can never be grasped at the centre of their being by what is less than personal: 'Only a person can heal another person.' Einstein's naturalism, therefore, is no more able to put us in touch with the depth and ground of being than is supranaturalism (*TC*, 131–2).

Tillich's 'third way', on the other hand, seeks to transcend both naturalism and supranaturalism. His proposal is that 'personality' is indispensable to any truly revelatory symbolizing of being-itself, and that a mature faith will acknowledge that God is more than personal – God is 'superpersonal'. God is not literally *a* person but instead the depth and ground of all personality. But any ultimate concern that is less than personal becomes a mere object. As such, Tillich seems to be suggesting, it can only have the effect of depersonalizing its devotees. Late in his life, Tillich came to appreciate the work of Teilhard de Chardin, the famous Jesuit palaeontologist (1881–1955). Like Einstein and Tillich, Teilhard de Chardin had acknowledged the powerful attraction of naturalism, but after nearly succumbing to its seductions he concluded that such a world-view functionally obliterates what is personal.[6] Like Teilhard de Chardin, Tillich concluded that in order for a culture to sustain and confirm the value of personality its religious expression must not allow the ground of being to be symbolized by anything less than personal. Even though contemporary scientific naturalism rightly rejects supranaturalism, therefore, Tillich would agree with Teilhard de Chardin that naturalism also must be rejected on the grounds that it does not allow sufficient room in its metaphysics for the reality of personality (*TC*, 128–32).

THE SUPRANATURALIST OPPOSITION TO SCIENCE

Long before naturalism raised its modern protests against theology, some theologians, religious educators and church officials had laid the foundation for such a reaction by challenging the legitimate method of science and its well-authenticated discoveries. Historically, such opposition is obvious in the Catholic church's confused treatment of Galileo, but it continues today in the rejection of evolutionary biology by Christians and other theists. At one level the reaction consists of a resistance to changes in the particular cosmography in which a set of religious symbols had been comfortably embedded for centuries. For example, much of the Western religious world's initial hostility to Copernicus, Brahe, Kepler and Galileo stemmed, in Tillichian terms, from an anxiety that the new pictures of the universe could no longer mediate the power of being to the faithful with the same fidelity as could the ancient impression of the fixity of the heavens.

However, at another level theists often spurn science because the explanatory power of natural accounts seems to threaten what they take to be the causal supremacy of God. Accordingly, theists have reacted defensively to claims that the laws of physics can explain the motions of the heavens, that chemistry can explain the origin of life, that natural selection can account for the diversity of species or that cognitive science can help us understand how the human mind works. In their obsession with saving a causal niche in the world for divine action, they have sought out either 'gaps' in science's understanding of nature or a position of primacy in a series of natural causes in which to locate the special influence of God. Their assumption has been that the more robust scientific explanations tend to become, the less authoritative theological explanation will be.

According to Tillich, however, any fear that theological explanation may be supplanted by advances in scientific understanding of natural causes can only come from a theologically unacceptable supranaturalist point of view. Supranaturalist opposition to purely scientific explanations, as though the latter logically constitute a threat to the authority of theology, can occur only under the false assumption that theology can compete with science in the task of providing natural explanations. Yet, as Tillich's theology argues, such an assumption denies genuine divine transcendence by in effect insisting that God be part of the continuum of natural causes. Supranaturalism rightly expresses the religious intuition that the world's existence is contingent upon a power of being that transcends it.[7] But by making God the first in a series of causes, supranaturalism, especially as expressed in the cosmological arguments for God's existence, ironically ends up naturalizing God. In effect it turns God into a spatialized and temporally definable causal substance to be understood in terms of the categories applicable only to finite being. All attempts to prove God's existence as a first cause, Tillich emphasizes, implicitly make the divine a part of nature. The danger in thinking of God as a first cause is that the ultimate depth and ground of being is assigned the greatly diminished role of playing only a part – even if the most important part – in a series of purely natural causes.

This idolatrous way of thinking about God, Tillich argues, is the root cause of modern naturalistic atheism. Supranaturalism deserves the naturalistic reaction, and theology needs to take the latter's atheism seriously as a necessary step in the movement towards an adequate understanding of God's relationship to nature and of theology's relationship to science. Tillich's third way, that of standing between naturalism and supranaturalism, seeks to 'liberate the discussion from the oscillation between two insufficient and religiously dangerous solutions' (*ST* II, 7). Tillich realizes, of course, that his third way is not entirely new. Augustine, Aquinas, Luther, Zwingli, Calvin and Schleiermacher all gave imperfect versions of it. But in an age of science, theology must be more careful than ever to remove all vestiges of supranaturalism in order to avoid the understandable naturalist reaction. It can do so, however, only if it thinks of God not as outside the world but as the world's depth and ground, as the power of being, or as being-itself. Supranaturalism is correct in emphasizing that God is not identical with nature and that God transcends the world. But naturalism is correct in rejecting a divine 'superworld' pictured as existing alongside nature. God cannot transcend nature if God is not already immanent in nature. 'In this respect God is neither alongside things nor even "above" them; he is nearer to them than they are to themselves. He is their creative ground, here and now, always and everywhere' (7).

What are the implications for science and religion of Tillich's 'third way'? Since no issue is as central to the contemporary science–religion exchange as that of how to understand divine action in relation to nature, one must ask how, and how well, Tillich's thought addresses this concern. Today most philosophers and many scientists can find no 'evidence' of divine action in nature, and so they view theology as having no significant explanatory function. Naturalism has been content to specify in a purely physical way how phenomena, including living, thinking, ethical and religious beings, have come to be and why they possess the traits they do. Today, even more than in Tillich's time, evolutionary naturalists claim to be able to provide the *ultimate* explanation of all living phenomena in terms of adaptive Darwinian processes. Is it possible then to understand divine action in such a way that theological explanation will not seem to be either superfluous altogether or in conflict with science?

I believe that Tillich would begin his response to this question by warning those involved in the science–religion dialogue that the very question 'How does God act in nature?' can easily presuppose a supranaturalistic understanding of God. It seems that almost every precise answer one might give to the question of divine action is likely to make God appear to be one cause among others. In the worst case, supranaturalism makes divine action a rival of any scientific understanding of causation in nature. For example, it proposes that it is God *rather than* chemical processes that gave rise to life, or it is divine design *rather than* evolution that created humans. Such claims, of course, only provoke the naturalistic retort that it is chemical processes *rather than* divine activity that brought about the first living entity, or it is natural selection *rather than* God that produced our ears, noses, brains and so on.[8] But even in the best cases, where theology employs the classical distinction between primary (divine) and secondary (natural) causes, supranaturalist interpretations of divine action still tend to make the divine 'primary cause' into one among other actors on the stage of nature. It is especially this sort of understanding that has made theology marginal in modern and contemporary academic settings.

If the question 'How does God act in nature?' is to have any real meaning, Tillich would locate it (existentially) in the fact that the question expresses an awareness of the threat of non-being implied in the very notion of causation and in every quest for explanations (*ST* I, 192–8). We humans ask about causes, including the ultimate cause of events in nature, not only to satisfy mundane curiosity but even more because we are tacitly aware of the abyss of non-being over which we and the whole of nature are perched. An underlying anxiety accompanies every human search for explanation, and both naturalism and supranaturalism only exacerbate this anxiety by their idolatrous positing of something less than being-itself as the response to the threat of non-being.

Neither nature as a whole nor a divine first cause can surmount the condition of finitude, that is, of being subject to the threat of non-being. Naturalism, especially in the light of recent physics and cosmology, leads us only deeper into the abyss of non-being when it presents our resourceful but ultimately extinguishable cosmos as the foundation of all being and all causes. And supranaturalism, by trying to be causally specific about how God acts, reduces the infinite power of being to something finite, thus meriting the opposition it receives from naturalism. Tillich's third way, on the other hand, suggests that beneath all quests for explanation, including those of science, there lies a tacit search for the depth and power of being-itself which alone can conquer the threat of non-being implied in the very idea of causation.

Only the experience of the 'shock' of non-being that arises in our encounter with finitude can awaken us to the depth, ground and power of being (*ST* I, 110–13). 'In revelation and in the ecstatic experience in which it is received, the ontological shock is preserved and overcome at the same time' (113). In the naïve question 'How does God act in nature?', Tillich discovers a deep anxiety about finitude and the threat of non-being. From the beginning of the modern age up until today some religious scientists, along with a number of theologians, have been obsessed with specifying how God acts in nature, but whenever their proposals have been taken literally rather than analogously they have understandably invited the scorn of naturalists. Thus, Tillich would view recent speculative attempts to locate divine action in the hidden realm of quantum events as theologically misguided.[9] Even though what occurs in this misty physical domain is inaccessible to direct observation, it is no less part of nature than rocks and rivers, and any attempt to connect God's creative or providential influence so closely to a specific dimension of nature ends up promoting the same naturalizing of God that is characteristic of all supranaturalism. It is not surprising then that contemporary scientific naturalists and followers of Paul Tillich alike reject this new version of physico-theology.

For Tillich, it is more than enough that God is the ground and power of being, and so any attempt to specify divine action in terms of natural categories will only diminish the sense of God's power and love. Theology's discourse about the power of being is always reliant on symbolic expression, and in an age of science the more literally theology takes its ideas about divine action, the more likely it is that these will be interpreted as scientific in nature. When such confusion occurs, the stage is set either for a new burst of supranaturalistic zeal or a severe naturalistic rebellion against any attempts by theology to do the work of science.

THE CONFLICT OF NATURALISM WITH SUPRANATURALISM

From a Tillichian point of view, many of the public jousts identified as instances of an underlying 'conflict' between science and religion are in fact masquerades for an ongoing dispute between scientific naturalism on the one hand and religious supranaturalism on the other. Nowhere is this camouflage more evident than in the current debate between evolutionary materialists and anti-Darwinian advocates of 'intelligent design'. Even though journalists typically identify this dispute as a conflict between science and religion, much more is involved. On one side of the 'Darwin wars' stand religious supranaturalists who view evolutionary biology as a mask for materialist metaphysics, and on the other are the naturalists who believe that evolutionary biology can provide the ultimate explanation of all characteristics of living phenomena (especially, though not exclusively, by invoking the mechanism of natural selection). Both sets of combatants are driven by ideological investments that sidestep the real question of science's relationship to theology.

There can be no doubt that many Darwinians have unthinkingly folded their biological understanding of evolution into a blatantly naturalist (and usually materialist) belief system. And this amalgam of science and naturalist belief drives some of their opponents in the religious world to take reactionary refuge from Darwinism in a supranaturalistic version of theism disguised as 'Intelligent Design Theory'.[10] So the present controversy over intelligent design is not a true conflict between science and theology, but an egregious instance of the clash between two world-views, scientific naturalism on the one hand and supranaturalism on the other.

From a Tillichian point of view, there is no question that for many people the Darwinian picture of life opens up an enormous abyss. Evolutionary biology involves an unprecedented degree of sheer contingency, and tracing the trail of accidental factors in the life-story back into the past opens the abyss wider and wider. The anxiety is especially pronounced in the case of those who invoke 'intelligent design' as though it were a scientific alternative to Darwinian biology. Intelligent design, no matter how much its proponents deny that it is a theological notion, functions as a symbol of the power of being in the face of anxiety, but like other forms of supranaturalism it implicitly naturalizes the divine by situating a symbol of ultimacy (intelligent design) in the realm of scientific causation. But in this categorical slot it cannot conquer the threat of non-being, since it cannot escape finitude itself.

On the other hand, in the light of Tillich's analysis of anxiety and courage it must be said that evolutionary materialism is also idolatrous. Its purely naturalistic explanation of living 'design' has an enormous appeal not only because of its intellectual simplicity, but even more because the materialist world-view also apparently responds powerfully to the existential threat of non-being. The image of an eternally enduring – even if essentially lifeless and mindless – material universe communicates something of the power of being to many a scientific naturalist. If the materialist spectre of a universe of matter rolling on eternally and meaninglessly were unable to assuage anxiety in some way, its devotees would immediately abandon it. But naturalism's almost mystical temptation to dissolve finite freedom in the impersonal oceanic abyss of matter can lead only to the loss of the self.

In conclusion, then, neither naturalism nor supranaturalism can be religiously satisfying in the final analysis. And the dispute between them distracts the participants from looking carefully at the deeper question of how science relates to religion.

Notes

1 See also *CB*, 20–3.
2 See, for example, Hawking (1992), 140–1.
3 See Haught (2006).
4 See, for example, Goodenough (1998) and Raymo (1998).
5 Einstein (1954), 11.
6 Teilhard de Chardin (1999), 185–7.
7 A sense of nature's contingency is the kernel of truth in all cosmological arguments for God's existence, the value of which consists not in any answers they give, but only in their expressing the *question* of being that arises from an accurate understanding of everything finite. See *ST* I, 208–10.
8 As in Cziko (1995).
9 See, for example, the essays in Russell, Clayton, Wegter-McNelly and Polkinghorne (2001).
10 See P. E. Johnson (1991), Moreland (1994), Behe (1996), Dembski (1999) and Wells (2000). See also the critique of intelligent design by Pennock (1999).

Further reading

Adams, James Luther (1965). *Paul Tillich's Philosophy of Culture, Science, and Religion*. New York: Harper & Row.

Drummy, Michael (2000). *Being and Earth: Paul Tillich's Theology of Nature*. Lanham, Md.: University Press of America.

Grigg, R. (1985). *Symbol and Empowerment: Paul Tillich's Post-Theistic System*. Macon, Ga.: Mercer University Press.

Haught, John F. (2006). *Is Nature Enough? Meaning and Truth in the Age of Science*. Cambridge: Cambridge University Press.

Wiebe, P. (1984). 'Tillich and Contemporary Theory of Science' in *Theonomy and Autonomy: Studies in Paul Tillich's Engagement with Modern Culture*, ed. J. C. Carey, 19–33. Macon, Ga.: Mercer University Press.

15 Tillich in dialogue with psychology

JOHN DOURLEY

IMPLICIT PSYCHOLOGY

Tillich's dialogue with psychology has many faces. It can be understood in the light of his conversations with specific psychologists and their schools. It can be understood in terms of his sustained efforts to establish the legitimate boundaries between religious and psychological healing.[1] Finally, there is the tribute he paid to Carl Jung on the occasion of the latter's death indicative of Tillich's late theological appreciation of and intellectual affinity with Jung's understanding of the human psyche (*CGJ*, 28–32). Yet there is a dimension to Tillich's relation to psychology that precedes these specifics. It lies in the way his theology itself is infused with a profound psychological sense lending to the foundations of his thought a compelling impact on the psyche of his reader. In his description of existential thinking Tillich refers to Boehme, Schelling, Baader and even Heidegger as philosophers who used 'psychological notions with a non-psychological connotation'. Such thinkers have 'developed an ontology in psychological terms' ('Existential Philosophy: Its Historical Meaning' in *TC*, 94, 96). Tillich himself stood in this tradition.

Tillich's unforced synthesis of ontology and psychology is evident throughout his work. It is, perhaps, most prominent in his understanding of faith as humanity's ultimate concern. Such a conception of concern, in admitted continuity with Schleiermacher's 'feeling of unconditional dependence', becomes for Tillich humanity's universal, religious and psychological experience of alienation from and drive towards its essential nature grounded in the divine (*DF*, 1–4, 38–40). Again, Tillich's 'proofs' for the existence of God combine the psychological and ontological. For Tillich, the ontological argument proves nothing. Rather, it points to the immediate fact of humanity's inborn religious and psychological experience of the Unconditional (*ST* I, 207). The cosmological argument then becomes a psychological reflection on the anxieties of existential life and the quest for the courage that will allow the human to bear them. His version of the teleological argument addresses the anxiety of meaninglessness and the quest for the 'ground of meaning' (209–10).

In his systematic work Tillich blends psychological with ontological notions in his treatment of the seemingly most obscure realms of the Christian tradition. In a daring gambit to ground even the doctrine of the Trinity in human psychological experience Tillich contends that humanity's native experience of the divine is latently Trinitarian. Such experience rests on the sense of divinely grounded opposites pulsating in the depths of human life. Such human experience encompasses both the dark and the light, the overwhelming and the sustaining, dimensions of divine life. Such a God is as close to the irrationalities of the unconscious as to the light of reason (250). When Tillich turns to his conception of regeneration, a divinely enabled self-acceptance in the light of one's continued unacceptability becomes the psycho-theological equivalent of the traditional theological doctrine of *simul justus et peccator* (*ST* III, 224–5). His thought on sanctification as process pays explicit tribute to the influence of contemporary depth psychology (231–4). Finally, his doctrine of the *kairoi*, the recurrence in one's time of the fullness of time in the original Christ-event, speaks of an experiential capacity to read the 'signs of the times' out of a synergy of psychological and spiritual insight (370–1).

For these reasons any discussion of Tillich's dialogue with psychology as an area beyond his discipline should bow first to his integration of a psychological perspective into the very fabric of his theology and its philosophical foundations.

TILLICH AND THE NEW YORK PSYCHOLOGY GROUP, 1942–5

Tillich had been intellectually interested in psychology in his native Germany prior to his emigration to the United States in 1933 and had known Erich Fromm in Frankfurt. This interest became more than academic through his participation in an ongoing discussion group made up of psychologists of many persuasions who met twenty-nine times in New York City throughout the academic years from 1941–2 to 1945. Tillich, the only non-psychotherapist, attended twenty-one of these meetings. Among the more famous of the participants were Erich Fromm, Rollo May and Carl Rogers. The broad focus of the group was on the inter-relation of religion and health, with a special interest in depth

psychology. Each year was devoted to a specific aspect of this relationship: 1942 to the psychology of faith, 1942–3 to the psychology of love,
1943–4 to the psychology of conscience and 1944–5 to the psychology of
helping. Tillich presented three papers throughout the life of the group.
His topics were the concept of faith in the Jewish–Christian tradition,
the ontology of love and the nature of conscience.[2]

Commentators agree that Fromm and Tillich were the natural leaders of the group and represented profound but somewhat conflicting
positions.[3] Fromm, consistent with his published works, looked upon
a transcendent divinity as necessarily an authoritarian divinity and so
an impediment to human dignity and true freedom. For Fromm, God
served as a symbol for the best of humanity and the realization of its
potential. Tillich too was sensitive to religion as fostering human development but refused to identify this valued dimension of religion with
the solely human.[4] It would appear that in this debate Fromm's conception of divinity was what Tillich would deem heteronomous and would
reject for a theonomous divine presence addressing consciousness from
its residual being in humanity's depth.

The group represented an emerging and substantial liberalism rejecting a theological parochialism for a more inclusive and extensive
embrace of the living currents in their contemporary culture. They
understood depth psychology, psychoanalysis and the relation of both to
religion to be vital contributors to the then current societal well-being.[5]
The Tillich of these meetings was already sensitive to the fact that
'troubled Christians began seeking help not from ministers, but from
psychoanalysts'.[6] That the psychological and theological communities
appreciated this fact and had to respond to it remained a life-long concern
for Tillich. And yet it never led him into a sustained personal analysis.[7]

THE INTERFACE WITH PSYCHOLOGY IN THE *SYSTEMATIC THEOLOGY* AND OCCASIONAL WRITINGS

In his conception of the multidimensional unity of life Tillich understands life to have evolved from the inorganic through the organic
and the psychological to the spiritual as the distinguishing note of
the human. Rather than understand these levels hierarchically Tillich
unites them in the centre of life under the dominance of spirit. This
understanding of the centredness of all the dimensions of life in the
spirit allows Tillich to distinguish between the psychological and spiritual dimensions of life while affirming that they are in fact inseparable

in existential life (*ST* III, 25–7, 36–7). The divine Spirit grasps the human spirit in the revelatory and salvific experience and leads it, however fragmentarily, into the integration of opposites, especially those of power and meaning, that constitute the base dynamic of divine life. Thus the human spirit, as the centre of all dimensions of human life, is grasped by the divine Spirit in the transformative or salvific moment of an ecstasy beyond the capacity of the human spirit itself to generate. Yet at the same time Tillich's ontology of the inherence of all finite and human being in their divine ground must contend that the divine Spirit grasps the human spirit in the revelatory and ecstatic event from within and through the depths of the human spirit: 'in the human spirit's essential relation to the divine Spirit, there is no correlation, but rather mutual immanence' (114).

In short, their mutual immanence enables Tillich to describe the grasping of the human spirit by the divine Spirit through a power working from within the human. This process has an obvious affinity with major themes in depth psychology but, for Tillich, does not reduce salvific transformation to a purely psychological event. Thus, Tillich can present the revelatory instance and the ecstasy it occasions as beyond the capacity of the psyche to produce even as such experience is always worked by the Spirit through its natural inhesion in the human. Further, Tillich argues, such revelation is of the mystery of being. It arises from and responds to the deepest ultimacy in the human and so is not qualified or determined by ongoing psychological knowledge and research, or by specific psychological traditions. The theologian need not attack Freud or defend Jung since neither, Tillich contends, addresses the power at work in the ecstasy of revelation (*ST* I, 130–1). In this vein he will write that Otto's description of the ambivalent experience of the holy as at once *tremendum* and *fascinosum* should never be described as merely psychological, because Otto's phenomenology rests on the experience of the abysmal and supportive nature of divine life itself (216). And yet the feeling remains that Otto and Tillich present a cogent ontological description of humanity's experience of the ambivalence of divine life in terms of psychological experience and language, and, in so doing, elevate the psychological to the domains of the ontological and religious. Such elevation simply sustains Tillich's point that, even in the revelatory event, the psychological and the spiritual cannot be clearly distinguished in existential humanity.

The same intimacy and difference between the psychological and the theological remain in much of Tillich's work. Sometimes the psychological is clearly distinguished from the theological, while on other

occasions Tillich would seem wholly to absorb such modern psychological conceptions as the unconscious into the substance of his theological treatment of God, Trinity and the sacramental. When he addresses
modern depth psychology from the perspective of his methodology of
correlation, the discoveries of the unconscious are held over against
theology and demand the theologian's response to them. In this context
depth psychology reveals the structures of the 'old aeon'; 'the determinism of the deeper psyche on the conscious mind and will'; 'the reality
of the demonic in everyone'; and 'an infinite libido whose insatiability
drives to the death wish' (ST II, 27, 42, 207; 'The Theological Significance of Existentialism and Psychoanalysis' in TC, 119). The theologian
must then acknowledge thc reality of the newly discovered 'collective
unconscious' and its power, and respond to it out of the resources of
the Christian tradition (ST II, 27). In this sense the theologian is almost
gifted by the abiding negativities of life revealed by depth psychology
to which the reality of New Being is to be addressed. When he subjects
modern psychology to his method of correlation, Tillich has little to
say about the capacities of the deeper psyche itself or of its ground to
address and heal the human difficulties that modern psychology has
revealed. The negative sides of humanity unveiled by depth psychology
serve either to confirm Christian positions on fallen humanity or to
provide a challenge to or foil for Tillich's answering theology.

Also helpful to the theologian, in a slightly different context, is
the healing impact of psychology on Christian theologically induced
pathology. Tillich refers to psychology's 'often shocking insights' into
the consequences of traditional theology's reduction of the human relation to God to a personal relation to God as 'Father' or 'Lord'. Such
reduction is pathologizing because it ignores the transpersonal nature
of God as being-itself or the ground and order of all that is. In so doing it
inserts the divine–human relation into subject–object categories whose
religious consequence is atheism and whose psychological consequence
is pathology (ST I, 245, 288–9). Tillich's theology stands as a rejection of
all forms of biblical and theological literalism, but he explicitly refers to
the pathology of literalism in relation to the symbols of heaven and hell
and of a final split between the saved and the damned. Psychology itself
is to overcome the neurosis bred by all literalism but especially in the
area of the afterlife (ST III, 416, 418–19). Tillich also praises Freud in particular for corroding a conception of saintliness based not only on sexual
repression, but also on the repression of many legitimate expressions of
the essential dimensions of the human spirit and its vitality (211). In continuity with this point Tillich credits 'the psychoanalytic movement'

and 'analytic psychology' with undermining Christian, Roman, Protestant and humanistic moralism and asceticism by showing the intimate connections between the spiritually sublime and the total vitalities of human life, among which Tillich would undoubtedly include the sexual. Henceforth no image of Christian perfection can afford 'to neglect analytic psychology's insights into the psychodynamics of repression' (240).

In the foregoing discussions Tillich holds psychology apart from religion and theology as either that body of recently uncovered knowledge that his methodology of correlation must address from a Christian perspective or as an agency enabling the theologian and psychologist to identify and corrode theologically induced pathology. But there are elements of Tillich's thought that go further. They introduce psychological elements into the fabric of his doctrine of God and of the Trinity. This fusion of theological and psychological realms is evident when Tillich symbolically equates meontic nothingness or infinite potentiality with the unconscious and so effectively with the dynamic element or first moment within the intra-Trinitarian dialectic (*ST* I, 179–80). He continues blending the psychological with the theological in his association of the 'collective unconscious' with the universal presence of the divine. This feature of the unconscious enables the individual to participate in the totality through the individual's connectedness with the unconscious. As the substratum generative of all consciousness, the collective unconscious would then be closely associated, if not identified, with the abysmal dimension of the ground of being urging and enabling the identity of microcosm with macrocosm, the individual with the totality, a point at the heart of Tillich's theology and Jung's psychology (261).

Tillich further remarks that the presence of God as Spirit to human life encompasses the unconscious: 'as Spirit he is as near to the creative darkness of the unconscious as he is to the critical light of cognitive reason' (250). This intimacy of the Spirit with the unconscious takes on added weight when Tillich further contends that humanity has a latent sense not only of God but of the movements of the life of the Trinity itself. What he calls the human 'intuition of the divine' has perennially distinguished between the divine depth and its meaningful expression in *logos* (250). Such human intuition of the divine depth would imply that the experience of the first moment in Trinitarian life is the experience of the unbounded and universal potential of the unconscious driven by its own dynamic to give itself form or expression and so complete itself in divine and human consciousness (279).

The originary foundation of consciousness in its unconscious precedent enhances Tillich's compelling sacramentalism. He lauds 'the twentieth-century rediscovery of the unconscious' as deepening the religious appreciation of the 'sacramental mediation of the Spirit', and goes on to associate the agency of the unconscious with his understanding of Catholic substance, religion's universal sacramental matrix (*ST* I, 279; *ST* III, 122). Catholic substance, for Tillich, directs one to the point of intersection of the divine with the human. As such it constitutes the basis of religious experience, itself always to be freed from potential idolatry through its interplay with the Protestant principle. In these passages Tillich equates the power of the sacramental with the unconscious depths of the human and contends that if these depths are not active in the mediation of the Spirit to consciousness, the resultant experience of the Spirit will become a sterile intellectualism or moralism. Tillich could hardly pay higher tribute to the unconscious as the basis of sacramental power in all its forms.

Tillich not only relates the unconscious to the possibility and necessity of sacramental experience, but also to mystical experience. Throughout much of his work he contends that Protestantism has weakened its spirituality by its rejection of mysticism. He specifically suggests that the turn of certain levels of the upper classes of Protestant society to the 'alliance of psychoanalysis and Zen Buddhism' compensated for the absence of an unmediated religious experience that a vital mystical sensitivity could provide (*ST* III, 243). These passages link sacramental and mystical experience with each other and tie each to their mutual origin in the unconscious.

Again, in his most extensive treatment of sanctification, most of the 'principles determining the New Being as process' make explicit reference to the insights of depth psychology. The spiritual cultivation of the deeper awareness of oneself, 'the voiceless voice of a concrete situation', Tillich relates directly 'to contemporary depth psychology' (231–2). He links the freedom of sanctification to depth psychology's ability to liberate the individual from the compulsions that impede growth in the freedom of the Spirit (232). Recounting the radical transformations in the lives of Socrates and Paul, Tillich grants to depth psychology the same power of conversion, not through a solely cognitive effort, but through the recovery and psychological re-enactment of the 'pains and horrors' of past traumatic experience (*ST* I, 96). The relatedness characteristic of growth in the Spirit breaks self-seclusion in the individual and in the other, and is 'interdependent with the psychotherapeutic analyses of the same structures' (*ST* III, 234). This relatedness is based on the conscious relation to one's own depth, the vertical dimension in life, as the basis of one's relatedness to the other. Such relatedness can support a healthy solitude that is not loneliness and avoids the pathologies of grandiose self-elevation and demeaning self-humiliation (234–5).

Effectively, Tillich is here applying to growth in the Spirit not only the insights of contemporary depth psychology, but also his own metaphysics of ground. This ontology bases all positive relation to the other on a preceding resonance with the ground of one's personal existence as the ground of all existence. In this synthesis, ontological, psychological and theological affirmations tend to become one. This unity is evident in Tillich's depiction of growth in the Spirit as growth towards the essential self powerfully manifest in those moments when it shines through 'the contingencies of the existing self' (235). In the context of Tillich's wider theology the primordial expression of the essential self in the second moment of the Trinitarian life is that which the human spirit is moved to recover in existence. Here he clearly states that the experience of this self can be anticipated in and through the distortions of the existential self in the present life. In these reflections Tillich should be credited with laying the ontological and theological foundations of modern self psychologies. Here his thought has a discernible affinity with Jung's conception of the self as both eternal and seeking fuller incarnation in existential consciousness.[8]

In a major article Tillich addresses the connections between contemporary theology, existentialism and psychoanalysis. The latter term he broadens to 'therapeutic psychology' and 'depth psychology' to include more than the classical Freudian position (*TC*, 112). Tillich identifies the common root of existentialism and the psychologies of depth in their opposition to the reduction of humanity's cognitive potential to the power of consciousness and particularly to that technical consciousness characteristic of modern industrial society. The target of the joint criticism of existentialism and depth psychology is that of a prevailing cultural mindset severed from its own depths and so reducing human consciousness to an objectivity shorn of the irrational or pre-rational (114). Such truncating uprootedness extends to the religious sphere. In their common effort to recover a lost and even irrational subjectivity, the efforts of existentialism, theology and depth psychology enter into a relationship of 'mutual interpenetration' (114).

Tillich credits Freud and his discovery of the unconscious as the major psychological contributor to an appreciation of both the irrational element within the human psyche and the darker sides of that psyche

(116–17). At the same time he is critical of Freud and certain other existentialists such as Sartre and Heidegger for their failure to identify essentialist elements as the basis of their own response to the human predicament they so acutely document. Tillich identifies the self-contradiction in their work in his contention that an essentialist element, whose reality and effectiveness they deny in principle, is surreptitiously present as their most significant resource in their reply to the distortions of existential life (120). In this article Tillich emphasizes his appreciation of Freud's discoveries of the depth of human estrangement and especially of the connection between a libido beyond satiety and the death wish. The theologian of correlation must address these culturally significant discoveries from a Christian perspective, but, true to this methodology, Tillich concludes that the answer to the questions that existentialism and depth psychology pose comes ultimately not from themselves but from 'somewhere else' (125). The location of the somewhere else brings up the question of the relation of religious to therapeutic healing, and where and why the borders of their competence are to be drawn.

RELIGIOUS AND THERAPEUTIC HEALING: THE RELATION OF EXISTENTIAL TO NEUROTIC ANXIETY

In at least three loci throughout his corpus Tillich reflects in some depth on the relation of religious healing, the *salus* of salvation, to the healing offered by the medical and psychological communities.[9] His reflections are based on his theological and ontological anthropology, which rest on the distinction between existential and essential humanity. The negativities giving rise to the anxieties of existence are ontologically traced to existential humanity's universal remove from its essential truth in the ground of its being. Such anxiety centres on the realities of death, guilt, meaninglessness, the always possible disintegration of life's polarities and the vicissitudes of living in the confines of space, time and finitude. These are among the major, but by no means the only, sources of anxiety that existential humanity must confront. In the face of such terror Tillich concludes, 'Finitude in awareness is anxiety' (*ST* I, 191). This anxiety is visible even in the biblical picture of Christ (*ST* II, 124–5). Tillich terms such anxiety 'existential anxiety', distinguishes it from 'neurotic' or 'pathological' anxiety and claims that only the mediation of the essential, the role of religious healing, can relieve existential anxiety at its root (*CB*, 64–5, 72).

In this first position in relating religious to psychological healing Tillich will attribute the alleviation of existential anxiety to the realm of religion as the bearer of the essential or 'New Being' and contend that medical and psychological healing in themselves cannot effect the recovery of the essential in existence. Consequently, medical and psychological approaches should neither discount nor attempt to subsume the religious alleviation of existential anxiety. With his precise ontology of anxiety the sphere Tillich initially delineates as the legitimate domain of religious healing is that of the mediation of the essential. Yet even here he will at least hold open the possibility that the mediation of the essential could alleviate specifically psychological and medical problems (73, 74).

In his second position Tillich moves to determine the legitimate domain of medical and psychological healing. This is in the area of 'pathological' as opposed to 'existential' anxiety. Neurotic anxiety is a pathologizing response to existential anxiety, one that limits in various degrees the freedom, dignity and, especially, the courageous self-affirmation of those victimized by it. Tillich does not exempt certain forms of restrictive religiosity as major contributors to neurotic anxiety (73). In his work *The Courage to Be* he elaborates on how the various neurotic responses to death, guilt and meaninglessness serve seriously to impede the ability of the individual to affirm one's truth with a courage derived ultimately from the 'God above the God of theism' (186, 187, 190). Medical and psychological procedures can effectively address neurotic anxiety. Such procedures usually lie beyond the capacities of the religious minister as such. Religious ministry should thus acknowledge the competency of the psychologist in the realm of neurotic anxiety, although some individuals may serve effectively in both roles (*ST* III, 281–2). Put succinctly, priest and psychologist or doctor should acknowledge, at least in principle, the specific areas of their respective competence and honour the difference between them.

At this point, after he so clearly distinguishes how religious and psychological healing are to be related in their difference and interface, Tillich seems to blur the distinctions he has so painstakingly made when he concedes that the priestly mediation of the essential can bring relief from neurosis and that the psychologist can mediate the essential and so effect that religious healing theology relates to salvation (*CB*, 74, 77). From the viewpoint of medical and psychological healing Tillich is here making an immense concession, which should be given more examination than it has to date. For, on the basis of his ontology of anxiety, one can move to establish the criterion that any psychology would have to meet if it were, in fact, to be an agent of the essential. Such a psychology would have to reject any form of supranaturalism, which would understand healing to be effected by a power invasive of the human from beyond the human. For Tillich, this would be an instance of a dehumanizing heteronomy allegedly acting on behalf of health. At the same time such a psychology would have to avoid a purely naturalistic understanding of healing, which would deny to the human a native relation to the divine as humanity's ultimate healing resource. This position would be consistent with Tillich's understanding of theonomy and the depth of reason, inasmuch as both insinuate a healing divine agency continuous with the depth dimension of humanity.

Within this framework depth psychology could truly mediate to a suffering humanity a reconnection with its essential truth in its own depths from which the healing approach of the divine would touch and transform the human mind and body. In Tillich's spirit, such an understanding of psychology's mediation of the essential self to existential and embodied consciousness would never move beyond a fragmentary approximation of the individual's full essential truth. Inflation would be avoided because growth into the essential is without end. In Tillich's sense, the fullness of the essential self would continue to stand as both an inexhaustible potential, whose ongoing admission into consciousness consciousness would resist only at its peril, and as a source of judgement of the ever present incompleteness of the individual's realization of the essential self in existence. A number of psychologies of the self, and especially Carl Jung's, would meet Tillich's criteria for a psychology in touch with the power of the self understood to transcend the ego from within the greatly extended boundaries of the psyche and to offer to, and demand of, the centre of consciousness, the ego, a response to its proffered healing power and expansive compassion.

AFFINITIES AND DIFFERENCES: TILLICH'S ADDRESS ON THE OCCASION OF JUNG'S DEATH

Although Tillich paid high tribute to Freud for breaking out of the culturally debilitating entrapment of modern rationalism and technical reason by plumbing the depths of pre-rational subjectivity, the deeper allegiance of his theology with psychology was with Carl Jung's. He made this clear in his address to the memorial meeting held on 1 December 1961 to honour Jung on the occasion of his death. Here Tillich developed the religious and theological significance of archetypal psychology with a profundity and clarity greater than that usually shown by Jung himself. In this address Tillich distinguishes, as would Jung, between the archetypal ground of the symbol and the symbol itself as an expression of this ground. The symbol's origin from the archetypal ground accounts for its substance and historical endurance. The fecundity of the archetype accounts for both the variability of the symbol and for the limitation of such variability by the limiting structure the archetype gives to its symbolic expression (*CGJ*, 30). Tillich then moves beyond Jung's usual comfort zone by identifying the ontological, epistemological and religious implications of Jung's understanding of the relation of the archetypal ground to its symbolic expression. Tillich locates the enduring power of the symbolic in its archetypal ground, now elevated to the religious stature of 'the creative ground of everything that is', and compares such a ground to the Christian understanding of the Logos as the site of the primordial expression of the 'essences of all things' (32). Effectively, Tillich is here summarily providing Jung with the ontology and theology that Jung's work entails but that Jung denied or qualified, namely, that the archetypal dimension of the unconscious generates the symbols in what Tillich calls 'revelatory experiences' and Jung calls the experience of 'the *numinosum*' as the basis of human religious experience itself (32).[10] This insight could immensely foster what Tillich calls the 'inter-theological' discussion of symbols between differing communities bonded by them (31). The identification of the common and human source of symbols could lead to their mutual appreciation by members of communities bonded by differing symbol sets and undermine the enmity that currently exists between such communities towards patterns of mutual embrace. In his final lecture (delivered just days before his death in 1965) Tillich in fact did move to this position in denying the need of the Christian tradition to claim for itself the status of an exhaustive and final revelation and in casting the future of religious studies in the light of the comparison of the great religious symbol systems (*FR*, 81, 91, 93).[11]

Tillich's theology and Jung's psychology share wider structural affinities. As early as the first volume of the system Tillich had identified the collective unconscious as 'the great symbol-creating source' (*ST* I, 241). Tillich's identification of the collective unconscious as the origin of symbols describes Jung's understanding of the impact of the unconscious on consciousness through the symbol especially as carried by the dream. Tillich's delineation of the experience of symbolic–revelatory and so salvific events and Jung's understanding of the numinous as characteristic of archetypal impress on consciousness are difficult to distinguish and may well point to the same experience. More, both thinkers are drawn to the radical immanental and experiential presence of the divine to the human obvious in Tillich's major symbols of God as the ground of being and depth of reason and in Jung's assertion that the divine and the human, the unconscious and consciousness, are 'functions' of each other in an all-containing psyche.[12] Nevertheless, from these foundational affinities possibly insuperable differences follow.

The greatest difference can be surfaced through a reflection on the psycho-religious implications of Jung's treatment of the Trinity. For Tillich, the Trinity symbolizes the process of divine life in which the disintegration of opposites is present as a possibility but defeated from eternity through the agency of the Spirit (*ST* I, 249–52). In the wake of its victory the Spirit leads the human into a participation in this eternally worked integration fragmentarily in time and fully in eternity. For Jung, the symbol of Trinity is, at best, a preliminary symbol to a fuller integration of opposites latent in the divine and to be realized under a more encompassing Spirit in the human. His realization that not all of creation has a presence in the reigning symbol of the creator led Jung to move from a trinitarian to a quaternitarian conception of divinity.

In his formal treatment of the Trinity Jung first understands the symbol to point to the foundational dynamic of the human psyche, the commerce between the unconscious and consciousness worked by the self. The unconscious (Father) generates consciousness (Son) and is united with its expression in the self (Spirit).[13] On wider reflection throughout his works Jung considers this understanding of the Trinity defective, because it fails to locate in a creating divinity the totality of what is so present in creation, namely the feminine, the material and bodily, and the demonic. This real absence of so much of created reality in the symbol of the creator moves Jung to a quaternitarian paradigm as the foundation of a new and superseding myth now fostered by the unconscious, at least in Western society, in compensation for the currently painful one-sidedness of the Christian myth.[14] This superseding myth would locate the opposites missing in the Christian tradition, the feminine, evil, and material creation, in the unconscious as the creative origin of all that is. Created consciousness would then be tasked with the differentiation and reunification of these divinely grounded opposites towards the emergence of a Spirit more inclusive in its embrace of those realities that the Christian myth cannot include in God as creator and so in the syntheses of opposites worked by the Christian Spirit. This Spirit would embrace and unite the male and female, the spiritual and the bodily, and, finally, good and evil in the form of a symbolic union of Christ and Satan, the light and dark brothers and sons of a common Father.[15] Not only would this Spirit be richer than the Christian Spirit, it would also imply that the redemption of the divine and the human are two sides of the same process.

In this matter Jung's appropriation of Boehme is more faithful to the latter's spirit than is Tillich's. Boehme is prominent throughout Jung's pages and named by Tillich as an intellectual 'grandfather'.[16] Jung takes from Boehme the archetypal theme that divinity becomes self-conscious in a human consciousness suffering in itself the union of the eternally unreconciled opposites in divine life. This side of Boehme is exploited in far more rational discourse by Hegel and implies that divinity is itself enriched through the unity of its opposites in historical humanity. Tillich, standing in a position of Trinitarian orthodoxy, cannot easily admit the implications of this position either ontologically, psychologically or theologically, since it would mean that God was driven to create in order to complete itself in creation. Jung and Boehme introduce the ideas of divine necessity in creation and the dependence of God on the outcome of history, ideas that Tillich could approach but never embrace throughout the vast majority of his work and systematics.[17] To put their differences succinctly, from Tillich's perspective an eternally integrated God leads the creature into the integration of divine life. In Jung's perspective a non-integrated God creates in order to find integration in humanity in a process redemptive of both.[18]

However, while the foregoing difficulties between Jung's self psychology and Tillich's theology appear to be residual and without easy reconciliation, they might be modified by a consideration of the radical new directions that certain aspects of Tillich's theology took in the final pages of his *Systematic Theology*. Here Tillich introduces his conception of essentialization. To this late point in his thought Tillich had resisted process theology, because it would seem to tie God's fate to the human historical response to the divine overture: 'A conditioned God is no God' (*ST* I, 248). But with his conception of essentialization Tillich affirms that the realization of the essential in historical humanity through the human response to its allure in existence contributes to the 'blessedness' and to the being of divinity and humanity preserved in eternity (*ST* III, 420–2). In the end Tillich ties the realization of God's well-being to the historical process as its deepest meaning without which history would become 'a divine play of no essential concern for God' (422). Tillich's mature reversal on this point would approximate the affirmation at the heart of Jung's psychology that divinity creates to realize itself in the consciousness of the creature in processes of mutual redemption as the base meaning of both incarnation and history.

At a less cosmic level, Tillich's reflections on the redemptive process to be found in certain psychologies and certainly in self psychologies is substantial in itself and yet remains to be fully implemented in practice. His late appreciation of archetypal theory might put him in a position to use it radically to recast the relative roles of priestly and psychological healing. Both psychologist and priest could be seen in the service of what Tillich identifies as the divinely grounded essential self. Both psychology and religious ministry would be enriched with this unforced fusion of their roles. Would a psychology such as Jung's, informed, in Tillich's estimate, by a sense of the mystery of being and the capacity to access it, not be as effective a servant of the essential and its healing power as a specifically religious approach? And would a specifically religious approach not have to bow to Tillich's position that in the existential situation the spiritual can be distinguished but never dissociated from the psychological? Tillich leaves the door slightly ajar on these issues. It may be time to throw it fully open.

Notes

1   Dourley (1997), 211–22.
2   Stokes (1985), 109–20.
3   Ibid., 120.
4   Cooper (2005), 14–15.
5   Stokes (1985), 137–8.
6   Ibid., 139.
7   Ibid., 118–19.
8   Jung (1958), XI, 265.
9   Dourley (1997), 212, n. 1.
10 See also Jung (1958), XI, 7.
11 See also Dourley (2004).
12 Jung (1958), VI, 243.
13 Ibid., XI, 129–37.
14 Ibid., 164–87.
15 Ibid., 175.
16 Ferre (1966), 11.
17 Dourley (1995a), 429–45.
18 Dourley (1995b), 51.

Further reading

Cooper, Terry D. (2006). 'Paul Tillich and Psychology: Historic and Contemporary Explorations' in *Theology, Psychotherapy, and Ethics*, ed. Terry D. Cooper. Macon, Ga.: Mercer University Press.

Dourley, John (1997). 'Issues of Naturalism and Supranaturalism in Tillich's Correlation of Religious with Psychological Healing'. *Studies in Religion* 26: 211–22.

Irwin, Alexander C. (1991). *Eros Towards the World: Paul Tillich and the Theology of the Erotic*. Minneapolis, Minn.: Fortress Press.

May, Rollo (1973). *Paulus: Reminiscences of a Friendship*. New York: Harper & Row.

16 Tillich in dialogue with Japanese Buddhism: a paradigmatic illustration of his approach to inter-religious conversation

MARC BOSS

In the Bampton Lectures, delivered in the autumn of 1961 at Columbia University, Tillich exemplifies his views on inter-religious dialogue with a conversation between a Christian and a Buddhist ('A Christian–Buddhist Conversation' in *CEWR*, 53–75). Portrayed as 'one of the greatest, strangest, and at the same time most competitive' religious traditions, Buddhism assuredly plays a major part in Tillich's late reflections on Christianity's encounter with the world religions (54). His visit to Japan in the late spring of 1960 has often been presented as the starting-point of this special interest in the Christian–Buddhist dialogue; but, as Terence Thomas has compellingly argued, 'this visit to Japan was more of a culmination than a venture into a new world' ('The Protestant Principle and the Encounter of World Religions' in *ERQR*, xi). The first part of this chapter will examine in some detail Tillich's concrete practice of dialogue with major representatives of Japanese Buddhism both before and during his visit to Japan. The second part will analyse his systematic reflections on Christian–Buddhist dialogue. The conclusion will briefly evaluate its significance for Tillich's late theology of religions.

TILLICH'S CONCRETE PRACTICE OF CHRISTIAN–BUDDHIST DIALOGUE

The meetings with Daisetz Suzuki and Shin'ichi Hisamatsu in the 1950s

In an account of his trip to Japan written for his friends Tillich relates his meetings with two influential Zen masters whom he had encountered before: '[Daisetz T.] Suzuki, whom [he] knew well from New York and Ascona', and '[Shin'ichi] Hisamatsu, whom [he] knew from Harvard'.[1] Suzuki had been appointed at Columbia University in 1951, while Tillich was still teaching at Union.[2] Their meeting in New York had most probably been facilitated by their common friend, the psychotherapist Karen Horney.[3] Their meeting again in Ascona

(Switzerland) was occasioned by their common participation in the Era-
nos Lectures in 1953. The encounter with Hisamatsu took place in the
autumn of 1957, while he was a Visiting Professor at Harvard University
for a semester.

Grace Cali, who served as Tillich's secretary at Harvard, reports
that 'The visit of the great Japanese Zen Master, Hisamatsu, created
more than a mild stir at Harvard . . . His several visits with Professor
Tillich bore out my feeling that this encounter was deeply stirring to
the theologian.'[4] Cali further reports that Suzuki came to Harvard along
with Hisamatsu and his translators. In early October 1957, a few days
after Hisamatsu delivered his first lecture in the presence of 'the full
faculty and student body of the Divinity School', Suzuki and Tillich
were both invited to participate in a symposium on 'New Knowledge
in Human Values' organized by Abraham Maslow at the Massachusetts
Institute of Technology (MIT). Cali recalls Tillich and Suzuki speaking
at the same session in strikingly similar terms: 'Both men unequivocally
rejected [the idea] that a scientific approach to human values was possible.' She finally stresses that 'the mental ferment of that 1957 autumn
[was] memorable for Tillich as he exchanged views with these Eastern
thinkers'.[5]

In his Matchette Lectures, which he delivered in April 1958, a few
months after his encounter with Hisamatsu, Tillich gives an interesting
account of what this encounter meant to him: 'In the last few months
I had three memorable evenings, memorable for myself, when I talked
for several hours with the master of Zen Buddhism, Hisamatsu, and
his two interpreters' (*ERQR*, 28). Tillich goes on to affirm, as he often
does, that personal encounters produce deeper understanding of alien
traditions than books do. But in this special case the human and religious
qualities of the conversation partner seem to have more cognitive value,
in Tillich's eyes, than the verbal information conveyed: '[I]f you meet a
person who really has the qualities of a saint, which this man has, then
the simple reality of his being gives you more insight into the nature of
that for which he lives than any external knowledge' (28).

The Harvard conversations with Hisamatsu
and his interpreters

The conversations with Hisamatsu, in which the two interpreters,
Jikai Fujiyoshi and Richard DeMartino, also played an active part, dealt
with a great variety of questions, ranging from practical spirituality (how
to find calmness in the midst of an active daily life) to more theoretical
discussions on the Zen concept of a Formless Self or on the Christian

notion of evil ('Dialogues, East and West. Conversations between Dr Paul Tillich and Dr Hisamatsu Shin'ichi' in *ERQR*, 75–170).

Tillich and Hisamatsu both engaged in these conversations with similar attitudes of open-mindedness. At the beginning of the first conversation each affirms that he has come to learn from the other, and each seems determined to put to the test whatever pre-established idea he has about the tradition of the other. Hisamatsu, for example, is quite familiar with Rudolf Otto's interpretation of Meister Eckhart, but he wants Tillich to tell him whether 'this is a proper presentation of Eckhart' (86). Likewise, Tillich submits to Hisamatsu's judgement what he has formerly learnt about the secularization of Japanese art from his friend Friedrich Spiegelberg (98). These initial exchanges about Eckhart and about the history of art allow the partners of dialogue to ensure that they speak more or less the same language, that some 'principle of charity' is at work, or, in Tillich's own words, that a 'common ground' has been found 'which makes both dialogue and conflicts possible' (*CEWR*, 62). In their second and third conversations Tillich and his Buddhist conversation partners uncover some proximities of thought that, for Hisamatsu at least, seem to be quite unexpected.[6] But they also realize that substantial differences oppose them in their most basic religious commitments: '[I]t is not that you cannot maintain your position,' says Hisamatsu at a certain point in their discussion about the nature of evil, 'it is more that we are unable to accept your position' (*ERQR*, 86). Tillich and his Buddhist dialogue partners nevertheless show a remarkable ability to reach agreement on what exactly their disagreement is about. Whereas Tillich identifies the ontological status of the 'particular' as a 'pivotal theme' of their discussion, DeMartino agrees that this is indeed a 'critical' difference between the Christian theologian and the Zen master: 'You experience the particular *in* its ultimate significance; Dr Hisamatsu "experiences" the particular *as* "ultimate," as a "nonparticular-particular," or as the "Self that is Not-Itself"' (140, 161).

DeMartino, whose contribution becomes decisive in the third conversation, rightly suspects in Tillich's insistence that the particular receives its ultimate significance as particular 'a subtle reminder that whereas the concrete individual gets lost in Zen, with [Tillich] it does not' (162).[7] In the Matchette Lectures Tillich retrospectively suggests that he felt compelled, in the course of his discussions with Hisamatsu, to hold firm to 'the ethical valuation of the individual over against his devaluation', to stress 'the personal character of divinity' over against the idea of a 'transpersonal absolute', to maintain 'the infinite distance of the individual person from the personal Divine Being because of his guilt and the need for forgiveness over against the elevation of the saint into the Formless self', and to give positive value to 'the individual person over against the transpersonal . . . self, in which everything individual and particular is overcome' (27–8).[8] Tillich also mentions the doctrine of creation and the question of the ultimate significance of history as further points on which he could not follow his Buddhist conversation partners (27). But in all these issues – even, indirectly, in the two latter ones – it is clear that the question of the ontological status of the 'individual' or the 'particular' was a central, and somewhat obsessive, concern for Tillich.

DeMartino meets this concern with notable acuteness by reporting a discussion he had earlier the same year with Martin Buber at Columbia University. There he made the case that if a Zen master proclaims, 'I am thou', it is not to be understood as meaning that the 'I' should 'cancel out the "thou".' To counter such 'reductionistic' misinterpretations of non-duality, he told Buber that 'any exclusively undifferentiated non-duality in which everything is reduced to a sheer sameness is branded in Buddhism a "false sameness" – precisely because particularity is annihilated' (142). This is also Hisamatsu's answer to Tillich's worrying that individuality might disappear in the Formless Self: '[W]ith the unfolding of the Self-Without-Form, individuality is not eliminated' (146). As a consequence of these elucidations of Zen's non-duality Tillich admits, 'I must try to learn with my dualistic mind how the individual – or "particular" – is simultaneously preserved and not preserved' (148).

The last significant step in the process of identifying some crucial point of disagreement occurs as Tillich remarks that in statements such as 'I am you' or 'Paul Tillich is Richard DeMartino', the copula may indicate either 'identity' or 'participation' (158). Identity, as Tillich understands it, qualifies the Zen master's claim that the statement 'I am you' is but a consequence of the central affirmation that 'I am the "ultimate" – or selfless Self.' Although Hisamatsu and DeMartino are both quite reluctant to adopt the term 'identity' to qualify their own position, they resolutely reject the position Tillich presents as its alternative:

> *Tillich*: I never would suggest that I am the ultimate. "I am you" because I participate as you do in the ultimate.
> *DeMartino*: Zen's "nonduality" is not a "participation."
> *DeMartino to Hisamatsu* (in Japanese): For Dr Tillich, you are I and I am you since you and I both "participate" in the ultimate "Self of No-Self."
> *Hisamatsu* (in Japanese): No; it is not participation.

(159)

With this strong and unambiguous statement that Zen's non-duality cannot be explained in terms of 'participation' as Tillich understands it, the dialogue has uncovered a central point of disagreement. Given the far-reaching consequences Tillich will draw from this statement in his later lectures, it can be plausibly argued that the Harvard conversations with Hisamatsu and his interpreters had a decisive and lasting impact on his understanding of the constitutive difference between Christianity and Buddhism.

The trip to Japan: visited places and major encounters

'Something very exciting has happened' (*ENGW* V, 348). These are the words in which Tillich announced to his friends that he had been invited to lecture for two months in Japan. The invitation, which also included his wife, Hannah, was addressed to him in the summer of 1959. It emanated from a 'Committee for Intellectual Interchange' established both in New York and Tokyo.[9] During the ten weeks they stayed in Japan the Tillichs were essentially based in Tokyo (3 to 23 May and 13 June to 2 July), but they also spent approximately three weeks in Kyoto (23 May to 12 June), and one in the mountain resort of Karuizawa (3 to 8 July).[10] From Tokyo they undertook two excursions to the ancient capital, Kamakura, including a meeting with Suzuki 'in one of the temples of Kamakura where he [had] his house and a rare library of Buddhist and Western literature'.[11] During their stay in Kyoto they also paid a visit to Hisamatsu. Hannah Tillich reports that their meeting with Hisamatsu took place at 'the famous Garden of Royan-Ji, the rock garden with the centuries-old wall sheltering its far side'.[12]

The Tillichs encountered representatives of Shintoism, as they visited 'the Meiji shrine in Tokyo and the Ise shrine in the South'.[13] In a conversation with Japanese Christians in Kyoto Tillich confessed that he could hardly identify Shinto's 'religious element'.[14] 'Shinto is a riddle to me . . . [M]y categories simply are not sufficient tools to grasp the situation here.'[15] The Tillichs also had the opportunity to meet representatives of so-called 'New Religions', such as the Tenrikyo and the Rissho Koseikai. In his report Tillich underlines their strong appeal to the Japanese masses.[16] To different degrees, all these encounters and conversations certainly helped Tillich to measure the complexity of the religious situation in Japan. Nevertheless, on 16 June, in a letter sent to Grace Cali from Tokyo, Tillich wrote in a somewhat telegraphic style: 'Most important for me: The discussions with the Buddhist scholars, most of them marvelous people.'[17]

Christian–Buddhist conversations in Japan

Tillich's discussions with Hisamatsu and Suzuki were undoubtedly of special importance to him. On 7 June, in a conversation at the Christian Center for the Study of Japanese Religions in the Kyoto area, he said that when he was first confronted with popular Buddhist piety in Kamakura, he asked himself: 'How would the two Buddhists whom I know and love, Mr Hisamatsu and Mr Suzuki, react to this; how do they feel about this?'[18] During that same conversation Tillich mentioned that he had received an answer to this question from Hisamatsu, earlier on the same day, in a group discussion in which he and the Zen master were both participating:

> [He] said that the most primitive piety . . . could be the way of awakening the Buddha spirit in every human being. Now in this way the whole of popular piety, if I understood him rightly, was left so much to itself without help from the religious leaders that I had a feeling my question was quite to the point and that he either could not answer it or set the question aside because it was not a problem for him.[19]

As we have already noticed, Tillich's 'Informal Report' also briefly mentions his conversations with Suzuki and Hisamatsu. The report contains no substantial information about his discussion with Suzuki in Kamakura, but it gives a highly instructive account of what Tillich himself describes as an 'especially memorable discussion' with Hisamatsu at the rock garden of Royan-Ji: 'The chief priest of the temple and Mr Hisamatsu and I fell into a discussion of over an hour about the question of whether the rock garden and the universe are identical (the Buddhist position) or non-identical but united by participation (my position).'[20] Three years after their first encounter in Harvard the Zen master and the Lutheran theologian had obviously not forgotten this critical issue of their earlier discussions. In another passage of his report Tillich refers to this distinction between identity and participation as the fundamental contrast underlying the other differences he observed between Christianity and Buddhism:

> The discussions with the Buddhists have shown me that their main points of difference with Christianity are always: the different valuation placed on the individual, the meaning of history, interpersonal relations, religious and social reformation, and finitude and guilt. It is the contrast between the principle of identity and the principle of participation.[21]

Tillich saw the principle of identity at work not only in Zen, but also, to some lesser degree, in Shin Buddhism (also referred to as Jodo Shinshu, the True School of the Pure Land), which he knew to be the most radical form of Pure Land Buddhism and the 'opposite pole of the Zen denominations' in Japan.[22] In his report Tillich mentions that he and his wife had a 'special relation' with this tradition, since Kosho Otani, whose father was the 'archibishop of a large section of Jodo Shinshu', used to live in their house in New York while he was studying at Columbia University.[23] It was he who arranged the discussion between Tillich and about twenty Buddhist scholars and fifty students that was held on 6 June at Otani University, the Jodo Shin Sect Buddhist university in Kyoto. Transcripts of this discussion were published in the journal *Japanese Religion* in 1961. It is unfortunately the only text of a group discussion between Tillich and Buddhist scholars that has come down to us.[24] In the course of this discussion Tillich discovered that his interlocutors were little concerned about the question of Gautama's historical existence, even though one of them admitted that this question 'should be seriously acknowledged instead of glossed over'.[25] As he asked if Buddhism knew anything comparable to the Reformation in Christianity – i.e. a distinctly religious movement attempting to fight 'the demonization or distortion of religion' – he was told that Shin and Zen Buddhism were both such movements, that both tried to de-demonize earlier forms of Buddhism, although Shin was finally more successful because of its sociological roots in the lower classes and 'its emphasis upon personal faith in the grace of Amida Buddha'.[26] Another participant corrected this somewhat apologetic account by stressing that this can be said only 'from an ideal point of view'.[27] Finally, Tillich asked a question of crucial importance, in the context of Otani University, about the significance of prayer in Buddhism:

> I can understand how it is that a Jew, a Christian, or a Muslim prays, because praying always leads people to another ego, a Thou, and it is thus an ego–thou relationship. To whom does someone pray on the basis of Buddhism? I understand very well that a Buddhist can meditate and I believe that in Christianity meditation is far too much neglected because the personal symbolism of the divine has overlaid the suprapersonal in much Christian thinking, especially in a country like the United States where the tradition of personalism is so strong. But on the other hand, in the official doctrine and theological background of Buddhism the personal element is almost swallowed by the suprapersonal element – let's

call it the Buddha principle or the Amida principle, but not a figure which can be looked at like a person. Nevertheless, there is much prayer going on. How can this be united with the fundamentals of Buddhist theory? Or, to formulate the question more precisely, "to whom does a Buddhist pray if he prays instead of meditating?"[28]

Here Tillich expresses again his concern about the possibility of an I–thou relationship in Buddhism. His Harvard conversations with Hisamatsu had convinced him that Zen leaves little or no place for such a relationship. But he knows that Jodo Shinshu calls for 'complete surrender to the compassion of the Buddha Power', that it relies on faith in the so-called 'other-power' in contrast to the 'self-power' of Zen.[29] This element of faith in Jodo Shinsu seems to imply some kind of I–thou relationship with the 'Buddha Power'. Tillich's question about the significance of prayer in Buddhism attempts to clarify the nature of this relationship. The first answer he receives is that Shin 'denies the whole concept of prayer' and 'admits only an expression of gratitude or thanksgiving for the grace of Amida Buddha'.[30] But this answer does not satisfy Tillich, since even an expression of gratitude inevitably 'includes some ego–thou relationship'.[31] Thanksgiving, he assumes, is but another form of prayer, so that even he or she who prays in that special, anti-superstitious, way 'cannot escape the personalized "thou"'.[32] Another participant recognizes that in many forms of Buddhism prayers are offered to Buddha, bodhisattvas or 'even to Shinto Gods', but that such practices are only 'made possible by the belief that Buddhahood has manifested itself in human form', which means that 'whatever may be the figure to whom one prays, one actually prays to the spirit of Buddha'.[33] Is this also the case in Shin's practice of thanksgiving and, if so, does it mean that the I–thou relationship, which seems implied in such practice, has at last no ultimate significance even for Shin Buddhists? The discussion came to a close before questions like these could be further investigated. But at the end of his visit to Japan Tillich appears to have reached the conclusion that Pure Land Buddhism ultimately rests upon the 'principle of identity'. This can be inferred from the account he gives, in a passage of his report, of a conversation he had with a 'Pure Land Buddhist scholar' about 'the possibility of communion' between individuals or persons. '[This scholar] made the statement, "If the individual self is a substance [in the sense of 'standing upon itself'] then no communion is possible"; to which I replied that "only on this basis is communion – in contrast to realizing identity – possible."'[34] Communion, for Tillich, implies both separation and its overcoming by participation, so that his main criticism of Zen Buddhism applies here to Shin Buddhism as well.[35]

In all the dialogues with Zen or Pure Land Buddhists that we have examined – that is, in all those of which a record has been kept – Tillich seems to put himself in the position of defending a rather staunch personalism whose Buberian overtones can hardly be overlooked. This position of his might appear somewhat startling to those of his fellow Christian theologians who constantly underline – and castigate – his own valuation of the 'transpersonal' (or of the synonymous 'suprapersonal') as a polemical enterprise directed 'against the philosophical and theological personalism of [the twentieth] century, against talk of I and Thou and of the "encounter" between God and humanity'.[36] But Tillich's unusual insistence, in his conversations with Buddhists, on the personal dimension of our relation to the ultimate shows – more convincingly perhaps than any abstract statement – that his well-known claim about the ultimate being more than personal should never be dissociated from his corollary claim that the ultimate cannot be anything less than personal (*ERQR*, 48–50; *ST* I, 245).

Another surprising characteristic of these conversations – especially those which occurred in Japan – is that Tillich, in contrast to many of his later commentators, did not see the question of being and non-being as a central issue.[37] The questions he asked again and again were 'How do the leading Buddhists deal with popular piety?' and 'Is there any event in Buddhism which is comparable to Protestantism?'[38] As he was asked, at the Christian Center for the Study of Japanese Religions, why these questions were so important to him, he answered:

> You see, a discussion about being and non-being also occurred this afternoon, and it was in the usual manner of philosophical discussion – I could have done that in Cambridge as well as here. What I want to understand here in Japan is the actual religious power or non-power of Buddhism. I am after this all the time.[39]

SYSTEMATIC PERSPECTIVES ON CHRISTIAN–BUDDHIST DIALOGUE

Kingdom of God, participation and *agape* versus Nirvana, identity and compassion

Tillich's most comprehensive attempt to systematize his various experiences in Christian–Buddhist dialogue is to be found in the third of his Bampton Lectures. Delivered a year and a half after his visit to Japan, this lecture, entitled 'A Christian–Buddhist Conversation', is entirely dedicated to this endeavour, since it aims at identifying the *telos* (i.e. the 'intrinsic aim of existence'), which works as an organizing principle in each of the two religions:

> In the dialogue between Christianity and Buddhism two *telos*-formulas can be used: in Christianity the *telos* of every*one* and every*thing* united in the Kingdom of God; in Buddhism the *telos* of every*thing* and every*one* fulfilled in the Nirvana.
>
> (*CEWR*, 64)

The italics in the pronouns are meant to signal that the opposition between personal and transpersonal reality determines a shift of emphasis in the two contrasted approaches to the ultimate expressed in the symbols Kingdom of God and Nirvana: 'The Ultimate in Christianity is symbolized in personal categories, the ultimate in Buddhism in transpersonal categories' (65–6). As he turns to the ethical implications of this basic difference between the two religions Tillich notices that the symbols Kingdom of God and Nirvana rest on two different ontological principles, which are 'participation' and 'identity':

> One participates, as an individual human being, in the Kingdom of God. One is identical with everything that is in Nirvana.
>
> (68)

More clearly than the principle of participation, the principle of identity leads to a 'sympathetic identification with nature' to which Tillich grants a positive ethical value, since it helps to prevent the 'technical control of nature which dominates in the western world' (69). In interpersonal ethical issues, however, Tillich's comparative appraisal of the two principles confers a higher value – or, at least, a higher efficiency – to participation over against identity:

> One can say, in considerably condensed form, that participation leads to *agape*, identity to compassion.
>
> (70)

Buddhist compassion is here construed as 'a state in which he who does not suffer under his own conditions may suffer by identification with another who suffers' (71). Christian *agape*, as Tillich understands it, transposes the structure of grace into the sphere of ethics: grace is unconditional acceptance, but it aims at transforming him or her who receives it. Likewise, *agape* entails both 'the acceptance of the unacceptable' and 'the will to transform individual as well as social structures' (72). The

ethical contrast between compassion and *agape* involves thereby a further contrast between the Buddhist and the Christian approach to the
concrete reality of historical life: compassion leads to 'salvation' from
historical reality, whereas *agape* leads to its 'transformation'.

Internal polarities: the 'silent dialogue' within Buddhism and Christianity

The Shin Buddhist scholar Taitetsu Unno has noticed that Tillich's
understanding of Buddhist compassion 'may not be totally inaccurate',[40]
as far as it refers to the Zen tradition 'represented by Shin'ichi Hisamatsu
and his lineage', but hardly does justice to 'other major streams of
Japanese Buddhism, including the Pure Land tradition, especially as
found in Shin Buddhism'.[41] Unno stresses in particular that, in Shin Buddhism, the concept of compassion involves the same two characteristics
that Tillich attributes to *agape*: the gracious acceptance of the unacceptable, and the will to transform both individual and social structures.[42]
If Tillich's understanding of compassion appears inadequate from a Shin
point of view it is not only, as Unno charitably suggests, as the result
of an insufficient acquaintance with this tradition. Although the record
kept of his conversation with Shin Buddhist scholars at Otani University shows no trace of any discussion about Shin's aptitude to transform
reality out of its own religious substance, the document suggests – and
so does the 'Informal Report' – that Tillich was reasonably well informed
about Shin's exclusive and radical insistence on grace. This means that
Tillich deliberately ignored this soteriological particularity of Shin Buddhism as he undertook to define the Buddhist concept of compassion
over against the Christian concept of *agape*.

It would, however, be a mistake to consider that Tillich pays no
attention whatsoever to such internal differences. The confrontation he
organizes between Buddhism and Christianity rests on what he calls a
'dynamic typology'. What makes this typology 'dynamic' is the estab-
lishing of 'contrasting poles' within each of the two religions (*CEWR,*
55). 'Under the method of dynamic typology every dialogue between
religions is accompanied by a silent dialogue *within* the representatives of each of the participating religions' (57). This means that the
polarities that Tillich sees at work in the contrast between Buddhism
and Christianity are equally at work as polarities internal to each
tradition.

Even though Christianity is predominantly determined by the
'personalistic symbol' of the Kingdom of God, it also leaves room
for 'transpersonal categories' such as the *esse ipsum* of 'the classical

Christian doctrine of God' (64, 66–7). Conversely, it seems obvious to Tillich 'that in Mahajana Buddhism the Buddha-Spirit appears in many manifestations of a personal character' (67). Even though the Buddhist principle of identity entails a more positive relation to nature than the Christian principle of participation, the latter principle can nevertheless 'reach a degree in which it is often difficult to distinguish it from the principle of identity, as, for example, in Francis of Assisi' (69). Similarly, even though Buddhist compassion longs primarily for 'salvation from reality', it does not always lead to an ascetic rejection of the phenomenal world, but it can also 'lead to the affirmation of the activities of daily life – as, for instance, in Zen Buddhism' (73). Tillich believes nevertheless that such attitudes are inspired by an ideal of 'ultimate detachment' rather than by some positive valuation of historical reality as such (73). On this specific issue Tillich sees a 'silent dialogue' going on within Christianity, but not within Buddhism.

History and social transformation

The question of history and of its meaning for social transformation is the major theme of the final pages of 'A Christian–Buddhist Conversation'. Refusing to reduce history to 'the scene in which the destiny of individuals is decided', Tillich describes it as 'a movement in which the new is created and which runs ahead to the absolutely new' (*CEWR*, 72). The transformation of reality that is at work in this movement is what the biblical tradition expresses in the symbol of 'the new heaven and the new earth'. Tillich mentions here only one of the various implications of this 'vision of history':

> With respect to the mode of the future, it means that the Kingdom of God has a revolutionary character. Christianity, insofar as it works in line with this symbol, shows a revolutionary force directed towards a radical transformation of society.
>
> (72)

This is a remarkable reminder of the vision of history that Tillich developed after the First World War in his religious socialist writings. His own insistence on the 'revolutionary character' of this vision and on the 'revolutionary force' it conveys for a 'radical transformation of society' has hardly been noticed in the countless discussions that 'A Christian–Buddhist Conversation' has engendered in the last forty years. Yet this issue plays a crucial role in the very last stage of the dialogue outlined in the Bampton Lectures. The significance of this last stage, which is meant to lead the dialogue between Christians and Buddhists to 'a preliminary end', lies in what Tillich sees as their common need to overcome any kind of religious 'indifference towards history' (75, 74). Such indifference, to be sure, exists in Christianity as well as in Buddhism. Tillich observes that there are 'strong, sometimes even predominant' counter-tendencies to 'the revolutionary dynamics in Christianity' (73). In such cases, he admits, 'the revolutionary impetus of Christianity is repressed' (73). But to be repressed it has to be there as a constitutive element. This, for Tillich, is not the case with Buddhism:

> The conservative tendencies in the official churches have never been able to suppress this [revolutionary] element in the symbol of the Kingdom of God, and most of the revolutionary movements in the West – liberalism, democracy, and socialism – are dependent on it, whether they know it or not. There is no analogy to this in Buddhism.
>
> (72–3)

Whether Tillich was right or not in this assumption about Buddhism – and there are good reasons to believe he was not – might be regarded as a minor issue at this point.[43] It is important to notice, however, that Buddhism's alleged indifference towards history is not here considered an obstacle to its internal transformation, by 'history itself', in the process of its dialogue with Christianity:

> For history itself has driven Buddhism to take history seriously, and this at a moment when in the Christian West a despair about history has taken hold of many people. Buddhist Japan wants democracy, and asks the question of its spiritual foundation.
>
> (74)

Tillich believes that Japanese democracy, which has been forced upon the Japanese people by the conqueror, lacks a spiritual foundation. It is in need, so he further assumes, of 'something which has appeared only in the context of Christianity, namely, the attitude toward every individual which sees in him a person, a being of infinite value and equal rights in view of the Ultimate' (74). This is certainly one of the main reasons Tillich, in his dialogues with Buddhists, constantly insisted on the personalistic element of his Christian faith over against the transpersonal element emphasized by his conversation partners. He was indeed convinced that major political issues were involved in these apparently speculative discussions about the ontological status of the individual.

The 'mission' of religious socialism and the encounter of world religions

Tillich's statement about a lack of spiritual foundation in Japanese democracy seems to imply that the Japanese should become Christians in order to become better democrats. But Tillich decidedly rejects this idea that the Japanese should be converted to Christianity. What 'has appeared only in the context of Christianity' is not Christianity as such, but a religious criterion that is to be applied to all religions, including Christianity. Tillich's most clear-cut statement about this essential point is not to be found in 'A Christian–Buddhist Dialogue' but in the last pages of another lecture, which was also delivered in the autumn of 1961, under the title 'Christian and Non-Christian Revelation':

> The Japanese . . . have a democracy, but this democracy is without roots and those who have a real consciousness of the situation are worried how it might be possible to save democracy if there are not these spiritual roots for it. Now, should we tell them that they should all become Christians and then democracy will be a wonderful thing in Japan? To say such a thing is obviously meaningless . . . Were I a missionary [to] the Japanese people . . . I would say, "We don't want to bring you another religion. We want to point to a criterion which is the criterion over and against all religions, including our own. If you accept this criterion you may judge yourselves as much as you judge us and perhaps we can unite in the acceptance of this criterion, because this criterion is nothing other than the majesty of the divine or holy itself against any particular form in which it appears".
>
> (*ERQR*, 72–4)

Although the discourse about 'mission' developed in this passage is often regarded as a late development in Tillich's thought, a case can be made that every single element of that discourse is already to be found in his early writings on religious socialism.[44]

In the 1920s and 1930s Tillich invites religious socialists to work in any 'confession' as long as the latter accepts to be submitted to the criterion of the 'prophetic-Protestant principle' ('Basic Principles of Religious Socialism' (1928) in *PolE*, 88; 'Religious Socialism' (1931) in *PolE*, 54). In 'Religious Socialism' (1931) he asserts that the 'radical character' of this principle precludes any 'confessionalism' that would claim absoluteness for itself:

[I]t establishes a point within the system of every confession at which it transcends itself and opens itself to the meaning of the other confessions . . . Therefore, religious socialism is not bound to a confession. It does not encroach upon the concrete confession of the individual; and for this reason it calls itself religious, and not Christian, Catholic, or Protestant socialism

(PolE, 54).[45]

It is to be noticed that the word 'confessionalism', in this context, refers to both intra- and inter-religious relationships. It is indeed well known that, in the years immediately following the First World War, the socialists who gathered with Tillich in the so-called Kairos Circle of Berlin called themselves 'religious' rather than 'Christian' in order to take into account the Jewish faith professed by some members of their movement. But recently edited archival material of this period reveals that the religious socialist movement of Berlin considered the possibility of including other religions as well.

In a manifesto that Tillich wrote for the group in 1919 – as an explicit counter-thrust to the Tambach Conference, which had been held earlier in the same year in Switzerland – it is said that 'confessional mission is bound to fail' if the paradox expressed in the prophetic-Protestant principle is to be taken seriously ('Die prinzipiellen Grundlagen und die nächsten Aufgaben unserer Bewegung (I)' (1919) in ENGW X, 249). This paradox implies that a radical no and a radical yes are simultaneously pronounced on both Christian and non-Christian beliefs, practices and institutions:

Our No is more radical than the Swiss No. It stops before nothing, be it the personal life, ecclesiastical forms, or the ethics of the Sermon on the Mount . . . To this absolute No corresponds the absolute Yes, the Paradox. As nothing can stop the No nothing can stop the Yes . . . The No is addressed to the saint and the Yes to the criminal; the No is pronounced on the Bible and the Yes on the book of charms; the No is over Luther and the Yes over the frantic Astharte Priests.

(241)

Because 'community', as religious socialism understands it, is based on this paradox, it should ignore any kind of confessional confinement. As a consequence, such community cannot 'exclude Jews and Buddhists' if they share the basic orientations of the religious socialist movement:

Either we exclude Jews and Buddhists who share the basic orientations of our movement – then we have not even attained the socialist ideal of humanity – or we accept them, as our principle would command us to do. In the latter case, Christianity is no more the expression of a religion limited by confessional boundaries, but of the universal religion of humanity on the ground of which the particular confessions, the Christian among others, raise up . . . This double significance of 'Christian' is unavoidable, at least in theory. In practice, it would be preferable to use the term 'religious' and to understand the word 'Christian' in a confessional sense . . . Therefore, if a name has to be found, it would be more accurate to speak of a religious socialist movement.

(247–8)

The mention of the Buddhists alongside the Jews in the context of this discussion has of course a paradigmatic function. It shows that the religious inclusiveness expressed in the term 'religious socialism' was potentially unlimited, even if, at that time, non-Christian religions – apart from Judaism – were considered 'provisionally without practical significance' (*ENGW* X, 257). Some decades later, when Tillich wrote in his introduction to the third volume of the *Systematic Theology* that 'a Christian theology which is not able to enter into a creative dialogue with the theological thought of other religions misses a world-historical occasion', it had become evident to him that the time of the practical insignificance of these other religions was over (*ST* III, 6).

CONCLUSION

In what is certainly the most famous passage of his very last lecture Tillich observes, 'in terms of a kind of an apologia yet also a self-accusation', that the main focus of his *Systematic Theology* was 'the apologetic discussion against and with the secular' rather than the questions raised by Christianity's encounter with world religions (*MW/HW* VI, 439). Mircea Eliade is certainly to be trusted when he reports, in his tribute at the Rockefeller Chapel memorial service, that Tillich wished to rewrite his *Systematic Theology* in the light of his encounter with other religions.[46] When he was asked, shortly before his death, whether Tillich was really serious about such a bold statement, Eliade answered that he was 'deadly serious'. And he went on to insist, 'I thought he was going to have time to do it, because although he was 78 in 1964, he didn't look that way . . . I was sure that Paul Tillich would have another six or seven years in which he could at least have a small *Systematic Theology* reworked in light of this experience.'[47]

Unfortunately, Eliade never specified what novelties such an alternative *Systematic Theology* would have brought up or what corrections of earlier positions it would have implied. In the abundant literature generated by these open questions two major responses have been advanced in order to identify the nature of the shift that seems to have taken place in Tillich's late thinking. The first, which locates the shift at a methodological level, states that Tillich moved from an aprioristic and normative approach towards other religions to a more empirical and descriptive approach.[48] The second response, which places the shift at a doctrinal level, holds that Tillich moved from an 'inclusivist' to a 'pluralist' theology of religions.[49] But the case can be made that neither of these two answers do justice to Tillich's theological interpretation of the history of religions and its highly sophisticated epistemological framework.[50] The shift, in the light of Tillich's dialogue with Japanese Buddhists, is neither methodological nor doctrinal, but kairological: it has to do with Tillich's perception of a new world-historical situation, which, almost half a century before, he had foreseen – and expected – in his religious-socialist writings.

Notes

1   Under the title 'Informal Report on a Lecture Trip to Japan, May 1 to July 10, 1960' Tillich related in some detail his visit to Japan and his impressions about it. An abridged version of this text is available in Hannah Tillich (1976), 93–115. The complete text has been published in German translation in *GW* XIII, 490–517.
2   See Thomas (1984), 196.
3   Ibid., 195–6.
4   Cali (1996), 72.
5   Ibid., 73.
6   '*DeMartino*: "[T]he concept of being necessarily implies non-being." *Tillich*: "I agree very much. Therefore I deny that there is being without non-being even in God." *Hisamatsu* (in Japanese): "Oh, does Dr Tillich also think so?"' *ERQR*, 116.
7   DeMartino, whom Tillich describes as an 'old pupil' of his (Hannah Tillich (1976), 100), worked as an interpreter for Suzuki and Hisamatsu in North America. Tillich praised his co-authored book with Suzuki and Erich Fromm (DeMartino, Suzuki and Fromm (1960)); see Cali (1996), 72.
8   Tillich, it must be noted, takes here the contrast between Christianity and Buddhism to be but a particular expression of what he describes as a more general contrast between 'East' and 'West'.
9   Hannah Tillich (1976), 93.
10 See Siedler (1999a), 187 and (1999b), 124–32. Siedler, who has established, on the basis of archival material, a detailed chronology of Tillich's visit to Japan, shows that Tillich's 'Informal Report' is not to be read as an

exhaustive account of his many encounters and activities in Japan. The original introduction of Tillich's report also contains a warning confirming this point (*GW* XIII, 490).

11 Hannah Tillich (1976), 101.

12 Ibid., 118. Masao Abe reports that the Tillichs also visited the monastery of Myoshinji Temple under Hisamatsu's guidance, Abe (1966), 129.

13 Hannah Tillich (1976), 107.

14 Ibid., 62.

15 Ibid., 59–60.

16 Ibid., 108.

17 'Letters from Japan' in Cali (1996), 111. Tillich also stresses that his discussions in Japan took place 'mostly with Buddhists', *ERQR*, 61.

18 Wood (1961–2), 58.

19 Ibid., 57.

20 Hannah Tillich (1976), 99.

21 Ibid., 104–5.

22 Ibid., 100.

23 Ibid., 99–100.

24 Masao Abe refers to several other 'conferences and meetings with Buddhist scholars' organized by 'Professors Nishitani, Takeuchi, and other members of Kyoto University' (Abe (1966), 129). Tillich, who briefly mentions these discussions in his 'Informal Report', speaks appreciatively of Nishitani's 'incisive and logical' mind and describes him as 'a philosopher with a Buddhist speculative background but also with a deep understanding of both old and modern western philosophy' (Hannah Tillich (1976), 101).

25 Wood (1961/2), 50.

26 Ibid., 51–3.

27 Ibid., 53.

28 Ibid.

29 Hannah Tillich (1976), 100.

30 Wood (1961–2), 54.

31 Ibid., 55.

32 Ibid.

33 Ibid., 54.

34 Hannah Tillich (1976), 101.

35 Confirmation of this can be found in the conclusion of 'A Christian–Buddhist Conversation', where a stylized version of the same dialogue takes place between a 'Christian philosopher' and a 'Buddhist priest', without any reminder of the Pure Land tradition.

36 Bayer (1994), 241, quoted and translated by James (2003), 143.

37 See, for example, Gilkey (1988) and Masao Abe's 'Response' to Gilkey, ibid., 11–15.

38 Wood (1961/2), 57.

39 Ibid., 58.

40 Unno (2001), 166.

41 Ibid., 165.

42 Ibid., 175–6.

43 See, for example, Unno (2001), 174 and Abe (1985), 179–85.

44 Terence Thomas, for instance, reads this passage as a corroboration of his thesis that Tillich developed a 'pluralistic' theology of religion in at least some of his latest works; see his 'Introduction' in *ERQR*, xxiii; see also Thomas (1995), 41–2. Tillich himself addresses the problem of the spiritual foundations of Japanese democracy in terms that explicitly refer to some of his early German works: 'I would suggest that there is a way to approach this problem, a way which came to me about fifty years ago when I first talked about the Protestant principle' (*ERQR*, 72).

45 Tillich, however, insists that 'the confessional character of every concrete religion' should not be 'abandoned in favour of a "rational supraconfession-alism"' (*PolE*, 54). No less than his critique of confessionalism, Tillich's corollary critique of 'rational supraconfessionalism' (or 'rationalist inter-confessionalism', as he also calls it) runs through his entire work, from the first religious-socialist essays that he wrote in 1919 (*GW* II, 27; *ENGW* X, 245) to the conclusions of his Bampton Lectures (*CEWR*, 97) and of his last lecture in Chicago (*MW/HW* VI, 441).

46 'Paul Tillich and the History of Religions' in *FR* 33–5.

47 Brauer (2001), 223.

48 See, for example, Thomas (1992), 5.

49 See Dourley (2004) and Thomas (1995). For a critical discussion of Thomas's argument, see James (1997), especially 37–42.

50 See Boss (2001), 177–95.

Further reading

Abe, Masao (1985). *Zen and Western Thought*. New York/Honolulu: Macmillan/ University of Hawaii Press.

Boss, Marc (2001). 'Religious Diversity: From Tillich to Lindbeck and Back' in *Religion in the New Millennium: Theology in the Spirit of Paul Tillich*, ed. Raymond F. Bulman and Frederick Parrella, 177–95. Macon, Ga.: Mercer University Press.

Gilkey, Langdon (1988). 'Tillich and the Kyoto School' in *Papers from the Annual Meeting of the North American Paul Tillich Society, Boston, Massachusetts, December 1987*, 1–10. Charlottesville, Va.: The North American Paul Tillich Society, Inc.

Ihuoma, Sylvester I. (2004). *Paul Tillich's Theology of Culture in Dialogue with African Theology: A Contextual Analysis*, Tillich-Studien, vol. XI. Münster: LIT Verlag.

James, Robison B. (2003). *Tillich and World Religions: Encountering Other Faiths Today*. Macon, Ga.: Mercer University Press.

Siedler, Dirk Christian (1999a). *Paul Tillichs Beiträge zu einer Theologie der Religionen*. Berlin: Alektor Verlag.

Thatamanil, John J. (2006). *The Immanent Divine: God, Creation, and the Human Predicament. An East–West Conversation*. Minneapolis, Minn.: Fortress Press.

Thomas, Terence (1999). *Paul Tillich and World Religions*. Cardiff: Cardiff Academic Press.

17 Tillich and feminism

RACHEL SOPHIA BAARD

Feminist theology's engagement with male theologians is usually characterized by a mixture of appreciation and uneasiness, and feminist dialogue with Paul Tillich is no exception to this rule. Feminists often object to the abstract nature of Tillich's theology, to androcentric assumptions in his thought and to elements in his personal life that suggest an objectification of women. Yet there has also been some appreciation of Tillich from feminist theologians such as Mary Daly, Judith Plaskow, Susan Lichtman and Mary Ann Stenger. As a matter of fact, feminists might find more points of contact with Tillich than with many other male theologians. These points of contact include a commonly shared concern with issues of social justice, a methodological openness to human experience, an ontology that lends itself to feminist appropriation and even traces of proto-feminist awareness in Tillich. One might posit that his characteristic openness to the political movements around him might have eventually led him into more lengthy conversation with feminist theology, had it been more of a presence during his lifetime. Such a conversation would not be confined to conceptual points, but would take explicit notice of the presence of presuppositions and social locations, thereby including a focus on personal, methodological and doctrinal issues.

PERSONAL CONVERSATIONS

Interpreters who operate with presuppositions that are similar to those of the author with whose work they are engaging usually focus on the content of his or her texts without much critical interrogation of the author's character. However, when interpreters and authors do not share a similar social space, and particularly when there is a power difference, the author's personal ethos (broadly understood to include personal and social elements) is more readily recognized as an aspect of intellectual discourse. This should not be seen as justification for *ad hominem* attacks on an author, nor as a negation of the importance of the actual content of an author's work, but simply as a recognition that the latter does not exist in a vacuum. Given the very different social spaces occupied by feminists and Western male theologians, it is not surprising that feminist theologians often operate with a strong hermeneutic of suspicion when they engage with 'malestream' texts. This hermeneutic of suspicion is shaped by experiences of cultural patterns that privilege male perspectives, by women's relative lack of power in public life and by widespread violence against women. When feminists then focus not only on texts, but on the ethos of an author such as Tillich, it is not a matter of unscholarly prejudice, but of an approach to texts grounded in the very real power relations within which human beings live.

Hannah Tillich's memoirs sketched the picture of a man who engaged in numerous extra-marital affairs and dabbled in pornography and sado-masochism.[1] Defences of Tillich ranged from attempts to malign Hannah, therapeutic approaches that focused on Tillich's puritanical upbringing and his traumatic experiences in the First World War, socialist arguments against bourgeois marriage, feminist retrievals of sado-masochism and arguments that Tillich's erotic misconduct should be seen as the other side of an erotic virtue.[2] However, not all of these responses are equally persuasive, and some are even offensive from a feminist perspective. Feminist distrust of patriarchal patterns of sexual domination or injustices against women in traditional marriages is evoked by the picture of Tillich that emerges from the memoirs, and this distrust will not simply disappear, even if one might be sympathetic to Tillich and intrigued by his ideas.

Nevertheless, this does not mean that the conversation between Tillich and feminism need come to a screeching halt at this point. Three observations might help to move the conversation forward. In the first place, perhaps the best way to look at the sexual aspect of Tillich's ethos is in terms of the concept of the boundary. Tillich himself entitled his brief autobiography *On the Boundary*, and his work is often described in terms of geographical and theological boundaries. In its simultaneous semblance of bourgeois 'respectability' and *avant-garde* openness, Tillich's sexual ethos tragically reflects this focus on the boundary on a more personal level. The boundary can be, and usually was in the life of Paul Tillich, a place of creativity, even of the approach of New Being. But when navigated unsuccessfully the boundary can also be a place where the New does not happen and where, instead, the uncreative clichés of *both* sides of the Old are repeated. Indeed, Tillich himself wondered,

'Was my erotic life a failure, or was it a daring way of opening up new human possibilities?'[3]

Two critiques of Tillich's sexual ethos suggest that Tillich did not succeed in 'opening up new possibilities' in his erotic life, but instead echoed the tired old clichés on both sides of the sexual boundary. Mary Daly argues that his pornographic and sado-masochistic exploits reflect patriarchal constructions of sexuality in terms of domination – something that has been criticized by feminist scholars in their attempts to formulate new perspectives on the erotic.[4] Thus, on the '*avant-garde*' side of the sexual boundary, one could argue that Tillich's actions do not reflect the kind of New Being that feminists would espouse. With regard to the 'traditional' side of the sexual boundary, Alexander Irwin accuses Tillich of an inability to live up to the demands of justice within the setting of personal relationships.[5] Although the Tillichs had agreed on an open marriage, Hannah Tillich's memoirs indicated some unhappiness about this arrangement. Paul Tillich's apparent insensitivity to that, and his insistence that they keep the outward appearance of the marriage intact while not acting in accordance with that appearance, can indeed be offensive to feminist sensibilities. Despite the warm friendships and rich relationships he was capable of having with women, it seems that Paul Tillich was not able to live consistently in a new way that would not repeat patriarchal forms of sexuality that either objectify women or see them as helpmates for the attainment of the goals of a man's life.

However, a second observation is in order. It is the fairly obvious reminder that ethos cannot be reduced to sexuality. Ethos is a multifaceted concept that encompasses various levels of a person's character. Describing ethos only in terms of sexuality would be a reflection of the modern confounding of morality with sexuality. In contrast, in classical rhetorical theory and moral philosophy ethos was a notion that was tied up with the social causes one embraced, the values one embodied and the actions one took. It particularly had to do with the kind of practical virtues that would help in forming prudent public decisions, virtues such as justice, courage, temperance, generosity, magnanimity, magnificence and prudence.[6] Paul Tillich, for all his faults, his abstractions and his residues of patriarchal thinking, nonetheless embodied many of these classical virtues. For example, Tillich's theological vision testifies to the virtue of magnificence, which can be described in terms of 'having a vision of what elevates the human spirit'.[7] Furthermore, Tillich's biographers repeatedly refer to his magnetic and warm personality and the impact that he had on people – in other words, to his generosity and magnanimity.[8] Ann Belford Ulanov writes of the Tillich she knew as a student:

> He cared about Being and about particular human beings. He
> always saw the specific person there before him and addressed his
> remarks to the other person's deepest self. I remember when I first
> met him as a student at Radcliffe, how generously and with what
> seriousness he listened to me, as he did to almost all young
> persons. He was much more than the recent gossip about his
> problems with women suggests. He saw women as individual
> persons, complete in their own right, and he called them forward
> from the distant background position into which they were so
> often thrust, to affirm their own being.[9]

It is also clear that Tillich possessed the virtues of justice and courage, i.e. a concern for human well-being and the ability to do what is right even at personal cost. After all, we are talking here about a man who was blacklisted by the Nazis and who had to emigrate from his beloved Germany because of the firmness of his moral convictions. This is the man who formulated so clearly the Protestant principle, 'that element of perpetual critique that stands against the ever-present threats of idolatry and utopianism' – a principle that is central to Mary Ann Stenger's feminist interpretation of Tillich.[10]

Thirdly, assessments of Tillich's ethos may also benefit from the insights of postmodern critical rhetorical theory, which, true to its overall philosophical paradigm, rejects the idea of the isolated Cartesian subject who exists above time and space. Likewise, the notion of ethos goes well beyond the isolated individual. As Susan Jarratt and Nedra Reynolds point out, the concept of ethos 'theorizes the positionality inherent in rhetoric – the speaker having been created at a particular site within the contingencies of history and geography . . . one always speaks from a particular place in a social structure'.[11] Within this framework, the notion of ethos is rendered an aspect of a broad hermeneutic of suspicion that would ask about the power relations and systems of oppression that lie behind discourses. When ethos is understood in terms of where the author is situated in systems of power and oppression, it becomes clear that dialogue between feminist theology and male theologians will always be fraught with difficulties. Male theologians are in deeper trouble with feminist theologians than can be indicated by merely pointing at sexual misconduct. And yet it is exactly at this point that it becomes clear that Tillich himself might actually be in less trouble with feminists than some of his colleagues. Although perception of an author's ethos is central to the interpretation of his ideas, the reverse is also true: interpreters will interpret an author's ethos in light of his intellectual work. Two aspects in particular of Tillich's work indicate that he transcended the patriarchal ethos to which feminists object: his method of correlation is indicative of an ethos of openness to the reality of human life; and there are many indications in the contents of his thought, as well as in the causes he espoused, of an ethos focused on justice. As such, his work embodies the kind of prophetic ethos that one also finds in feminist theologies.

Tillich's failure successfully to inhabit all the boundaries of life was in a paradoxical way consistent with this prophetic ethos. Tillich's theology was not a theology of certainty, but a theology of search, of going the road less travelled, of risking 'being in touch with the unrepeatable tensions of his present'.[12] Those tensions included the post-First World War social upheavals in Europe and the rejection of everything bourgeois. Tillich's willingness to risk life within the tensions of the various boundaries within which his life was situated, instead of opting for settling on either side, is exactly what makes his writings compelling. Tillich's 'erotic solution', flawed as it was, seems to have been born from the same searching passion of the spirit that makes his work so intriguing to the kind of dialogue partner that is not satisfied with traditional answers to human questions on existence – such as feminists.

METHODOLOGICAL CONVERSATIONS

The emphasis on women's experience as a methodological starting-point for feminist theology means that the latter recognizes the importance and inevitability of doing theology from a particular social location. To some extent, this particular emphasis stands in contrast to Tillich's method, which correlates answers derived from Christian texts with questions raised by analysis of the 'universal' human situation. Feminist scholars argue that the assumption of a universal human situation tends to universalize the experience of Western males – it thus hides patriarchal interests and exhibits androcentric tendencies. Indeed, charges of such patriarchal and androcentric thinking are frequently levelled at Tillich by his feminist interpreters. Moreover, Tillich's description of the 'situation' in terms of philosophical concerns is quite different from the feminist emphasis on concrete, rather than philosophical, situations.

Nonetheless, some feminist theologians have found Tillich's method 'less inadequate' than other twentieth-century theologians'.[13]

Indeed, Tillich shares with feminist approaches a basic tendency to see theology as a response to human situations (although Tillich's version is best called 'apologetic theology'), rather than as an interpretation of 'the tradition' (what Tillich called 'kerygmatic theology'). In Tillich's chosen approach, 'the form of the questions . . . is decisive for the theological form in which the answer is given' (although the converse is also true, that 'the substance of the question is determined by the substance of the answer') (*PTM*, 24, 25). One should note that this approach, even if it is not yet David Tracy's 'mutually critical correlations', is nevertheless 'not the mere juxtaposing of a Christian answer with a human problem' but rather 'an interpretive art requiring sensitive readings of both human situations and also of Christian symbols in the tradition'.[14] As Tillich himself remarked, his method is 'a genuine pragmatism which refuses to close any door' (17).

For feminist theologians, the 'human situations' that are to be interpreted include women's experiences of their everyday realities. This emphasis is sometimes phrased in a way that seems to suggest the absolutization of women's experience as a separate source for theology alongside revelation as traditionally understood. Tillich's critique of idolatry might serve as an important warning against any tendencies to view women's experience as normative and absolute in this way, as Mary Ann Stenger argues.[15] Furthermore, Tillich's own remarks on method might be helpful to express feminist method in a more coherent way. Tillich warns against seeing experience as a positive source and norm of systematic theology. By experience he means 'participation in the reality within which theology speaks' (22). He emphasizes that '[n]ot experience, but revelation received in experience, gives the content of every theology' (23). Thus, revelation is the moment, the place, where the finite and the infinite meet, not where the finite is simply declared infinite or the infinite is transformed into the finite. This is similar to how he describes the notion of the *kairos*, that 'moment rich in content and significance', when 'the eternal breaks into the temporal, and the temporal is prepared to receive it' (33, xix).

How would this compare with feminist approaches to the task of theology? The point of emphasizing female experience as the methodological starting-point for feminist theology is that of retrieving silenced voices and showing that revelation is received also in female experience. This is not a matter of putting the finite and the infinite on the same level (against which Tillich warns), but of pointing to those moments of revelation, i.e. moments in which the finite and the infinite meet, that have been ignored by 'official' tradition (*ST* I, 65). In short, feminist method sees revelation as happening in the midst of women's experience. This is the *kairos* of feminist theology: the event of a growing feminist consciousness in which revelation happens in and through women's lives.

In his method of correlation, Tillich helped to develop a broad stream of theology that does not see its task as one of 'speaking into' human situations from the vantage point of the Bible or the 'official' tradition (which is, as feminists point out, largely a male tradition), but as one of recognizing that the content of theology is revelation received in experience, both the revelatory experiences of the classical traditions and those of long-ignored voices and new situations (*PTM*, 23). Feminist theological method, while not directly derived from Tillich, is broadly similar, although it also challenges the overly abstract and androcentric perspective on the human situation found in Tillich's thought. In its turn, Tillich's warnings against idolatry and his remarks about method can caution feminist theology to keep in mind that female experience is a vehicle for revelation and not revelatory in and of itself.

THEOLOGICAL CONVERSATIONS

The best-known feminist interpretation of Tillich's doctrinal thought is Judith Plaskow's treatment of his doctrines of sin and grace.[16] Plaskow argues that Tillich's continued reliance on the concept of hubris is indicative of an androcentric hamartiological framework. Feminist theologians have argued that the focus on 'pride' or self-elevation as the root of sin tends to aggravate the general female tendency to negate the self, a tendency Plaskow refers to as 'passivity'.[17] From this perspective, various feminist theologians have also criticized the emphasis on passive receiving of grace in the Protestant doctrine of justification – a doctrine that is central to Tillich's theology. Plaskow is therefore dismissive of Tillich's doctrine of grace, seeing his emphasis on divine acceptance as fostering passivity in women and thus aggravating female pathologies.[18] Mary Daly has similar concerns. She describes Tillich's doctrine of acceptance as a masochistic torture chamber in which the female victim is condemned to live with the 'knowledge' that she is really guilty and deserving of condemnation, despite the belief that a loving God forgives her.[19]

Despite these remnants of androcentric thinking in Tillich, there are other feminist theologians who see potential in both his doctrine of sin and his doctrine of grace. Susan Lichtman points out that if we keep in mind that the Greek term for sin, *hamartia*, means 'missing the mark', then one can posit that self-abnegation and self-worship are simply two opposite ways of 'missing the mark'. In other words, she writes, 'both the prideful person, and the passively dependent one, portray a person alienated from his/her own true nature'.[20] Indeed, Tillich is at times able to recognize not only the sins of the powerful, but also the 'sins of weakness' (*IH*, 93).

Tillich's ontological insights, and particularly his notion of 'estrangement', should have enabled him to escape the problematic androcentrism of the traditional Augustinian emphasis on pride. In this regard his description of humans' essential nature in terms of three sets of polar ontological elements in the first volume of his *Systematic Theology*, especially the polar elements of individualization and participation, is particularly significant (*ST* I, 174–86). In the existential state of estrangement these two polar ontological elements risk breaking down into either loneliness, 'in which world and communion are lost', or collectivization, 'a loss of individuality and subjectivity whereby the self loses its self-relatedness and is transformed into a mere part of an embracing whole'. Both of these are moves towards 'not being what we essentially are' (199). Within the logic of this ontology, estrangement can include both the extreme individualization that is called pride and a loss of the self in extreme participation that feminists point to as the more typical female sin.

However, in his discussions of sin in the second volume of the *Systematic Theology* Tillich reverts to the traditional Augustinian concepts of pride, concupiscence and unbelief as the various forms of estrangement, with pride as the primary form (*ST* II, 47–55). Tillich makes a distinction between pride, a moral concept, and hubris, an ontological concept, which he translates as 'self-elevation' and which can appear in acts of humility, as well as in acts of pride. However, he not only describes hubris largely in terms of pride, but from a feminist perspective the very choice of hubris as the basic category for both opposites is problematic. Given his above-mentioned ontological insights about the tension between over-identifying the self and losing the self, it seems contradictory to go on to discuss sin in terms that emphasize hubris. Of course, self-elevation can indeed sometimes take the form of a false humility, which can hide spiritual pride, and this might be what Tillich had in mind in his description of humility as a form of hubris. But his focus on only that particular kind of false humility as a sinful form of humility indicates that he remained in the sphere of androcentric thinking in his discussion of actual sins.

Nevertheless, there are points of contact between Tillich's analysis and feminist perspectives on the doctrine of sin. The focus on estrangement from the ground of being is a move away from a moralistic doctrine of sin. In this existential concept, Tillich formulated in a new way the classical Christian insistence that wrongful acts are not the real problem, but rather the manifestations of a more fundamental problem, a brokenness, a chasm between humanity and the divine, between the finite and the infinite. This was traditionally called 'original sin', a doctrine that is rejected by some feminist theologians because of the way in which it has functioned to justify the oppression of women. Yet, perhaps ironically, even feminist theologians who reject the doctrine of original sin (and not all do) still insist that the real 'problem' is some kind of brokenness in need of healing. For example, Rita Nakashima Brock writes that 'sin is a sign of our brokenheartedness, of how damaged we are . . . something to be healed'.[21] As such, Tillich's notion of estrangement might provide a helpful bridge between feminist views on sin and the valuable classical insight that sin is not simply a matter of individual acts.

Just as the feminist conversation on Tillich's doctrine of sin needs to continue, so also does that on his doctrine of grace. When his doctrine of grace is seen within the overall logic of his ontology, it becomes clear that it represents the best in the Protestant take on grace, while escaping some of its androcentric assumptions. The main reason for this is his perspective on God. Tillich rejects the notion of God as the highest of all beings, and in line with that he does not view the classical spatial metaphor of divine transcendence in terms of God as the 'totally other', the 'highest' being who is, metaphorically speaking 'above' everything else and not of this world. Instead, his description of God as being-itself, the power of being in everything else and as such the power of resisting non-being – in short, of God as the ground of being – points to a God that 'transcends every being and also the totality of beings' (*ST* I, 237). Again, one finds a similar perspective on God in feminist theologies. Rosemary Radford Ruether expresses her feminist perspective on God in language quite evocative of Tillich: 'The God/ess who is primal Matrix, the ground of being-new being, is neither stifling immanence nor rootless transcendence.'[22]

As ground of being, Tillich's God is not the male monarch who comes from 'on high' to reach out to the humbled sinner. Such a view of God and of divine grace all too easily justifies hierarchy and can also lead to a depiction of grace that smacks of sado-masochism. These sado-masochistic overtones are strikingly present in Karl Barth's depiction of the true recipient of divine grace as a 'non-willing, non-achieving, non-creative, non-sovereign' female figure, symbolized by Mary.[23] This female figure passively awaits and receives the 'grace' coming from above, from the Word, the male figure of Christ.[24] When coupled with the classical emphasis on pride as sin and the concomitant notion that the self must be shattered, one ends up with a 'grace' that shatters a self who passively awaits this treatment.[25]

The theological matrix within which Tillich's embrace of the Protestant doctrine of justification is located helps to overcome this somewhat sado-masochistic depiction of grace. The God Beyond God who is also the ground of being is a God whose transcendence lies in immanence. Although less personal than traditional theistic images for God, this vision of God allows for a more intimate divine presence, the presence of the God that is not the Totally Other who 'comes down on' the passive recipient of grace, but is the transcending-yet-immanent reality in which the accepted one is rooted. Rita Nakashima Brock's phrase, 'original grace', by which she means a 'primal interrelatedness', a healing reality that begins at birth, is an apt description of the kind of dynamic present in Tillich's doctrine of grace.[26] Within Tillich's system, the relationality of original grace is formulated in terms of the ground of being overcoming our estrangement from ourselves, others and being-itself, i.e. overcoming the condition of 'original sin', and rooting our very selves in an alternative condition, that of acceptance. As such, grace is presented as that which enables New Being.

Linked to this emphasis is, of course, Tillich's Christology, which deserves further feminist reflection. It is in Christ as New Being, 'the one in whom the conflict between the essential unity of God and man and man's existential estrangement is overcome', that one finds the courage to be – in other words, the courage to be the self that both belongs to the world and transcends it, the self who is both individual and participant (*ST* II, 125; *ST* I, 169–70). The New Being, the Christ, in whom 'the eternal unity of God and man becomes actual under the conditions of existence without being conquered by them', enables self-integration, the holding together of the ontological elements of individualization and participation under the ambiguous conditions of life (*ST* III, 270). Given the tension in feminist thought between affirming relationality as a female virtue and emphasizing autonomy as a female need, a Christology that envisions the New Being in terms of such self-integration is worth examining.

Moreover, Tillich's distinction between the historical person, Jesus of Nazareth, and the Christ-event as an intersubjective, communal

phenomenon transcends the image of Jesus as the heroic male individual that has been so problematic for feminist theology (*ST* II, 97–
9).[27] One finds in Rita Nakashima Brock's discussion of Christ as the
Christa/Community a similar emphasis on a Christology 'not centered
in Jesus, but in relationality and community as the whole-making, healing center of Christianity'.[28] Brock's emphasis on the manifestation
of erotic power in the Christa/Community is also evocative of Tillich's
affirmation of the creative power of *eros* (*LPJ*, 117).[29] As Alexander Irwin
has argued, feminist theologians might well take note of Tillich's affirmation of *eros* as a theological principle, given their rejection of the
agape/eros distinction as a false dichotomy.[30]

Clearly Tillich's ontology lends itself to feminist appropriation, as is
attested both by the dynamics it lends to his views on God, Christ, sin
and grace, and by its direct appropriation by Mary Daly for her analysis
of patriarchy as that which destroys women's participation in being and
of feminist consciousness as participation in New Being. Although she
accuses Tillich of being unaware of the gender aspects of his ontological
theology, she recognizes in one of her earlier works, *Beyond God the
Father*, that 'his manner of speaking about the ground and power of being
would be difficult to use for the legitimation of any sort of oppression'
and that it is 'potentially liberating in a very radical sense'.[31] The later
Daly is far more critical of Tillich (especially of his personal life),[32]
yet even in the book where she lodges her central critiques of Tillich,
Gyn/Ecology, traces of his ontological language can still be seen, such
as when she speaks of the self-affirming being of women's participation
in the divine.[33]

Daly is not quite correct when she says that Tillich is unaware of
the gender aspects of his ontological theology, however. There are a
few traces of such an awareness in his thought. The most significant
is a short discussion of the Trinity and the issue of exclusively male
God-language in the third volume of the *Systematic Theology*. Tillich
suggests that the emphasis on God as ground of being could be one way
to address the problem of exclusive male symbolism for God (*ST* III, 293–
4). Tillich's brief treatment of this issue reflects certain gender stereotypes: he writes that 'the concept "ground of being" . . . points to the
mother-quality of giving birth, carrying, and embracing', which he then
contrasts with the stereotypical 'demanding father-image of . . . God'.
However, these stereotypes also occur in feminist discussions of the
issue of inclusive God-language and are to some extent inevitable if
the stereotypical father imagery of classical theism is to be balanced.
More disturbing, perhaps, is Tillich's slightly anxious reference to this

maternal ground of being as 'calling back, resisting independence of the created, swallowing it', which echoes the age-old misogynist theme of the dangerous devouring woman (294).[34] Nevertheless, Tillich's aware-ness of the problem of God-language is a striking anticipation of later feminist concerns that the symbol of an exclusively male God 'func-tions to support an imaginative and structural world that excludes or subordinates women'.[35]

Tillich also finds in the self-sacrifice of Christ a symbolism that tran-scends male–female dichotomy and thus enables less masculine ways of talking about the Trinity. He sees self-sacrifice as breaking the 'contrast of the sexes', since Christians of both sexes can participate in the symbol of the suffering Christ 'with equal psychological and spiritual intensity' (294). However, feminist theologians have been very critical of both the notion of self-sacrifice and the idealization of the suffering Christ, given the traditional self-sacrificial ideal of womanhood.[36] Thus, while feminists might appreciate Tillich's sincere efforts to transcend gender dichotomies, they would challenge his assumption that participation in a symbol of sacrifice is equally liberating for both sexes.

A more promising avenue for thinking about God in female terms, apart from the symbol of God as ground of being, is Tillich's focus on the Spirit. Although feminist theologians are wary of finding in the Spirit a 'feminine element' in God, the feminist sensibilities inherent in Tillich's pneumatology have to do with the 'ecstatic character of the Spiritual Presence which transcends the alternative of male and female symbolism' (294).[37] He even shows awareness of the problematic way in which gender dualism links rationalism to males and emotionalism to females. It is this dualism that is transcended in the ecstasy of the Spiritual Presence. Although Tillich does not develop these themes, his awareness of issues that would later occupy feminist theologians provides an interesting point of contact from where feminist dialogue with Tillich can develop further.

Finally, it is worth mentioning an intriguing passage in *The Social-ist Decision*, where Tillich laments female participation in the political romanticism that deprives women of their rights (*SD*, 152–3). Tillich attributes this to the 'powers of origin possessed by woman by virtue of her resonance with eros and motherhood', which he believes make women prone to reject the rationalistic system of socialism, even if it is socialism that has worked for women's emancipation. There are some disturbing elements in this analysis: although Tillich often transcends gender dualism, as mentioned above, his basic analysis in *The Socialist*

Decision seems to be premised upon such dualism. The romantic myth of origin is associated with women, and this, he writes, should be broken 'by the unconditional demand [that] is the root of liberal democratic, and socialist thought in politics' (5). The myth of origin also finds its fulfilment in the rational demand. Given traditional associations of rationality with masculinity and his own association of the myth of origin with women, these images show the continued presence of underlying gender dualism in his thought. Moreover, his view that women do not embrace socialism and liberal political thought reflects the German context within which the text was written and is belied by the socialist and liberal leanings of much later feminism. Despite these problems, we see in Tillich sincere efforts to transcend the gender dualisms of Western thought, as well as efforts to value the traditionally feminine. The oscillation between those two impulses should not be attributed to androcentrism on his part, for it reflects the tensions within feminism itself, which is often divided between so-called 'equality' feminism and so-called 'difference' feminism. In the final analysis, it remains significant that Tillich states explicitly that '[s]ocialism cannot possibly tolerate the restoration of male patriarchalism' (152–3).

In conclusion, there exists a surprising amount of common ground between Paul Tillich and some of the leading feminist thinkers of recent decades, as well as avenues for further reflection. These include: similar theological concerns; a methodological concern for human experiences in the task of theology; and an effort to live creatively and in a new way within the 'boundaries of our habitations'.[38] Like Tillich, feminist theologians struggle to live creatively on the boundaries between adherence to and criticism of the church, between classical and renewing theological thinking, between old and new ways of being in intimate relationships with others. Tillich may not always have been entirely successful in his efforts at living on the latter boundary, and his lack of success has indeed exposed him as still steeped in the Western patriarchal system. Likewise, Tillich may not always have escaped androcentric assumptions in his thought, nor focused sufficiently on the concrete human situations to be correlated with the symbols of Christianity. Yet in other ways he managed to transcend the tired old clichés and live and write in ways that signalled New Being. Feminist theologians and this very German twentieth-century theologian may have little in common at first glance, but both conversation partners share a commitment to live creatively within the tensions of their day, and, as such, they have much to say to – and learn from – one another.

Notes

1 Hannah Tillich (1973).
2 May (1973), Heyward (1989), Irwin (1991) and Althaus-Reed (2000).
3 May (1973), 65.
4 Daly (1988), 94–5.
5 Irwin (1991), 117.
6 Hauser (1986), 96–8.
7 Ibid., 98.
8 Pauck and Pauck (1976).
9 Belford Ulanov (1985), 120.
10 Stone (2002), 230. See Paul Tillich, 'The Protestant Principle and the Pro-letarian Situation' in *ProtE*, 61–81. On Mary Ann Stenger's work, see, inter alia, Stenger (2002).
11 Jarratt and Reynolds (1994), 47.
12 Taylor (1987), 11. Tillich's historical focus is particularly clear in his essays on the *kairos* and 'the present crisis' in *ProtE*, 32–51 and 237–69.
13 E.g. Daly (1973), 200 n. 10.
14 Taylor (1987), 126–7.
15 Stenger (2002), 117, 129–39.
16 Plaskow (1980).
17 See Saiving (1960), 100–12, Plaskow (1980), 14, Nelson Dunfee (1982) and Potter Engel (1998).
18 Plaskow (1980), 157.
19 Daly (1988), 377.
20 Lichtman (1989).
21 Brock (2000), 7.
22 Radford Ruether (1993), 85.
23 K. Barth (1956), 188ff.
24 K. Barth (1961), 161.
25 E.g. Daly (1984), 2.
26 Brock (2000), 8.
27 On a basic statement of the problems inherent in a masculinist Christology, see Radford Ruether, 'Can a Male Savior Save Women?' in (1993), 116–38.
28 Brock (2000), 52. This distinction is also at the heart of Mark Kline Taylor's suggestions for a praxis-oriented Christology in M. K. Taylor (1990).
29 As Alexander Irwin notes, *eros* is an oft-mentioned concept in Tillich's thought, from early lectures and works to his *Systematic Theology*. See Irwin (1991), 4.
30 Ibid., 121–96.
31 Daly (1973), 20.
32 Daly (1988), 94–5, 435–6 n. 40.
33 Ibid., 111.
34 See Sprenger and Kramer (1971), I, 9, Noddings (1989), 49, Furlong (1992), 8 and Diamond (1996), 36–7. It would be far-fetched to say that Tillich suffered from a fear of women, but the fact remains that his description of the swallowing ground of being finds echoes in ancient misogynist themes that seem to point to male anxieties. This is particularly the case when one

couples that with his reference to the ground of being as the abyss, 'the abysmal character of the divine life', which makes revelation mysterious, and which is then contrasted with the logical and spiritual character of the divine life, which makes revelation possible (*ST* I, 156).

35 Johnson (1995), 4–5. See also McFague (1982).
36 This has been expressed particularly in feminist critiques of sacrificial theories of atonement. See Heyward (1982), 54–7, Brown and Parker (1989), 1, Williams (1993), 199–202 and Brock (2000), 56. On the link between an ethos of female self-sacrifice and violence against women, see, inter alia, Gudorf (1992), 91 and Mananzan (1994), 44–52.
37 Johnson (1995), 50–4.
38 This is the striking title of Delwin Brown's book on continuity and change in religious traditions. See D. Brown (1994).

Further reading

Irwin, Alexander C. (1991). *Eros Towards the World: Paul Tillich and the Theology of the Erotic.* Minneapolis, Minn.: Fortress Press.
Lichtman, Susan (1989). 'The Concept of Sin in the Theology of Paul Tillich: A Break from Patriarchy?' *The Journal of Women and Religion* 8: 49–55.
Plaskow, Judith (1980). *Sex, Sin and Grace: Women's Experience and the Theologies of Reinhold Niebuhr and Paul Tillich.* New York: University Press of America.
Stenger, Mary Ann and Ronald H. Stone (2002). *Dialogues of Paul Tillich.* Macon, Ga.: Mercer University Press.

18 Tillich and the postmodern

JOHN THATAMANIL

> If I were still writing a theology – I am sometimes tempted to do just
> that – the expression 'Being' should not figure in it . . . There is nothing
> to be done here with Being.
>
> Martin Heidegger[1]

> But there is no pure revelation. Wherever the divine is manifest, it is
> manifest in 'flesh,' that is, in a concrete, physical and historical reality,
> as in the religious receptivity of biblical writers.
>
> Paul Tillich (*BR*, 5)

Paul Tillich has been summarily tossed into the dustbin of history by
any number of schools and figures who are resolutely and perhaps inordi-
nately fond of the prefix 'post-'. For postmoderns, Tillich is too ontotheological and too indebted to German Idealism to pass as a contemporary.[2]
For postliberals, Tillich is an arch-modernist, a correlational thinker
whose methodology surrenders theology's independence, integrity and
authority by subjecting its formulations to alien and extrinsic criteria.[3]
The radically orthodox who make strategic use of selected postmodern
themes, albeit with considerable critical reserve, have no truck with
Tillich. In a time when academic theology is dominated by postmoderns, postliberals and the radically orthodox, Tillich's legacy appears
marginal and imperilled. Does postmodernism mark the death-knell of
Tillichian theology? Does Tillich's commitment to formulating theology in conversation with secular modernity relegate him to oblivion in
a time now widely regarded as postmodern, if not postsecular?

In this chapter I argue against any premature closure that would
relegate Tillich's corpus to a dead and bygone past. My intention is not
to birth a more-postmodern-than-thou Tillich: his theological contributions are too multifaceted to be characterized as either univocally modern or postmodern. What matters, at any rate, are not these overused
labels of uncertain extension; what matters is that contemporary theologians must not disfigure theology's future prospects by amputating

usable resources on the grounds that they are putatively dated and so obsolete. Characterizing Tillich as straightforwardly postmodern would be anachronistic and calling him modern altogether trite. A careful, albeit selective, examination of central themes and motifs in Tillich's theology demonstrates that he defies such conventional categories. As a thinker whose life and thought were always 'on the boundary', Tillich escapes contemporary classifications just as he eluded those of his own time.

POSTMODERN: MAKING DO WITH AN IMPOSSIBLE TERM

The term 'postmodern' is a vexing and impossible one, not because it is indefinable, but because it has been defined in such multifarious and incompatible ways as to defy synthesis. Those who define the term with the greatest ease are the least persuasive. For Graham Ward, the postmodern issues from the 'implosion of secularism'. Ward demonstrates well that mapping what this collapse entails is no simple matter, but that he is able to specify so easily that 'it is the many consequences of that implosion that postmodernism explores and postmodernity expresses' is unconvincing.[4]

That the postmodern ruptures the complacent and self-sufficient confidence of certain forms of secular reason is beyond doubt; whether it marks the end of the secular as such remains to be seen. A subtler reading of the postmodern as a cultural and intellectual trajectory suggests that it poses a threat to all – theists and atheists alike – who are committed to leaving in place stark and impermeable boundaries between the secular and the religious. The term 'undecidability', much beloved by Derrideans, better illuminates the fecundity of the postmodern. Postmodern reflection overturns attempts to isolate and thereby to quarantine the religious from the secular, the supranatural from the natural, belief from knowledge. If the term 'postmodern' is at all usable,[5] its power, especially in its deconstructive modality, resides in its capacity to demonstrate that life and thought resist neat and fastidious boundaries, categories and systems. Postmodern reflection is haemorrhagic.

Insofar as modernity sought in the name of Enlightenment reason to secure thought by an appeal to firm foundations, by an appeal to clear and distinct premises modelled on the indivisible Cartesian self's self-evident presence to itself, the postmodern marks the crisis of modernity. That crisis does not amount to the birth of a new irrationalism; on the contrary, postmodern thinkers are soberly aware of the false securities

and concealed enthusiasms of an instrumental reason that aspires to
sovereignty but at tremendous cost – the dismissal of all that it cannot control and domesticate. The ethical force of postmodern criticism
rests precisely in its resistance to modernity's totalizing aspirations,
most especially modernity's confidence in technical reason's capacity
for controlling knowledge.

POSTMODERNISM AND ONTOTHEOLOGY

In the broad family of postmodern philosophers and theologians who
think and write in the wake of Martin Heidegger, Emmanuel Levinas and
Jacques Derrida, the postmodern critique of reason's pretensions, especially with respect to thinking about God, has been encapsulated under
the rubric of 'ontotheology'. These thinkers insist that understanding
God as being perpetuates thinking in which otherness in general and
the otherness of God in particular fades from view. The argument, to
be traced to Heidegger, claims that any thinking of God that identifies God with being will constrain and even determine the conditions
under which God is permitted to appear. Any theology that would per-
mit God to be so confined not only opts for the priority of the same
over the other but is also guilty of idolatry. God is not permitted to
surprise us, as we by our metaphysics have appointed the conditions
for God's arrival. To counter such an unholy compact between metaphysics and theology, philosophers such as Heidegger, Levinas, Derrida
and Jean-Luc Marion are committed to thinking otherwise than being
in order to let the divine Other appear as it will. Levinas and Marion in
particular appeal to neo-Platonic tropes in order to fund reflection that
would move beyond being to the good and so break the stranglehold of
ontotheology.

But just what precisely is meant by the term 'ontotheology'? In
contemporary philosophical discourse the term has attained to an infe-
licitously broad range of meaning, one that extends well beyond the
generous amplitude given to the term by Heidegger himself. In our time
'ontotheology', at its worst, functions as a very long, philosophical four-
letter word and is invoked to dismiss any mode of philosophical reflection that one happens to oppose. Any thinking is ontotheological *to the
extent* that it seeks to do the following: establish an absolutely secure
ontological foundation by depicting God as the first being, the being who
is the cause of all other beings, and, by naming God as first cause and
causa sui, recruits God to serve as an ultimate principle of intelligibility
that renders the world comprehensible and subject to rational control.
The upshot of these moves is to give rise to a conception of reality,

empirical and ultimate, as transparent to calculative reason. Ontotheo-logical thinking risks prioritizing the one over the many, the self over the other and sameness over difference.

I use the qualifying phrase 'to the extent' to avoid giving the impres-sion that reflection can be entirely free from ontotheological elements. A more likely scenario is that thought – and perhaps language and gram-mar themselves – stands compromised by the effects of our aspiration for security, certainty and control. A strategy that would avoid a naïve aspiration for total purity from the ontotheological would strive instead for thinking that allows the ontotheological to be subverted by elements that resist it.

Not every attempt to think the relationship between God and the world by appeal to ontology is ontotheological. If one's ontological aspi-rations are taken to be hypothetical and so vulnerable to correction, and if speculative thinkers remain haunted by the possibility that they might be thrown off the lowly donkey of metaphysical reason by a bril-liant darkness that exceeds sight, then it is possible to imagine forms of metaphysical reflection that avoid the sin of epistemological founda-tionalism and avoid also the sin of circumscribing the conditions under which the divine might appear.

Jean-Luc Marion agrees that not every appeal to being is captive to ontotheology. Despite his decisive option for the good over being, Marion allows the following:

> Even if Dionysius (or some other) understood the question of God on the basis of Being, this simple fact would not be enough to establish that he is inscribed within onto-theo-logy. That is . . . if an onto-theology wants to attain conceptual rigor and not remain at the level of a polemical caricature, it requires first a concept of being, next a univocal application of this concept to God and creatures, and finally the submission of both to foundation by principle and/or cause. If these conditions are not met, if in contrast Being remains an inconceivable *esse*, without analogy . . . then the mere fact that Being comes up is not enough to establish an onto-theo-logy.[6]

IS TILLICH GUILTY OF ONTOTHEOLOGY?

How does Tillich fare when assessed by these criteria? Tillich, for obvious reasons, is regarded as the paradigmatic thinker of God-as-being, and his appeal to the notion of God as being-itself appears to be a bla-tant violation of Heidegger's call for a theology that breaks company with being. Tillich's theology appears, at least at first glance, to be the very embodiment of what is now widely regarded as an obsolete and unsustainable kind of metaphysical theology. But if we elect Marion's perspective over against Heidegger's unequivocal exile of being from theology, it may be possible to see again in Tillich a theologian who makes room for divine otherness despite his characterization of God as the ground of being and being-itself. After all, Tillich's theology of God as being-itself can be understood rightly only if his indebtedness to apophatic theology is not forgotten.

But will Tillich's indebtedness to the apophatic absolve him of the charge of falling victim to ontotheology? As is well known, Derrida routinely worries that apophatic theology decouples God and being only to reassert that God enjoys being beyond being, namely superessential being. And Heidegger's question lingers as well. Before the God who is the ground of being, can we fall to our knees in awe? Can we 'play music and dance before this God'?[7]

Heidegger's query forces Tillichians to confront a host of questions that have dogged Tillich's project from its inception, questions that inevitably follow any theology that wishes to call God being-itself, questions that antedate both Tillich and Heidegger by centuries. What does the God of the philosophers have to do with the God of Abraham, Isaac and Jacob? Or in a form more ancient still, what does Athens have to do with Jerusalem? Tillich adamantly refused this dichotomy and sought to reconcile philosophy and revelation. If we read Heidegger's attempt to rid the term *being* from theology as a Pascalian option for the revealing God over against a philosophical God, and if we regard the disjunction between Jerusalem and Athens to be the *sine qua non* of any theology that would escape ontotheology, then Tillich must be convicted as guilty beyond reasonable doubt. But if it turns out that we cannot be rid of ontotheology simply by forswearing Athenian citizenship, then Tillich's integrative theological project might yet find a way to escape the charge.

How does Tillich manage to escape the ontotheological so conceived? Firstly, although Tillich does insist on referring to God as being-itself, he is clear this non-symbolic term does not yield conceptual knowledge of God. One must say that God is being-itself – because God is the source of being for all beings – but one does not thereby know what being-itself is, as the term's meaning remains shrouded in mystery. Being-itself turns out to be a singular term in Tillich's lexicon, one that serves to demonstrate that all (subsequent) talk about God has to be symbolic. In this respect Tillich's thought reverses Hegel's priority of the concept over the symbol. By enacting this reversal of Hegel, Tillich goes a very long way towards sabotaging an idolatry of the conceptual, one that would grant to mind the capacity to adequate itself to the divine nature. Ultimately, Tillich's thought is deeply indebted to apophatic theology in which all names, conceptual and symbolic, are ruptured and broken.

Secondly, Tillich's theology of God is concerned to speak of God *both* as ground *and* as abyss, as *Grund* and as *Ungrund*. Such a God does not serve neatly as a foundation for secure knowledge claims. Thirdly, Tillich's God is neither an infinite being nor an existent. As such, Tillich is cognizant of the inadequacy of any thinking that would reduce God to the status of a supreme being who is the first cause and *causa sui*. Fourthly, Tillich is convinced that neither the categories of causality nor of substance are applicable to divinity and that they can be ascribed to God only in a symbolic vein. Fifthly, Tillich is a wholly impure thinker – a thinker of boundaries and margins, a thinker who knows that any attempt to separate the Jew from the Greek is bound to fail. In addition to being an émigré, caught between 'native and alien land', he is also caught 'between theology and philosophy'.[8] Tillich is resolutely 'jewgreek'. Indeed, he is more. Towards the end of his life, Tillich's thought moved well beyond a Mediterranean ambit (a circumference within which most postmoderns who speak fondly of the radically Other remain imprisoned) because of his broad engagement with the history of religions. Even in this final stage of his thought, Tillich's thinking remains within the circle of faith. His theological encounters with other religions do not take place on neutral, rational territory. Like Anselm and Augustine, Tillich's systematic theology is an expression of ultimate concern. Theology, for Tillich, rests on a venture, on an existential risk, a Kierkegaardian leap, and not on any appeal to clear and distinct ideas, not even the idea of being. For these many reasons, Tillich cannot easily be classified as a thinker who is owned by the ontotheological.

ONTOTHEOLOGY AND GOD AS BEING-ITSELF

In the first volume of the *Systematic Theology*, Tillich spoke emphatically about God as being-itself. Given the importance of his statement, it is worth citing Tillich at some length:

> The statement that God is being-itself is a non-symbolic statement. It does not point beyond itself. It means what it says directly and properly; if we speak of the actuality of God, we first

assert that he is not God if he is not being-itself. Other assertions
about God can be made theologically only on this basis . . .
Theologians must make explicit what is implicit in religious
thought and expression; and, in order to do this, they must begin
with the most abstract and completely unsymbolic statement
which is possible, namely, that God is being-itself or the absolute.

(*ST* I, 238–9)

Six years later Tillich clarified his basic contention. Firstly, he insists
that it is precisely because God is being-itself and not a determinate
being of any sort that every statement about God must be symbolic.[9]
Secondly, Tillich contends that 'being-itself' is not itself a concept that
generates determinate knowledge of God. Being is a concept, but it is
entirely unlike all others. Why? Because being is presumed in every
act of thinking but cannot itself be thought; being remains mysterious. Being 'remains the content, the mystery, and the eternal *aporia* of
thinking' (*ST* II, 11). And because being-itself remains a mystery, only
symbolic language about God as being-itself will do.

    In response to critics who object to Tillich's talk about God as being-
itself, Tillich takes up the question, 'whether there is a point at which
a non-symbolic assertion about God must be made' (9). To this query
Tillich responds, 'There is such a point, namely, the statement that
everything we say about God is symbolic. Such a statement is an assertion about God which is not itself symbolic' (9). But having made this
statement, Tillich is immediately aware of a problem, and I take his
awareness of the problem to be expressive of a desire to avoid an ontotheological turn: 'if we make *one* non-symbolic assertion about God, his
ecstatic-transcendent character seems to be endangered' (9).

    Several observations are relevant at this juncture. Firstly, Tillich
is aware of the risk that theologians run should they claim that any
statement about God is unsymbolic. So, Tillich is intent on demonstrating that the concept of being-itself functions primarily as a conceptual
hedge against deficient ontic notions of deity, rather than as a notion
that yields determinate knowledge of God. Secondly, Tillich's statement
in the second volume of the *Systematic Theology* is not an equivocation. His argument is that human beings are driven by ultimate concern
to ask the question of being and non-being and in this way express a
longing to be reunited with that from which they are separated but to
which they nonetheless belong. When we refer to the divine reality, not
as given in religious experience but as thematized in theological reflection, when we designate conceptually the logical object of our existential

longing, Tillich suggests, we are forced to include in theological speech a non-symbolic moment:

> In the moment, however, in which we describe the character of this point or in which we try to formulate that for which we ask, a combination of symbolic with non-symbolic elements occurs. If we say that God is the infinite, or the unconditional, or being-itself we speak rationally and ecstatically at the same time. These terms precisely designate the boundary line at which the symbolic and the non-symbolic coincide. Up to this point every statement is non-symbolic . . . Beyond this point every statement is symbolic . . . The point itself is both non-symbolic and symbolic.
>
> (9–10)

Tillich's language is admittedly difficult at this juncture, but he is being as precise as possible. Theological reflection will necessarily – whether it appeals to metaphysics or not, whether it appeals to a causal doctrine of creation or not – have to speak of God as the object of our longing and then distinguish what we take God to be from other possible referents. When God becomes a referent in any conceptual discourse, we will have to speak of God as non-symbolically as possible for the sake of clarity and precision. Tillich believes that an analysis of human experience suggests that the most adequate conceptual terms are those that render explicit what is implicit in religious experience: that God is the whence of our being and the world's being, our source, 'the one in whom we move and have our being' (Acts 17:28). Hence, the term 'being-itself'.

It should be noted – as more than a passing remark – that this Lukan–Pauline borrowing from the sixth-century poet–philosopher Epimenides is a quintessential scriptural moment that gives the lie to the overly neat and simple-minded separation of Jerusalem from Athens, of Jew from Greek, a separation that Tillich would not countenance. The biblical witness is itself hybrid. The decisive question is whether in the midst of such impurity and hybridity it is Jerusalem that absorbs and transfigures Athens (while also being transformed by Athens) or whether Athens absorbs and domesticates Jerusalem. Tillich would have little patience with those who believe that the question of ontotheology can be resolved simply by rejecting Athens and opting for the Bible.

Conceptual clarity, attained by means of non-symbolic communication, is itself a barrier to idolatry, a barrier to speech that would reduce God to the status of an ontic being. By specifying that God is the 'structure of being' Tillich means to make clear that 'God is not subject to

that structure', as any of the later Heidegger's gods most definitely would
be. But our conceptual tokens can become idolatrous should we fail to
understand their limited scope and function. Tillich is emphatic on this
score and notes that his theology *'only starts* with the statement that
God is being-itself . . .' before moving on to discourse about God as Life
and Spirit.[10] Indeed, Tillich understood that any naming of God whatsoever must be situated within a larger appreciation of God as beyond
all names:

> God is beyond even the highest names which theology has given to
> him. He is beyond spirit, beyond the good. God is, as Dionysius
> says, super-essential . . . He is not the highest being but beyond any
> possible highest being. He is supra-divinity, beyond God, if we
> speak of God as a divine being . . . Thus, all the names must
> disappear after they have been attributed to God, even the holy
> name "God" itself. Perhaps this is the source – unconsciously – of
> what I said at the end of my book, *The Courage to Be*, about the
> "God above God", namely, the God above God who is the real
> ground of everything that is, who is above any special name we can
> give to even the highest being.
>
> (*HCT*, 92)

Tillich recognizes that all talk about God, symbolic or non-
symbolic, has to be interrupted and must ultimately be found wanting. Even symbolic language, language that participates in the reality
to which it points, functions best when it is broken.[11] From Dionysius,
Tillich has learned a very great deal, including Dionysius's insistence
that even number does not mean the same thing when applied to God
as when applied to mundane realities. God is beyond one and three. In
all this, Tillich follows Dionysius faithfully.

But we are still left wondering about what Tillich means when,
in the second volume of the *Systematic Theology*, he seems to step
back from his earlier characterization of being-itself as wholly non-
symbolic. More precisely, what does Tillich mean when he claims that
to speak of God as being-itself is to speak rationally and ecstatically at
the same time? The most compelling way to an answer lies not through
Tillich but by considering how his terminology has come to function
in religious circles, both in his time and ours. Talk about God as the
power of being, God as the ground of being, ultimate concern, and faith
as the state of being grasped by an ultimate concern – all these locu-
tions have become commonplace not just in theological circles but in
the religious life of Christian communities. These terms are employed

not only to do theological work, but they have also become the stuff of sermons, liturgies and prayers. Tillich is rightly famous for maintaining that symbols cannot be invented by calculative deliberation. They are born and they die; they come unbidden and depart unbidden. Strangely, it has turned out that the conceptual terminology of the one who spoke in this way about the life of symbols has taken on symbolic power, and Tillich's own categories enable us to understand why that has transpired.

To speak of God as being-itself is a conceptual exercise and hence a non-symbolic operation, but to speak of God at all from within the theological circle is to speak in faith on behalf of faith. When a concept is employed in the service of faith, it does not behave. It transgresses against its assigned function and can become a symbol. The one who employs the concept does not retain mastery over it; on the contrary, one finds oneself overmastered by it. The one who says/confesses 'God is being-itself' – despite appearances to the contrary – is not necessarily up to something materially different from St Peter who confesses 'You are the Christ, Son of the living God.' Peter's confession acknowledges that he has found New Being in Christ. The one who states that God is being-itself confesses that he or she has being alone, that he or she is able to resist annihilating nothingness and find the courage to keep on keeping on only in and through God who is the source of his or her being. That is why speech about God as being-itself is, at once, rational and ecstatic. When such modes of speaking coincide, language resists attempts at good housekeeping, and the conceptual and the symbolic spill over into each other. The language of Athens is transfigured by the language of Jerusalem. It is after all possible to pray in Greek as well as in Hebrew.

At this point, a further question intervenes: why do we need the conceptual in theology? Cannot theology live by the resources of the symbol alone without recourse to conceptual idolatry? Why not clarify and elaborate the meaning of symbols by examining the material practices of the church which lives out the meaning of its symbols in and through just those material practices? On this account, we understand what the symbol of the Eucharist means not by appeal to ontology but by examining how the church eats, how the church feeds and whom it feeds. There is much to be said for this line of argument, which appeals to practice as a way to bypass conceptual idolatry. This appeal to practice is driven by the desire to avoid not just idolatry of speech, but also the idolatry of injustice, of worshipping Moloch or Mammon while claiming to worship the Christ. To all this I say, Amen!

But Tillich knew something that appears to be forgotten by contemporary theologians who wish to reside wholly and purely in Jerusalem, wholly and purely in the symbolic realm, wholly and purely in practice, whether they be postmodern or postliberal. Such purity is neither possible nor desirable. There is indeed no pure revelation. Where the divine is manifest, it is manifest in flesh, and that flesh includes the concept. The Logos that has become flesh deigns in its materiality to take on even the lowly concept. And thank God, because none of us are citizens of Jerusalem alone. Those who would seek to avoid Athens altogether in the name of avoiding ontotheology need to be reminded that the inscription on the cross was written not just in Hebrew, but also in Latin and Greek.

Tillich's correlational theology risks translating Gospel into current philosophical idioms – not because he believes that any such idiom is adequate to the truth of the Gospel – but because he is convinced that apart from some such material incarnation, the Gospel could not be received. On a Tillichian reading, the refusal to risk conceptual translation is as Gnostic a practice as to maintain that Jesus only appeared to be human.

GOD AS *GRUND* AND *UNGRUND*

One does not have to appeal to Tillich's apophatic sensibility alone to make a case against those who would characterize him as an ontotheologian. Also critical is his rejection of every conception of divinity as *actus purus*. Those most allergic to theologies of God as being-itself seem to assume – probably on the basis of scholastic precedent – that every conception of God as being-itself necessarily entails a commitment to a conception of divinity as pure actuality free of potentiality. On this matter, Tillich is emphatic and unambiguous: 'The God who is *actus purus* is not the living God' (*ST* I, 246). Hence, Tillich believes that any adequate theology must appeal to figures like Schelling, Boehme and before them Duns Scotus who have insisted on preserving a negative element in divinity. Tillich's commitment to this principle is manifest in his claim that being itself 'includes nonbeing'. He writes, 'one could say that being includes nonbeing but nonbeing does not prevail against it. "Including" is a spatial metaphor which indicates that being embraces itself and that which is opposed to it, nonbeing. Nonbeing belongs to being, it cannot be separated from it' (*CB*, 179). Tillich goes on to say that 'The self-affirmation of being without nonbeing would not even be self-affirmation but an immovable self-identity.

Nothing would be manifest, nothing expressed, nothing revealed' (179).

If characterizing God as 'being-itself' amounts to an exclusion of non-being and dynamism from the divine life, then the term is manifestly deficient. For this reason, Tillich insists that theologians must include Scotus's affirmation of God as will alongside a Thomistic affirmation of God as intellect. Aquinas, Tillich contends, erred in subordinating will to intellect in the divine life 'when he accepted the Aristotelian *actus purus* as the basic character of God' (*ST* I, 247). This is not to say that Tillich affirms the priority of will over intellect. On the contrary, he affirms the equiprimordiality of will and intellect, of dynamics and form.

Tillich's rejection of an *actus purus* divinity means that his God is very much *Grund* as well as *Ungrund*, meaning-rich depth as well as dynamic abyss. Precisely Tillich's inclusion of non-being within the divine life renders Tillich's God anything but the immutable *causa sui* God of the philosophers. Tillich's God is at once Pascal's fire and being-itself. Tillich's God is not just the basis of the rational structures of reality but also the One who destabilizes and ruptures extant orders for the sake of richness and novelty, novelty driven by the eschatological drive for the Kingdom of God. Hence, Tillich's God can in no way be reduced to an ontotheological foundation on which one can establish absolutely secure knowledge claims in Cartesian fashion.

By now it should be apparent that Tillich's God is simply not the ontotheological God that Heidegger rejects. His divinity is not a being, not even a supreme being. Tillich's God is not *causa sui*, nor can his divinity be univocally named the cause of the world. Nor can the term *being-itself* be applied univocally of both God and the world. Tillich is explicit on all of these matters. To construe God as the world's cause is to draw God into the series of causes and effects and render God once again into an ontic reality, into a being, albeit the first or supreme being. Hence, Tillich insists, should causality be applied to God at all, it must be understood only as a symbol rather than as a category (239). The relation between God and the world is one of participation, and participation is a relation whose intimacy and depth exceeds causality. In sum, Tillich's objections to regarding God as the world's *prima causa* mirror many of Heidegger's reservations.

Perhaps the most compelling evidence that Tillich was moving entirely beyond an earlier and more modernist conception of the theological task – that the primary work of theology is to render faith intelligible to secularity – can be found in his final gambit towards developing a theology formulated in conversation with the history of religions. In his last days, Tillich acknowledged that the scope of his theological project was limited because it was formulated largely in conversation with secular modernity. Theology's future, he argued, will require something more, a genuine encounter with other religions of the concrete spirit. Tillich's call for and commitment to such a project, taken together with Tillich's actual engagement with Eastern traditions, especially Zen Buddhism, demonstrates that he was well ahead of his time in this regard. Philosophers and theologians who today fancy themselves postmodern, who speak of leaving behind the Cartesian priority of self by recognizing the absolute dignity and inviolability of the Other, are rarely to be found in conversation with actual religious others. A full forty years after Tillich's passing, few Christian theologians, postmodern or otherwise, have engaged another religious tradition with the seriousness with which Tillich engaged Buddhism.

Postmodern theologians must do more than chide Tillich for his modernist theological project. Contemporary theologians would do well to recognize that we have, by and large, failed to transform and in turn be transformed not just by Athenian Greek but also by Sanskrit theological traditions, by Chinese philosophy, by Tamil devotionalism and by a still more robust and yet-to-be-attained polyglot profusion – a linguistic dissemination that encounters not just other idioms but all that follows in the train and wake of these other idioms – including, not least of all, other conceptual tools that will rupture the idolatries that inevitably follow from a triumphalist monolingualism that presumes that we can pray to God only in Hebrew or, as is true in our time, only in English. Locking oneself away in Jerusalem – as if that were possible – as an attempt at avoiding the ontotheological ailment is no cure. Tillich knew better than to long for such fictive purities, and so should we!

Postmodern commitments to principles of difference and otherness can only be fulfilled if Western thinkers adopt something like what Richard King calls 'postwesternism', a more radical departure from extant modes of reflection than can be found in the (counter)canons of postmodern thought:

> What is needed . . . is an approach which takes into account the postmodernist critique of the Enlightenment and the colonial discourses perpetuated by it, while at the same time constructing a cultural space based upon indigenous insights and orientations from the non-western world which is no easily assimilable by western culture, in either its modernist or postmodernist incarnations. Thus, what I am suggesting is . . . that something

akin to 'postwesternism' be developed, that is, an approach which takes into account the changing formation of international politics, globalization and inter-cultural dialogue, and which is overtly motivated towards facilitating a postcolonial 'inter-culturalism' with the goal of an end to the political, economic and philosophical hegemony of the western world.[12]

Inasmuch as we can glimpse in Tillich's work a move in this direction, his theology anticipates postwesternism and so marks an important step beyond the culturally circumscribed work of interrupting the hegemony of Enlightenment reflection.[13] In this respect, as in many others, post-modern theologians have yet to learn from Tillich, a theologian whom they are altogether too eager to supersede.

Notes

I would like to thank Ellen Armour, Rob James, Harold Oliver and Thomas Reynolds for reading this chapter in one or other of its many versions.

1 Quoted in Hart (2000), 82.
2 Charles Winquist, for example, declares, 'Tillich is not a postmodern theolo-gian. He clearly works within the ontotheological tradition. The hermeneu-tical strategies within his thinking are elaborative rather than deconstruc-tive.' See Winquist (1995), 62. Importantly, that is not Winquist's final word with respect to Tillich's ongoing relevance. Rather than dismissing Tillich outright, he argues that there is much in Tillich's thought that disrupts the ontotheological: 'His specific philosophical indebtedness to the ontotheo-logical tradition of nineteenth-century German idealism and more general mortgage to the autonomous subject of Cartesianism are allied with a theo-logical exigency in his thinking that subverts and transcends the totalization and exclusivity of these philosophical traditions' (63). Among the subversive features that Winquist sees in Tillich's theology are the disruptive power of his figurations of ultimacy, his eschatology, his method of correlation which 'makes his work continually subject to reformulations of the philosophi-cal problematic and also subject to cultural change' (63) and Tillich's keen awareness regarding the awkwardness of naming God. On all these matters I am in profound agreement with Winquist. I disagree with him only in his unequivocal dismissal of 'being' as a regressive ontotheological feature of Tillich's theology.
3 See, for example, Kevin Vanhoozer's misleading claim (in an otherwise important and compelling essay) that 'Paul Tillich's method of correla-tion . . . let modern culture and thought forms set the agenda by asking the questions which theology then answered . . . Tillich is illustrative of the modern tendency to let some *logos* or other swallow up the biblical *mythos*.' See Vanhoozer (2003), 19. For a nuanced treatment of Tillich's trenchant cri-tique of modernity, as opposed to Ernst Troeltsch's endorsement of the same, see Scharlemann (2004).
4 Ward (2001), dxv.

5 The very viability of the term is open to question when one considers that even Derrida, who is considered by many the postmodernist par excellence, rejects the applicability of the term to his thought. He confesses, 'I am not sure what this word means and I am not sure that it is useful to understand what is going on today' (Derrida (1999), 182).

6 Marion (1999), 30–1.

7 Heidegger (2002), 72.

8 On Tillich's sense of his own marginality, see his autobiographical work, *OB*.

9 Tillich is explicit on this matter and contends, 'The unsymbolic statement which implies the necessity of religious symbolism is that God is being-itself.' See Paul Tillich, 'Reply to Interpretation and Criticism' in Kegley and Bretall (1956), 334. My thanks to Robison James for bringing this important claim to my attention.

10 Paul Tillich, 'Rejoinder' to Robert P. Scharlemann, 'Tillich's Method of Correlation: Two Proposed Revisions' in Scharlemann (2006) 40–1. Emphasis added.

11 One should, on good Tillichian grounds, say that symbols function properly *only* when they are broken, that is to say when one recognizes the symbol as a symbol that points beyond itself. But Tillich allows that there are some who, remaining in thrall to 'natural' literalism, have yet to recognize myths and symbols for what they are. Tillich also recognizes that there are 'reactive' literalists who simply refuse to allow symbols and myths to be broken and, by clinging to literalism, risk idolatry (*DF*, 51–3).

12 King (1999), 233.

13 For a work that takes up Tillich's mandate for theology done in conversation with the history of religion, see my book, *The Immanent Divine*, which puts Tillich's theology into conversation with Sankara's Advaita Vedanta and opens both to mutual transformation through dialogue. See Thatamanil (2006).

Further reading

Crockett, Clayton ed. (2001). *Secular Theology: American Radical Theological Thought*. London: Routledge.

Grigg, R. (1985). *Symbol and Empowerment: Paul Tillich's Post-Theistic System*. Macon, Ga.: Mercer University Press.

Hart, Kevin (2000). *The Trespass of the Sign: Deconstruction, Theology and Philosophy*. New York: Fordham University Press.

Stenger, Mary Ann and Ronald H. Stone (2002). *Dialogues of Paul Tillich*. Macon, Ga.: Mercer University Press.

Thatamanil, John J. (2006). *The Immanent Divine: God, Creation, and the Human Predicament. An East–West Conversation*. Minneapolis, Minn.: Fortress Press.

Bibliography

Abe, Masao (1985). *Zen and Western Thought*. New York/Honolulu: Macmillan/ University of Hawaii Press.

Adams, James Luther (1965). *Paul Tillich's Philosophy of Culture, Science, and Religion*. New York: Harper & Row.

Adorno, Theodor W. ed. (1967). *Werk und Wirken Paul Tillichs. Ein Gedenkbuch*. Stuttgart: Evangelisches Verlagswerk.

Albrecht, Renate (1987). 'Paul Tillich – His Life and His Personality' in *Religion et Culture*, ed. M. Despland, J.-C. Petit and J. Richard, 7–16. Quebec: Presses de l'Université Laval/Éditions du Cerf.

and Werner Schüßler (1986). *Paul Tillich. Sein Werk*. Düsseldorf: Patmos.

(1993). *Paul Tillich. Sein Leben*. Frankfurt am Main: Peter Lang.

Alston, William P. (1972 (1967)). 'Tillich' in *Encyclopedia of Philosophy*, ed. Paul Edwards, VII, 125. New York: Macmillan.

Althaus-Reed, Marcella (2000). *Indecent Theology: Theological Perversions in Sex, Gender and Politics*. New York: Routledge.

Arendt, Hannah (1958). *The Human Condition*. Chicago, Ill.: University of Chicago Press.

Augustine (2000). *Confessions*, trans. Maria Boulding. New York: New York City Press.

Badiou, Alain (2001). *Ethics: An Essay on the Understanding of Evil*, trans. Peter Hallward. New York and London: Verso Books.

(2005). *Being and Event*, trans. Oliver Feltham. New York: Continuum.

Barker, Jason (2002). *Alain Badiou: A Critical Introduction*. Modern European Thinkers. London: Pluto Press.

Barth, Karl (1956). *Church Dogmatics* vol. I, part 2, trans. G. T. Thomson and Harold Knight, ed. G. W. Bromiley and T. F. Torrance. Edinburgh: T&T Clark.

(1957). *Church Dogmatics* vol. II, part 1, trans. G. W. Bromiley, ed. G. W. Bromiley and T. F. Torrance. Edinburgh: T&T Clark.

(1961). *Church Dogmatics* vol. III, part 4, various translators, ed. G. N. Bromiley and T. F. Torrance. Edinburgh: T&T Clark.

(1986). 'The First Commandment as an Axiom of Theology' in *The Way of Theology in Karl Barth: Essays and Comments*, ed. H. Martin Rumscheidt, 63–78. Allison Park, Pa.: Pickwick Publications.

Barth, Ulrich (2003). 'Die sinntheoretischen Grundlagen des Religionsbegriffs. Problemgeschichtliche Hintergründe zum frühen Tillich' in Ulrich Barth, *Religion in der Moderne*, 89–123. Tübingen: Mohr.

Baumgarten, Barbara Dee (1994). *Visual Art as Theology*. New York: Peter Lang.

Bayer, Oswald (1994). *Theologie*. Handbuch Systematischer Theologie, ed. Carl Heinz Ratschow, vol. I. Gütersloh: Gütersloher Verlagshaus.

   (2008). 'Grundzüge der Theologie Paul Tillichs, kritisch dargestellt'. *Neue Zeitschrift für Systematische Theologie und Religionsphilosophie* 50.

Begbie, Jeremy (1987). 'Theology, Ontology and the Philosophy of Art with Special Reference to Paul Tillich and the Dutch Neo-Calvinists', PhD Diss., Aberdeen.

Behe, Michael J. (1996). *Darwin's Black Box: The Biochemical Challenge to Evolution*. New York: The Free Press.

Bertinetti, Ilse (1990). *Paul Tillich*. Biographien zur Kirchengeschichte, ed. H.-U. Delius. Berlin: Union Verlag.

Bixler, Julius ed. (1961). *The Search of God and Immortality*. Boston, Mass.: Beacon Press.

Boss, Marc (2001). 'Religious Diversity: From Tillich to Lindbeck and Back' in *Religion in the New Millennium: Theology in the Spirit of Paul Tillich*, ed. Raymond F. Bulman and Frederick J. Parrella, 177–95. Macon, Ga.: Mercer University Press.

Braaten, Carl E. (1967). 'Preface' and 'Introduction' in *P*.

Brauer, Jerald C. (1989). 'Tillich at Chicago'. *Newsletter of the North American Paul Tillich Society* 15: 4, 2–10.

   (2001). 'Still Creative. Paul Tillich at Chicago' in *Spurensuche. Lebens- und Denkwege Paul Tillichs*, ed. Ilona Nord and Yorick Spieger. Münster: LIT Verlag.

Brock, Rita Nakashima (2000). *Journeys by Heart: A Christology of Erotic Power*. New York: Crossroad.

Brown, Delwin (1994). *Boundaries of Our Habitations: Tradition and Theological Construction*. SUNY Series in Religious Studies, ed. Harold Coward. Albany: State University of New York Press.

Brown, Joanne Carlson and Rebecca Parker (1989). 'For God So Loved the World?' in *Christianity, Patriarchy and Abuse: A Feminist Critique*, ed. Joanne Carlson Brown and Carole R. Bohn. Cleveland, Ohio: The Pilgrim Press.

Brunner, Emil (1929). 'Die andere Aufgabe der Theologie'. *Zwischen den Zeiten* 7: 255–76.

Bryson, Lyman ed. (1944). *Approaches to World Peace*. Fourth Symposium. New York: Harper.

Buber Martin (1979). *I and Thou*, trans. Walter Kaufmann. New York: Charles Scribner's Sons.

Büchsel, F. (1923). 'Die Stellung der Theologie im System der Wissenschaften. Eine Auseinandersetzung mit Paul Tillichs *System der Wissenschaften*'. *Zeitschrift für Systematische Theologie* 1: 399–411.

Bulman, Raymond F. (1981). *A Blueprint for Humanity: Paul Tillich's Theology of Culture*. Lewisburg, Pa.: Bucknell University Press.

   and Frederick J. Parrella eds. (2001). *Religion in the New Millennium: Theology in the Spirit of Paul Tillich*. Macon, Ga.: Mercer University Press.

Bultmann, Rudolf (1959). 'Preaching: Genuine and Secularized' in *Religion and Culture. Essays in Honor of Paul Tillich*, ed. Walter Leibrecht, 236–42. New York: Harper & Row.

Cali, Grace (1996). *Paul Tillich First-Hand: A Memoir of the Harvard Years.* Chicago, Ill.: Exploration Press.

Camus, Albert (1942). *Le mythe de Sisyphe. Essai sur l'absurde.* Paris: Gallimard.

Caputo, John D. (1997). *The Prayers and Tears of Jacques Derrida: Religion without Religion.* Bloomington, Ind.: Indiana University Press.

Carey, John J. ed. (1978). *Kairos and Logos: Studies in the Roots and Implications of Tillich's Theology.* Macon, GA: Mercer University Press.

 ed. (1987). *Being and Doing: Paul Tillich as Ethicist.* Macon, Ga.: Mercer University Press.

Clayton, John P. (1978). 'Was heißt "Korrelation" bei Paul Tillich?' *Neue Zeitschrift für Systematische Theologie* 20: 175–91.

 (1980). *The Concept of Correlation: Paul Tillich and the Possibility of a Mediating Theology.* Berlin: Walter de Gruyter.

Cobb, Kelton (1995). 'Reconsidering the Status of Popular Culture in Tillich's Theology of Culture'. *The Journal of the American Academy of Religion* 63: 53–84.

 (2005). *The Blackwell Guide to Theology and Popular Culture.* Oxford: Blackwell.

Coetzee, P. H. ed. (2003). *The African Philosophy Reader.* Second edn. New York: Routledge.

Cooper, Terry D. (2005). 'Paul Tillich and the New York Psychology Group, 1941–45'. *Bulletin of the North American Paul Tillich Society* 21: 14–15.

 (2006). 'Paul Tillich and Psychology: Historic and Contemporary Explorations' in *Theology, Psychotherapy, and Ethics*, ed. Terry D. Cooper. Macon, Ga.: Mercer University Press.

Cowan, Wayne ed. (1966). *Witness to a Generation: Significant Writings from Christianity and Crisis (1941–1966).* New York: Bobbs-Merrill.

Crockett, Clayton ed. (2001). *Secular Theology: American Radical Theological Thought.* London: Routledge.

Cziko, Gary (1995). *Without Miracles: Universal Selection Theory and the Second Darwinian Revolution.* Cambridge, Mass.: MIT Press.

Daly, Mary (1973). *Beyond God the Father: Toward a Philosophy of Women's Liberation.* Boston, Mass.: Beacon.

 (1984). *Pure Lust: Elemental Feminist Philosophy.* Boston, Mass.: Beacon.

 (1988). *Gyn/Ecology: The Metaethics of Radical Feminism.* Boston, Mass.: Beacon.

Danz Christian (2000a). 'Der Begriff des Symbols bei Paul Tillich und Ernst Cassirer' in *Die Prägnanz der Religion in der Kultur. Ernst Cassirer und die Theologie*, ed. D. Korsch and E. Rudolph, 201–28. Tübingen: Mohr Siebeck.

 (2000b). *Religion als Freiheitsbewußtsein. Eine Studie zur Theologie als Theorie der Konstitutionsbedingungen individueller Subjektivität bei Paul Tillich.* Berlin/New York: Walter de Gruyter.

 (2004a). 'Theologie als normative Religionsphilosophie. Voraussetzungen und Implikationen des Theologiebegriffs Paul Tillichs' in Danz (2004b), 73–106. Vienna: LIT Verlag.

ed. (2004b). *Theologie als Religionsphilosophie. Studien zu den prob-lemgeschichtlichen und systematischen Voraussetzungen der Theologie Paul Tillichs*, Tillich-Studien, vol. IX. Vienna: LIT Verlag.

(2005a). *Gott und die menschliche Freiheit. Studien zum Gottesbegriff in der Neuzeit*. Neukirchen-Vluyn: Neukirchener Verlag.

(2005b). 'Die Krise der Subjektivität und ihre geschichtsphilosophische Überwindung. Überlegungen zu Paul Tillichs frühen religiösen Sozialis-mus' in *Krisen der Subjektivität. Problemfelder eines strittigen Paradig-mas*, ed. I. U. Dalferth and P. Stoellger, 157–74. Tübingen: Mohr Siebeck.

(2005c). 'Glaube und Autonomie. Zur Deutung der Rechtfertigungslehre bei Karl Holl und Paul Tillich' in *Wie viel Vernunft braucht der Glaube? Internationales Jahrbuch für die Tillich-Forschung*, vol. I, ed. C. Danz, W. Schüßler and E. Sturm, 159–74. Vienna: LIT Verlag.

(2005d). 'Die Krise der Subjektivität und ihre geschichtsphilosophische Überwindung' in *Éthique sociale et socialisme religieux. Actes du XVe Colloque International Paul Tillich, Toulouse 2003*, ed. M. Boss, D. Lax and J. Richard, 157–74. Münster: LIT Verlag.

(2006a). 'Symbolische Form und die Erfassung des Geistes im Gottesverhältnis. Anmerkungen zur Genese des Symbolbegriffs von Paul Tillich' in *Das Sym-bol als Sprache der Religion. International Yearbook for Tillich-Research*, vol. II, ed. Christian Danz, Werner Schüßler and Erdmann Sturm, 59–75. Münster: LIT Verlag.

Werner Schüßler and Erdmann Sturm eds. (2006b). *Das Symbol als Sprache der Religion. International Yearbook for Tillich Research*, vol. II. Münster: LIT Verlag.

DeMartino, Richard, Daisetz Suzuki and Erich Fromm (1960). *Zen and Psycho-analysis*. New York: Harper & Bros.

Dembski, William (1999). *Intelligent Design: The Bridge Between Science and Theology*. Downers Grove, Ill.: InterVarsity Press.

Derrida, Jacques (1999). 'Response to David Tracy' in *God, The Gift, and Post-modernism*, ed. John D. Caputo and Michael Scanlon. Bloomington, Ind.: Indiana University Press.

Despland, M., J.-C. Petit and J. Richard eds. (1987). *Religion et Culture*. Quebec: Presses de l'Université Laval/Éditions du Cerf.

Diamond, Stephen A. (1996). *Anger, Madness, and the Daimonic: The Psycholog-ical Genesis of Violence, Evil, and Creativity*. Albany, N.Y.: State University of New York Press.

Dillenberger, John (1987). *A Theology of Artistic Sensibilities: The Visual Arts and the Church*. London: SCM.

Dixon, Jr, John (1963). 'Is Tragedy Essential to Knowing? A Critique of Dr Tillich's Aesthetic'. *The Journal of Religion* 43:4, 271–84.

Dourley, John (1974). 'Trinitarian Models and Human Integration'. *Journal of Analytical Psychology* 19.

(1995a). 'Jacob Boehme and Paul Tillich on Trinity and God: Similarities and Differences'. *Religious Studies* 31: 429–45.

(1995b). 'Humanity, The Trinity's Missing Fourth, The Psycho-Spiritual Impli-cations of Jung's Quaternitarian Psyche'. *Pastoral Sciences* 14.

(1997). 'Issues of Naturalism and Supranaturalism in Tillich's Correlation of Religious with Psychological Healing'. *Studies in Religion* 26: 211–22.

(2004). 'Toward a Salvageable Tillich: The Implications of His Late Confession of Provincialism'. *Studies in Religion* 33: 3–26.

Drummy, Michael (2000). *Being and Earth: Paul Tillich's Theology of Nature.* Lanham, Md.: University Press of America.

Dumas, Marc (1993). *Die theologische Deutung der Erfahrung des Nichts im deutschen Werk Paul Tillichs (1919–1930).* Frankfurt am Main: Peter Lang.

Durkheim, Émile (1960). *Division of Labor in Society (1893),* trans. George Simpson. New York: The Free Press.

Dussel, Enrique (1998). *Ética de la liberación en la edad de la globalización y de la exclusión.* Madrid: Editorial Trotta.

Einstein, Albert (1954). *Ideas and Opinions.* New York: Bonanza Books.

Eliade, Mircea (1966). 'Paul Tillich and the History of Religions' in *FR.*

Ferre, N. (1966). 'Tillich and the Nature of Transcendence' in *Paul Tillich: Retrospect and Future.* Nashville, Tenn. and New York: Abingdon Press.

Fichte, Friedrich Joseph Wilhelm von (1908–12). *J. Fichtes Werke in 5 Bänden,* ed. V. F. Medicus. Leipzig: Felix Meiner.

Fischer, H. (1992). *Systematische Theologie. Konzeptionen und Probleme im 20. Jahrhundert.* Stuttgart/Berlin/Cologne: Kohlhammer.

Foerster, Herbert (1965). *Die Kritik Paul Tillichs an der Theologie Karl Barths.* Diss., Göttingen.

Ford, L. S. (1970). 'Tillich's One Nonsymbolic Statment: À Propos of a Recent Study by Rowe'. *Journal of the American Academy of Religion* 38: 176.

Foster, A. Durwood (2007). 'Tillich and the Historical Jesus'. *Bulletin of the North American Paul Tillich Society* 33:1, 6–14.

Furlong, Iris (1992). 'The Mythology of the Near East' in *The Feminist Companion to Mythology,* ed. Carolyne Larrington. London: Pandora Press.

Gatens, Moira (1998). 'Modern Rationalism' in *A Companion to Feminist Philosophy,* ed. Alison M. Jaggar and Iris Marion Young, 27–8. Oxford: Blackwell.

Geertz, Clifford (1973). *Interpretation of Cultures.* New York: Basic Books.

Gilkey, Langdon (1982). 'Tillich: Master of Mediation' in *The Theology of Paul Tillich,* ed. Charles Kegley. Second edn. New York: The Pilgrim Press.

(1984). *Reaping the Whirlwind: A Christian Interpretation of History.* San Francisco, Calif.: HarperSanFrancisco.

(1988). 'Tillich and the Kyoto School' in *Papers from the Annual Meeting of the North American Paul Tillich Society, Boston, Massachusetts, December 1987,* 1–10. Charlottesville, Va.: The North American Paul Tillich Society, Inc.

(1990). *Gilkey on Tillich.* New York: Crossroad.

(2001). 'The Religious Situation at the End of the Twentieth Century' in *Religion in the New Millennium: Theology in the Spirit of Paul Tillich,* ed. R. F. Bulman and F. J. Parella, 7–18. Macon, Ga.: Mercer University Press, 2001.

Gisel, Pierre (2002). 'Première guerre mondiale et apories de la modernité' in *Mutations religieuses de la modernité tardive,* ed. M. Boss, D. Lax and J. Richard, 50–77. Tillich-Studien, vol. VII. Münster: LIT Verlag.

Goodenough, Ursula (1998). *The Sacred Depths of Nature.* New York: Oxford University Press.

Graf, F. W. and A. Christophersen (2004). 'Neukantianismus, Fichte- und Schellingrenaissance. Paul Tillich und sein philosophischer Lehrer Fritz Medicus'. *Zeitschrift für Neuere Theologiegeschichte* 11: 52–78.

Grigg, R. (1985). *Symbol and Empowerment: Paul Tillich's Post-Theistic System*. Macon, Ga.: Mercer University Press.

Gudorf, Christine E. (1992). *Victimization: Examining Christian Complicity*. Philadelphia, Pa.: Trinity Press International.

Gustafson, James M. (1992). *Ethics from a Theocentric Perspective*, 2 vols. Chicago, Ill.: University of Chicago Press.

Haigis, Peter (1998). *Im Horizont der Zeit: Paul Tillich Project einer Theologie der Kultur*. Marburg: N. G. Elwert Verlag.

Hardt, Michael and Antonio Negri (2000). *Empire*. Cambridge, Mass.: Harvard University Press.

    (2004). *Multitude: War and Democracy in the Age of Empire*. New York: Penguin Press.

Hart, Kevin (2000). *The Trespass of the Sign: Deconstruction, Theology and Philosophy*. New York: Fordham University Press.

Hauerwas, Stanley and William H. Willimon (1989). *Resident Aliens: Life in the Christian Colony*. Nashville, Tenn.: Abingdon Press.

Haught, John F. (2006). *Is Nature Enough? Meaning and Truth in the Age of Science*. Cambridge: Cambridge University Press.

Hauser, Gerard (1986). *Introduction to Rhetorical Theory*. Philadelphia, Pa.: Harper & Row.

Hawking, Stephen (1992). *A Brief History of Time*. New York: Bantam Books.

Heidegger, Martin (2002). 'The Onto-theo-logical Constitution of Metaphysics' in *Identity and Difference*, trans. Joan Stambaugh. Chicago, Ill.: University of Chicago Press.

Heinrichs, J. (1970). 'Der Ort der Metaphysik im System der Wissenschaften bei Paul Tillich'. *Zeitschrift für Katholische Theologie* 92: 249–86.

Henel, Ingeborg (1981). *Philosophie und Theologie im Werk Paul Tillichs*. Frankfurt am Main: Evangelisches Verlagswerk.

Heyward, Carter (1982). *The Redemption of God*. Washington, D.C.: University Press of America.

    (1989). *Touching Our Strength: The Erotic as Power and the Love of God*. San Francisco, Calif.: Harper & Row.

Hopkins, Dwight W. (2005). *Being Human: Race, Culture and Religion*. Minneapolis, Minn.: Augsburg Fortress.

Hopper, David (1968). *Tillich: A Theological Portrait*. Philadelphia, Pa.: JB Lippincott.

Ihuoma, Sylvester I. (2004). *Paul Tillich's Theology of Culture in Dialogue with African Theology: A Contextual Analysis*. Tillich-Studien vol. XI. Münster: LIT Verlag.

Irenaeus (2004). 'Against Heresies' in *The Writings of Irenaeus. Ante-Nicene Christian Library Translations of the Writings of the Fathers down to AD 325*, vol. V, trans. Alexander Roberts and W. H. Rambaut. Whitefish, Mont.: Kessinger Publishing.

Irwin, Alexander C. (1991). *Eros Towards the World: Paul Tillich and the Theology of the Erotic*. Minneapolis, Minn.: Fortress Press.

Jahr, H. (1989). *Theologie als Gestaltmetaphysik. Die Vermittlung von Gott und Welt im Frühwerk P. Tillichs*. Berlin/New York: Walter de Gruyter.

James, Robison B. (1997). 'Tillich on "The Absoluteness of Christianity"': Reconceiving the Exclusivist-Inclusivist-Pluralist Scheme' in *Papers from the Annual Meeting of the North American Paul Tillich Society, Philadelphia, Pennsylvania, November 1995*, ed. Robert P. Sharlemann, 35–50. Charlottesville, Va.: University of Virginia.

(2003). *Tillich and World Religions: Encountering Other Faiths Today*. Macon, Ga.: Mercer University Press.

Jantzen, Grace M. (1999). *Becoming Divine: Toward a Feminist Philosophy of Religion*. Bloomington, Ind.: Indiana University Press.

Jarratt, Susan C. and Nedra Reynolds eds. (1994). 'The Splitting Image: Contemporary Feminisms and the Ethics of êthos' in *Ethos: New Essays in Rhetorical and Critical Theory*, ed. James S. Baumlin and Tita French Baumlin. Dallas, Tex.: Southern Methodist University Press.

Jenson, Robert (1997). 'Karl Barth' in *The Modern Theologians*. Second edn, ed. David Ford, 34. Oxford: Blackwell.

John, Peter (2003). 'Tillich: The Words I Recorded, the Man I Knew'. *Newsletter of the North American Paul Tillich Society* 29:1, 4–11.

Johnson, Elizabeth A. (1995). *She Who Is: The Mystery of God in Feminist Theological Discourse*. New York: Crossroad.

Johnson, Phillip E. (1991). *Darwin on Trial*. Downers Grove, Ill.: InterVarsity Press.

Jung, Carl Gustav (1958). *Collected Works*, 20 vols. Princeton, N.J.: Princeton University Press.

Kegley, Charles W. (1960). 'Paul Tillich on the Philosophy of Art'. *The Journal of Aesthetics and Art Criticism* 19:2, 175–84.

and Robert W. Bretall eds. (1956). *The Theology of Paul Tillich*. New York: Macmillan.

Kelsey, David (2005). *Imagining Redemption*. Louisville, Ky.: John Knox Press.

Khal-Tambwe, Willy Nunga (in press). *Mission chrétienne et people premier*.

King, Richard (1999). *Indian Philosophy: An Introduction to Hindu and Buddhist Thought*. Edinburgh: Edinburgh University Press.

King, Jr, Martin Luther (1968). 'Remaining Awake Through a Great Revolution. A sermon. The National Cathedral, Washington, D.C., March 31, 1968'. *Congressional Record* 9 April 1968.

Klemm, David E. (2004). 'Introduction: Theology of Culture as Theological Humanism'. *Literature and Theology* 18:3, 239–50.

and William H. Klink (2003). 'Constructing and Testing Theological Models'. *Zygon* 38:3, 495–528.

Klemm, David E. and William Schweiker (2008). *Religion and the Human Future: An Essay on Theological Humanism*. Oxford: Wiley-Blackwell.

Klotz, Leopold ed. (1932). *Die Kirche und das Dritte Reich: Fragen und Forderungen deutscher Theologen*. Gotha: Klotz.

Leese, K. (1926).'Das System der Wissenschaften'. *Christliche Welt* 40: 317–25, 371–5.

Leiner, Martin (2007). '"Kein Gott, der den Menschen Fragen stellt?" Jüdische und literarische Anfragen zur theologischen Methode und zur Gotteslehre Paul Tillichs'. *Tillich Preview* 1.

Levinas, Emmanuel (1996). *Emmanuel Levinas: Basic Philosophical Writings*, ed. Adriaan T. Pepperzak, Simon Critchley and Robert Bernasconi. Bloomington, Ind.: Indiana University Press.

Lichtman, Susan (1989). 'The Concept of Sin in the Theology of Paul Tillich: A Break from Patriarchy?' *The Journal of Women and Religion* 8: 49–55.

Luther, Martin (1883). *Weimarer Ausgabe*, 127 vols. Weimar: Verlag Hermann Böhlaus Nochfolger.

McEnhill, Peter and George Newlands (2004). *Fifty Key Christian Thinkers*. London: Routledge.

McFague, Sallie (1982). *Metaphorical Theology: Models of God in Religious Language*. Philadelphia, Pa.: Fortress Press.

Mananzan, Mary John (1994). 'Feminine Socialization: Women as Victims and Collaborators' in *Violence Against Women. Concilium*, 1994/1, ed. Elisabeth Schüssler Fiorenza and Mary Shawn Copeland, 44–52. Maryknoll, N.Y.: Orbis Books.

Marc, Franz (1978). *Schriften*, ed. Klaus Lankheit. Cologne: DuMont.

Marion, Jean-Luc (1991). *God without Being. Hors-texte*. Chicago, Ill.: University of Chicago Press.

    (1999). 'In the Name: How to Avoid Speaking of "Negative Theology"' in *God, The Gift, and Postmodernism*, ed. John D. Caputo and Michael J. Scanlon, 30–1. Bloomington, Ind.: Indiana University Press.

Matthews, Thomas F. (1967). 'Tillich on Religious Content in Modern Art'. *Art Journal* 27:1, 16–19.

May, Rollo (1969). *Love and Will*. New York: W. W. Norton.

    (1973). *Paulus: Reminiscences of a Friendship*. New York: Harper & Row.

    (1988). *Paulus: Tillich as Spiritual Teacher*. Revised edn of May (1973). Dallas: W. W. Norton.

Medicus, F. (1902). *Kants Philosophie der Geschichte*. Berlin: Reuther & Reichard.

    (1905). *J. G. Fichte. Dreizehn Vorlesungen*. Berlin: Reuther & Reichard.

Milbank, John, Catherine Pickstock and Graham Ward eds. (1999). *Radical Orthodoxy: A New Theology*. London: Routledge.

Moreland, James Porter ed. (1994). *The Creation Hypothesis: Scientific Evidence for an Intelligent Designer*. Downers Grove, Ill.: InterVarsity Press.

Morgan, David (1996). 'The Enchantment of Art: Abstraction and Empathy from German Romanticism to Expressionism'. *Journal of the History of Ideas* 57:2, 317–41.

Moritz, H. (1960). *Sein, Sinn und Geschichte beim frühen Tillich*. Diss.: Leipzig.

Moxter, M. (2000). *Kultur als Lebenswelt. Studien zum Problem einer Kulturtheologie*. Tübingen: Mohr Siebeck.

Nelson Dunfee, Susan (1982). 'The Sin of Hiding: A Feminist Critique of Reinhold Niebuhr's Account of the Sin of Pride'. *Soundings* 65: 316–27.

Neugebauer, G. (2006). *Offenbarung und Geschichte. Tillichs frühe Christologie vor dem Hintergrund seiner Schellingrezeption*. Diss.: Halle/Saale.

Nietzsche, Friedrich (1984). *Human, All Too Human: A Book for Free Spirits*, trans. Marion Fabor with Stephen Lehmann. Lincoln, Nebr.: University of Nebraska Press.

Noddings, Nel (1989). *Women and Evil.* Berkeley, Calif.: University of California Press.

Nörenberg, K.-D. (1966). *Analogia Imaginis. Der Symbolbegriff in der Theologie Paul Tillichs.* Gütersloh: Gütersloher Verlagshaus.

Novak, Michael Anthony (2007). 'Salvador Dali's *The Sacrament of the Last Supper*: A Theological Re-assessment' at http://ethicscenter.nd.edu/archives/documents/Novak.pdf

Nuovo, Victor (1987). 'Tillich's Theory of Art and the Possibility of a Theology of Culture' in *Religion et culture: actes du colloque international du centenaire Paul Tillich, Université Laval, Québec 18–22 août 1986*, ed. Michel Despland, Jean-Claude Petit and Jean Richard, 393–404. Quebec: Presses de l'Université Laval/Éditions du Cerf.

O'Keefe, Terence (1987). 'The Metaethics of Paul Tillich: Further Reflections' in *Being and Doing: Paul Tillich as Ethicist*, ed. John J. Carey. Macon, Ga.: Mercer University Press.

O'Meara, Thomas F. (1985). 'Tillich and the Catholic in Substance' in *The Thought of Paul Tillich*, ed. James Luther Adams, Wilhelm Pauck and Roger Shinn. New York: Harper & Row.

Ortiz, Gaye W. and Clive Marsh eds. (1997). *Explorations in Theology and Film.* Oxford: Blackwell.

Palapathwala, Ruwan (2001). 'Beyond Christ and *System*: Paul Tillich and Spirituality for the Twenty-First Century' in *Religion for the New Millennium: Theology in the Spirit of Paul Tillich*, ed. Frederick J. Parrella and Raymond F. Bulman, 205–20. Macon, Ga.: Mercer University Press.

Palmer, Michael (1984). *Paul Tillich's Philosophy of Art.* Berlin/New York: Walter de Gruyter.

(1990). 'Paul Tillich's Theology of Culture' in *MW/HW* II, 1–31.

Parrella, Frederick J. (1994). 'Tillich and Contemporary Spirituality' in *Paul Tillich: A New Catholic Perspective*, ed. Raymond F. Bulman and Frederick J. Parrella. Collegeville, Minn.: The Liturgical Press.

(2004). 'Paul Tillich and the Doctrine of the Trinity: A Catholic Perspective' in *Trinität und/oder Quaternität – Tillichs Neuerschließung der trinitarischen Problematik/Trinity and/or Quaternity – Tillich's Reopening of the Trinitarian Problem*, Tillich-Studien, vol. X, ed. Gert Hummel and Doris Lax, 280–98. Münster: LIT Verlag.

Pauck, Wilhelm and Marion Pauck (1976). *Paul Tillich: His Life and Thought*, vol. I, *Life*. New York: Harper & Row.

Pennock, Robert T. (1999). *Tower of Babel: The Evidence Against the New Creationism.* Cambridge, Mass.: MIT Press.

Plaskow, Judith (1980). *Sex, Sin and Grace: Women's Experience and the Theologies of Reinhold Niebuhr and Paul Tillich.* New York: University Press of America.

Potter Engel, Mary (1998). 'Evil, Sin, and Violation of the Vulnerable' in *Lift Every Voice: Constructing Theologies from the Underside*, ed. Susan Brooks Thistlethwaite and Mary Potter Engel, 159–71. San Francisco, Calif.: Harper & Row.

Radford Ruether, Rosemary (1993). *Sexism and God-Talk: Toward a Feminist Theology.* Boston, Mass.: Beacon.

Ratschow, Carl Heinz (1980). 'Paul Tillich. Ein biographisches Bild seiner Gedanken' in *Tillich-Auswahl*, 3 vols., ed. M. Baumotte, vol. I, 11–104. Gütersloh.

Raymo, Chet (1998). *Skeptics and True Believers: The Exhilarating Connection Between Science and Religion*. New York: Walker and Company.

Re Manning, Russell (2005). *Theology at the End of Culture: Paul Tillich's Theology of Culture and Art*. Leuven: Peeters.

(2006). 'The Place of Christ in Tillich's Theology of Culture' in *Christus Jesus – Mitte der Geschichte!?/Christ Jesus – Center of History!?* Tillich-Studien, vol. XIII, ed. Peter Haigis, Gert Hummel (†) and Doris Lax, 34–53. Münster: LIT-Verlag.

Reimer, A. James (1988). *Paul Tillich and Emanuel Hirsch: A Study of Theology and Politics*. Lewiston, Maine: The Edwin Mellen Press.

Repp, M. (1986). *Die Transzendierung des Theismus in der Religionsphilosophie Paul Tillichs*. Frankfurt am Main: Peter Lang.

Rex Crawford, W. ed. (1953). *The Cultural Migration: The European Scholar in America*. Philadelphia, Pa.: University of Pennsylvania Press.

Richard, Jean (1986). 'Theology of Culture and Systematic Theology in Paul Tillich'. *Église et Théologie* 17: 223–32.

Robinson, James M., ed. (1968). *The Beginnings of Dialectical Theology*. Richmond, Va.: John Knox Press.

Royce, Josiah (1982). *The Spirit of Modern Philosophy* (1892). New York: Dover.

Russell, Robert John, Philip Clayton, Kirk Wegter-McNelly and John Polkinghorne eds. (2001). *Quantum Mechanics: Scientific Perspectives on Divine Action*. Vatican City State: Vatican Observatory Publications, and Berkeley, Calif.: Center for Theology and the Natural Sciences.

Saiving, Valerie (1960). 'The Human Situation: A Feminine View'. *The Journal of Religion* 40:2, 100–12.

Scharf, Uwe-Carsten (1999). *The Paradoxical Breakthrough of Revelation: Interpreting the Divine–Human Interplay in Paul Tillich's Work 1913–1964*. Berlin/New York: Walter de Gruyter.

Scharlemann, Robert (1969). *Reflection and Doubt in the Thought of Paul Tillich*. New Haven, Conn.: Yale University Press.

(1984). *The Being of God: Theology and the Experience of Truth*. San Francisco, Calif.: HarperSanFrancisco.

(1985). 'The Religious Interpretation of Art' in *The Thought of Paul Tillich*, ed. James Luther Adams, Wilhelm Pauck and Roger Lincoln Shinn. San Francisco, Calif.: Harper & Row.

(1987). 'Demons, Idols, and the Symbol of Symbols in Tillich's Theology of Politics' in *Religion et culture: actes du colloque international du centenaire Paul Tillich, Université Laval, Québec 18–22 août 1986*, ed. M. Despland, Jean-Claude Petit and Jean Richard, 377–92. Quebec: Presses de l'Université Laval/Éditions du Cerf.

(2006). 'Christianity and the End of Modernity' in *Religion and Reflection: Essays on Paul Tillich's Theology*, ed. Erdmann Sturm, 231–52. Münster: LIT Verlag.

Schelling, F. W. J. (1977). *Philosophie der Offenbarung*, ed. Manfred Frank. Frankfurt am Main: Suhrkamp.

Schleiermacher, Friedrich Daniel Ernst (1960). *Der christliche Glaube. Nach den Grundsätzen der evangelischen Kirche im Zusammenhange dargestellt,* vol. I, ed. M. Redeker. Berlin: Walter de Gruyter.

Schneider-Flume, Gunda (1979). '"Entsprechungsdenken" und Sündenerkenntnis. Die Auswirkungen der Methode der Korrelation auf das Sündenverständnis in der Systematischen Theologie Paul Tillichs'. *Zeitschrift für Theologie und Kirche* 76: 489–513.

Schüßler, Werner (1986). *Der philosophische Gottesgedanke im Frühwerk Paul Tillichs (1910–1933). Darstellung und Interpretation seiner Gedanken und Quellen.* Würzburg: Königshansen und Neumann.

(1987). 'Where Does Religion Come from? Paul Tillich's Concept of *Grundoffenbarung*' in *Religion et culture: actes du colloque international du centenaire Paul Tillich, Université Laval, Québe 18–22 août 1986,* ed. Michel Despland, Jean-Claude Petit and Jean Richard, 159–71. Quebec: Presses de l'Université Laval/Éditions du Cerf.

(1989). *Jenseits von Religion und Nicht-Religion. Der Religionsbegriff im Werk Paul Tillichs.* Frankfurt am Main: Athenaeum.

(1991). 'Review of Ilse Bertinetti, *Paul Tillich.* Biographien zur Kirchengeschichte, ed. H.-U. Delius. Berlin: Union Verlag, 1990'. *Dialog. Mitteilungsblatt der Deutschen Paul-Tillich-Gesellschaft,* Neue Folge 12, 10.

(1997). *Paul Tillich.* Munich: Beck.

(2006). 'Chiffre oder Symbol? Die Stellung von Karl Jaspers und Paul Tillich zur Frage der "analogia entis"' in *Das Symbol als Sprache der Religion. International Yearbook for Tillich Research,* vol. II, ed. Christian Danz, Werner Schüßler and Erdmann Sturm, 135–53.

and Erdmann Sturm (2007). *Paul Tillich. Leben – Werk – Wirkung.* Darmstadt: Wissenschaftliche Buchgesellschaft.

Schütte, H.-W. (2004). 'Subjektivität und System. Zum Briefwechsel Emanuel Hirsch (1888–1972) und Paul Tillich (1886–1965)' in *Theologie als Religionsphilosophie. Studien zu den problemgeschichtlichen und systematischen Voraussetzungen der Theologie Paul Tillichs,* Tillich-Studien, vol. IX, ed. Christian Danz, 3–22. Vienna: LIT Verlag.

Schweiker, William (1995). *Responsibility and Christian Ethics.* Cambridge: Cambridge University Press.

(1998). *Power, Value and Conviction: Theological Ethics in the Postmodern Age.* Cleveland, Ohio: The Pilgrim Press.

(2005). *Theological Ethics and Global Dynamics: In the Time of Many Worlds.* Oxford: Blackwell.

Seigfried, A. (1978). *Gott über Gott. Die Gottesbeweise als Ausdruck der Gottesfrage in der philosophisch-theologischen Tradition und im Denken Paul Tillichs.* Essen: Lugerus Verlag.

Shakespeare, William (2002). *The Complete Sonnets and Poems,* ed. Colin Burrow. Oxford: Oxford University Press.

Siedler, Dirk Christian (1999a). *Paul Tillichs Beiträge zu einer Theologie der Religionen.* Berlin: Alektor Verlag.

(1999b). 'Paul Tillich in Japan. Eine Chronologie'. *Tillich Journal* 3: 124–32.

Simpson, M. (1967). 'Paul Tillich: Symbolism and Objectivity'. *The Heythrop Journal* 8:3, 293–309.

Sprenger, J. and H. Kramer (1971). *Malleus Maleficarum*, trans. Montague Summers. New York: Dover Publications, Inc.

Steinacker, Peter (1989). 'Passion und Paradox – Der Expressionismus als Verstehendshintergrund der theologischen Anfänge Paul Tillichs. Ein Versuch' in *God and Being/Gott und Sein. The Problem of Ontology in the Philosophical Theology of Paul Tillich/Das Problem der Ontologie in der philosophischen Theologie Paul Tillichs. Beiträge des II. Internationalen Paul Tillichs-Symposions in Frankfurt am Main 1988*, ed. Gert Hummel, 59–99. Berlin: Walter de Gruyter.

Stenger, Mary Ann (2002). 'Theology and Feminism' in *Dialogues of Paul Tillich*, ed. Mary Ann Stenger and Ronald H. Stone. Macon, Ga.: Mercer University Press.

and Ronald H. Stone (2002). *Dialogues of Paul Tillich*. Macon, Ga.: Mercer University Press.

Stiernotte, Alfred (1964). 'Tillich Rounds out His System'. *Journal of Liberal Ministry* 4: 132–3.

Stoker, Wessel (2006). 'Does Tillich's Theology of Art Have a Future? In Response to Russell Re Manning, *Theology of the End of Culture: Paul Tillich's Theology of Culture and Art*' in *International Yearbook for Tillich Research*, ed. Christian Danz and Werner Schüßler, 197–208. Vienna/Berlin: LIT Verlag.

Stokes, A. (1985). *Ministry after Freud*. New York: The Pilgrim Press.

Stone, Ronald H. (1980). *Paul Tillich's Radical Social Thought*. Atlanta, Ga.: John Knox Press.

(2002). 'The Aims of World War II' in *Dialogues of Paul Tillich*, ed. Mary Ann Stenger and Ronald H. Stone, 230. Macon, Ga.: Mercer University Press.

Stout, Jeffrey (2004). *Democracy and Tradition*. Princeton, N.J.: Princeton University Press.

Sturm, E. (1995). '"Holy Love Claims Life and Limb": Paul Tillich's War Theology'. *Zeitschrift für neuere Theologiegeschichte* 2: 60–84.

(2001). 'Paul Tillichs Heidegger-Rezeption'. *Kulturwissenschaftliche Studien* 7: 24–37.

(2004). 'Selbstbewußtsein zwischen Dynamik und Selbst-Transzendenz des Lebens und unbedingter Realitätserfassung. Paul Tillichs kritische Rezeption der Religions- und Lebensphilosophie Georg Simmels' in *Theologie als Religionsphilosophie. Studien zu den problemgeschichtlichen und systematischen Voraussetzungen der Theologie Paul Tillichs*, Tillich-Studien, vol. IX, ed. Christian Danz, 23–47. Vienna: LIT Verlag.

ed. (2006). *Religion and Reflection: Essays on Paul Tillich's Theology*. Münster: LIT Verlag.

Tanner, Kathryn (1997). *Theories of Culture: A New Agenda for Theology*. Minneapolis, Minn.: Fortress Press.

Taylor, Charles (1975). *Hegel*. Cambridge: Cambridge University Press.

Taylor, Mark C. (1987). *Erring: A Postmodern A/Theology*. Chicago, Ill.: University of Chicago Press.

(1992). *Disfiguring: Art, Architecture and Religion*. Chicago, Ill.: University of Chicago Press.

Taylor, Mark Kline (1987). *Paul Tillich: Theologian of the Boundaries.* Minneapolis, Minn.: Fortress Press.

(1990). *Remembering Esperanza: A Cultural-Political Theology for North-American Praxis.* Maryknoll, N.Y.: Orbis Books.

Taylor, Mark Lewis (2005). *Religion, Politics and the Christian Right: Post-9/11 Politics and the Christian Right.* Minneapolis, Minn.: Fortress Press.

Teilhard de Chardin, Pierre (1999). *The Human Phenomenon,* trans. Sarah Appleton-Weber. Portland, Oreg.: Sussex Academic Press.

Thatamanil, John J. (2006). *The Immanent Divine: God, Creation, and the Human Predicament. An East–West Conversation.* Minneapolis, Minn.: Fortress Press.

Thatcher, A. (1978). *The Ontology of Paul Tillich.* Oxford: Oxford University Press.

Thiessen, Gesa (1993). 'Religious Art is Expressionistic. A Critical Appreciation of Paul Tillich's Theology of Art'. *Irish Theological Quarterly* 59:4, 301–11.

Thomas, Terence (1984). 'On Another Boundary: Tillich's Encounter with World Religions' in *Theonomy and Autonomy, Studies in Paul Tillich's Engagement with Modern Culture,* ed. John Carey, 196. Macon, Ga.: Mercer University Press.

(1992). 'The "New Being" and the Encounter of Religions'. *Newsletter of the North American Paul Tillich Society,* 18:2.

(1995). 'Convergence and Divergence in a Plural World' in *Spirit and Community: The Legacy of Paul Tillich's Thought,* ed. Frederick J. Parrella, 18–42. Berlin and New York: Walter de Gruyter.

(1999). *Paul Tillich and World Religions.* Cardiff: Cardiff Academic Press.

Thompson, I. E. (1981). *Being and Meaning: Paul Tillich's Theory of Meaning, Truth and Logic.* Edinburgh: Edinburgh University Press.

Tillich, Hannah (1973). *From Time to Time.* New York: Stein & Day.

(1976). *From Place to Place.* New York: Stein & Day.

Tönnies, Ferdinand (1887). *Gemeinschaft und Gesellschaft.* Leipzig: Feues Verlag.

Tracy, David (1987). *Plurality and Ambiguity: Hermeneutics, Religion and Hope.* San Francisco, Calif.: Harper & Row.

Turner, Denys (1995). *The Darkness of God.* Cambridge: Cambridge University Press.

Ulanov, Ann Belford (1985). 'The Anxiety of Being' in *The Thought of Paul Tillich,* ed. James Luther Adams, Wilhelm Pauck and Roger Lincoln Shinn, 120. San Francisco, Calif.: Harper & Row.

Unno, Taitetsu (2001). 'Compassion in Buddhist Spirituality' in *Religion in the New Millenium: Theology in the Spirit of Paul Tillich,* ed. Raymond F. Bulman and Frederick J. Pareella, 166. Macon, Ga.: Mercer University Press.

Urban, W. M. (1940). 'A Critique of Professor Tillich's Theory of the Religious Symbol'. *The Journal of Liberal Religion* 2:1, 34–6.

van Dusen, Henry Pitney (1945). *The Christian Answer.* New York: Charles Scribner's Sons.

Vanhoozer, Kevin J. (2003). 'Theology and the Condition of Postmodernity: A Report on Knowledge (of God)' in *The Cambridge Companion to*

Postmodern Theology, ed. Kevin J. Vanhoozer. New York: Cambridge University Press.

Ward, Graham (2001). 'Introduction: Where We Stand' in *The Blackwell Companion to Postmodern Theology*, ed. Grahman Ward. Malden, Mass.: Blackwell.

Wehr, Gerhard (1979). *Paul Tillich in Selbstzeugnissen und Bilddokumenten*. Rowohlts Monographien 274, ed. K. Kusenberg. Reinbek bei Hamburg: Rowohlt.

Wells, Jonathan (2000). *Icons of Evolution: Science or Myth?* Washington, D.C.: Regnery.

Wenz, Gunther (1979). *Subjekt und Sein. Die Entwicklung der Theologie Paul Tillichs*. Munich: Chr. Kaiser Verlag.

Wiebe, P. (1984). 'Tillich and Contemporary Theory of Science' in *Theonomy and Autonomy: Studies in Paul Tillich's Engagement with Modern Culture*, ed. J. C. Carey, 19–33. Macon, Ga.: Mercer University Press.

Williams, Delores (1993). *Sisters in the Wilderness: The Challenges of Womanist God-Talk*. Maryknoll, N.Y.: Orbis Books.

Winquist, Charles E. (1995). *Desiring Theology*. Chicago, Ill.: University of Chicago Press.

Wittekind, F. (2004). '"Sinndeutung der Geschichte." Zur Entwicklung und Bedeutung von Tillichs Geschichtsphilosophie' in *Theologie als Religionsphilosophie. Studien zu den problemgeschichtlichen und systematischen Voraussetzungen der Theologie Paul Tillichs*, Tillich-Studien, vol. IX, ed. Christian Danz, 135–72. Vienna: LIT Verlag.

(2005). 'Die Vernunft des Christusglaubens. Zu den philosophischen Hintergründen der Christologie der Marburger Dogmatik' in *Wie viel Vernunft braucht der Glaube? Internationales Jahrbuch für die Tillich-Forschung*, vol. I, ed. C. Danz, W. Schüßler and E. Sturm, 133–57. Vienna: LIT Verlag.

Wolterstorff, Nicholas (1995). *Divine Discourse: Philosophical Reflections on the Claim that God Speaks*. Cambridge: Cambridge University Press.

Wood, Robert (1961–2). 'Tillich Encounters Japan' in *Japanese Religions*, vol. II, nos. 2–3, 48–71.

Ziche, P. (2004). 'Orientierungssuche im logischen Raum der Wissenschaften. Paul Tillichs System der Wissenschaften und die Wissenschaftssystematik um 1900' in *Theologie als Religionsphilosophie. Studien zu den problemgeschichtlichen und systematischen Voraussetzungen der Theologie Paul Tillichs*, Tillich-Studien, vol. IX, ed. Christian Danz, 49–68. Vienna: LIT Verlag.

United States v. *Seeger*, 380, U.S. 163, 1965.

Index